ELIZABETHAN
NON-CONFORMIST TEXTS

ELIZABETHAN NON-CONFORMIST TEXTS

VOLUME I
Cartwrightiana
Edited by Albert Peel and Leland H. Carlson

VOLUME II
The writings of Robert Harrison and Robert Browne
Edited by Leland H. Carlson and Albert Peel

VOLUME III
The writings of Henry Barrow
1587–1590
Edited by Leland H. Carlson

VOLUME IV
The writings of John Greenwood
1587–1590
Edited by Leland H. Carlson

VOLUME V
The writings of Henry Barrow
1590–1591
Edited by Leland H. Carlson

VOLUME VI
The writings of John Greenwood and Henry Barrow
1591–1593
Edited by Leland H. Carlson

ELIZABETHAN NON-CONFORMIST TEXTS

VOLUME V

The writings of Henry Barrow
1590–1591

Edited by Leland H. Carlson

LONDON AND NEW YORK

First published 1966
by George Allen & Unwin Ltd
This edition reprinted 2003
by Routledge
2 Park Square, Milton Park, Abingdon, Oxfordshire OX14 4RN
Simultaneously published in the USA and Canada
by Routledge
711 Third Avenue, New York, NY 10017
Transferred to digital print 2013

Routledge is an imprint of the Taylor & Francis Group, an informa business

First issued in paperback 2013
© 1966 George Allen & Unwin

Typeset in Times by Keystroke, Jacaranda Lodge, Wolverhampton

All rights reserved. No part of this book may be reprinted or reproduced or utilised in any form or by any electronic, mechanical, or other means, now known or hereafter invented, including photocopying and recording, or in any information storage or retrieval system, without permission in writing from the publishers.

British Library Cataloguing in Publication Data
A catalogue record for this book is available from the British Library

Library of Congress Cataloging in Publication Data
A catalog record for this book has been requested.

ISBN 978-0-415-31993-5 (hbk)
ISBN 978-0-415-86452-7 (pbk)

Publisher's note
The Publisher has gone to great lengths to ensure the quality of this reprint but points out that some imperfections in the original book may be apparent.

THE WRITINGS OF
HENRY BARROW
1590-1591

Edited by
LELAND H. CARLSON
PH. D.

Published for
THE SIR HALLEY STEWART TRUST

GEORGE ALLEN AND UNWIN LTD
RUSKIN HOUSE
MUSEUM STREET LONDON

THIS VOLUME IS DEDICATED TO
SIR JOHN ERNEST NEALE
ASTOR PROFESSOR OF ENGLISH HISTORY

UNIVERSITY COLLEGE, UNIVERSITY OF LONDON
1927-1956

WITH GRATITUDE FOR AND PLEASANT MEMORIES OF

THOSE STIMULATING ELIZABETHAN SEMINARS

PREFACE

THIS is Volume V in the series on "Elizabethan Nonconformist Texts." Volume I was issued in 1951 with the title, *Cartwrightiana*. In 1953 Volume II was published, *The Writings of Robert Harrison and Robert Browne*. In 1962 two volumes were issued, Volume III being *The Writings of Henry Barrow, 1587-1590*, and Volume IV being *The Writings of John Greenwood, 1587-1590, together with the Joint Writings of Henry Barrow and John Greenwood, 1587-1590*. Volume VI will be forthcoming in about a year, with the title, *The Writings of John Greenwood and Henry Barrow, 1591-1593*. Volume V has eleven items and Volume VI will have approximately thirty-five items. Also, a bibliography will be included in Volume VI for the four volumes on the works of Barrow and Greenwood.

The principles of editing in Volume V are the same as those enumerated in the preface of Volume III.

I feel a special debt of gratitude to Mrs. Orin Tramz for accurate and speedy typing of difficult Elizabethan material. For a much-appreciated sabbatical year I thank President E. C. Colwell. For the many keepers of books and custodians of precious manuscripts I have pleasant memories of efficient service. To Sir John Neale, Joel Hurstfield, and S. T. Bindoff I am grateful for discussions of Elizabethan problems and for long friendships. To R. B. Wernham I am indebted for a document location. And to the publisher, Sir Stanley Unwin of the firm, George Allen and Unwin Ltd., to Barbara Clapham and the trustees of the Sir Halley Stewart Trust, I express my sincere thanks.

LELAND H. CARLSON.

December 12, 1964.
School of Theology at Claremont
Claremont Graduate School
Claremont, California

CONTENTS

PREFACE   vii

INTRODUCTION   1

   THE WRITINGS OF HENRY BARROW, 1590-1591

 I. A Plaine Refutation of Mr. George Giffarde's
    Reprochful Booke, Intituled, *A Short Treatise
    against the Donatists of England*   25

 II. A Refutation of Mr. Giffard's Reasons con-
    cerning Our Purposes in the Practise of the
    Truth of the Gospel of Christ   332

                     APPENDICES

 III. George Gifford's Controversy with Barrow   365

 IV. George Gifford's Controversy with Greenwood   368

 V. Sir Robert Sidney to Lord Burghley, April 21,
    1591   370

 VI. Sir Robert Sidney to Lord Burghley, May 31,
    1591   371

 VII. Sir Thomas Bodley to Sir Robert Sydney,
    May 20, 1591   372

 VIII. Governor Bradford's Account of *A Plaine
    Refutation*   373

CONTENTS

  IX. George Gifford's Writings   378

   X. Barrow's Citations from Scripture   381

  XI. George Gifford's Will   382

INDEX   386

INTRODUCTION

Barrow begins his *A Plaine Refutation* by an appeal to Lord Burghley, to whom the book is dedicated. During the autumn of 1590 Barrow had written two letters to Burghley and had submitted his treatise, "The First Part of the Platforme" to him. But Burghley disliked the revolutionary programme presented in the "Platforme" and the second part was never written. Nevertheless, Barrow continued his appeal to the Lord Treasurer, who was distantly related by his marriage to Mildred Cooke. Burghley had the reputation of a moderate, disliked some of the policies of Archbishop Whitgift, possessed the full confidence of the Queen, and advocated a policy of caution, conservatism, and tolerant understanding.

Barrow complains of the malignant adversaries who have misrepresented the views of the Separatists. In two books written by Dr. Robert Some, and in two books written by George Gifford, the Separatists are denounced as Anabaptists, Donatists, sectaries, schismatics, and heretics, as seditious persons who seek the curtailment of the Queen's prerogative. No opportunity has been given the Separatists to defend themselves from the clamours of pulpit and press. They have now been in prison for more than three years, without trial either by a civil court or by the word of God. In order that both sides may be heard, that equity may be done, that truth in all its simplicity may prevail, Barrow beseeches the Lord Treasurer to be a means to the Queen for the holding of a public conference for the settlement of all the issues that have arisen, so that the will of God may be known and practised.

Following his appeal to Lord Burghley, Barrow addresses himself to the reader. The time of apostasy and desolation foretold by John the Seer in the Book of Revelation is at hand.

The falling away from the gospel is evident in the two books of Gifford whose eyes are bound and whose mind is impervious to reason. His shameless slanders and patent falsehoods are apparent to all. The Separatists neither believe nor teach any Anabaptistical doctrine of perfection in this life; man indeed is not immune from sin. Again, the Separatists cannot be charged with schism. Seeing that Gifford has defended the Church of England for its separation from the Roman church in its apostasy, may not the same right be accorded to the Separatists? Neither can Mr. Gifford charge his opponents with derogating from the Queen's power. Did he not himself zealously seek the reformation of the church until the times changed? May not the Separatists seek a reformation, in season and out of season, not to minimize the Queen's power but to maximize God's word? Therefore, in accusing the Separatists of Anabaptism, Donatism, and Brownism, does not Mr. Gifford slander and deceive?

Gifford had argued that the Church of England suffered from some light imperfections, from a few faults in ecclesiastical government, with the implication that these could be corrected and that separation for trivial causes was not justified. Barrow replied that Gifford himself had spent fifteen years fighting these "light imperfections". Was he merely tilting with windmills? Was he not aware of the difference between things fundamental and things indifferent?

A modern wit suggested that there were only two things he disliked in his friend: what he said, and what he did! This in effect is Barrow's extreme position towards Gifford. The entire worship is popish, erroneous, superstitious. The membership in the church is confused, mixed, uncovenanted, and profane. The ministry is imposed on the church without a requisite calling. And the discipline is basically, essentially wrong.

Throughout the long polemic Barrow constantly attacks. Even when he is defending his position, he returns to his

Introduction

aggressive posture. Thus, Gifford is forced into a defensive position. Gifford labours under this handicap. Futhermore, he is dealing with an opponent who has endured three years of imprisonment, and he is writing against a man regarded by some as a martyr. He is in the unfortunate position of defending Marian martyrs and condemning Separatist martyrs. He is also vulnerable because of his own record. Barrow reminds him of his own difficulties with the hierarchy. He had been suspended as vicar at Maldon but now is in league with Bishop Aylmer. He was a petitioner to Parliament in 1587 but now is a practitioner of those errors he sought to remedy. He now defends what he previously attacked. In other words, he is a time-server, a sycophant of his Ordinary, a seeker after promotion, and a turncoat in the best tradition of Master Andrew Perne at Cambridge.

The First Principal Transgression

The first major accusation levelled against the Church of England is that it is guilty of false worship. It is false because it is invented by man, is erroneous, and is imposed upon the people by the hierarchy and the Catholic tradition mediated through the *Book of Common Prayer*. Barrow begins his argument by seeking to establish a major premise — to build a foundation. This he finds ready-made in the Scripture. The written Word of God is the pattern, prepared by the prophets and apostles, and Jesus Christ is the Great Designer. Barrow's view of Scripture is that of Thomas Cartwright, of Theodore Beza, of John Calvin. In asserting that "everie part of the Scripture is alike true, inspired of God, given to our direction and instruction in all things," he is a man of his age who has substituted the absolute authority of the Bible for the absolute authority of the church. There is no suggestion that the books of the Bible may have local, temporal, or historical relevance. No thought of progressive revelation is revealed in his writings. Hence for him "the least departure from God's Word is an error; the least transgression of God's lawe is a sinne; the reward of the least error or sinne is eternal death " unless God's mercy and Christ's merits intervene. But such mercy and merits are not imputed to the impenitent and the obstinate. Since Barrow found it easy to regard those who disagreed with him as proud and stubborn, he naturally concluded that they lacked the necessary foundation. Therefore the ideological and spiritual edifice which they erected was built on shifting sand.

Gifford's answer is that Anglican worship is derived from the Bible, despite some imperfections, wants, spots, blemishes and faults which are not of the essence of worship. To a man like Barrow such exceptions were fatal. The spots and blemishes become incurable botches of Egypt, malignant Roman ulcers. The *Book of Common Prayer* is the basis of Anglican worship; it is derived from the papal liturgies; it is the invention of men; therefore it is idolatrous.

There must be Scriptural sanction for all aspects of worship. Therefore Barrow asks Gifford if the New Testament provides for such Romish fasts as Embers, Saints' Eves, or Lent. If the origin of such fasts is not apostolic but papal, then the worship of the Church of England is imposed by men, not God. Where does the Scripture authorize special feasts such as Christmas, Candlemass, and All-Hallows, Lady days, Saint days ? Why should St. George, or St. Michael and all angels, or the innocents, or certain dead saints be especially singled out by men ? Why should direful comminations be used at Lent instead of Christ's discipline ? Should a civil action such as rogations be a part of worship ? Perhaps a parish clerk occasionally needs to ascertain the boundaries of a parish, but should this action become a popish procession, with special collects en route over cattle, corn, and grass ? Is not the rite of purification or churching of women a Jewish remnant ? Are not tithes an integral part of the Levitical priesthood ? And if the priesthood, sacrifices and decimations of the old dispensation are all removed with the advent of Christ's gospel in a new dispensation, why are they retained ? Should not fees for marrying, purifying, burying be abolished ? Should

Introduction

not clergymen be supported by the free-will offerings of the faithful rather than by taxes on all, believers and unbelievers ?

Barrow reveals himself as a son of the radical reformation in his views on absolution. Only God can forgive all sin. Therefore, in assuming power to forgive all sin, the priest is guilty of sacrilege and of usurpation of divine power. The arrogant practice of binding and loosing, retaining and forgiving, is sheer popery. But to Gifford this critical attitude ran counter to the power of binding and loosing conferred on the disciples by Jesus Christ in Matthew 18:18. Either the power given to the disciples ended with their generation, or it descended to their successors. The implication seems clear that for Barrow it did not descend to subsequent generations, and such an interpretation the Anglicans naturally rejected. To Barrow all members of the church had the power and obligation — equally with the greatest minister of the church — to forgive wrongdoers upon repentance. This power included the right to reprove and cast out even the minister himself. All binding and loosing was effected by the word of God, not by mortal man, who was merely an agent whether he was a priest or the least of God's servants.

Private communion Barrow condemns as popish and superstitious. The Lord's Supper is to be celebrated only in a public communion of the faithful, and is not to be administered in a private dwelling to a sick person. Such a practice is suggestive of the rite of extreme unction, implies the idea of necessity, and nourishes superstition.

Barrow is equally critical of the Anglican doctrine and practice of baptism. Why should there be in addition to public baptism such a practice as private baptism by women, or midwives ? Is baptism by supposition to be tolerated ? Is not baptism by a bishop — confirmation or bishoping — a work of supererogation and therefore superstitious and superfluous ? Can any prudent man explain why the law of the church requires popish gossips or sureties, instead of the parents, to answer for the child that he doth forsake the devil and all his works ? Is not the entire doctrine of the Church of England, with its practice of hasty baptism by a woman, in time of danger, suggestive of the teaching that baptism is a cause of salvation ? And is this not popish, a denial of the Pauline, Augustinian and Calvinistic teaching of God's eternal election as the sole cause and foundation of salvation ?

In summarizing Barrow's denunciation of the false worship, we may reduce his reasons — some trivial and others inconsistent — to several main allegations. First, the worship of the Church of England is too closely associated with that of the Roman Catholic Church. Reformation has fallen far short of the Reformed ideal. Again, the use of the Apocrypha for public reading is indefensible. Thirdly, the arbitrary selection of Scriptural readings for their yearly calendar omits much of the Bible and presents the rest out of context. Fourthly, the prayers are prescribed and mechanical, the devices of men, mere reading of other men's words, and not the spontaneous outpouring of the Spirit. And lastly, the rites of the Church are administered in a false, superstitious, popish, and unscriptural manner.

The Second Principal Transgression

In the Church of England the profane multitude is received and retained without any attempt to separate the godly and the ungodly. One is born into the church, baptized indiscriminately into its membership, and retained in its bosom. When the Church of England established its independence from the Roman Catholic Church in 1559 by the Act of Supremacy and the Act of Uniformity, no attempt was made to ascertain who were true believers, who remained secret papists, who were heretics, or who were Laodiceans. All were received indiscriminately into the body of the Elizabethan church. The result was that a few Catholics migrated to the Spanish Netherlands, a few refractory priests and professors lost their positions, but the overwhelming mass of people and clergy continued in

Introduction

the new establishment. Hence the confusion, sacrilege, and secularization of the Church of England. Hence the profanation of the whole nation.

Barrow raises some difficult points by his accusation. Who should belong to the church? Is membership an inheritance, a gift, an achievement, a godly privilege or a profane requirement? The medieval tradition was that of uniformity and universal membership. But the monolithic structure had collapsed. Uniformity was shattered by the advent of the Lutherans, the Calvinists, the Anabaptists, the Anglicans, and the Puritans. Universal membership remained an ideal, but the seamless garment had been badly rent, and the pieces had rough edges. The ecclesiastical schisms were not the only problem. There were centrifugal forces which the men of the sixteenth century could not understand, much less control. Capitalism, commerce, voyages of discovery, and nationalism were bringing changes. Printing, popular reading of the Bible, theological differences, the priesthood of new and unorthodox believers, prophesying movements, pulpit oratory, and pamphlet controversies were uniting unwittingly to produce a silent revolution — the modern mind.

If the ideal of uniformity could not prevail on an international scale, it must continue on a national basis. *Cuius regio, eius religio.* Richard Hooker, moderate, reasonable, tolerant, conceived of the state civil and the state ecclesiastical as two sides of the same coin. The Elizabethan hierarchy and the secular government shared this view. Nevertheless, doubts continued to grow. If the pope could not legislate, could the magistrate open windows into man's soul? If the magistrate happened to be imprudent, dilatory, or ungodly, was it necessary to tarry for the magistrate? English Presbyterians laboured from 1570 to 1590 to change the system from within, but the efforts of Aylmer, Bancroft, Whitgift, and the Queen frustrated these hopes. For the nonconformist the alternative was conformity or separation. And for the Separatist the alternative was intolerance and persecution, or exile and drift into the Anabaptiscal doctrine of separation of church and state.

This was the dilemma of Barrow. He believed sincerely in a church which comprised a fellowship of select, peculiar, separated persons. God's covenant or promise of love and protection belonged only to the faithful, who loved Him and kept His commandments. The seals of this covenant were the sacraments of baptism and the Lord's Supper. No one could enter into this covenant relationship except by a true voluntary outward profession of faith and a vow of obedience. No one could remain in this covenant who broke the commandments or walked in spiritual darkness. God's covenant was made with Israel, but only those were of Israel who kept the faith and obedience of Abraham. To suggest, as Gifford did, that all were within the covenant, was to forget that the Israelites waxed proud, turned to idolatry, and committed fornication with the daughters of the Egyptians, the Chaldeans, and the Assyrians — thus incurring the wrath and punishment of Jehovah.

Gifford upheld the view of Elizabethan society. Both Anglicans and Presbyterians believed in a comprehensive church but disagreed on polity. Both Gifford and Whitgift shared the Calvinist view that the tares and the wheat should grow up together. Barrow disagreed on this interpretation of Calvin, and contended that the tares represented the world, not the profane element in the church. This Barrowist view was exported to Plymouth by the Pilgrim Fathers and to New England generally by many of the Puritans, who arrived at Boston with hazy non-separating sentiments but who quickly adjusted to the stricter views of Barrow, Brewster, and John Cotton. The dilemma of the New England Separatists became acute as the second and third generations assumed control. Was the function of the church merely to edify the saints? Was its true task simply that of keeping the elders warm and spiritually cozy? Out of this problem of providing for the ongoing of the church came the compromise known as the

Introduction

Half-Way Covenant. The later conflicts about restricted or open communion, the appeal to the unconverted by Solomon Stoddard (1643-1729) through revivals, and the return of Jonathan Edwards to the stricter viewpoint brought the wheel around full circle. In effect, the Gifford-Barrow conflict was not new. Origen was condemned for his universalist doctrines; Augustine conflicted with Pelagius on irresistible or resistible grace; Dutch Calvinists won out over Arminius; and Arminianism triumphed in the later period of Archbishop Laud and John Wesley.

The question of the true membership of the Church of England is related to the origins of the Elizabethan Church. Since the change from Catholicism to Anglicanism was effected by statute in 1559, the debate centred on the Catholic church prior to the change. Gifford's view was that the Roman church constituted a true church. Barrow asserted that the Roman church was a false church though God's elect were a remnant within the church. If the Roman church was a true church, how can Gifford justify his separation from it?

For Barrow the condition of the Church of England is similar to that of the Roman Catholic Church. The Lord has many thousands of his elect among both churches. Therefore, one must not presume to judge of God's secret election, known to Himself and to be revealed in His good time. It is a question rather of the open, patent, odious sins of the profane multitude. One cannot justify the easy membership of atheists, papists, idolators, heretics, drunkards, adulterers, bawds, whores, whoremasters, thieves, and gamesters. Such persons should be removed from the membership of God's people, but they should be allowed to attend the public services though forbidden the sacrament of the Lord's Supper until they amend their lives.

What concerns Barrow is the lack of proper discipline in the Church of England. Discipline is the proper function of the entire congregation, which holds the power of excommunication. This power the parish assembly does not have. The spiritual courts exercise this function, and they excommunicate for contumacy, for non-attendance at the courts, and for non-payment of fines. Such action does not solve the problem. It is palliative, trivial, and monetary. What is needed is a reformation of life, not a financial penalty. The power of excommunication belongs to every member of the church acting together. It does not belong to the pope, the bishop, the presbytery, the chancellor, the commissary, or the archdeacon.

The Third Principal Transgression

Having concluded that the membership of the parish assemblies consists of an admixture of profane and pious, secular and religious persons, Barrow affirms them to be a flock of wild and unclean beasts. Part of the problem is that these flocks are guided by shepherds who have led the sheep astray. Therefore, Barrow launches into a somewhat unfair examination and extreme criticism of the ministry of the Church of England.

To establish the true norm of the ministry, Barrow sets forth what he conceives to be the New Testament pattern. Therein he finds apostles, prophets, and evangelists, who were appointed for the establishing of the church. Their function having been fulfilled, their offices have ceased. What remains is a five-fold structure of pastors, teachers, elders, deacons, and widows or relievers or deaconesses. These are to be selected and ordained by individual congregations, and they are to be subject to the scrutiny and censure of the members, if necessary. Pastors, teachers, and elders are overseers, episcopoi, superintendents, whose functions are, respectively, exhortation, teaching of doctrine, and ruling. Deacons and relievers are of another order, with functions of distributing benevolences and ministering to the sick.

By contrast the ministry of the Church of England is

Introduction

composed of a reigning, a collegiate, and a servile order. The reigning order is constituted by two archbishops — the primate metropolitan of all England and the metropolitan for the north — as well as palatine and ordinary lord bishops. Assisting these rulers are chancellors, commissaries, special judges, archdeacons, high commissioners, and attendant court officials, such as advocates, proctors, registrars, notaries, summoners, and pursuivants.

A second order is that of the collegiate or idle ministry. In the universities these are masters and presidents of houses, fellows, doctors of divinity, bachelors of divinity, masters of arts, bachelors of arts, and clerks. In the cathedral churches these are lord bishops, deans, sub-deans, prebendaries, canons, and all their attendants. The third order consists of the parish ministry, which includes parsons and rectors, vicars and curates, deacons, churchwardens, sidesmen, questmen, and parish clerks.

Barrow believes that the various kinds of bishops have forgotten their true function as overseers of one congregation. He finds their names, titles, and dignities both blasphemous and unwarranted. Pontifical prelates and lordly bishops are arrogant and presumptuous. They have lost their humility and sense of service. They have overstepped their true area of jurisdiction to become privy councillors, members of parliament, judges in civil causes. Instead of serving one congregation, by whom they should have been called, they aspire to rule hundreds of parish churches, by whom they have not been called. They fulfill no apostolic, prophetic, or evangelistic function. They have no time for saving souls and edifying the saints because they are too busy citing, summoning, silencing, sequestering, suspending, depriving, excommunicating, absolving, and imprisoning dissenters. They have forgotten their Master who washed the feet of his disciples, and they have followed after false gods, such as palaces, pomp, lordly state, money, promotions, pleasure, power, and ambition. They have taken both swords into their hands, as Innocent III and Boniface VIII once did, and thus have perpetuated a monstrous confusion of civil and spiritual offices.

Barrow is critical of chancellors and commissaries and their courts. Their titles are not found in the New Testament. Their offices are spiritual, but they are administered by laymen. They arrogate to themselves not only ecclesiastical matters but also civil and judicial causes, thus encroaching upon the jurisdiction of the Queen and the common law courts. Procedure is corrupt and justice is venal. Even worse is the Court of High Commission, which has become an arm of the bishops, though a few lay judges are retained for fashion's sake. Its composition is mixed, its functions are confused and overlapping, its use of the *ex officio* oath is a scandal, and its arbitrary citations and imprisonments are an insult to justice.

Barrow's remarks about the archdeacon are interesting and informative. Although the office of deacon is found in the New Testament, that of the archdeacon is not. This would be excusable if the latter were foremost in distributing alms, but he is more interested in collecting fines. Not only does he exercise jurisdiction over other deacons, but he holds sway over parsons, vicars, churches, and large parts of shires. He is in effect a deputy bishop, an archidiaconal officer, and a powerful judge.

In discussing the collegiate ministry of the universities, Barrow does not find much fault with titles or offices. Instead, he digresses to a discussion of the curriculum and student practices. He is critical of the grammar schools, where Latin is learned from profane authors and lascivious poets. When the student arrives at the university he is salted and matriculated. Then he continues with the study of logic and rhetoric. His approach to philosophy is through Aristotle, from whom he learns ethics, economics, politics, and science. Much of what he learns about meteorology, astronomy, and astrology Barrow characterizes as curious and profane arts, unfit for a

Introduction

Christian, more so for a Christian clergyman. Accompanying the usual education at the universities are the ceremonies, academic dress, student disorders, peculiar customs, special organizations, and all the specious debates, in a language the people do not understand, and on theses which are self-evident or patently absurd.

Barrow's comments on education may be taken *cum grano salis*. He may be reflecting his own experiences at Clare College, Cambridge, where he spent four years in study, roistering, and dissipation. His own legal and secular studies may have led him to the conclusion that education should be centred around the Bible, especially after his dramatic conversion. He was accused of denigrating universities and education, but he stated that he did not condemn lawful arts and necessary sciences. He expressly advocated the teaching of languages and other godly arts not only in the universities but in every city. He probably was short-sighted in his views that only necessary and godly arts be studied, inasmuch as his view of " necessary " was restricted. Perhaps he was supercritical of the vain, curious, and unlawful arts, but he never criticized Clare College and Cambridge in the spirit revealed by Edward Gibbon in his criticism of Magdalen and Oxford.

With his usual asperity Barrow pours scorn upon the cathedral clergy. The dean has not likeness to a Christian deacon. With his velvet cushion, his cloth of estate, and his silver mace, the dean is an unlikely person for the distribution of alms to the poor. Sub-deans are unheard of in the Scripture. Prebendaries are idle bellies. Prebends are offices not infrequently given to civilians, or lay parsons. But in a church where ecclesiastical officials exercise civil power, Barrow ironically asks, why should it be unusual for lay officials to hold ecclesiastical offices ? And in a cathedral church, where Satan's throne is to be found, occupied by a lord bishop, and surrounded by loitering priests, one may expect all the abuses associated with the abbots, monks, friars, and nuns in the days of Henry VIII, who abolished the monasteries. Equally desolate will be the kingdom of these new abbey lubbers, Barrow predicts.

Having expressed his strictures on bishops and collegiate clergy, Barrow turns to the ordinary parson of the parish. The parson is not a true pastor, either in name, or function, or calling. The pastor is called to preach, to exhort, and to guide the flock. But the parson too frequently is a dumb dog — an unpreaching minister — who reads an appointed service from the *Book of Common Prayer*. The pastor keeps himself free from civil entanglements, but the parson is involved with rents, tithes, rates, homilies, and injunctions. A pastor is a bishop, an overseer, but a parson stands subject to his bishop. A pastor is called by his congregation, but a parson is imposed on the people, presented by a patron who holds the advowson. A pastor is ordained by his people, but a parson is ordained and instituted by a bishop. A pastor is called to a specific flock, but a parson is not called to any particular church. Perchance, he may become a house priest, a domestic chaplain, a schoolteacher, or a deputy. A pastor is paid by the benevolence of his congregation. A parson is paid by the endowed income of his living, which may be £100 in a small hamlet and £10 in a large community. Such inequities lead to a desire to move to better churches, though the sheep be utterly deserted. Indeed, because of the system of endowed livings, many of which were too poor to support a worthy incumbent, the churches were administered by vicars, readers, lay parsons with little education, and even scandalous hirelings. Pluralism, non-residence, and dissatisfaction were inevitable consequences of the Tudor historical contingencies.

The Fourth Principal Transgression

The fourth principal cause of separation from the Church of England is that the government, the regimen, the discipline of the church, is not in accordance with the pattern of the primitive church as set forth in the New Testament.

In this point Gifford labours under certain handicaps. He

Introduction

had been known during the 1580's as one who actively advocated and supported a reformed Presbyterian model. He had virtually admitted that the poor church suffered and groaned under the yoke of antichristian government. He had witnessed the successful efforts of Whitgift, Aylmer, and Bancroft to check the classis movement. He had seen the wheel of fortune turn in the death of John Field (1588), in the arrest of John Udall and the imprisonment of Thomas Cartwright with other Presbyterian leaders (1590). Thus, his position in 1590 was changed from that of 1587, and he was in danger of being regarded as a turncoat, an ecclesiastical chameleon which adjusted to the new situation.

Gifford argued that the Church of England was in substance and matter the true spouse of Christ, even though it lacked the form prescribed in the New Testament. He had formerly supported Cartwright's position that this form was permanent and immutable, but he was acutely aware of the teaching of Archbishop Whitgift and Bishop Cooper that the form of church government may vary from country to country, from century to century. Therefore, he hesitated, and he was frustrated by his own doubts. May the form be variable? Is church government, unlike doctrine, a thing indifferent, of the category of *adiaphora*? If church vestments, rites, ceremonies, and liturgies were subject to prescription and alteration, why not the form of church government? If the Queen and church had won the battle on these issues in the period 1564-1588, would they not also prevail in the issue of polity? Time and circumstances seemed to favour the established usage.

Gifford contends that the church may labour under outward bondage and yet be the true church. Barrow replies that churches in all times have suffered outward persecution from civil governments. The real issue is that the Church of England suffers from inward bondage, that her officials exercise both civil and ecclesiastical functions, that the persecution stems from the spiritual officials within, not from the secular enemy without. In the prevailing Erastianism, the church has lost her freedom and her very soul. She is subject to the laws, traditions, and devices of men, not to the word of God. In obeying the magistrates, she follows the hireling instead of the true shepherd. Even worse, in yielding to the dictates of men, the church violates the demands of her own conscience. Since all the laws and ordinances of the New Testament, however small and external, bind the court of conscience, according to Barrow, not much jurisdiction over the affairs of the church is given to the courts of men. The church will always suffer outward bondage, but it should never tolerate an inward antichristian yoke.

The essence of government and discipline is the power given by Christ to the church for the selection and testing of church officials — whether they be called bishops and priests and deacons, or pastors, teachers, and elders. This power is equally given to the church for the guidance of the laity by means of admonition, suspension, and excommunication. This may be regarded as the matter, the gist, the substance of ecclesiastical government, polity, discipline. So far is there agreement among the prelatical, the reformist, and the separatist traditions. But when the crucial question is posed as to who shall possess and administer this power, the answers differ. For the Anglicans, the bishop is the source of power. For the Presbyterians, the presbytery or synod is the true court. For the Separatists, the church or congregation is the rightful judge. Thus, the conflict between the Episcopal, Presbyterian, and Congregational systems involves the question of whether one man, a committee, or an entire group shall wield the sceptre.

Barrow's criticism of the discipline of the Church of England is that it is too sparing in its use of excommunication for sin and heresy, too quick in its use of suspension for trivial causes such as non-payment of fees or contempt of court by non-appearance before the archdeacon, commissary, or chancellor. Barrow dislikes the system of easy absolution by payment of money. In fact, Barrow, who in his strict, absolute, critical temperament is painfully aware of the egregious sins as well

Introduction

as the frailties of others, is really provoked by the laxity of the system. He yearns for a system where each person is subject to the watchful guidance and censure of his fellow members in the church. He could forsee all the advantages for nation, individual, truth, and morality, but he could not forsee the difficulties, such as the nature of human nature, censoriousness, misunderstanding, and pride.

Barrow attacks the teaching that church government is subject to change and circumstance. When God, the Great Architect, commanded the building of the Tabernacle, he prescribed the exact specifications to his servant Moses. Provision was made for the least pin, tape, and hook. Nothing was left to the discretion or determination of men. When the Great Creator fashioned the human body, as the habitation of the spirit, he left no power to mortal man to alter the members, not even to make a single hair. *A fortiori*, how much more did God the Great Architect prescribe the pattern for the spiritual body, the church. Barrow waxes lyrical in describing this heavenly pattern, this perfect archetype, which was delivered by the Holy Ghost to the Apostles, which was set forth by the Apostles in the New Testament, which was confirmed by the death of Christ, and which was sealed by signs and wonders from heaven. What monstrous presumption do these earthly architects reveal in setting aside this eternal blueprint! Are they greater than Moses? Are they wiser than Solomon? Are they more favoured than the Apostles? God forbid. The true city is four square, immovable, proportionate, beautiful, ravishing to the senses. What barbarous havoc would it be to substitute an ugly, deformed hovel for the heavenly edifice.

Barrow charges Gifford with inconsistency. If he defends the discipline of the Church of England as being from Christ, as being of the substance of the true church, then why did he and his fellow reformists sue unto Parliament to remove this discipline? Can it be wrong in 1585 and right in 1590? Is the discipline of Christ subject to the vicissitudes of the times?

Could it be that the threat of a prison cell in Newgate or the Fleet is sufficient to " colour " the pure and absolute teachings of Christ ? What a hypocrite is Gifford! What a graceless man is this apostate! Is he not a dry, withered, fruitless tree, twice dead, plucked up by the roots ?

Barrow reserves his sharpest criticism for the functioning of the discipline in the Church of England. As a student of law, and as a member of Gray's Inn, he was familiar with the history and practice of common law. He was thankful for Magna Carta, for Parliament as an expression of the public will, and for the common law courts as agencies of justice derived from custom and statutes. But he was contemptuous toward the hierarchy of archbishops, bishops, deans, chancellors, commissaries, officials, and archdeacons. He hated the spiritual courts, such as the Court of High Commission, the Court of Audience, the Court of Faculties, the Court of Arches, the lesser courts of chancellors, commissaries, and archdeacons. He denounced the unfair oath *ex officio* and refused to take it. He characterized the spiritual courts as stage-like, pompous, popish, and arrogant. To him their procedure was insolent, lawless, noisy, and undignified. He resented the jurisdiction exercised by the Court of High Commission as an encroachment on the royal prerogative, in defiance of Magna Carta, of Parliament, of the Privy Council; in disregard of the higher law of man and of God.

He terminates his argument with Gifford by denying not only the form but also the substance or matter of the Church of England. Since the membership is a mixed company of believers and unbelievers, since the ministry is imposed by bishops and patrons rather than called by the church, since the worship is popish and stinted, and since the discipline is defective, he reaches the easy conclusion that the Church of England is a false church. This being so, he concludes that Gifford began his book without counsel, continued it without grace, and ended it without truth.

Introduction

A Refutation of Mr. Giffard's Reasons Concerning Our Purposes in the Practise of the Truth of the Gospel of Christ

Barrow made four accusations or charges of principal transgressions against the Church of England. These constitute the outline and substance of his book, *A Plaine Refutation*. But he also set forth his positive programme of purposes in five articles. The gist of these articles is that the Separatists seek the kingdom of Christ, that they plan to worship God in the manner prescribed in the Bible, that they intend to establish by covenant a fellowship of believers who in turn will elect their leaders, that they desire to introduce the New Testament polity and discipline, and that in accordance with this faith and order, by the assistance of the Holy Ghost, they promise to lead their lives and, if necessary, to leave their lives.

Gifford replied to these articles, but it was not easy to differ with such obvious purposes as seeking the kingdom of Christ and worshipping God in the New Testament manner. He therefore took issue with the Separatists in their third, fourth, and fifth articles, which announced a complete separation from the Church of England and the establishment of a new, gathered, covenanted, congregational, independent, church.

The burden of Gifford's accusation is that the Separatists as private men were taking ecclesiastical responsibility into their own hands and that they usurped the functions of the chief magistrate. It is to these two points that Barrow addresses himself after making a few observations on Gifford's handling of the five articles.

Barrow replies that private men in all ages constitute the church. Where two or three or fifty private men assemble in the name of Christ, there is the nucleus of a possible church. In the church at Antioch, it was the church of private men that fasted, prayed, and ordained Barnabas and Saul (Acts 13:3). Did not all the primitive churches originate with private men, who selected and consecrated their leaders? Only gradually and regrettably did the bishop arrogate to himself the power that the church had exercised. Many early bishops were elected by the voice of the people, by acclamation, even by force against the wishes of the candidate himself.

Barrow insists that when the church was established under Elizabeth, it derived no power or status or apostolic succession from the Roman Catholic Church, for the popish church was a false church. Only private men within the church in all ages constitute the true church. The martyrs in Queen Mary's days were but private men, separated from the established Roman Church. Yet the martyrs are the glory of the Church of England. If the martyrs, as the leaders of private men, separated from the corruptions of the Roman Church, may not the suffering Separatists withdraw from the corruptions of the Anglican Church? The question is not easy to resolve. We may well ask ourselves: if Gentile separated from Jew, if Antioch from Jerusalem, if Peter from James, if West from East, if Roman Catholic from Greek Orthodox, if Anglican from Roman, if Separatist from Anglican, who then is the schismatic?

The other question is both difficult and touchy. Do not the Separatists " runne before the prince's commandement "? In other words, do not the Separatists usurp the power of the Queen, limit her prerogative, and intrude themselves into the seat of the magistrate? Barrow was aware of the dangers and pitfalls involved in the question, but he dealt with it boldly, perhaps recklessly, in an age that knew not any " heretical " doctrine of separation of church and state.

Private men are commanded by God to establish His ministry and government. The Apostles did not sue to parliaments for permission to establish the Christian Church. The early followers of Christ did not wait upon Nero, or Decius, or Diocletian to sanction their missionary work. They obeyed a higher law and a more majestic governor.

Introduction

No earthly prince may negate God's commandment. If the magistrate fails to promote God's will, if he establishes a false church, then Christians may not interfere with the magistrate nor with the false church, nor with the false ministry, but they may and must forsake the false to seek the true church. The same commission given to the Apostles is given to all men at all times to seek first the kingdom of God and His righteousness. Private men must seek "the true worship of God in the true church, though all the princes of the world, whether believers or infidels, should forbid the same." Therefore, Gifford's distinction that the church may reform under heathen and popish princes but not under Christian magistrates, though they err in some points, is false. If it is unlawful to disobey a Christian prince, it is equally unlawful to disobey a heathen or popish prince. The only recourse for the conscientious Christian and the true church is to do God's will without exception, without tarrying for the magistrate, without resistance to the prince, and without fear of Christian suffering even unto death. When Barrow was hanged on April 6, 1593, he exemplified his own teaching.

THE WRITINGS OF
HENRY BARROW
1590-1591

I

A PLAINE REFUTATION

Barrow's work, *A Plaine Refutation of Mr. George Giffarde's Reprochful Booke*, printed at Dort in the Netherlands in 1590-1591, is a composite work. Besides Barrow's treatise, *A Plaine Refutation*, it contains " A Brief Summe of the Causes of Our Seperation, and of Our Purposes in Practise, Withstood by George Gifford, Defended by Henry Barrow as Followeth". This is a recapitulation with new material of the controversy with Gifford in 1587-1588, and is printed in Carlson, *The Writings of Henry Barrow*, 1587-1590, pp. 118-150. It also contains " A Refutation of Mr. Giffard's Reasons Concerning Our Purposes in the Practise of the Truth of the Gospel of Christ," also by Barrow, and two treatises by Greenwood, " A Breife Refutation of Mr. George Giffard His Supposed Consimilitude betwene the Donatists and Us," and also his " A Fewe Observations of Mr. Giffard's Last Cavills about Stinted Read Prayers, and Devised Leitourgies." Thus there are in all three works by Barrow and two by Greenwood.

In the 1591 edition the arrangement is as follows :

Title page. *Verso* is blank.
Dedication to Lord Burghley — ii *recto* — iv *verso*.
" Wisdome to the Reader " — A *recto* — A iv *verso* — B *recto* — B ii *verso*, 12 pages.
" A Brief Summe of the Causes " — pp. 1-20.
" A Plaine Refutation " — pp. 21-186.
" A Refutation of Mr. Giffard's Reasons " — pp. 187-206. (The title is not given in the 1591 edition, but it is in the 1605 edition).
" A Breife Refutation " — pp. 207-234.
" A Fewe Observations " — pp. 235-255.

The 1605 edition is a careful re-issue of the 1591 work, with one major change. It eliminates Greenwood's "A Fewe Observations" and replaces it with Barrow's "A Few Observations to the Reader of M. Giffard His Last *Replie* [A SHORT REPLY].

The title page of the 1591 edition has the word "consimilituda" which becomes "consimilitude" in the 1605 edition. Also, in the re-issued work there is an additional one-paragraph introduction or statement to the reader. I have collated the two editions and checked eight copies of the book. Aside from the differences noted, there are a few minor variations in spelling, punctuation, and overturned letters, but only significant departures from the 1591 text have been noted.

For many decades the copy of the 1591 *A Plaine Refutation* at the Huntington Library has been regarded as a unique copy, and it is so listed in the *Short-Title Catalogue* (no. 1523). It came into the library of Sir Thomas Egerton, Attorney-General, perhaps in 1593 after the trial of Barrow and Greenwood. Thus, the book became a part of the family library at Bridgewater House, and in February, 1917, the book was in the collection sold to Henry E. Huntington. This is the only copy of the 1591 edition in the United States, but fortunately there are other copies of the first edition in Lambeth Palace Library, in the Norwich Public Library, and in the Lincoln Cathedral Library. The book is also available in University Microfilms, Ann Arbor, Michigan, reel 172.

The 1605 edition is available in the British Museum, Lambeth Palace Library, Durham Cathedral Library, the University of St. Andrews, and Archbishop Marsh's Library at Dublin.

The copies of the book at the Bodleian Library, Trinity College, Dublin, the University of Edinburgh Library, have the date 1606, but otherwise are identical with the 1605 edition. It is probable that in the course of printing the book late in

A Plaine Refutation

1605 or early in 1605/6 that the date was changed to 1606. American copies of the 1605 edition are available at Yale and the Library of Congress, and there is a 1606 imprint at the Boston Public Library and also at the Union Theological Seminary Library in New York.

[AA 1 recto]

A PLAINE
REFVTATION
OF M. G. GIFFARDES
reprochful booke, intituled
a short treatise against the Donatists
of England.

Wherein is discouered the forgery of the whole Ministrie, the confusion, false worship, and antichristian disorder of these Parish assemblies, called the Church of England.
Here also is prefixed a summe of the causes of our seperation, and of our purposes in practise, which M. GIFFARD hath twise sought to confute, and hath now twise receiued answere, by HENRIE
BARROWE.

Here is furder annexed a briefe refutation of M. Giff. supposed consimilituda [sic] betwixt the Donatists and vs. Wherein is shewed how his Arguments haue bene & may be
by the Papists more iustly retorted against
himself & the present estate of
their Church, by
I. GREN.

Here are also inserted a fewe obseruations of M. Giff. his
cauils about read prayer & deuised
Leitourgies.
[Dort], 1591

A Plaine Refutation

" Good Reader,[1] the treatises here insuing (being some while since intercepted)[2] are now republished for thy good, together with a few observations of Mr. Giffard his last *Reply*, not printed heretofore.[3] Read and ponder them with judgment and indifferencie, and as thou findest them to accord with the word of God, so acknowledge and accept them: but not in any thing wherin they do erre therefrom; as al men's writings are subject to errour. It shal bee thy part therfore in these, as in al the writings of any men, to consider and examine them by the Scriptures and word of God, which is alone the word of truth; and so far to receive them, and no furder but as they agree therwith. The Lord give thee understanding and grace to to [*sic*] follow the truth in love, to the salvation of thy soule, by Jesus Christ. Amen. 1605.

[AA 2 *recto*][4] To the right honorable pere [peer] and grave Counselor Sr. [Sir] William Cecill, Knight of the most noble order, Baron of Burleigh, Lord High Treasurer of England, etc., grace and wisdome be multiplied from God our Father and from our Lord Jesus Christ.

Proverbs 18:17. *Justus qui primus in lite sua, donec advenit proximus eius et pervestiget illum.*[5]

Hitherto (Right Honorable) have our malignant adversaries [Robert Some and George Giffard] had their full scope against us with the lawe in their owne handes, and have made no spare or conscience to accuse, blaspheame, condempne, and punish us, yea, to pronounce and publish us as damnable hereticks, schismatikes, sectaries, seditious, disobedient to princes, deniers and abridgers of their sacred power, etc., to the eares and eies of all men openly in

---

[1] This introductory paragraph or preface is in the 1605 edition of *A Plaine Refutation* but not in the 1591 edition. The writer is Francis Johnson, who had collaborated in the seizure and destruction of the 1591 edition. Thus, his work in 1605 atoned for his anti-Separatist action in 1591.

[2] About 2,000 copies of Barrow's *A Brief Discoverie of the False Church* were confiscated in April, 1591, and burned in June. This work was not re-issued. About 1,000 copies of *A Plaine Refutation*, containing three treatises by Barrow and two by Greenwood, were also confiscated and burned at the same time. This is the work which was re-published.

[3] Barrow's *A Few Observations to the Reader of M. Giffard His Last* REPLY [A SHORT REPLY] replaced Greenwood's *A Fewe Observations* in the 1605 edition.

[4] The first eight pages have no number or signature designation. I have designated them as AA1, AA2, AA3, and AA4, *recto* and *verso*, since they precede A1 *recto*.

[5] He that pleadeth his cause first seemeth just; but his neighbor cometh and searcheth him out.

their pulpits, and in their printed bookes, published by the consent and approbation of their church.¹ No trial all this while upon anie sute or complaint graunted us: either civile, that we might know for what cause and by what lawe we thus suffer, which yet is not denied the most horrible malefactors and offendors: or ecclesiasticall by the word of God, where place and freedome might be given us to declare and pleade our owne cause in sobrietie and order: that so the meanes appoincted of God for our recoverie might be used, and wee (wherein we should be found to erre or transgresse) might be convinced to our faces by the Scriptures, and left inexcuseable. But in stead of this christian course, they have shut us up now more than three yeares² in miserable and close prisons from the aire, from all exercise, from all companie or conversation with anie person, from all meanes so much as to write, yncke and paper being taken and kept from us, [AA 2 *verso*] and a diligent watch both by our keapers held over us, and also continuall searches upon one pretence or other made, where we were rifled from time to time of all our papers and writinges they could find.³ And being thus streightly kept and watched from speaking or writing, their conscience yet giving them no rest in all their prosperitie and pleasures, whilest we the Lord's poore witnesses against their sinnes breathed (not to speake of their secret and indirect meanes wherby they sought to take away our lyves), they suborned (amongst sondrie others) two special instruments, Mr. Some and Mr. Giffard, to accuse and blaspheme us publiquelie

---

¹ This is a reference to Richard Alison, George Gifford, and Robert Some, who had already written on behalf of the Church of England against the Separatists.

² From October 8, 1587, or November 19, 1587, to October 8, 1590, or November 19, 1590, would be exactly three years of imprisonment for Greenwood and Barrow. Barrow is writing about December, 1590, or during the early months of 1590/1.

³ This strict policy of keeping ink and paper from the prisoners, searching their rooms and rifling their papers, probably dates from the autumn of 1588, when both Barrow's *marginal* notes and *interleaved* notes on Dr. Some's *A Godly Treatise Containing and Deciding Certaine Questions* (1588) had been seized by the prison authorities. Undoubtedly these searches were more systematic after September, 1590, by which time Barrow and Greenwood's two books, *A Collection of Certaine Sclaunderous Articles Gyven Out by the Bisshops*, and *A Collection of Certain Letters and Conferences*, had been published. During the autumn Barrow completed *A Brief Discoverie of the False Church*, and smuggled it out sheet by sheet with the aid of Daniel Studley. When it is remembered that there are in all 270 printed pages in this book, this must have been no easy task to escape the vigilance of the keepers.

A Plaine Refutation

to the viewe of the world, etch [sic] of them in two bookes,[1] the one [Dr. Some] labouring to prove us Anabaptists, the other [Mr. George Giffard] Donatists in the same. Which bookes they have preferred especiallie to your Honor,[2] as the chiefe obstacle that hindered them from their violent and bloudie course, of the same intent (no doubt) that their predicessors the chiefe priestes and pharasies accused our Saviour unto Pilat, and the Apostle Paule unto the Romane governours. Yet even all this, we hope, the Lord hath disposed to the furder manifestation of his truth, by directing our adversaries to bring our criminations before your Honor. Of whose wisdome and equitie we have so great experience and assurance, as we cannot from henceforth doubt to be condempned unheard, or to find therein worse usage, than our Saviour and the Apostles found at those heathen rulers.

Wherfore we addressed our selves (by such meanes as the Lord administred, and as the incommodities [sic] of the place, and the infirmities of our decaied bodies and memories would permit) to our defence, or rather to the defence of that truth, wherof God hath made and set us his unworthie witnesses, though as signes to be spoken against, and as monstrous persons in this sinful generation. And have hereunto undertaken Mr. Giffard's two reprochfull blasphemous bookes: shewing the true causes of our separation from the parish assemblies, confirming and approving the same to be both true and sufficient [AA 3 *recto*] by sondrie weightie reasons and expresse Scriptures; refelling[3] by the like all the frivolous cavills and injurious sclanders which Mr. Giffard hath there brought to hide their sinnes, deface the truth, and to defame us. As also shewing such apparant dissimilitude betwixt the Donatists and us, both in the causes of our and their seperation, and in the manner of our and their proceedings, and in sondrie errors they held, as no

---

[1] Robert Some published his *A Godly Treatise Containing and Deciding Certaine Questions* about May, 1588. A year later his second book appeared, *A Godly Treatise, Wherein Are Examined and Confuted Many Execrable Fancies Given Out by H. Barrow and J. Greenewood.* Gifford's *A Short Treatise* appeared about May, 1590, and his second work against the Separatists, *A Plaine Declaration That Our Brownists Be Full Donatists*, appeared about February, 1590-1 (not May 4, 1590, as is stated in *A Short-Title Catalogue*, item 11862).

[2] Some's *A Godly Treatise, Wherein are Examined and Confuted Many Execrable Fancies* (1589) is dedicated to Sir Christopher Hatton and Sir William Cecil, chancellors of Oxford and Cambridge University. Gifford's *A Short Treatise* (1590) is dedicated to Sir William Cecil, Lord Burghley.

[3] Refuting, confuting, disproving.

man of anie knowledge or judgment before attempted, or shall hereafter be able (with anie truth or conscience) to compare us unto them herein, or to excuse Mr. Giffard for this his unchristian deeling with us. All whose unsanctified reproches wherwith his bookes through everie sentence are seasoned in stead of better grace, hereupon fall to the ground, and remaine upon his owne, and not upon our accompt. This defence when whe [we] had through the mercifull hand of our God finished, though not with anie shew of humane wisdome or arte, so much as in simplicitie of the truth and innocencie of our heartes, wee held it our dutie to present in like maner in al reverence and humilitie unto your honorable view and grave consideration. That both sides beeing heard according to equitie, and our answeres as well as their criminations duly expended, your sentence, or at the le[a]st [your] approbation, might proceede according to the truth. Craving herein no furder favour, than according to the equitie of our cause and innocencie of our doings: nor yet shunning any furder triall of the one or the other, that your Honor shall appoinct or thincke meet; whether with these our adversaries, or anie other that shall be contrarie minded, whosoever. Beeseaching your Honor's perdon for this our bould presumption, the rather because such necessitie was layed upon us by the hand of God, through the importunate chalenges and insolent provocations of these our accusors: whose mouthes must either be stopped, or else through our default the holy truth of God, which we beleeve and professe, yea, and our innocencie be betrayed to the perpetual infamie of these our reprochfull adversaries, to our owne [AA 3 *verso*] present perill and future judgment, to the scandall of all that professe the same truth with us, but chiefly to the offence and torning backe of many, even of the whole land, from the streight waies of the Lord, even the waies of life and peace. All which mischiefes (we trust) shalbe prevented by these our simple indevours, the Lord giving testimonie and blessing to his owne word. The truth wherof shall shine forth in our simplicitie, the power therof be made manifest in our weakenes, to the discoverie and reformation of these publique enormities in the false worship, open sacrilege, antichristian ministerie and heinous disorder exercised and soffred in this land, and to the discipation of all the delusions and vain promises and perswasions of these false prophetts, wherwith they have a long time (for their owne fleshlie pompe and filthie lucre) seduced the whole land, drawen them into, and held them in the wrath and heavie judgments of God. That so the mightie hand

A Plaine Refutation

of God working in the heart of our sovereigne prince and nobles, especiallie through your Honor's faithfull counsell and furtherance; and also in the heartes of all the Commons, when the truth of these things shal be shewed unto them, a general and sincere conversion to the Lord may be made, even from all things that now are, or hereafter shall be found contrarie to his holie will, whither in the publique estate of all, or in the private estate of anie. For sure, as everie perticular person goeth forward from faith to faith as knowledge is increaced, everie day teaching other unto eternal life, so in the publique estate of the church no change that is made according unto the truth, as the publique error is espied, ought to be held strange or dangerous. But most heavenlie is that harmonie, where all the members kint [knit] together in the same faith, both in general and perticular, with one accord goe forward in their callings and duties, still amending what is found amisse, and daylie indevouring to doo better. Then should [AA 4 *recto*] there not be found anie such unchristian contention abought the truth, pleading and spurning against the truth, or persecution for the truth. Then should the Lord's dreadful judgments, which now hang over the whole land for these sinnes, be avoided, and his blessings in stead therof be multiplied. But sure in the meane time until these sinnes be removed out of God's sight and redressed, there is no peace to be looked for or asked of the Lord, there is no pleading with or against Him, howsoever the false prophet may goe abought to heale the hurte of this people as a light evill, saiing, "peace, peace, when there is no peace,"[1] and to repair the breaches that are as the sea, with untempered stuffe and vaine visions tending unto abdication. Wherfore, to the torning away of so great evills, and the procuring of so great and inestimable benefites to our sovereign queene and countrie, as we have not with-holden our utmost indevours to the discoverie of the publique enormities and sinnes of these times, in all truth and freedome, being readie yet furder to witnesse and approve the same, if such neade be, to the face of our greatest adversaries and gainsayers, by the evidence of God's word. So now it remaineth that we instantly beseach your Honor, even in the name of God, before whome we shall all of us shortly appeare to our accompt and judgment, by whome this chardge is layed upon you (the cause being now brought, and by both sides, aswell our adversaries as us, layed open before your Honor) that you would

[1] Jeremiah 6 : 14 and 8 : 11. See also Ezekiel 13 : 10.

now be a meanes to her right excellent Majestie that these weighty and dangerous matters may be no longer wrapped up or put off in securitie and silence (lest these our soffrings and testimonies rise in judgment with this generation), but may rather be furder inquired and discussed, and order and redresse taken according to the will of God. Which shall no doubt torne [turn] to the high glorie and most acceptable service of God and of your prince, to the unspeakable [AA 4 verso] benefite of this whole land, and to the happie discharge of your dutie and conscience to your eternall praise in this life and in the life to come.

   Your lordship's most humble and addict in the Lord:
   HENRIE BARROWE and JOHN GRENWOOD
    for the testimonie of the gospel in close prison

[A 1 recto] *Wisdome to the reader from the Father of lightes, to discerne of these times, and to judge of themselves what is right.*

Math. 24
Mark 13
Psa. 74
Dan. 7, 9, &
11 Cap.

II Thes. 2
II Tim. 3

Revel. 6

Revel. 8

Revel. 9

Seing the Scripture speaketh evidently of the generall defection and apostasie under Antichrist, and of the abhominable desolation and havock that he should make in these dangerous and latter times; where the sunne should be made blacke as a sack-cloth of haire, the moone be made as blood, the starres cast to the earth, the heaven departe away as a booke wrapped up, every mountaine and isle be moved out of their place. And all these things are most perticularly and most lively described in the booke of the Revelation: of Antichriste's beginning, increace, exaltation, abolishing. How a great part of the trees and all greene grasse should be blasted, a great [third] parte of the sea become blood, and of the creatures that lived therin dye, and a greate parte of the shippes therof be destroied; the third parte of the rivers and of the fountaines of waters be torned into wormwood, and manie men die of the bitternes therof. How that fallen apostatat starre should open the bottomles pitte, the sunne and aire be darkened with the smoke therof, the earth pestered with the swarme of poisoned stinging scorpions, and crowned armed locustes that came out of the smoke of the pitte; and of those innumerable warriours upon those strange horses that destroied such multitudes of men. How the

A Plaine Refutation

beast should get unto him manie [seven] heads and mo [ten] hornes, and upon his hornes crownes: how he should be inthronised, receive the dragon his large power and high commission: how he should warre with the sainctes, and open his mouth into blasphemie against God: how he should erect his image, and give his marke: how he should kill as manie as will not worship his image, and suffer none to buye or sell, but such as receive his marcke. How that greate harlot that sate upon manie waters, so gorgiously araied and adorned, the mother of all the whoredomes and abhominations of the earth, with that goulden cuppe full of abhominations and filthines of her fornication in her hand, wherwith she made droncken all the inhabitantes of the earth, should sit upon the beast, and be made droncken with the blood of the sainctes and martyres of Jesus. Revel. 13

Revel. 17

And yet furder: how the vials of God's wrathfull judgments should by his faithfull messengers and witnesses be powred forth upon the earth, upon the sea, upon the rivers and fountaines of water, upon the sunne, upon the throne of the beast, upon the greate river Euphrates, and into the aire with the peculiar and fearfull plagues denounsed and to be executed hereupon. As also how the great Babilon should be discovered, forsaken, pleaded against, condempned, consumed, fire cast upon her and all her wares, the greate milstone upon her and al her children, and inhabitantes to presse her downe to hell. Revel. 16

Revel. 18

To conclude: how Christ himself and his holye armie mounted upon the white horse of his word, should warre against the beast, and [A 1 *verso*] against the kinges and nations that were gathered togither by the false prophet into battell against Christ and his armie, how he should smite the heathen with the sharpe sword that issueth out of his mouth, rule them with a rod of yron, and tread them in the wine-presse of his fierce wrath: how he should give the flesh of all this people with their kinges, capitanes and mightie men as a praye [prey] to the fowles the uncleane spirites: and how he should take the beast, and with him the false prophet that wrought signes before him, wherein he deceived them that re- Revel. 19

ceived the beaste's marck and worshipped his image, and cast these both alive into that lake of fire burning in brimstone.

Who now (if not such to whome the Scriptures are hidden, and this booke sealed) could in this generall falling away from the gospel, this generall departure of the true established churches out of the inhabited, this universall corruption and confusion of all estates, degrees, persons, callings, actions, both in the church and commune welth, in this estate, in this defection, seeke for or pleade for a true visible established church, the true ministerie of the gospel, true worship, ministration, sacraments, government, order? Or who (that were not droncke and had all their senses bound and intoxicate with the whore's cuppe) could affirme this confuse Babel, these cages of uncleane birdes, these prisons of foule and hatefull spirits, to be the spouse of Christ, the congregations of the sainctes, the true established and rightly ordered churches of Christ? Is it likely that these men have as yet read the whore's misterie written in her forehead, or as yet know what belongeth to the true established church, worship, administration, sacraments, ordinances, government of Christ? Though they have in his Testament which is dayly read amongest them, an exact and absolute patterne of al these things before their eies: and have not in their churches anie one thing in their practise and proceedings, not one pinne, naile, or hooke according to the true patterne: yea, though they heare the trompets of the Lord blowen against them, though they see the viallz of the Lord's wrath powred upon them, and all their doings, yet stop they their eares and wincke with their eies, lest they should see with their eies, and heare with their eares, and understand with their heartes, and be converted and healed. And therfore are so farr from finding place to repentance, that they open their mouthes into blasphemie and railings; especially these men that have the marcke of the beaste, upon whome that evill and malignant sore is fallen, as you dayly see and heare in their bookes and pulpets.

And how well these governours, mariners, merchant-

A Plaine Refutation

men, and all that trafique on this sea, can endure the borning [burning] of these their pleasant gainefull wares, how they waile, howle, and crye out when this heavenly fire is cast out into their shippes: let the behaviour of these bishopps their hierarchie and priestes towards the servants of God, that speak against their antichristian proceadings, shew, and how they bestir them to quench the burning of the harlot, smiting and rending Christ's poore Revel. 12:15 witnesses with tongue, tooth, and naile, casting out of their mouthes a flood of raylings, reproches, sclanders, [A 2 recto] criminations against them of poysoned bitters [sic] waters, corrupt doctrines, blasphemous opinions, unsufferable perverting and abusing the Scriptures to hide, tolerat[e], or defend the antichristian forgeries, abhominations, disorder and enormities of their church and ministrie, that are discovered and condempned by the word of God in the mouthes of us his simple witnesses.

Of this sort (amongst manie other such like) are two bookes notoriously infamous, lately published by one George Giffard, a priest of their orders, against certeine Christians, whome he calleth Brownists, Donatists. In the one of these bookes[1] he laboureth to defend and cleare the parish assemblies of the Church of England, of such heinous crimes as the said Christians object against them, and forsake them for, witnessing and suffring in bandes and persecution against the same under the handes of these popish prelats and Romish priestes. In the other booke he indevoreth to recover the blame he justly suffred in the first for reproching, sclandering, blaspheming, accusing these faithfull and innocent Christians, appliing himself to prove them Donatists by comparing together them from poinct to poinct.[2] Both which bookes are here answered,[3] and now at length published to the perusing and judgment of al men. Where they shal see how well he hath de-

---

[1] *A Short Treatise against the Donatists of England, Whome We Call Brownists* (1590).
[2] *A Plaine Declaration that Our Brownists Be Full Donatists, by Comparing Them Together from Point to Point Out of the Writings of Augustine.* This work was issued about February, 1590/1.
[3] Barrow's *A Plaine Refutation* answers Gifford's *A Short Treatise*, and Greenwood's *A Breife Refutation* replies to Gifford's *A Plaine Declaration.*

livered and acquitted thier church, in the first: as also how justly he hath proved his charges, accusations, and blasphemies in the first and second.

The fower principall transgressions wherwith we charge, and for which we forsake parish assemblies: namely, the prophanenes, wickednes, confusion of the people which are here received, reteined and nourished as members: the unlawfullnes of their whole ministrie which is imposed upon them, reteined and mainteined by them; the superstition and idolatrie of their publique worship in that devised leitourgie which is imposed upon them; and the forgerie of their antichristian ecclesiasticall government, to which al their churches stand subject;[1] are such and so apparant, as not only prove these parish assemblies not to be true established churches of Christ; but if it were admitted (which can never be proved) that they somtimes had bene true established churches; yet these transgressions obstinatly stood in and defended, are sufficient causes of our separation from them in this degenerate estate. For where such prophane confuse multitudes without anie exception, separation, or choice, were all of them immediately from publique idolatrie at one instant received, or rather compelled to be members of this church in some parish or other, where they inhabited, without any due calling to the faith by the preaching of the gospel going before or orderly joyning togither in the faith, there being no voluntarie or particular confession of their owne faith and duties made or required of any; and last of all, no holy walking in the faith found amongst them. Who can say that these churches, consisting of this people, were ever rightly gathered or built according to the rules of Christ's Testament? Or who can say that this people in this estate are [A 2 verso] the communion of sainctes? Or who (without sacrilege) in this estate can

---

[1] These are the familiar four causes which emerge in Barrow's writings. After refuting some of Gifford's arguments, Barrow deals with these causes or principal transgressions in the following order: 1. false worship; 2. false membership; 3. false ministry; 4. false discipline. These constitute the main outline of the entire book.

administer the holy things of God unto, or in the same communicate with this people? Likewise, where these parishes have a false and antichristian ministerie imposed upon them, who can say that they are the true established churches of Christ? To the building and ministery wherof Christ hath ordeined, instituted, and prescribed a certaine ministrie unto the worlde's end? Or who (withoutsacrilege) may joyne unto, or communicate with a false and antichristian ministrie? Christ also hath given unto his church perpetuall and alsufficient rules in his holy word for the whole administration and government of his established churches, to which they are bound, wherby they ought to buyld, proceede, and walke. Those churches then that receive an other leitourgie, an other foundation, other rules for their administration and government, cannot be said the right and true established churches of Christ. Neither may anie faithfull man joyne unto them in this administration and government, without heynous impietie and denying the faith. The more particular proofe aswell of these arguments as of these transgressions, insue hereafter in this treatise. These reasons all men may see prove directly these parish assemblies not to be the true established churches of Christ to which anie faithfull Christian may joyne himself in this estate; especially when all reformation unto the rules of Christ's Testament is not only denied, but resisted, blasphemed, persecuted.

How then are Mr. Giffarde's eies bound and covered with the spirit of slumber, that still dreameth of a true church, ministrie, sacraments, worship, government, in this estate; and will not be wakened by these reasons, or anie thing that can be said or alleged against their ungodly doings; though he can neither approve these his strong conceived imaginations by the rules of God's word, nor disprove these evident charges in the fower principall transgressions by us alledged against their parish assemblyes. Which yet he indevoreth to put away and shift off by shameles sclanders and open untruthes; giving out: that we condemne a church, for that wicked men come with the godly to the publique exercises of religion: for that there are some ungodly men of the church;[1] for that there are some wantes in the calling of the ministers,[2] and in the outward discipline:[3] as also, some imperfections or corruptions in the worship, which are not fundamental.[4]

The untruth wherof, our verie propositions (though we should no furder answer) sheweth to his face. Where we charge, and the word of God condemneth their assemblies, for that they consist of prophane multitudes never orderly gathered unto, or walking in the faith. There shall whilest the church consisteth of mortall men alwayes be wicked in the church. But Christ hath his fanne in his hand to make cleane his barne flore. And hath given power and commandement to his church to cast out the wicked from amongst them. We acknowledge that the prince ought to compell al their subjects to the hearing of God's word in the publique exercises of the church: yet cannot the prince compell any to [A 3 *recto*] be a member of the church, or the church to receive any without assurance by the publique profession of their owne faith, or to reteine anie longer, than they continue and walke orderly in the faith.

Againe, we condemne not their assemblies for some faltes in the calling of the ministrie; but for having and reteining a false and antichristian ministrie imposed upon them. Such we here prove their whole ministrie to be in office, entrance, and administration. In like maner, we forsake not their assemblies for some faltes in their government or discipline, but for standing subject to a popish and antichristian government. And such we here prove theirs to be in the officers, courtes, proceedings. Neither refreine we their worship for some light imperfections (as he saith) but because their worship is superstitious, devised by men, idolatrous, according to that patched popish portesse,[5] their service booke, according unto which their sacraments and whole administration is performed, and not by the rules of

---

[1] *A Short Treatise*, pp. 47-70.
[2] *Ibid.*, pp. 70-82.
[3] *Ibid.*, pp. 82-90.
[4] *Ibid.*, pp. 7-17 especially, but also pp. 17-46.
[5] Portas, a breviary — *The Book of Common Prayer*.

A Plaine Refutation

Christ's Testament. Such we here prove their booke, worship and ministration to be.

We also before set downe unto him sundry popish, idolatrous, and blasphemous abuses in their worship and ministration: as their idoll Lent, Ember and Eave fastes; their idoll feastes; popish and Jewish Easter, Pentecost, Christmasse, etc.; their idoll Ladie dayes, Sainctes' dayes, Innocentes' dayes, Angells' dayes, Soule dayes. Their false maner of administring their sacramentes with such idolatrous and popish ceremonies and trinckets, the font, signe of the crosse, gossips, etc. Their midwives' baptisme, confirmation: their housling the sick with the other sacrament: their Juish and popish ceremonies, vestures, etc. Their purification, offertories, chrismes, etc.[1] Their mariing, buriing, limiting or conjuring the fieldes, made a parte of the publique worship, and of the pastor's office, etc. These abhominations Mr. Giffard will at no hand have called popish, idolatrous or blasphemous. We impudently lye (he claims), and unsufferably sclander in so saiing. He therfore indevoreth to pourge them of all popish and superstitious opinions and abuses, shewing how cleare the Church of England is of the same. Yet will not Mr. Giffard be thought to plead for or justifie anie publique abuse of the church, but only to plead against the Brownists that speake worse of these things than they are. For these are no fundamental errors, such as polute the worship, but only light imperfections, etc. Well, we will refer the discussing of the nature of them how heinous they are, unto their due place. Only here we would know of Mr. Giffard what foundation these things themselves have in the word of God, and what warrant he can there shew for them. If he can justifie them by the word of God, then verely our offences are no lesse than he hath said, that blame them to be idolatrous, popish, blasphemous. But if these trumperies have no foundation or commandement in God's word, but are the devises of men; then we would know whither God requireth or

---

[1] This is a summary of Barrow's reply to Gifford's answer. See Leland H. Carlson, *The Writings of Henry Barrow, 1587-1590*, p. 131.

accepteth such worship at their hands? And whither being made the publique worship of God and administration of their church, they be not idolatrie? And then how they may offer, or [A 3 verso] the faithfull be constrayned to such idolatrie, to such worship, as God neither requireth non [nor] accepteth? And with what conscience he can, or how he dare stand a minister of that leitourgie and worship, which the [he] cannot approve by the word of God, and which he would not be thought to allowe of, the abuses therof being so manifest and odious in his owne eies? Especially now with what conscience he can thus blaspheme and condempne us for refreining that worship which he cannot approve, and doth not alowe. Or how he can so earnestly inveigh against those most forward and zealous hearers, who though they will heare their sermons, yet withdraw from the booke service, for the errors and evills they see therin. This Mr. Giffard in the Epistle to his second booke, saith, is a more grievous sinne than they suppose.[1] In deed, if the poore soules knew what they did or ought to doo in refreining the publique false worship of the church, they would and could have no spirituall communion with those ministers or people that still exercise and will not be withdrawen from the same false worship, which they condempne and forsake; nor yet would or might they heare their learned sermons that are joyned and conformed to the same idolatries and abuses.

But to the matter; untill Mr. Giffard can prove by the word of God this publique worship and administration according to their service booke in those poinctes wherin we blame them, there is no cause he should exercise it himself, allure others therunto, or condempne us for refreigning the same as we are commanded of God in as manie places as true worship is injoyned, and false worship forbidden. In all this then he but bewraieth his owne shame and hipocrisie in condempning and blaspheming us for doing the will of God, in aluring others to false worship and idolatrie; and in doing that

[18] *A Plaine Declaration*, Ai verso.

A Plaine Refutation

himself for filthie lucre and feare of the world, which he for shame of the world dare not alow, neither can justifie.

Yea, and whatsoever he colourably pretendeth and aledgeth in his second booke to cover and excuse the shame and infamie of his former;[1] yet is he become an earnest pleader for all the corruptions and abuses of his church, not granting unto us anie one of the abuses we reprove to be unlawfull and ungodly, lest we should therupon urge him to have the same left and refreined (though not publiquely put downe and reformed as he accuseth) by the faithfull: and so they should be condempned for the practise, and we justified for the refreining these things. Therfore he is driven to plead for, mitigat, excuse, to tollerate with his uttermost shiftes and cavills all these abhominations whatsoever. Which yet are so heinous and of so high a nature, as no pretexts of the prince's or churche's power, of ceremonies, of things indifferent, no distinctions of substance and forme, of fundamental and not fundamental errors and corruptions, etc., can hide, but they are found heinous transgressions of the law of God, detestable abuses of the worship of God. And he in practising and pleading for them is found but as the dogge retorned to his owne vomit; as the false prophet that teacheth the prince to set a scandall before the people, and that seduceth the people to eate their idolothites.[2] [A 4 recto]

Yea, he is yet furder driven, openly to justifie the ministrie and regiment of these arch and lord bishops and their hierarchie to be of Christ, against which he erewhile also amongest the rest of that faction was an earnest sutor to the parliament to have them utterly

---

[1] The second book is *A Plaine Declaration*; the former is *A Short Treatise*.
[2] Things offered to idols. The reference to the false prophet is from Revelation 2 : 14, and pertains to Balaam. In Numbers, chapters 22-24, the conduct of Balaam seems exemplary, but Jehovah was displeased when Balaam accompanied the princes of Moab (22 : 22), although Jehovah seems to have given permission to go (22 : 20). Balaam was slain by the people of Israel. (31 : 8). In Joshua 13 : 22 Balaam is termed a soothsayer. See also II Peter 2 : 15 and Jude 1 : 11; Deuteronomy 23 : 4, Joshua 24 : 9, 10, Nehemiah 13 : 2, Micah 6 : 5.

removed out of the church and abolished,[1] their offices, ministrie, courtes, government, which could not be done without most heinous impietie, open barbaritie and violence to the church and unto Christ himself, if they had bene of Christ, as he now pretendeth. Againe if they were not of Christ but of Antichrist (as they all of that sect then upon certeine knowledge and assurance affirmed) how, and with what conscience could the Reformists themselves submit unto their decrees, power and government, receive their ministrie of them, exercise their ministrie under them, sweare and performe their canonical obedience unto them ? Let Mr. Giffard with all his conning reconcile this in truth and good conscience; howsoever he hath reconciled himself to that apostatical throne, from which he was revolted.[2] And in testimonie of his unfeined fidelitie and in hope of some promption [promotion], hath written these blasphemous bookes in his gracious lord's defence, against the Brownists; yea, and rebuked in the Epistle to his second booke[3] al such as speake against the bishops, etc., which yet shall never be able to hide or excuse his open contrarietie, perfidie, apostasie, yea, that which yet is more fearefull, his open restreint, blasphemie, and despight of that truth which he sometimes gladly acknowledged and professed. Unto all which he is driven, by opposing himself against these Brownists, in the defence of their worship, leitourgie, and ministrie, which al should fal to the ground with their lords the bishops' throne. For if they fall out to be antichristian and no true ministers according to the rules of Christ's Testament, then must that ministrie which is made by them, standeth subject unto them,

---

[1] This probably refers to the Presbyterian Supplication to Parliament and to the Bill and Book, presented to the House of Commons on February 27, 1586/7, by Anthony Cope. Gifford was a Presbyterian Puritan, had participated in the classis movement, and had been suspended by Bishop Aylmer for nonconformity. See Albert Peel, *The Seconde Parte of a Register*, II, 208-218. See also Benjamin Brook, *The Lives of the Puritans*, II, 273-278 ; John Strype, *Whitgift*, III (1822), printed a speech critical of the Bill and Book.
[2] See further, J. E. Neale, *Elizabeth I and Her Parliaments, 1584-1601*, pp. 145-152.
[3] *A Plaine Declaration*, p. 18.

A Plaine Refutation

etc., needz be antichristian also. Then have they and their ministrie not to intermedle with the government and administration of Christ's church; much less to make [for] them lawes, a leitourgie, and worship.

Neither staieth Mr. Giffard himself here in the defence of this present worship, leitourgie, hierarchie, courtes and their procedings, ministrie and their administration, but yet is dryven for the defence of all these, to justifie the church of Rome (even in their greatest and deepest apostasie) to be the true visible established church of Christ, to have the true seale of the covenant, etc. And in deed this it standeth him upon to prove, seing their whole ministrie were immediately derived and received from their mother of Rome, as also their whole government, courtes, etc., and no smal parte of their worship and ministration togither with the whole people, parishes and synagogs as they now stand. He wanteth not learned proves [proofs] to bring this abought: as that the apostasie should arise, and Antichrist sit in the church of God. Yea, he proveth both the church of Rome and of England at once by the schisme of Israell, the apostasie of Juda, etc., which yet in those estates were pronounced churches by the prophetts. He proveth them within the covenant by the second com-
[A 4 verso] mandement, where the promise is made to the thousand generation.[1] As also by the greatest corruptions and faltes that he can anie where reade, of the primative churches. These miserable reasons and examples are the maine pillers and ground-worckes of al their buildings, and his writings; which being pulled downe, their whole frame falleth to the ground at once, and is irreparable. For this I refer the reader to their due place in the Second Transgression, where they are largely refuted and answered.[2]

An other pitifull reason he bringeth in his Proeme to the Reader,[3] of an humane bodie consisting of maimed or deformed members: which yet so long as

---
[1] Deuteronomy 7 : 9 ; I Chronicles 16 : 15 ; Psalms 105 : 8.
[2] See *infra*, pp. [51-101].
[3] *A Short Treatise*, Ai verso.

life remaineth in it, is said an humane bodie. So the church, though it consist of mained [maimed] and deformed members, yet whilest it hath the life, *viz.*, true faith in Christ in it, it is to be held a true church. I will not here stand to show how untowardly he hath drawen this comparison beyond the Apostle's scope and proportion, Romans 12. Nor yet how manie errors and inconveniences would insue of such racking of allegories. Only to his reason we answere; that if in his first proposition he meane by deformed members, such as have not their right and true shape that God hath appoincted to humane members, but a strange and diverse forme; as the feet of a beare, the mouth and teeth of a lion, though it have the face of a man, the haire of a woman, etc., then hold we it not a naturall, but a monstrous bodie. So we say, that to the heavenly body of Christ may no monstrous deformed strange members be joyned, but only such members unto the publique ministrie as are described, Romans 12. Neither may that heavenly edifice be built of any other than lyving, holy, precious stones, I Peter 2, or be built in anie other forme, than that Christ hath prescribed, and the maister builders left unto us in his Testament, I Corinthians 3. They that misbuild the temple of God, destroy it. And they that destroy the temple of God, them shall God destroy.

[margin: Revel. 12 / Revel. 9 / Revel. 17]

Now then to his inference or instance. We denie this body of their church to consist of these true members spoken of, Romans 12. Neither of those living precious stones, I Peter 2. Neither to be built according to the true apostolike patterne, I Corinthians 3. But to consist of those monstrous members, Revelation 9 and Revelation 13, and of those prophane multitudes, Revelation 17, 18.[1] Remayning in confusion and disorder, Revelation 18:2. And therfore not to be held the heavenly body of Christ, but that monstrous body of that beast. Not that holy spouse of Christ, but that adulterous harlot. Not that compact citie, that heavenly Jerusalem, but that confuse Babilon.

---

[1] Revelation 17 : 15 and 18 : 2.

A Plaine Refutation

Furder, to that faith and life of the church he speaketh of; we confesse indeed, to the stopping of his sclanderous mouth that so untruly chargeth us, that no sinne or sinnes in anie church or Christian can disanull the covenant, where this true faith is found. But this we say, that true faith may not be severed from true repentance, even of all things they see to be contrary to God's word. True faith may never be severed from true obedience of whatsoever is shewed to be the will of God in his word. Faith without workes is dead. Now then to the faith of the [B 1 *recto*] Church of England, we finde it without workes, we find it without repentance. In their workes (as the Apostle saith) they denye God, howsoever in words they confesse him; in their deeds they are abhominable and unperswaded to everie good worke; howsoever they make a shew of godlynes, they denye the power therof. Yea, so far are they from suffring their workes to burne [to be tried by fire], being shewed and reproved unto them by the word of God, as they smite, persecute and blaspheme with all hostilitie and reproch those that but shew and reprove their sinnes. How then should they be thought to have this true faith, this true life in them? But the faith of their church remaineth to be furder examined and discussed in this booke, whither I refer for furder triall.

And now if this verbal faith and confession of justification by Christ, only make a church and a Christian (though they erre and transgresse in manie, yea, in anie other thing), as the life doth make a man, etc., how may we, that professe this faith and make this confession, be by Mr. Giffard accused, pronouced, condemned, divulged as damnable heretikes, Brownists, schismaticks, etc.? Shall this faith give life unto them, and not unto us? Or will he slay them that Christ gyveth life unto? And that before anie due conviction of anie one error or transgression deserving these hard censures and sentences? May he not evill accuse us of rash, furious, disorderly dealing, that thus uncharitably accuseth, condempneth, smitheth, before any triall? Yes, that thus presumptuously runneth before, and forestalleth

Rom. 2
James 2

Tit. 1:16

II Tim. 3:5
I Cor. 3

the judgment of their own church, pronouncing and divulging us damnable heretikes and schismatickes, before their church had detected, convinced and rejected us for any one error.

As to the heresies he accuseth us of, namely, to hould an Anabaptisticall perfection in this life and immunitie from sinne and from the superior powers that God hath set over us.[1] When he shall be able to shew by anie one sentence in our writings, or but necessarily to infer from the same, that we hould these heresies, let us then be held such, and Mr. Giffard no accuser and sclanderer. But if the contrarie appeare in all our writings and doings, then is it evident that he hath most maliciouslie sclandered us, to bring us in hatred with our sovereigne queene and the whole land. We may evill be accused to hould the error of perfection, for blaming their church for such heynous transgressions, or of Anabaptisticall freedom, for not being subject to their antichristian yoake, or for using the fourth and fifth chapter of the Epistle to the Galatians against their burdenous and ungodly traditions. These causes and Scriptures wil not beare up Mr. Giffard his malicious suspicions and chardges. Neither if we held these detestable heresies, could our sinnes or errors either excuse or lessen these transgressions of theirs. It is a bad foundation to build his credit upon the ruines of other men's; especially by such detraction and sclander.

The schisme he chargeth us with,[2] hath as litle ground or colour of truth. We willed him long since to prove these parish assemblies in this estate true and established churches, and then we would shew him how free we are of schisme. We depart not from anie part of the truth, [B 1 *verso*] or from anie that will walke holily and orderly in the same. The causes of our seperation from these parish assemblies we have shewed to be such as prove them no true established churches of Christ, or such where the faithfull may abide with anie promise or comfort. In seperating from them,

---

[1] *A Short Treatise*, Aii verso.
[2] *Ibid.*, Aii recto, 65-70.

A Plaine Refutation

then, we have not rent our selves from the church or body of Christ, but rather seperated the church from them: and obeyed the commandement of God that calleth us out from emongst them.

Againe, whilest Mr. Giffard standeth so much upon the name of a church, and giveth the same to the Romish synagog in their deepest apostasie, how will he escape himselfe, or cleare the Church of England from the blot of schisme, for seperating and withdrawing from the church of Rome? Anie excuse that he can make or devise, wil cleare us aswel as themselves. Let him looke therfore to the measure he meateth,[1] lest it be measured unto him againe with the same, not only in this matter of schisme, but even in that especial poinct of Donatistrie, which he of a singular judgment above all others of this time hath espied out, and taken no small paines to compare and liken us unto them from poinct to poinct. Forgetting in this heate of zeale and acuminate pregnancie[2] of his, how the papistes have continually battred them with the same ordinance, with much greater advantage than he hath us. In asmuch as he confesseth the church of Rome the true established church of Christ, with the true ministri and true seale of the covenant, etc. And in that they still reteine the same ministrie, government, courtes, officers, canons, orders, parishes, people, synagogs, etc., that the papistes used and left in this land, as the Donatists did. Wheras we on the contrarie do not seperate for the same causes, neither doo justifie or reteine the same ministrie, worship, leitourgie, officers, ordinances, governement, parishes, synagogs, that they use, etc., as the Donatists did. Neither do we hold such errors concerning the magistrates or ministry, etc., as the Donatists did, as is here more perticularly shewed in a peculiar treatise, whither I refer.[3] Only here observing, how the malicious man still (by the just judgment of God) falleth into the same pitte, which he digged for the innocent.

[1] Meteth — pays out, requites, makes return for.
[2] Sharp-witted suggestiveness.
[3] Greenwood, *A Breife Refutation of Mr. George Giffard*.

Henry Barrow

For whilest he would accuse us to derogate from the prince's authoritie, in not allowing her to make lawes for the church: and greatly to blemish her fame and diminish her love emongst her subjects, whilest we denie these parishes to be true established churches of Christ, he himself layeth upon her al these popish trumperies, idolatrous reliques, antichristian enormities and abuses of their church; and distaineth [defileth] her name and honor therwith (for the reformation wherof, this hipocrit somtimes stood a zealous sutor to the parliament).[1] Yea, he now maketh his prince an opposite adversarie unto Christ, one that will not be admonished, or be obedient to God's word. If these abuses he then complained of were just or tollerable, how could he sue to have them abolished; and that by a positive lawe? If they be contrarie to the word of God, how then can he now obey them, or blame us for refusing to [B 2 recto] obey them? The Lord deliver our sovereign queene from such sycophants, such impostors as these false prophets are, that are faithful neither to God nor her, but most dangerouslie seduce and highly abuse her gracious disposition, which hath ever bene inclinable to anie truth of God that hath bene sincerely shewed unto her. It is no shame, neither anie new thing, but a most high honor and praise for godly princes to redresse things that are amisse, when they are shewed by God's word. Neither is it anie injurie to the prince, when the faithful witnesse against and refreigne anie

---

[1] Especially to the parliaments of 1584-5 and 1586-7. There are two dissertations at the University of London which are relevant: Hazel Matthews, "Personnel of the Parliament of 1584-1585" (1948); Richard C. Gabriel, "Members of the House of Commons, 1586-7" (1954). See also J. E. Neale, *Elizabeth I and Her Parliaments, 1584-1601*, (1584-5), chapters IV, V; (1586-7), III; (1589), III. Some of the material which John Field collected for the Puritans' appeal to parliament is in Albert Peel (ed.), *The Seconde Parte of a Register, Being a Calendar of Manuscripts under That Title Intended for Publication by the Puritans about 1593, and Now in Dr. Williams's Library*, London, 2 vols. The most recent writing on the Puritan campaign in the parliaments of 1584-5 and 1586-7 is Patrick Collinson's essay, "John Field and Elizabethan Puritanism," *Elizabethan Government and Society, Essays Presented to Sir John Neale*, edited by S. T. Bindoff, J. Hurstfield, and C. H. Williams (1961), pp. 127-162. See also T. W. Davids, *Annals of Evangelical Nonconformity in the County of Essex*, pp. 77-84.

A Plaine Refutation

thing that is contrarie to God's word: or dishonor to the prince to amend the same, how long soever the abuse hath continued as this accuser and flatterer suggesteth. The rest of whose criminations and accusations against us, our indevours and proceadings, I deferr to answere untill we come to the articles.[1]

Yet now, that the groundworke and true causes of all his bitter invectives and grievous charges against us may appeare to all men; we have here set downe in print the originall and whole former passage betwixt us and him concerning these poinctes in controversie; that the reader may the better discerne and judge of these our present writings. And also see what cause ther was given him thus to accuse, reproch, and blaspheme us as heretickes, schismatickes, disobedient and injurious to princes, Anabaptists, Donatists, Brownists, with infinite vile and reprochfull objectives,[2] wherwith his treasurie is stored. If in those writings appeare no such matter, then we protest, that (to our knowledg) we never gave him cause thus to accuse and blaspheme us, he being a man altogither unknowen by person unto us, and never so much as seene, spoken unto, or medled with by us the writers of these things, otherwise, than by those writings here insuing; wherunto also we were provoked by himself, who would needs take upon him this quarrell. Which how christianly and soberly he hath handled and performed, let him of his owne mouth be judged, even by everie sentence of his bookes, which are referced[3] with most grievous and inaudible raylings; not so much as speaking of us in anie place therof without some hard, cruell, and dispightfull words and bitter revilings and cursings. All which in our innocencie, as the sparow and swallow by flying, we shall escape. And having therby discovered his spirit, easely passe over without regarding or answering the same. Turning

---

[1] Gifford replied to the five Barrowist articles or purposes in his *A Short Treatise*, pp. 90-104. Barrow set forth his answers in "A Refutation of Mr. Giffard's Reasons Concerning Our Purposes in the Practise of the Truth of the Gospel of Christ," which is printed in this volume, pp. 332-364.

[2] On page [22], Barrow speaks of "infinit reprochfull and horrible adjectives."

[3] Stuffed, crammed.

also from his person as much as may be, as from a most unreasonable and unhonest man, with whome we would be loath to have furder to doo; fixing our eies wholye upon the matter set before us; indevoring to make proofe and evident demonstration of these chardges, for which we forsake their assemblies, and have all this time suffred under their tyrannous handes. As also, to cleare our profession and proceadings herein of such calumniations and reproches, as this our malignant adversarie defameth them with. And this in all brevitie, truth, and good conscience, as so variable and infinite a matter wil permit. Wherin if in anie poinct we deale obscurely and insufficiently (for as the man is, such is his strength)[1] we desire that the [B 2 verso] truth may not suffer prejudice therby, but that the learned and wise reader wil rather confirme and repaire our weake or loose reasons: yea, by our insufficiencie be provoked even in zeale and love of the truth to handle it more exactly. Wherin we shall gladly gyve place, and much rejoyce.

But if in anie thing we be found to depart from the truth, we desire to be lovingly reduced, yea, condignly [condignly] reproved and censured, vowing (through God's grace) never to resist anie truth that shal at any time be shewed us, neither to refuse to be reformed. The lesse faltes, as the errors in the writing or print, we shall desire the reader charitably to construe and correct. And if ther be found or rather abound anie imperfect or redundant sentences, let those be imputed chiefly to the want of better skill in the writers, and partly to their decayed memories, to the inconveniencie of the place, the continual tossings and turmoiles, searches and riflings, and no peace or meanes given us either to write, or revise that we had written.[2]

To conclude, we beseach and admonish the reader,

---

[1] Judges 8 : 21.
[2] When the reader remembers the difficulties under which Barrow wrote, without a library or reference works, having to smuggle out his sheets as they were written, without being able to review or recast his manuscript, and having no opportunity to proof-read and revise his material, he will be surprised that there is not more redundancy and greater imperfections than there are.

A Plaine Refutation

not to be withdrawn from the truth by anie fore-conceived opinion either of our tenuitie [slightness] of giftes and base estate, or of the excellencie and multitude of our adversaries, for that were dangerous to themselves. But rather diligently to ponder their owne wayes and the issues therof, and where they finde themselves to erre, speedely to retorne to the truth without cunctation [delay] or excuse; that so they may finde peace and assurance to their owne soules. Which grace we even wish to our greatest enimies, and shall not cease to pray, that God may thus blesse our indevoures.

[In the 1591 and 1605 edition the following twenty pages (pp. 1—20) comprise "A Brief Summe of the Causes of Our Seperation, and of Our Purposes in Practise, Withstood by G.G., Defended by H.B. as Followeth." This treatise was written in 1588, and therefore is printed in volume III in its chronological place. See Leland H. Carlson, *The Writings of Henry Barrow, 1587-1590*, pp. 118—150.]

[21] A PLAINE REFUTATION OF MR. GIFFARD HIS REPROCHFUL BOOKE, INTITULED *A Short Treatise against the Donatistes of Englande, etc.*

You were before shewed,[1] that we judged none otherwise and no furder, than the expresse worde of God teacheth us to judg of you. That is, to knowe the tree by the fruicte, and the fruicte by God's worde. You were there shewed, that we judged not of God's secret election which he hath in al places amongst all sortes of men, but of the apparant odious sinnes of your congregations; from which whilest you wil not be purged, we may have no spiritual fellowship or communion with you in this estate. We shewed you, that notwithstanding all your wickednes, we never doubted,

---

[1] Barrow is referring to his manuscript reply to Gifford's manuscript answer. Both are printed in "A Brief Summe of the Causes of Our Seperation, and of Our Purposes in Practise, Withstood by G.G., Defended by H.B. as Followeth," in Carlson, *The Writings of Henry Barrow, 1587-1590*, pp. 118-150.

but the foundation of God stood firme, the Lord having manie thowsandes of his elect amongst you knowen to himself, though not apparant to our eies, whom he in his good time will call more neare unto him. And therfore we with extreame longing and love towardes you, sought and desired your convertion, that we might see that seale of God's grace upon your foreheades, wherwith all that name the name of Christ are sealed, *vzt.*, " to depart from iniquitie."

II Tim. 2:19

To this end we did, and still doe, reprove in the name of our Lord Jesus Christ these heinous transgressions in your publique assemblies, lying in your miserable prisons, the Lorde's witnesses against the same. To this end we exhort al men by al meanes, and admonished you of your present evil estate, as also blamed you for your former ungodlie and false surmises, collections, and chardges, wresting and depraving our wordes contrarie to al sense, equitie, and conscience.

We hoped that this thus far forth had sufficed, especiallie, seeing you rested in silence more than two yeares without any replie or contradiction.[1] Until now at length upon your submission made, and consultation had with your Ordinarie,[2] you disclosed this cocatrice egge, which you had so long sit upon, and all to sprinckled [*sic*] us with the viperous poyson therof. Terming us at the first dash Donatists, Brownists, Anabastites [Anabaptists], hereticks, [22][3] schismaticks, with infinit reprochfull and horrible adjectives joyned to the same, which you have aboundantly drawen out of the evil treasurie of your owne wicked heart, without cause given by us, or shewed by you. Continuing stil, and more and more abounding in the gall of bitternes, still chardging us with intollerable pride, presumption, intrusion into God's judgement seate, in falselie chardging, accusing, condemning your christian assemblies, that professe the gospel, etc.,[4] notwithstanding al we have said to

Math. 12:34, 35

---

[1] *A Short Treatise* appeared in May, 1590. Therefore, we may date Gifford's earlier manuscript answer about February, 1587/8.
[2] John Aylmer, Bishop of London.
[3] From page 22 to page 206, the running title is : " Mr. Giffard Refuted."
[4] *A Short Treatise*, p. 3.

A Plaine Refutation

cleare our selves of those crimes, and to prove in perticular the thinges we chardged you with; the truth wherof remaineth now to be skanned. In which blasphemous veyne of wryting you but fulfil the measure of your sinne, and those prophecies you were foretold of. " *They shall drincke and be moved and be madd, etc.*[1] *They shal gnawe their tongues for grief, and blaspheme the God of Heaven for their paines and for their soares, and not repent of their worckes.*"[2]

First then to this word [*principal*] wherat you so stomble, and from which you draw such hereticall conclusions. We give you to understand, that we used it onely to signifie and expresse unto you the fower cheif heades, from whence flowe, and whether [whither, to which] may be reduced all these several and infinite enormities and abuses, which abounde in your church. As to the nature and qualitie of these four, how far they extend, let the word of God judge. Yea, let anie by the same worde judge.

1. Whether such assemblies as were never dulie gathered unto Christ, but all the prophane and open wicked of the land receaved by constrainte into the bodie of your church as members of the same, immediatlie from open idolatrie and apostasie, without the preaching of the gospel going before to call them to the faith, or anie voluntarie profession made by themselves in particular of their owne faith; whether such congregations as these may in this confusion be held and esteamed the true and rightly planted churches of Christ.

2. Also, let anie by the worde of God judge, whether those congregations which have not that ministerie of the gospel that Christ hath in his Testament instituted to his church, but have and retaine an other strange and antichristian ministerie, even that the pope used and left in the land, may be held the true and rightly planted churches of Christ.

3. Moreover, let anie judge, whether those congre-

[1] Jeremiah 25 : 16.
[2] Revelation 16 : 10, 11.

gations which have not those orders and governement which our saviour Christ hath ordained and commaunded unto his church unto the worlde's end, but (rejecting that) have and retaine an other strange antichristian government, even that antichristian hierarchie the pope used and left in the land, may be held the true and rightly established churches of Christ.

4. Finallie, let anie (in whom is anie sparke of light) judge, whether those congregations that retaine and use an other leitourgie, that is, an other forme of publique administration and worship than Christ's Testament, especially such a patched, erroneous, idolatrouse, blasphemous thing as theirs is, and will not be reformed or withdrawen from the same, may be esteamed [23] the true and rightly established churches of Christ, such as Christe's faithful servantes may have communion and fellowship with in their administration of prayers and sacraments. But now where all these faultes concur, and have not onelie obstinacie, but tyrannie and persecution joyned to the same, who can doubt of the matter? Whether also your churches can remaine in these transgressions, or you maintaine the same, and not depart from the groundes and principles of christian religion and faith (which you boast to keepe), let anie which is anie thinge exercised in the worde of God, judge.

And thus by these few wordes are not onelie your three inevitable dangers (into one of which you would needes shove us) but even your whole blasphemous booke, avoyded at once. For whie should we now ether maintaine this heresie: 1. *That where the true faith is, ther can breake forth no great faultes, errors, and abuses*; or this absurde maner of speache: 2. *That all errors and deformities in religion, be heresies, blasphemies, and abhominations.* Or ells confesse: 3. *That with intollerable pride, presumption, and intrusion into God's judgment seate, we have taken upon us to judge and condemne whole assemblies which professe the faith of Christ sincearelie in all fundamentall poinctes.*[1] For holding that it cannot be held the true church of Christ rightlie planted and established, where

---

[1] *A Short Treatise*, p. 4.

A Plaine Refutation

the people were receaved into the bodie of the church before they were dulie caled unto the faith, or had made profession thereof: where they have not the true ministrie of Christ, but a strange antichristian ministerie imposed upon them: where they have not the governement of Christ, but of Antichrist over them: where their administration and worship is not after the gospel of Christ, but after their popish idolatrous leitourgie. Al this may safely be defended, without falling into anie such inconvenience as Mr. Giffard threatneth.

As to the heresie he speaketh of, we doubt not, neither ever thought, but the best church that consisteth of mortall men, may fall ether of negligence or of ignorance, into grievous offences, and dangerous errors. Yea, we doubt not but that some famous churches and Christians may fall into such errors, as he termeth fundamentall; the holding wherof should utterly subvert the faith. As in the church of Corinth, Galatia, Asia, there where [were] [those] that denied the resurrection; that revived the ceremonial lawes; that held the doctrines of Balaam and Nicholas.[1] But this we hold withal, that no true church or Christian will maintaine anie sinne or error, when it is evidentlie shewed and convinced unto them by the worde of God, much lesse persecute such as reprove and admonished [sic] them, as you doe. Or if they doe, whilest they remaine in that estate, they are not of us to be held the true churches of Christ. I Cor. 15 Gal. 3 and 4 chapters Revel. 2:14, 15

To your second chardge we answeare: that we have learned to put difference betwixt errour and heresie. All good men (as is said) doe and may erre, but no good man wil defend, or persist in his error, when it is shewed and convinced unto him. Obstinacie joyned unto error, after [24] it is duelie convinced, maketh

---

[1] Balaam influenced others to eat things sacrificed to idols, and to practice fornication. See Numbers 22 : 5-24 : 25; 31 : 8; Joshua 13 : 22; Revelation 2 : 14. Nicholas is associated with the Nicolaitans, who seem to have advocated a form of antinomianism or libertinism in religious rites. Among the Gnostics, there was one group called the Nicolaitans, which advocated the eating of things sacrificed to idols. See Revelation 2 : 6, 15 and Albert Hauck, *Realencyklopädie für protestantische Theologie und Kirche*, "Nikolaiten," XIV, 63-68 (1904).

Henry Barrow

<small>Titus 3:10, 11
Rom. 16:17
I Tim. 6:3 etc.
Deut. 17:12</small>

heresie. Furder we say, that anie error being obstinatly holden and taught, after it is duelie convinced and reproved unto him, maketh an hereticke, and heresie in that partie or in the congregation that so holdeth and teacheth it, and doth separate from the faith and communion of Christ. Wherfore we can but wonder at your ignorance, who stand for a teacher in your church, and yet hold some errors obstinatlie held and taught against the truth of God, not to be heresies, or (at the least) not to be fundamental; though you see by expresse rule everie hereticke after one and the second admonition, to be shunned.[1] Yet say we not, that though everie error thus obstinatlie held, be heresie, and everie transgression against the lawe, be sinne; that therfore all sinnes are equal, or all errors of like indignitie. The lawe and judgments of God teach us to put difference.

<small>Rev. 18</small>

Neither is ther cause whie you should chardge us or we confesse our selves guiltie of pride, presumption, intrusion into God's judgment seat, for condemning those assemblies which the whole worde of God condemneth in all their doings.[2] Greater is your pride, presumption, etc., that in this maner condemne and blaspheme the truth and servantes of God for reproving your sinnes, that thus plead for and coulor these filthie abhominations of your church, which are most odious to everie good conscience. But this knowe for certain, howsoever the shipmasters, maryners, and marchantmen of these wares howle and crye out; howsoever the false prophet labour to gilde and adorne the false church with the jewells, ornamentes and titles that belong to the true church; how much soever the harlot doe glorifie her self, and say in her heart that she sitteth as a queene, and is no widowe, and shall see no sorrowe;

---

[1] Titus 3 : 10.

[2] In the margin some contemporary reader has written : " often sayde, but never able to be proved." Francis Johnson, the possessor of one of the two copies saved from the fire, may be the writer. If so, the remark would be characteristic of Johnson as a Puritan or a forward preacher. Later he became the Separatist minister of the London Barrowist congregation, in September, 1592. See Ellesmere MS. 2115, in the Huntington Library, and Harley MSS. 6848, f. 34 *verso*, in the British Museum.

A Plaine Refutation

yet shal her plagues come in one daye, death, and sorrowe, and famine, and she shalbe burnt with fire, because the God that condemneth her is a strong Lorde.

In that you chardge us with the breach of the rule, Mathew 18 [verse 17], unto you, this still proceedeth of your former vayne conceipt, arrogating unto your churches such names, titles, prerogatives, duties, as belong and are only given to the true churches of Christ. Not being able nor endevouring to approve your churches by the Testament of Christ, although you were often required and urged by us so to doe, wherby all contention should soone have ceased, you beene cleared and justified, we justlie convict and chardged. In the meane while we affirme unto you, that these Rev. 11 golden rules onlie belong unto the true church of Christ, and that the court without the temple which is given to the Gentiles, is to be cast out, and not to be measured. The cannons of the pope, which your church imbraceth, more fitly agree unto you, than the rules of Christe's gospel, which your church rejecteth and blasphemeth. But that we maie the sooner see our fault, shew us [25] (we pray you) how we might execute this rule unto you, how we might tel it to your church,[1] how we might be heard and have redresse. For if by your church you meane the Convocation House,[2] you see how they have often openly rejected this sute. If you meane by your church the bishops (whom you cal the cheif governours of your church), you see they blaspheme this truth, caling the order of Christ's government, intollerable, dangerous to the subvertion of prince and

---

[1] A reference to Matthew 18 : 17, " tell it unto the church." If the bishop had usurped disciplinary power, what jurisdiction remained for the church ?

[2] The upper and lower house of the Convocation of Canterbury and of York. For a brief summary and bibliography, see " Convocations of Canterbury and York," in F. L. Cross (ed.), *The Oxford Dictionary of the Christian Church* (London, 1957), pp. 339 f. See also Edmund Gibson, *Synodus Anglicana*. Ed. Edward Cardwell (Oxford, 1854). Thomas Lathbury, *A History of the Convocation of the Church of England*. 2nd ed. (1853). Dorothy Bruce Weske, *Convocation of the Clergy* (1937).

state, etc.;[1] they hate, persecute, imprison al that speake for, or seek the same. But if nowe you meane by churches your parish churches, alas, you see they want [lack] power; they can mend nothing, be it never so heinous or hereticall; they must receave what their lordes the bishops impose, and endure til they redresse. How then, to whom, or to what end would you have us complaine unto your church in this estate; or with what equitie and conscience can you thus revile and condemne us for breaking Christ's order towardes your church, when you see your church wil not be subject unto Christe's order; but persecuteth us and all such as reprove their faultes and seek to doo Christe's will, because their worckes are evil and wil not endure the light, when they are never so litle examined therbye. As shal furder appeare but by a cursorie touching of these principal transgressions following.

THE FIRST PRINCIPAL TRANSGRESSION WHERWITH YOUR CHURCHES ARE CHARDGED, IS:

That they worship God after a false maner; their worship being made of the invention of man, even of that man of sinne, erroneous, and imposed upon them.

We leave your first answeare unto this transgression, and our replie upon your said answeare, to be perused and compared by the indifferent reader,[2] and now addresse our selves unto this your second defence.

First to make our accusation and his answere more cleare, Mr. Giffard translateth our proposition into a sylogism, thus:

Whatsoever assemblies worship the true God after a false

---

[1] Barrow is thinking of the Bishop of Winchester, Thomas Cooper; see his work, *An Admonition to the People of England*, pp. 73-84, 137-9, in the edition (1589) of 252 pp.
[2] Carlson, *The Writings of Henry Barrow, 1587-1590*, pp. 120-123.

A Plaine Refutation

maner, their worship being made of the invention of man, even of the man of sinne, etc., the same are not the true churches of God.[1]

But the assemblies as they generallie stand in England doe worship the true God after a false maner, their worship being made of the invention of man, etc.

Therfore the assemblies of England be not the true churches of God.

We finde Mr. Giffard so ful of *legier du main* [legerdemain, deception] that we had neede looke narrowlie to his fingers, lest by his sophistrie and diepe schole learning he beguile us, as the serpent by his craftines deceaved Evah, and turne [26] us not onlie from the true state of our controversie, but from the simplicitie that [is] in Christ. Mr. Giffard as it should seeme finding these propositions (as they were delivered him) al to[o] hard and heavie for him, hath sought to lighten his burden by leaving out such matter and words as pressed him most sore, and then would runne away with the rest as you see. The words he hath left out and ought to have joyned to everie transgression, are these: *willfully obstinate*, as appeareth in the verie next words immediatly going before these four propositions.

Furder, in repeating and urdging the transgression, he hath purposely left out these wordes, *and imposed upon them*, and in their place hath set *etc.*, which serveth not the tourne half so wel. These words we can at no hand spare him, and therfore must entreate him to add them to both his first and second proposition; which if he doe, he shall then finde the fearful conclusion to followe faster, than he with al his logique can avoide.[2] For if they remaine obstinate and incorrigible, yea, incurable in their sinnes, disobedient to the voyce of Christ, skorning his reprof, despising his grace, refusing to repent, having nether wil nor power to amend, be their sinne as smale in their owne eies as they can imagine, as litle as by their learned distinctions of

[1] *A Short Treatise*, pp. 7-8.
[2] Gifford omitted the last five words: "erroneous, and imposed upon them," but Barrow himself omitted the word "erroneous."

Henry Barrow

fundamental, etc., they can anie way make it; yet it being a transgression of God's most holie lawe, bringeth death; and being holden after this manner abovesaide, bringeth everlasting death; and doth in this estate separate them from the love, favour, and mercie of God, so far as we can judge. Ther can be no remission without repentance; nether can anie be said to repent, whilest they obstinatlie persist in wilful transgression; nor the Lord in that estate to accept anie offring at their hands, be their offrings otherwise never so perfect and according to the lawe, as the Scriptures plentifullie witnesse. So then, if Mr. Giffard had taken the matter with him, he should not thus have altred the whole state of our proposition, in steade of clearing it; nether should [he] have had anie cause thus to chardge it with heresie after his accustomed maner, or to have produced his scholastical or (as he useth it) we might more rightlie saye, papistical distinctions of fundamental errors and transgressions. Wherebie what ells should he inferr, or doth he labour to prove, if not, that some errors and sinns are (as the papistes say) mortal, others not deadlie? Or ells that which is more grosse, that some error or transgression might be built upon the foundation. Because some errors and sinnes are of higher nature and offence than other, or because that the best men and churches may fal into greivous errors and sinnes (which as we never denied, so we stil to the stopping of our adversaries' ungodlie mouthes, affirme). Yet hence it followeth not, that because the best men and churches that hold the foundation may erre and sinne, therfore anie error or sinne is of the foundation, or is not a transgression from the foundation.

The written worde of God, delivered by the prophets and apostles, is the foundation, Christ Jesus himself being the cheif corner stone. Everie part of the Scripture is alike true, inspired of God, given to our direction and instruction in all thinges. No [27] error or transgression can be joyned onto or built upon this foundation, no more than light and darknes can be mingled. The least departure from Gode's worde is an error; the least transgression of God's lawe is a sinne; the rewarde

A Plaine Refutation

of the least error or sinne is eternal death, if the mercy of God and the merites of Christ come not betwixt; 1 John 1:6 which mercy and merites belong not unto the impenitent and obstinate. Therfore they that obstinatlie hold anie error or transgression, and wil not by repentance be purged from the same, lose Christ, and so hold not the foundation. Now then, seing Mr. Giffard hath a special phantasie to drawe this transgression more than anie of the three prinsipal transgressions following, into forme of argument (because in his bad conscience he did foresee they would presse too sore), let the first proposition be drawn into forme of argument, thus:

> *Whatsoever assemblies worship God and administer according to an idolatrous leitourgie imposed upon them, and continue wilfullie obstinate in the said sinnes, are not in that estate to be esteamed or communicated with as the true churches of God.*
> *But your publique assemblies in England doo worship God and administer according to such an idolatrous leitourgie imposed upon them, and continue wilfullie obstinate in the saide sinnes.*
> *Therfore the publique assemblies of England are not in this estate to be held or communicated with as the true churches of God.*

But let us now retorne againe unto that argument which you have taken such paynes to drawe, and to confute in our names. The second or minor proposition therof you denie, *vzt.*, *that the Church of England doth worship God after a false maner, their worship being made of,* etc.; affirming your worship to be " the embracing of the holie Bible, and by the doctrine therof," etc. Wel, let the holie Bible be judge betwixt us in all controversies; and let your writing shewe how wel you have approved your worship in those perticular pointes which were recited and reproved unto you. But in our judgment you flee from this issue before you beginne, in that you make so lardge an exception of " imperfections, wantes, spots, blemishes, faultes, which destroy not the worship of God "; otherwise (you saye) our church doth worship God aright without heresie, blasphemie or idolatrie. Nowe surelie this is the odd and onlie exception that ever we heard of. Whie if al imperfections, wantes, spots, blemishes and faultes were taken away, we durst joyne in the rest of your [28] worship to you or the pope either. The rest that remaineth must then needes be free and pure from heresie, blasphemie, or idolatrie. It were a wonderful apostasie or heresie, where were no truth, especially when al corruption should be purged away. But if you meane that these faultes thus reproved by us, and holden by you, doe not corrupt God's worship amongst you; for the trial of this, let the nature and quality of them be dulie examined by the word of God, and we doubt not but a litle of such leaven shalbe fownd to make sowre the whole lumpe. Yea, that these spots and bleamishes you speake of (being lo[o]ked in that pure glasse) wil appeare the olde running issues, and incurable botches of Egipt, which they have derived from their mother of Rome, even of those malignant ulcers that are founde upon the men which have the marcke of the beast, and upon them which worship his image, for anie defence that you have or can make for them.

Gal. 5:9
Eccl. 10:1

Reve. 16:2

Yet unto the four apparant reasons in our general position of this transgression to prove your worship false and idolatrous, your peremptorie answere is: "that they but make apparant our vanitie and Anabaptistical error."[1] Our vanitie, in that the three first [reasons], 1. *of the invention of man*, 2. *of that man of sinne*, 3. *erroneous*, are al but one. Our Anabaptistical error is in the fourth, in these wordes *imposed* [*upon the people*]; wherin "we chalendge such a freedome to the church, as that nothing may be imposed upon the flockes, that the church-governours shal decree by the worde."[2] The three first of these reasons whereby his worship was proved to be idolatrous, he quietlie

---

[1] *Ibid.*, p. 9.
[2] Barrow is repeating Gifford's statement, but he has changed "yee challenge" to "we chalendge." The statement originally was probably in Barrow's manuscript reply, rephrased or paraphrased by Gifford, and repeated by Barrow.

A Plaine Refutation

suffring to passe and carry their conclusion, [he] laboureth to prove al [three reasons to be] but one. Because, saith he, *whatsoever man inventeth in the worship of God is erroneous; and whatsoever is erroneous therin was invented by man; for al false worship is man's invention, whether it be the invention of the man of sinne or anie other, it is al one before God, who respecteth not persons, but the wickednes of the sinne.*[1] Wel, howsoever we might insist and shew difference betweene that man of sinne, that Antichrist, and others that have not such cursed marckes upon them; howsoever also we might shew differences betwixt the devises of other more godlie men (which devises peradventure in themselves conteine no errors, until they be abused, set up, enjoyned and read in the church, etc.), and the pope's portesse [portas] from which execrable plant al these idolatrous graftes are fetched. Yet wil we not stand upon lighter matters with you, contending whether the reasons may be said three or one. It sufficeth us, and we content our selves to have proved and obteined, that the worship of your church is erroneous, it being made of the invention of man. And your self hath confessed, *that whatsoever man inventeth in the worship of God, is erroneous.*[2]

Nowe we may furder conclude from the second commandment, that whatsoever worship is devised by man; and whatsoever devise of man is put into the worship of God, is idolatrie. But a great part, if not the whole worship of your church, is devised by man, even by the man of sinne, etc. Therfore the worship of your church is idolatrie. Let your service booke prove our minor proposition, or [29] your answers to the perticulars, disprove it. And we in the meane time will procede unto your answere unto the fourth part of our proposition, " imposed upon them." Wherin you chardge us with this Anabaptisticall error, that we should chalendg such a freedome, as [a consequence of which] nothing might be imposed upon the church which the church governours should decree by the

---

[1] *A Short Treatise*, p. 9.
[2] *Ibid.*

worde. It should seeme certeinly you knowe not what truth or error meaneth. Or ells are so possessed with malice, as you make no conscience what truth you cal heresie, or heresie you cal truth, as appeareth by your unjust chardging of us, and your ungodlye defending al the abhominations of the tymes. Who but you could drawe this hereticall collection from our wordes? We in the same sentence, and in the verie next worde immediatlie going before, having protested your worship to be erroneous. How maie it followe, that because we denie errors to be imposed upon the church, therfore we denie that such thinges as the elders shal determine of by the worde of God, may be imposed upon the church? Whie what the elders decree by the worde of God, cannot be said to be the invention or the commandement of man, but of God, by whose direction they but pronounce and performe the will of God? But no error can be said to be of the worde of God, and everie invention of man (by your owne confession) is erroneous. Therfore we may stil and againe here conclude, that seing the worship of your Church of England is made of the invention of man, even of the man of sinne, erroneous, and imposed upon them, it is false and idolatrous, and such as no true elders may impose, or the true church of Christ receave. Furder we say, that no true elders of the church, nor the whole church it self, may decree or impose anie thing by way of lawe, which Christ hath not decreed and imposed in his worde. And if you hold otherwise (as your popish phrases, "decree, impose upon the flockes," seeme to import), then we affirme, that you both hold a papistical and Anabaptistical error, and utterlie not onlie corrupt the worship and government of Christ, but bring in a new worship and government by bringing in and setting up your owne decrees and devises as the papistes and Anabaptistes doe.

  Now cometh their leitourgie or service-booke, which containeth the publique worship and administration of their church, to be examined by the word of God. The defence wherof Mr. Giffard, though he be a sworne priest after and unto the orders therof, yet he verie

A Plaine Refutation

loathlie and doubtfullie undertaketh at the first entrance, as one that carieth a witnesse and a judge, that could tell an other tale in his owne conscience. He confesseth "that as no man's workes are perfect, so there are manie and great faultes in this booke," though (as it should seeme) none of those perticulars which we recited unto him (onlie the baptisme by weomen excepted) seing the [he] laboureth to defend all the rest. But we which for some errors and spots hould it to be an idolatrous booke, and the worship therof idolatrie, fal into the foule and detestable heresie of per-[30] fection. And in that we affirme it to be " a pregnant idoll, ful of errours, blasphemies, and abhominations," we doe falselie accuse, and impudentlie sclander.[1] These great wordes nether convince us, nor cleare you; let them therfore remaine upon your accompt. The truth of our chardges, and the qualitie of your transgressions, shall by and by appeare by the discussing the perticulars. And for all your greate threates of heresie, we still for the faultes we have alleadged (though there were no more, as by your owne confession ther are both manie more and greater) dare affirme your worship to be false, idolatrous, and abhominable. The worde of God caleth him an heretick that obstinatelie holdeth anie one error after due conviction, though he hold much truth besides. There is no heretick that doth not hold some, yea, much, truth. The word of God pronounceth them idolatours, that obstinately contynue in anie idolatrous and false worship, though they doe manie other things according to the rules of the worde; ells were not the papistes to be judged idolatours or heretickes. Shall all they now that judge according to the worde of God, be guiltie of that detestable heresie of perfection? What is this but to accuse God of heresie, whose judgments these are? Because we cannot be perfect here, therfore we ought not [ought not we] to contend towards perfection, by Rom. 12:9 leaving that which is evill, as it is shewed unto us, and endevouring to do that which is good? Might not the

---

[1] Carlson, *The Writings of Henry Barrow, 1587-1590*, p. 130.

masse-booke, and the most vile heresies, be thus defended and justified? Because they are not perfect, therfore they not evill? Because they cannot be perfect, therfore they will leave none evil?[1] This is Mr. Giffard's best divinitie he hath, to defend the worship of his church. But let us nowe come to the perticular defaults in their worship by us objected, and by him defended.

Mr. Giffard being demanded where he founde in the New Testament the Romish fastes of his church, as their Embers, Sainctes' Eaves, and Lent;[2] first confesseth, that in the whole Bible he can find no warrant for anie Romish fastes. But afterwardes (lest he should be unlike himself) sayth, that we injuriouslie sclander and belye their church in matching them with the blasphemous synagogue of Rome, seing they place not in abstinence from meates ether the worship of God, remission of sinnes, nor merite; seing they condemne the doctrine of devils, etc.[3] Whie should we by his rayling and subtile cavils be withdrawen from our present question, which because he dare not answere, and cannot approve his Embers, Sainctes' Eaves, and Lent fastes by Scripture, he seeketh to turne away, and to cavile about other doctrines, as the putting holines, merit, etc., in the abstinence and the restraint of meates, wherwith he was not chardged by us; yet wherof happelie (if he were narrowlie sought and followed) he could not so wel cleare his church, as he supposeth. We onlie made question of things done, and of the present practise of their church. Namelie, how we could approve [31] their Embers, Sainctes' Eaves, and Lents, which we caled Romish fastes, by the worde of God. At which wordes he picketh a quarrle, that he might not be urged to prove his Embers, Sainctes'

---

[1] " Because they are not perfect, [is it true that] therefore they [are] not evill? Because they cannot be perfect, [is it true] therefore [that] they will leave none [refrain from no] evil?
[2] *Ibid.*, pp. 130-1.
[3] *A Short Treatise*, pp. 10-11.

A Plaine Refutation

Eaves, Lent fastes by the Scripture. But let him cavil as much as he list at this worde *Romish*. Whersoever and whensoever they were invented, it is certaine they were brought into and left in the church by the pope, and are stil used (though not altogether after so idolatrous a maner) at the same holie tides as they were and are in the Romish church; and therfore are still to be caled upon his name, what prince soever after command them, or what church soever use them. And evill provide they for their prince's honor, that make her the author of such abhominable idolatrous stuffe, as these Romish fastes, your Embers, Sainctes' Eaves, Lents are, which he can no way colour or excuse by anie politicke lawes, or transfer the blame from their church therbie. No politick lawes can make that lawfull, which the word of God condemneth. No politick lawes can excuse the church from breaking the commandements of God. Nether may these fastes be esteemed civill actions, because the prince's lawe commandeth them. For so might all their worship of God be held civill actions, because the prince's lawes in like maner commandeth them. But these fastes are commanded and solemnly proclaimed in their church and that by the priest, as he is directed by his rubrick, orderly as they arise in their calendare. The people are sommoned to the sinagogue unto publique prayer, al commanded to fast, etc., shal we call this a civile action? Nay, sure it must be as much and as well ecclesiasticall as anie other part of the worship and administration of your church.

Well, and besides that you have receaved and derived these fastes from the church of Rome, let your special collects, upon your Sainctes' Eaves, your bitter commination and special communion upon your Ash Wednesday, with your epistle out of Joel 2:12. *Tourne you unto me with all your heartes, with fasting, weeping, and mourning, etc.*, your gospell out of Matthew 6:16: *When you fast be not sad as the hipocrites, etc.* Likewise your Collect and Gospell upon the first Sundaye of your Lent, making mention of Christ's forty dayes fast in the wildernes, desiring that your forty dayes fast may subdue the flesh, etc.¹ Let this your apish, or rather popish counterfeighting, let your special communions in your passion weeke, your Maundy Thurs-daye,² your Good Friday, etc., shewe how popishlie you keepe these your fastes.

Furder, let your generall inhibition of flesh and of mariage at these pope-holie tides, and your bishops' speciall dispensation for both, by their licences for money, shew, how popishlie your Church of England keepeth these idolatrous execrable fastes; and whether herein your church maintayneth not the doctrines of devills.

To conclude, let anie man by the Testament of Christ judge, whether these annuarie [annually] prescribed fastes by waye of lawe unto all congregations from yeare to yeare, at set tymes and ceasons, without anie present occasion so urging, be anie thing [32] like those holie christian fastes which the primative churches used, either according to their general or perticular occasions.

Next ensue your idoll feastes, your Al-Hallowes, Candlemas, several Ladie daies, Sainctes' daies, and dedicating your churches unto sainctes. Here you say we thunder out terror, as if the Church of England did worship idolles and celebrate feastes in the honor of false gods; and yet all is but a starck lye, and a wicked sclaunder.³ Here your evill conscience fearing the blow before it come, can provide no warde but your accustomed rayling, which is the way to make it more heavie and soare. If you had according to our re-

---

¹ See *The Book of Common Prayer.* For the " bitter commination," see section 25, " A Commination, or Denouncing of God's Anger and Judgements against Sinners." For the use of Joel 2 : 12 and Matthew 6 : 16, see section 15, " The Collects, Epistles, and Gospels, to Be Used at the Ministration of the Holy Communion, throughout the Year," for the first day of Lent — Ash-Wednesday.
Immediately following are the collect [and epistle] and gospel for the first Sunday in Lent.
² Maundy Thursday was the day before Good Friday. Because Christ washed the Apostles' feet at the Last Supper, the ceremony of washing the feet of poor persons on Thursday before Easter was instituted. The distribution of alms or " maundy money " was commonly associated with this ceremony.
³ *A Short Treatise,* p. 11.

A Plaine Refutation

questes approved your feastes and holie dayes of your church, etc., by the Testament of Christ, we had yeilded therunto; or how soever, you had therby beene freed from these feares and judgments that pursue your evill conscience. Then had you not upon this occasion needed or used these vayne protestations, how you hold but one only God, and one mediator betweene God and man, the man Jesus Christ, that God onely is to be worshipped through the mediation of Christ, that sainctes are not to be worshipped, no dayes to be celebrated in their honor, nor churches dedicated unto them.[1] How bitterlie then do you sclander? That you keep no such feastes, dedicate eaves, daies, and churches in their name, you can with no shame denie; for the present practize of your church through everie moneth in the yeare, sheweth this true. Onely nowe it remayneth in question, whether these feastes, etc., be consonant to Christe's Testament, or idolatrous. And you being requested, ought to have prooved this keeping these feastes, these holie Cessations[2] by way of lawe, this dedicating eaves, dayes and churches in sainctes' names, by the evident testimonie of God's word, before you had thus reviled us.

But surelie as you are more than loath to be drawen to the triall and proofe of this stuffe, so take we no delight to rake in this most noysome [ill-smelling] Math. 15:8 dounge of your solemne feastes and vaine worship, which you (as sweete odoures) offer up unto God in the name and mediation of his sonne Christ Jesus. What wil you answeare unto God (though you wil vouchsalf us none answeare) when he shall aske you who hath required these thinges at your handes? What will you then pleade for your Jewish feastes of Gala. 4:9 Easter and Penticoste? If you saye you keep them not after the maner of the Jewes, yet can you not be said to keep them according to Christe's Testament; for there you have no warrant for such feastes. What wil you pleade for your popish feastes of Christmass,

---

[1] *Ibid.*, pp. 11-12.
[2] Cessations, or ceasing from all labours to observe the feasts and fasts.

Al-Hallowes, Candlemass, etc., for your dividing and devising Christ's life into a stage-playe, celebrating his birth upon one daye, his circumcision upon an other, his epiphanie (as you cal it) upon an other, etc., yea, anie of these upon one special daye more than an other? But where have you learned to keepe them after your heathen and prophane maner, with garnishing your earthlie houses, decking your bodies with gaye clothes, great cheare in glottonie, excesse, ryot, idle games, dicing, daunsing, mumming,[1] masking, wassaling; what president [precedent] can you shew of [33] such worshipping and feasting, except it be that holie daye which the Israelites kept before the calf unto the Lorde in the wildernes? Exodus 32:5, 6. Where have you thus learned Christ? Is this to keepe the feaste with the unleavened breade of sinceritie and truth? To crucifie the old man? To be planted to the similitude of his death and of his resurrection, etc.? What can you there pleade for your superstitious devotions towards your Ladie, keeping a daye, an eave, a fast, a feast, a cessation from al labours, an especial worship to her annunciation, an other to her purification yeerly in your church? It were good you would consider of these things what you can answeare: for certis [assuredly] we poore ignorant Christians can see no other mystery in the matter, but that it is detestable idolatrye, even that verie powring out your drinck offrings and burning incense to the queene of heaven.

Jere. 44

Furder what wil you then say to your celebration of deade saincts, keeping one solemne daye unto them al at once? And againe severallie to John Baptist, and to the apostles as they are allotted in their pageant.[2]

---

[1] Mumming, or participating in a mummers' play, also refers to silly or hypocritical religious ritual.
[2] The Feast of All-Saints is celebrated on November 1; the Nativity of St. John the Baptist is observed on June 24.

A Plaine Refutation

George also your St. patron[1] must not be forgotten. A daye also is kept to the martyre Stephen,[2] an other daye to the Innocents,[3] with their daye, eave, fast, feast, cessation, special worship to everie one perticularlie. What warrant can you shew for this out of the Bible? The patriarckes, prophets, godly kings were never so celebrated: neither have you anie commandement or president [precedent] in al the Newe Testament thus to celebrate them. Paule and Peter whilest they were alive desired to be remembred and prayed for of the church, but never required anie such dutie being deade.

Furder, what wil you answeare for your keping a daye, cessation, etc., to St. Michael and al angells?[4] How wil you excuse your self of most high idolatrie, advancing your self in thinges you never sawe, rashlie puffed up of your fleshlie minde, and not holding the heade, depriving others of their crowne. It wil not then stand, to saye, you worship the Lorde by these devises; for so said your fathers in the wildernes. *To morrow the holy day of the Lorde.* The Lorde he wilbe worshipped according to his owne wil revealed to us in his worde; and not by our devises, how holie soever they seeme. If then God be not worshipped with this kinde of worship, their idolls are; or (to speake rather as the prophets and the apostles doe) the devil is worshipped therbie. Leviticus 17:7. Deuteronomy 32:17. II Cronicles 11:15. I Corinthians 10:20. And thus your owne

Collos. 2:18, 19

Exod. 32:5

---

[1] St. George, patron saint of England, is honoured by a feast on April 23. In 1348 the noble Order of St. George, or the Blue Garter, was created. There is some confusion on the identity of this saint with George of Cappadocia. See Peter Heylyn, *The Historie of . . . St. George* (London, 1631; second ed. 1633); John Milner, *An Historical and Critical Inquiry into the Existence and Character of Saint George, Patron of England* (1792); E. A. Wallis Budge, *George of Lydda, the Patron Saint of England* (1930); Isabel Hill Elder, *George of Lydda. Soldier, Saint and Martyr* (1949); Robert Chambers, *The Book of Days*, I, 539f.
[2] St. Stephen's day, December 26, in honour of the proto-martyr. See Acts 6:5-8:1; Chambers, *The Book of Days*, II, 763.
[3] Innocents' Day, or Childermass Day, is observed on December 28, to commemorate the massacre of children in Bethlehem, as ordered by King Herod the Great. See Matthew 2:16-18.
[4] St. Michael and All Angels, or Michaelmas Day, is observed on September 29. See Chambers, *The Book of Days*, II, 157, 387-388.

conclusion which you tooke so heynously, falleth apace upon you; and you have not brought one reason to save or cleare your self.

As to your doctrines by you verballie alleadged concerning God and his worship, the idolatrous Israelites and Jewes in their greatest schisme and diepest apostasy could have alleadged manie true doctrines also. But nothing is more sure than this; Christ is not a priest for such sacrifices as his Father is not pleased with. Nether is he a mediator of anie other testament than his owne. As to the dedication of your churches unto deade sainctes, and the caling them by their owne names, the first you say was the fault of the papistes, but you in caling them after the same names doe not sinne.[1] Was it a fault in your predecessors so [34] to dedicate and cal them, and shall it be no fault in you so to cal them as they had dedicated and left them unto you? But you so cal them only to distinguish them.[2] Whie [do you use] this excuse they also had? But they had furder superstition in these places and sainctes. And doe not you nourish the same superstition in the weake, and animate the papistes in their sinnes, by ratifying these their doings and calling your churches by the same names they baptized them in?

But might we ask you where you thus learned to cal and distinguish christian congregations in the Scriptures? Your answeare and place is readie, Luke [in] Acts 17 caleth a streate in Athens, Mars streate, and aske us if he therfore dedicated it to that heathen God.[3] We answeare you, that if Luke should so give the name and cal it speaking in his owne person for himself, he should sinne and commit idolatrie, in naming the creature of God after an idol, as you do in caling the daies and your churches after the names of such sainctes. David saith he wil not take the names of their idolls in his lippes. But Luke here recordeth the historie of such thinges as came unto Paule in Athens, and the vulgar

Psal. 16:4

---

[1] *A Short Treatise*, p. 12.
[2] *Ibid.*
[3] Acts 17 : 19 and 22 speak of Areopagus and Mars' Hill. In Acts 9 : 11 there is a reference to a street called Straight, in Damascus.

A Plaine Refutation

name of the place whether [whither] the Athenian philosophers ledd Paule, naming it after their maner, not that himself so caled it willingly, or to give us boldnes to do the like, but rather to manifest their fault and superstitious feare they stoode in of their idolls, as Paule, verse 22, sheweth,[1] by the reproofe of their fault, teaching us to avoyde the like. And can you collect that because Luke writeth that they of Athens named a streate after Mars, they of Alexandria signed [named] a ship unto Castor and Pollux, that Christians may by those places name or cal anie thing in their possession after idolls or dead sainctes? Is this the best doctrine you can draw, and use you can make, of this Scripture? Yet is it the only place of Scripture you have used to approve any part of your publique worship, which we had blamed unto you. We wil not stand to urge the poperie and superstition of some of the sainctes' names of your churches, how some of them are caled after Christ's sepulchre, others after al the rable of sainctes both men and weomen, sainctes in the pope's calendar; but proceade to the rest of your tromperie, as your comminations, rogations, purifications.[2]

Your comminations you saye are a part of canonicall Scripture, which is to be read in the church. Partes of canonicall Scripture, indeed they are, by you miserably dismembred and bownd up together, and wickedly used and perverted to such superstition and idolatrie, being used in the place and upon the daye of popish shrift. Or rather (as your portesse [portas] saith) in the place of the discipline of the church, and of the penance, used in the beginning of Lent. Thus in the best use of it by your owne confession it is an execrable idoll, in that it

---

[1] Acts 17 : 22.
[2] Comminations were recitals of divine threatenings against sinners, especially on Ash-Wednesday. God's cursing against impenitent sinners is in Deuteronomy 27. See "A Commination," in *The Book of Common Prayer*. Rogation days or Gang-days, were Monday, Tuesday, and Wednesday preceding Ascension-day or Holy Thursday. During Rogation week it was customary for the parson and parishioners to walk around the bounds of the parish. One reason for this perambulation was the avoidance of strife on boundaries. Another was the preservation of a correct knowledge of parochial property.

is brought into your church, and supplieth the place of Christe's discipline in his church, and is used in stead therof untill Christe's discipline may be restored againe (which you there say " is much to be wished "), it being nothing lesse than that which it standeth for, by your owne confessions in the preamble before your comminations.¹ It remayneth then the instrument of those idoll shepheardes to feede the [35] sheep of distruction with the curse of God, being sealed unto your whole church by your owne mouthes, all your church being generallye founde, and wilfullie remayning guiltie in som sinnes there condempned: as these publique idolatries, others, and each one in sundrie perticulars: as deceipt, wronge, whoredome, etc. We wil not here stand to discusse the follye and poperie of this solemne peice of your worship and administration. Penance and your Lent fast are grosse to everie one, in whom is anie light.

<small>Zechar. 11</small>

Your rogations you say are but limiting the boundes of everie parish, to avoyde contention.² But we would then knowe of you how it became an act of your church, a part of your pastor's office, to be done by the parson and the parish clarcke with the rest of the parishners, certaine psalmes, the letanie and collects being said over the grasse, corne, and cattayle, in place of the popish procession. Yea, there are of your priestes that wil not faile to reade a gospel when they come at a crosse way orderly. This is somewhat more than visiting the bowndes. Nether ever thought we that such civile actions had belonged to the church and ministrie. Christ would not be made a divider here on earth, there are civile judgment seates appoincted therunto. And howsoever this publique sollemne worship be commaunded by other injunctions of your church, and not by your service-booke, yet according to that booke is this solemne action performed.

<small>Luke 12:14</small>

---

¹ In the section, "A Commination," in *The Book of Common Prayer*, we read: "Brethren, in the Primitive Church there was a godly discipline, that, at the beginning of Lent" ... "until the said discipline may be restored again (which is much to be wished), it is thought good" ...

² *A Short Treatise*, p. 12.

A Plaine Refutation

Purifications you say are annexed to make up our ryming figure. For nether your Booke nor doctrine of your church alloweth anie other purification, than in the bloude of the lambe, etc.[1] Nether yet did the Jewes (from whom the pope [as it should seeme] derived this worship) hold anie other purification than in the bloude of that lambe, although they figured that bloude by sundrie rites and ceremonies, of which sort this maner of bringing weomen to the priest in the church after childbirth, and a certaine number of dayes expired, was. Yet seeing you wil at no hand be said to imitate the Jewes herein, you must then take it from the pope of necessitie, for other aucthor you can finde none for it, nether anie president [precedent] or warrant in the Testament of Christ. The weoman's monethlie restraint and separation from your church, her comming after that just tyme wympeled,[2] vealed [veiled], with her gosips and neighbours following her, her kneeling downe before and offring unto the priest, the prieste's churching, praying over her, blessing her from sonne and moone, delivering her in the end to her former vocation, shewe somewhat besides giving of thankes.[3] But if it should be admitted only a thanksgiving, we would then knowe of Mr. Giffard or his Ordinarie, how this perticular and ordinarie (though miraculous) matter, more than al other strange actes, wonderful and extraordinarie deliverances both by sea and by land, manie and great benefites of the Lord both to men and woemen, should be made a publique action of the church, an especial part of the publique worship and administration therof;

---

[1] *Ibid.*, p. 12.
[2] Enveloped in a wimple, covered with a shawl.
[3] The rite of churching, by which a woman one month after childbirth is received back into the church, with prayers and thanksgiving, and with accustomed offerings. See "The Thanksgiving of Women after Childbirth, Commonly Called the Churching of Women," in *The Book of Common Prayer*. The phrase "blessing her from sonne and moone" refers to Psalm 121 : 6. In present day versions of the *Book of Common Prayer*, Psalm 116 or 127 is used, but in the versions of 1549, 1552, 1559 and 1604 Psalm 121 was used. The change was made in the version of 1662. See William Keeling, *Liturgiae Britannicae, or the Several Editions of the Book of Common Prayer of the Church of England*, second edition (London, 1851), pp. 342-345.

[36] and what warrant they have in Christe's Testament for this. But if they there have none, whie other perticular and private benefites may not aswel be brought into the church also, and be enjoyned by lawe, as this; and then what end would there be of these devises, and what place to the publique ministrie of God's worde in the church?

Furder we would knowe of them whie these woemen should by lawe be constrained to defer their thanksgiving until the moneth be expired, or if they have given God thankes before, privatly, whie they should for his private and peculiar benefite be compelled to give thankes publiquely againe for the same, or rather to hire the priest to give thanks for her againe. Of these pointes touching this matter, we would crave Mr. Giffard's learned and direct answeare in his next booke.

Next come your tithes, offringes, mortuaries. These you saye are but for maintenance of your ministerie, and not as a matter tyed of necessitie unto a priesthoode, as in the time of the lawe; and if they were, the error were not fundamental.[1] We never doubted but that they were the maintenance of your ministerie; but whether the ministrie of Christ nowe under the gospell may be so maintayned, is the question. We reade in the Testament, that the ministrie of the gospel ought to be maintayned by the flockes unto which they attend, and that by the free and loving contribution of the faithful, according to the minister's necessitie, and the people's habilitye from time to time. We reade not in the Testament that this contribution ought to be imposed by waye of 1. lawe, or 2. bargaine, upon the people; as by paying tenthes, thirdes, forty or fifty powndes a yeare. We finde not in the Testament that the ministers of Christ ought to sel their administration, as the sacraments, etc. Nowe let the tithes, offrings, set wages of your ministrie (we meane the inferior common ministrie of parsons, vickars, roving curates, or hireling preachers, and not of the lordlie sort which live as princes in pallaces, nor of your collegiate priests in their dennes)

I Cor. 9
Gal. 6:6
I Tim. 6:8
Mat. 10
II Cor. 11:20
I Thes. 2:5
II Pet. 2:15
Jude 11, 12, 13

---

[1] *A Short Treatise,* pp. 12-13.

A Plaine Refutation

be examined by these rules, and tryed, whether they have anie foundation in the worde of God or no. As to their accursed covetousnes and odious portsale [public sale] not onlie of their owne tongues, but of that gospel and ministration (which they pretend) of your sacraments, baptisme, supper, churching, marriing, buriing, etc., and that to the most prophane and ungodlie for their tithes, offrings, wage, etc., Mr. Giffard shal never be able to hide from God, or excuse before men. It would require a lardge discourse to set downe how these their tithes accord in everie perticular unto the Levitical decimations; and how dangerous nowe, it were to revive, and unpossible to joyne these lawes unto Christe's ministrie and gospel. If that priesthode be removed, there must be of necessitie a removing of the lawe. They that revive anie part of the ceremonial lawe, are bounde to the whole lawe, and abolished from Christ. Let Mr. Giffard then looke whether this error be fundamental, as he caleth it, being obstinatelie held. The prince's commandement wil no more change the nature of this [37] lawe, than the commandement of Ezekia¹ and other godlie kings did before tyme, for so might al the lawes of God which princes should commande be transferred from God to men. If it be said they use these tithes, etc., otherwise, so also might the Galatians and Corinthians have said of such ceremonies as they would have joyned to the gospel.

^{Num. 18}

^{Hebr. 7:12}
^{Gal. 5:3, 4}
^{Phil. 3:2}

Nowe are we to take a viewe of your maner of visiting the sicke and houslling them with the sacrament. Your absolution, dirges, and funeral sermons over and for the deade. You confesse a maner of visiting the sicke prescribed, but you demande of us where we have seene it practized by, or urged at their handes which are able and diligent pastors, by these that have the government of your church.² Wee answeare, that it sufficeth to be commanded and prescribed by your service-booke unto all your ministers and churches, to the diligent observation wherof all ful preistes are sworne.

---

¹ Hezekiah. See II Chronicles 29.
² *A Short Treatise*, p. 13.

Furder your church-wardens and sidemen are sworne to present all defaultes therin at the arch-deacons' or commissaries' courtes. So that no marveyle though this booke be founde in the handes of the most diligent and able priestes, reading it over weomen at their churching, over the maried, over the sicke, over the deade, and where not. And for Mr. Giffard's satisfying, we give him to weite [wit, know], that as learned priestes as he, have used this booke to the visitation of the sicke. And nowe we would knowe of him whie these able priests should have more libertie to pray by the direction of the spirit for and with the sick, according to their present estate, than they are allowed by those that have the government of your church in the publique praiers of the whole church, according to the present estate therof. To conclude, we would knowe of him by what warrant in God's worde the church can prescribe and enjoyne such a form of visiting, etc.

As to their absolution which Mr. Giffard so slilye would passe over without speaking anie worde therof, let the reader understand that nothing can be more popish or blasphemous than it is: where a sacrilegious priest taketh upon him by the authoritie committed unto him, to absolve the sicke from all his sinnes. Hath anie mortal man power to forgive sinnes? Or is it not the office of God alone? Hath the priest power to forgive al sinnes, such as are not made unto him? What horrible blasphemie is this? To him that hath power to forgive all sinnes, to him we may make our prayers and supplication, him only may we worship. Hath the greatest minister of the church any more power to retaine or loose the sinne of the least member, than the said member hath to bind or loose his [the minister's] sinne? Doth not this rule of our Savior aswel extend unto him as to the least in the church: " If thie brother sinne against thee, rebuke him, and if he repent, forgive him " ? Hath not the church power to reprove and cast out their pastor if he so deserve? Is not al this binding and loosing donne by the worde of God, and not by anie power or excellencye of man? Hath not the worde of God the like power and effect against sinne

Luke 17:3
Rom. 16:17
I Tim. 5:20
Psal. 149:9

A Plaine Refutation

in the mouth of the least of God's servants, as in the mouth of the greatest? Let this collect then (wherbie the priest in their leitourgie [38] by the power committed unto him absolveth the sick of al his sinnes) remaine one witnesse (amongst manie other) of their poperie, and until more come, of most high blasphemie.[1]

Mr. Giffard taketh verie heinouslie at our handes this phrase of housling, with the sacrament, terming it a false packing in us, and goeth about to purge his church therof, by shewing how it denieth " all the wicked blasphemous corrupt doctrines of the papists touching the Lorde's Supper.[2] And also denieth, that a man is of necessitie to receave it at his death."[3] Thus ever with his impertinent matters he with-draweth and shrinketh from the present question. We must therfore still call him backe to the poynte, and demaund of him what warrant in Christ's Testament their church hath to institute a private communion, or to administer the Supper of the Lord in anie other place than where the church is assembled. This if he can doe, then indeed we have faulted in caling it an housel. But if he can shewe no warrant for this private domestical communion, then we must still blame this action as popish, superstitious, and irregular, what doctrines soever they hold of the Lord's Supper besides. Againe, though they exhort and perswade the sick person that this sacrament is not then of necessitie; yet if he be so superstitious to require it, the priest then is bownde of necessitie to deliver it him, though there be no more to receave than they two. And what is this but to nourish superstition, or to make the sacrament so delivered of great value and profit unto them. Thus jugleth and toyeth your church with the holy things of God at her pleasure.

The papistes you say that invented the purgatorie, had also their blasphemous diriges and prayers for the deade. But we are more than impudent in lying, to terme the

I Cor. 11:20

---

[1] " And by his authority committed to me, I absolve thee from all thy sins." See " The Order for the Visitation of the Sick," *The Book of Common Prayer*.
[2] *A Short Treatise*, p. 13.
[3] *Ibid.*

prayers which you use at burials, such : seing your church denieth the purgatorie, prayers for the deade, etc.[1] We will not requite you with evil wordes, but let the proofe of these matters declare who is a lyer and impudent. We would therfore first knowe of you where you have learned to make the burial of your deade an ecclesiasticall action, part of the pastor's office, and to make it an especial part of your worship, if not of the pope ? Then where you learned to burie in your hallowed churches and church-yardes (as though you had not fieldes and grounde to bury in) with a special dirige and leitourgie, with praiers, singers, ringers, mourners, beades-men, etc., if not of the pope ? It were too longe to shewe the originall and processe of this superstition, with the great advantage that cometh to the priestes therbie. It were needles also to shewe, howe this your leitourgie, dirige, and prayers, are fetched and peiced out of the pope's portesse [portas]. It were curious to relate the watching, preparing, arraying, crossing, dressing the corps[e] to the grave, also the array of the mourners with all the superstition of the heraldes, the attyre of the priestes and clarckes, with their tymes and place when and where to receave, when to rest, when to singe, to reade, to praye, when and with what wordes to cast on the [39] first shovel of earth by the hand of the priest, the grave being made east and west, etc. Onely this in general we say, that all these devises (seing God no where commandeth them in his worde) are vayne, superstitious, and fond [foolish], as whereby God's name is highly taken in vayne, prophaned, and abused ; yea, his Holy Spirit most impiouslie blasphemed and despighted. For whilest the whole land is of their church, and they bury all that dye in their church of their natural death after this maner with this leitourgie (but such as dye of any violent death, how christianly soever, they vouchsalf not thus to burye), pronouncing in the collect they use whilest earth is casting on, that God in his mercy hath taken to himself the soule of that their deare brother or sister departed, they therbie

[1] *Ibid.*, p. 14.

A Plaine Refutation

justifie the most wicked, gracelesse, impenitent wretches, atheistes, blasphemers, idolatours, papists, Anabaptists, heretickes, conjurers that dye in their sinnes, as though such could have anie benefite by the death of Christ, or the mercy of God belonged unto such as dye in their sinnes impenitent, except peradventure the prieste's prayers nowe, the holines of the grownd, and this christen buryal, etc., may helpe him; thus openlie contradicting the expresse word of God, and hardening all the rest of your prophane atheists, idolators, whoremasters, blasphemers in their sinnes. Likewise in an other collect, where they desire God, that they with that their departed brother may have a perfect consummation and blisse both in bodie and soule,[1] what do they but pray for the soule of the deade, seing they burye all with this collect, and some must needes dye apparantly wicked, and impenitent. Yea, what doe they hereby but establish a purgatory, or some such meane place, for in hel there is no redemption. Thus whither doth not man wander whilest he followeth his owne inventions, and forsaketh the straight pathes of the Lorde.

As to their venal funerall sermons, they have as litle grownde or warrant in the Scriptures, as their dirige and funeral collects have. Wel may they derive them from the funeral orations of the heathen orators, but no president [precedent] they have of the godlie in anie age so to bury their deade. We reade of no such matter at anie of the patriarches', prophets', or godlie kinges' burial. No, nor at the burial of our Saviour Christ, of the martyre Stephen, of the Apostle James, or anie of the faithful in those tymes; yet were there as godlie, religious, learned, and able men to doe it then alive and remayning, as they that thinck the best of themselves nowe, if the Holy Ghost had seene it so needful.

Next fellowe [followe] your corrupt maner of administring the sacraments, the font, the crosse in bap-

---

[1] "That we, with all those that are departed in the true faith of thy holy Name, may have our perfect consummation and bliss, both in body and soul, in thy eternal and everlasting glory." See "The Order for the Burial of the Dead," *The Book of Common Prayer*.

tisme, your gossips, and blasphemous collect used to this sacrament, your baptisme by weomen, bishoping, with other heretical collects of this booke, etc. When we shew (you say) whie the fonte is an abhomination, you shal knowe what to say.[1] How idolatrously the font was invented, brought into the church, hallowed, and used by [40] the pope, is evident to all men. Whether they fetched this from the Jewes' lavar, sea,[2] or base, we will not here dispute. Sufficeth it us that it is an idolatrous, popish, enchaunted, hallowed relique, wherin they put and kept their enchaunted hallowed water, and used it to manie execrable idolatries. Therfore it is an abhomination to the Lord, a detestable idoll that ought to be utterly abolished by the lawe of God, and ought not to be used in his church and worship.

<small>Deut. 7
II Kings 18:4
Rom. 14
I Cor. 8</small>

Furder seing it nourisheth the papists, the weake and ignorant in their fore-conceaved superstition, and is an offence unto the godly, if it were a thing in libertie, yet ought it not to be thus used, much lesse thus enjoyned and retayned by vertue of lawe upon all congregations. And seing in the best imagination of it, it is not an instrument of anie more necessitie or use unto this sacrament than anie other cleane and decent vessel,

<small>I Cor. 6:12</small>

seing also our Saviour Christ hath not separated anie vessel or water to this use, we cannot see how a fewe men may be thus bold to command this vessel upon all churches by waye of lawe, and to forbid all other unto

<small>Gal. 5:1</small>

this use. For what is this but to restraine that which God hath left in libertie, to controle God, and to make newe lawes for his church. And whie might they not by the same usurped power bring in what unnecessarie ceremonies they list, even al their fore-fathers' the Jewes' and popes' infinite traditions, aswel as these popish devises and Jewish ordinances above-said; aswel as these popish idolatrous reliques of fonte, bells, organs, musick, surplices, coapes, vestiments, habites, hoodes, cappes, tippetts, tires [attires, outfits], etc.

---

[1] *A Short Treatise*, p. 14.
[2] The laver was a vessel in Solomon's Temple in which were washed the sacrificial offerings. It was also a vessel in which a priest washed his hands and feet. Sea, or see, was a seat, a place of honour and dignity.

A Plaine Refutation

But if these least little thinges, which they call matters indifferent, wherin al men ought to obey, prove so heynous in God's eyes, so pernitious to the whole church, what shal we thinck of their simbolical ceremonies, tryflings, jocolings [jovialities, sportings], that they have added to their sacraments? As unto their baptisme a dialogue betwixt the priest, the clarcke, the God-fathers, God-mothers, and the infant; the signe of the crosse, the sanctifying or making holie their water, etc. Their fowre sortes of baptismes. Namely, 1. Their publique baptisme by the priest, etc. 2. Their hastie baptisme by weomen. 3. Their baptisme by supposition: *N. [Name] if thou be not baptised, I baptise thee, etc.*[1] 4. And their lorde the bishop his baptisme, or confirmation of Christ's baptisme.

Likewise in their sacrament of the Supper, their frivolous leitourgie stinting the priest when and how to stand at the north end of the table, what and when to saye and praye, when to kneele, when to tourne, when to glory God, etc. Also the vayne dialogue betwixt the priest, clarcke, and people. Their altering the wordes of Christ's institution, and delivering it after a popish maner. *The bodie of our Lord Jesus Christ, which was given for thee, preserve this thie bodie and soule unto everlasting life, etc.*,[2] and that kneeling, that they might adore the bread, or at least retaine a taste of their former superstition in tyme of high poperie, etc. Of this sacrament they have also divers kindes, with di-[41] vers leitourgies: as publique, or ordinarie; sollemne, upon certaine of their festivals; and private, or domestical. Not here to speake of their other half sacraments, as their penance or commination upon Ash-Wednesday, with their special leitourgie thereunto. Their solemnization of mariage in the bodie of their church upon the Lorde's daye or otherwise by the priest, with his booke and special leitourgie, with a ring

---

[1] " If thou be not baptized already, N. [Name], I baptize thee in the name of the Father, and of the Son, and of the Holy Ghost. Amen."

[2] " The Order of the Administration of the Lord's Supper, or Holy Communion," in *The Book of Common Prayer.* Compare Matthew 26 : 26; Mark 14 : 22; and Luke 22 : 19.

(as the element) to be laid upon the service-booke, which doth hallowe it in steade of holie water : with which ring the man must be taught of the priest to wedd his wief, etc. And the marryed offer unto the priest and clarck.

Touching the crosse, Mr. Giffard confesseth it to be most " blasphemously and horribly abused in poperye, they ascribing unto it power to drive out [and expell] devils, and worshipping it with devine honor."[1] We looked that after his accustomed maner he should have said, " but our church doth not so thinck of or worship the crosse, therfore you Brownists most impudentlye sclander, etc." But in steade of this he saith never a worde to the matter in perticular, save unto symbolical ceremonies in general he is of judgement, that the antient churches immediatlie after the apostles' tyme " did offend, in taking over much libertie to ordeine ceremonies symbolical." Yet he doubteth not, but " verie reverend godlie learned men, ledd by the example of those holye fathers [of olde], have judged it lawful for the churches to ordeyne such ceremonies."[2] We would first therfore knowe of those reverend godlie learned, and not of Mr. Giffard, whie they (nowe that al are christian and no heathen amongst them) retaine and enjoyne this superstitious signe of the crosse in the administration of their baptisme. Also whether they are not persuaded, that our Saviour Christe's institution which the Apostles taught and delivered unto the churches touching the administration of the sacraments, was perfect and fullie sufficient. If they so thincke of it, whether they judge it lawful for anie mortal men, or the whole church, willingly and wittingly to alter or add anie thing to, or plucke anie thing from, the said institution of our Saviour in the sacraments. Or if they so add, whether our Saviour doth accept and blesse it, as his owne institution. And if God doe not accept or blesse such sacraments, where his institution is thus wilfullie violated and changed, howe such adulterate

---

[1] *A Short Treatise*, p. 14. See William Bradshaw, *A Shorte Treatise of the Crosse in Baptisme* (1604), and Robert Parker, *A Scholasticall Discourse against Symbolizing with Antichrist in Ceremonies* (1607).
[2] *A Short Treatise*, p. 15.

A Plaine Refutation

sacraments may be said the true seales of God's covenant; especiallie where such a blasphemous, horrible, popish, idolatrous ceremonie is used, as Mr. Giffard confesseth this signe of the crosse to be, except it be better with them than it was with the papistes. Or howe may the faithful in this estate joyne unto them. And nowe it would be known of Mr. Giffard (seing he in his owne judgment condemneth these symbolical ceremonies) howe he dare thus presumtuously breake Christe's institution in delivering them after the maner prescribed, and joyne unto those men that enjoyne those ceremonies, against such of Christe's fai[t]hful servants as reprove them, stand, and [42] suffer against them. Is not this most fearefully and presumptuously to tempt God, to sinne against his owne conscience? It is no excuse unto him to saye, the best reformed churches doe use witnesses (he meaneth God-fathers, and God-mothers) in baptisme.¹ For his owne conscience knoweth and judgeth, that the best churches doo erre in so doing.

Furder, baptisme being publique, to be delivered openlie in the assemblie when the whole churche is mett together, what neede more witnesses of the matter than the whole congregation? But howe wicked and impious is that lawe of their church, which forbiddeth the parents to answere and undertake for the bringing up their owne children in the true faith and feare of God, and driveth them to bring popish gossips or sureties, who must both undertake, vowe, and answere for their childe, that he doth forsake the devil and his workes, etc. What can be more vaine, folish, and ridiculous?

To the baptisme by weomen you answeare, that it "is both condemned by the cheif governours of your church, and is not practized, except it be among the popish and superstitious ignorant sort."² First we must oppose the publique lawe of your church against those your governours, who we suppose (as confidentlie as you speake) wil not prove in the plural nomber, when *Mr. Giffard here confesseth both some members of their church to be popish, superstitious, and ignorant; and also this baptisme of their church to be such.*

¹ *Ibid.*
² *Ibid.*

the pointe commeth to scanning. Your lawe in three places of your portesse [portas] doth not onlie allowe the baptisme by weomen, but publiquelie justifie it, and maketh a kinde of necessitie of such privat baptisme: saiing, that if the child be in danger, they may baptise it at home without a minister, and " that in this case they have donne wel and according to due order, concerning the baptisinge of this childe, which being borne in original sinne and in the wrath of God, is nowe by the laver of regeneration in baptisme, receyved into the nomber of the children of God, and heires of life everlasting."[1] Wherin, besides that they most highlie breake and prophane the institution and ordinances of Christ concerning the publique seale of this holie covenant, in delivering it without a lawful minister, privatelie in a house, rashlie, and unreverently without due order, etc., they also consequently maintaine and teach these popish blasphemous errors therbye: that if the childe had dyed unbaptized, it had bene damned; and that baptisme is of necessitie to salvation: for ells what needed so great feare and haste, that they would not staye to bring the childe to the publique congregation, no, nor so much as for the minister to baptise it? Or how could there be so great cause and so greate necessitie in the matter as their book mentioneth, if they thought that the salvation of the childe honge [hung, depended] not upon the baptisme? Wherbie is manifestly convinced, as also by their wordes not secretlie implyed, that they hold baptisme the cause, and not the seale of salvation. For ells to the infant nowe dying, what good could baptisme doe? Or which waye could it be a " laver of regeneration " unto it, or receive it into the nomber of God's children? We had thought that the salvation of the childe had onlie honge [hung] upon the eternal election [43] and predestination of God, and that the

---

[1] "The Ministration of Private Baptism of Children in Houses," in *The Book of Common Prayer*. In the versions of 1549, 1552, and 1559, those that are present may call on God for his grace, and one of them shall name the child, and dip him in the water, and say the requisite words of the baptism. In the 1604 and subsequent versions, the action of baptizing is assigned to a lawful minister.

A Plaine Refutation

seale of the covenant had belonged unto it, by reason of the parents' faith, and is administred not as anie helpe or present benefite to the newe borne infant, so much as when it commeth to ryper age to be a contynual comfort and help unto it.

Bisshopping, Mr. Giffard saith, is litle used or urged in the Church of England, being loath belike to make anie defence therof. Yet it is certaine that the priest is in his portesse [portas] enjoyned to commaund, " that the children be brought to the bisshop to be confirmed, so soone as they can saye, in the vulgare tongue, the articles of their faith, etc."[1] Also in an other place of their said service-booke there is an expresse lawe: " that none shalbe admitted to the holye communion, until such time as he can say the catechisme, and be confirmed."[2] Howe accorde these lawes to Mr. Giffard's saying, that it is litle used? But what a monstrous matter is this confirmation of their church, where the baptisme of Christ is to be confirmed of a wretched man, if he were (as he is nothing lesse) a servant of Christe? Yea, that Christe's faithful servants (whom Christ hath alredie publiquely baptised, receyved, and engrafted unto himselfe) should be kept from the comfortable table of the Lorde, until they have a popish bisshop his confirmation. Not here to mention the binding of the faith of the whole church to an apocrypha catechisme.[3]

Yet to make this their confirmation either of greater estimation, or more execrable with all men, they add in the second cause manie speciall vertues therof. Namely, " that by their imposition of handes and praier, such as

---

[1] See the concluding page of " The Ministration of Publick Baptism of Infants, to Be Used in the Church," in *The Book of Common Prayer*. See also the first page of " The Order of Confirmation," *ibid*.
[2] See " The Order of Confirmation," especially the final sentence, in *The Book of Common Prayer*.
[3] *The Book of Common Prayer* of 1549 required confirmation for admittance to Holy Communion. The versions of 1552, 1559, and 1604 added the requirement of saying the catechism. In the 1662 version the requirement is made more flexible : " And there shall none be admitted to the Holy Communion, until such time as he be confirmed, or be ready and desirous to be confirmed."

are so confirmed by them, maye receave strength and defence against all temptations to sinne, and the assaultes of the worlde and the devil."[1] Surely if this be true, great is the bishops' faulte to neglect the practise therof; but howe great then our sinne, to blame and condemne such a wonderfull and excellent ordinance. But doubtles this is either too good or too bad to be true. If al they upon whom these bisshops shal laye their handes and praye over, shal " receave strength and defence against al temptations to sinne, and the assaults of the worlde and the devil," then shal al they that receave this confirmation be undoubtedlie saved. Yea, if anie of them whome the bisshop shal thus confirme, shal receive this strength and defence, etc., then have the bisshops greater power, and their prayers more vertue, than ever God gave to anie mortal man, yea, than ever he gave to our Saviour Christ himself; with whom though Judas were contynuallie conversant [with] his most heavenly doctrines and holie prayers, yet the devil entred into him and prevayled against him. Though Peter were a right deare and faithful servant of Christ, yet Sathan sifted him, and he fell. Yea, we had thought that our Saviour onlie had received this " strength and defence against al temptations to sinne, assaults," etc. And that al mortal men had bene dailye subject to sinne, temptation, etc., that our rejoycing might be of God, and not of our selves, and God's glorie be shewed and perfected through our weaknes. If these [44] vanuties [sic] of the biss[h]ops were true, then might it indeed rightly be called a confirmation, for then such as had that [confirmation] were sure and sure, there then to those should be no more use of Christe's merites, suffrings, or mediation, or of God's mercye. But because al men are continuallie prone unto, and even enclosed and compassed about with sinne, whilest they dwel in this mortal flesh, and have continual neede of God's mercy, and use of

---

[1] This is the third paragraph of the preamble to "Confirmation, Wherein Is Contained a Catechism for Children," in the 1549, 1552, 1559, and 1604 versions of *The Book of Common Prayer*. The preamble is dropped in the 1662 version.

A Plaine Refutation

Christ's merites, suffrings, and mediation, yea, because we see wel nigh al those whom the bisshops have thus confirmed, to be confirmed in al sinne and wickednes, and even the bisshops themselves the aucthors of this devise (from whom al this vertue and holines should flowe fourth unto others) to be them-selves the verie synkes and draynes of al abhomination, corruption, idolatrie, superstition, blasphemie, and open transgression of al God's lawes, we are confident in the truth and power of our Lorde Jesus Christ to witnesse against those abhominable ordinances of Antichrist, and against the Church of England for receiving the same, and maintayning the most impious blasphemous doctrines that ensue therof, as is above proved.

To the blasphemous collects in your sacraments and booke, you wishe we were as weary in lying and sclandering, as we should be to seeke and finde out one such.[1] You have in remembrance the collects wherin the priest by the aucthoritie committed unto him, dothe absolve the sicke of al his sinnes.[2] You must not forget your two collects said over the deade brother. The one, wherin you praise God for receiving to mercye his soule, lived he or died he never so prophane, blasphemouse, and impenitent a wretch. The other, wherin you praye for him, that you with him "may have a perfect consummation and blisse both in bodie and soule."[3]

Nowe to helpe your memorie a little furder, we woulde desire you to consider better of that glorious antheame you singe or saye in your publique communion, wherin "with angells and arch-angells and al the companie of heaven you laude and magnifie", etc.[4] Wherin we wil not demaunde of you howe, whilest you remaine in the flesh, you can have such familiar conversation with those heavenlie souldiours and elect spirits of the faithfull deceased, that you together with them can praise

---

[1] *A Short Treatise*, p. 15.
[2] See "The Order for the Visitation of the Sick," *The Book of Common Prayer*.
[3] See "The Order for the Burial of the Dead," *The Book of Common Prayer*.
[4] See "The Order for the Administration of the Lord's Supper, or Holy Communion," *The Book of Common Prayer*.

and laude God. Nether wil we presse you with the papistical and curious speculations in making digrees of angells, arch-angels, etc. But we would here knowe of you howe manie arch-angells you reade of and finde in the Scriptures,[1] and whether you knowe anie more heades of angells than Christ himself. Except peradventure your church have some especial prerogative from the apostatical sea [see], to make arch-bisshops and arch-angells.

Your collect also in baptisme of sanctifying the floud Jordan and al other waters to the mistical washing away of sinne,[2] some saye savoreth greatly of poperie, and retayneth the people in a superstitious opinion, that the water used in baptisme hath holines and some especial vertue in it above common water, especially when it is thus blessed by the priest, and taken out of the hallowed fonte, etc. But we wil not presse you herewith, nether yet stand to examine your collect upon your [45] St. Michael and All Angels' Day, how you make Michael a creature, and canonize him amonge the pope's saincts, and worship him amongst and together with all angels.[3] This shalbe no blasphemie, no poperie in your church. Nether wil we stand to unrip your popish patched letanie, or shew by what pope, and whie every part therof was devised and added, and wherfore it is good.[4]

As for the quick and the deade, for al that travaile by sea or by land, for all weomen labouring with childe, for all sicke persons and younge children, all prisoners and captives, for bishops and curates, for [from] lightnings and tempestes, for [from] plague, pestilence, and famine, for [from] battaile and murder, and for [from] sodeyne

---

[1] The word "archangel" occurs twice in the Bible, in I Thessalonians 4 : 16 and Jude 1 : 9. The first reference speaks of the Lord's descending "from heaven with a shout, with the voice of the archangel, and with the trump of God." The second refers to Michael the archangel. By contrast, the word "angel" occurs 294 times in the Scriptures.
[2] See the opening collect in "Of the Administration of Public Baptism." The language is changed in the 1604 version of *The Book of Common Prayer* to "didst sanctify water to the mystical washing away of sin."
[3] See "The Collects, Epistles, and Gospels to be Used throughout the Year," in *The Book of Common Prayer*.
[4] See "The Litany" in *The Book of Common Prayer*.

A Plaine Refutation

death, etc., all which things and what ells that you will request at his handes, Christ cannot but graunt you, when you so beconjure him " by the mysterie of his holie incarnation, by his holie nativitie and circumcision, by his baptisme, fasting, and temptation, by his agonie and bloudie sweate, by his crosse and passion, by his pretious death and buriall, by his glorious resurrection and assention, and by the coming of the Holy Ghost ".[1] And sweetlie you entreat him by them all severally and joyntely to deliver you from the evils above-said, and also from fornication and al other dea[d]ly sinnes. In which sofrage [suffrage][2] we wil not observe that you hold some sinnes deadlie, and others not deserving death, because you peradventure can shift it off with learning, howsoever it standeth in the pope's booke, or they that made it thought of it. Only we observe that this your holy letanie is a most rare and especiall confection, soveraigne good for all thinges at all tymes, but especially in the morning, and therfore it is so often enjoyned to be songe or said in your church everie weeke at their mattens.

Yet was there (by what adventure we knowe not) an unsavorie and unhappie sofrage [suffrage] stollen into your letanie in Kinge Edward's tyme, *against the tyrannie of the Bisshop of Rome and all his detestable enormities.*[3] Which sofrage because it was nether so canonical or holie, nether agreed unto the rest, and could not be songe with them in tune; or because it was over rough doctrine for sondrie of their weake brethren that then loved and yet love the pope and anie thing that commeth from him, with all their hearte; or ells (that which is more likelie) over plaine doctrine to make the people abhor all their Romish wares and marchantmen; the worthy bishops, most vigilant pastors and governours of

---

[1] Almost all of this paragraph is taken from " The Litany."
[2] A suffrage is a supplication or intercessory prayer. One of the rubrics in the 1549 Prayer Book is " The Litany and Suffrages."
[3] " From all sedition and privy-conspiracy; from the tyranny of the Bishop of Rome, and all his detestable enormities; from all false doctrine and heresy; from hardness of heart, and contempt of thy word and commandment, *Good Lord, deliver us.*"

your church, to avoide these inconveniences, of their pontificall aucthoritie dismissed it, thrust it quite out of their letanie, and utterlie abrogated and razed it out of their authenticall leitourgie. Wherin (nowe it hath bene by these learned men corrected, and this perrilous sofrage thrust out) it is impossible to finde ether heresie or blasphemie.[1]

But can there be more horrible and execrable blasphemie than thus to conjure and exercise [exorcise] Christ by his nativity, circumcision, baptisme, fasting, by his agonie, his sweate, his crosse, his death, his buryal, etc.?[2] What conjurers or enchaunters can exceede this? Where have they learned thus to praye? Thus to dismember and distort Christ, or thus idolatrouslie to applie and abuse these outwarde thinges which he did or were donne unto him in the fleshe? Why might they not aswel beseech him by his growing in age, his wal-[46]king, sleeping, weeping, etc., by his crowne of thornes, the spondge, nayles, speare? No mervaile they fetched this geare from the pope's portesse [portas]. Againe, where have they learned to pray for their forefathers' offences, if not of the pope? Where have they learned to pray for all that erre, all that travaile by land or water, for all that are sicke, in captivitie, tribulation, etc., when there is a sinne for which we are forbidden to praye, when there are many most ungodly and wicked persons going about and suffring for much mischief, thus traveyling, emprisoned, etc.? Pray they not for God's open enemies, for the breach of all God's lawes, for the overthrowe of all majestracie, publique peace and order, and for the destruction both of the church and common wealth therby? Also where learned they to pray against lightning, tempest, plague, famine, battle, etc., when they have no present neede, or have no present

---

[1] This supplication is in "The Litany" for 1549 and 1552, but the version of 1559 omitted it.

[2] "By the mystery of thy holy Incarnation; by thy holy Nativity and Circumcision; by thy Baptism, Fasting, and Temptation, *Good Lord, deliver us.*"

By thine Agony and bloody sweat; by thy Cross and Passion; by thy precious Death and Burial; by thy glorious Resurrection and Ascension; and by the coming of the Holy Ghost, *Good Lord, deliver us.*"

A Plaine Refutation

feare or danger therof?[1] Is not this to trifle, to abuse God's name? Can this prayer be of faith to praye against lightning in the middest of wynter, etc.? Is not this to forbid God to use his owne creatures to his owne will and glorie? Yea, to forbid him to restraine his creatures, or to punish his enemies by dearth, plague, warre? Finally, where learned they to praye against sodeyne death, that God should not call anie of this land, yea, of the whole world, sodeynly? Is not this to appointe God when and howe to call? Hath not God reserved these secret thinges in his owne hande only, forbidden men to be curious or inquisitive after them, and commanded them continually to watch and be readie, for in an howre that we thincke not, will our Master come as a theife in the night, etc.?

These are the publique prayers, doctrines, worship, and administration of the Church of England, which it not only tollerateth, but with an high hand commaundeth, maintayneth, enforceth upon all men. Of all these execrable wares standeth Mr. Giffard, a marchantman, retayling them to the misera[b]le people, being with none more or so much offended as with those who refuse and speake against this tromperie; whom how he rewardeth or refuteth, let this his blasphemous popish booke shewe. What defence he hath made for this worship and ministration, let the readers by this time judge, and howe smoothly he hath passed by and coulored, yea, swallowed up, all these abhominations, transferring all the blame and reproach upon the poor servants of Christ, that condemne this trash, and admonish him. Evill signes ether of a true minister, or true Christian. None speaking by the spirit of God justifieth error or blasphemeth the truth at any time. How far he hath sought to justifie these antichristian devises and popish enormities, and blasphemed us for speaking the truth, let his booke shewe.

Yet bringeth he against us a certaine secte in their church which condemne certayne thinges as corruptions

---

[1] "From lightnings and tempests; from plague, pestilence, and famine; from battle and murder, and from sudden death, *Good Lord, deliver us.*"

and such as neede reformation, and therfore would know how we could abandon al the assemblies for this Booke, seing manie disalowe manie thinges therin.[1] [47] To this he saith we make a double answeare: first, that using a part, they doe homage to the whole. Then, that the best part of this Booke is an abhomination to the Lorde, etc.[2] This dubblenes is of your owne heart, who dissembling with God and your owne conscience to avoyde open shame, care not what wrong you doe others, or what judgments you heape upon your self against the daye of wrath. Our answeare was but one, and this. That you knewe never a minister that useth not the Booke, that standeth not under this idoll: or that had throwne it out by the power of God's worde, or with-drawen the people from it with al their preaching these 29 yeares. But that they all administer by it, joyne their gospell to it, minister to that people that use it, etc. That the conningest of you that use the best and leave the rest, cannot make that best part you use other than a piece of swines-flesh, an abhomination to the Lorde. And that the perswation of your consciences could neither justifie your worship, cleare your selves, or satisfie others. Especially when we see your consciences to tollerate and to submit unto the whole, to use part in respect of your homage, and to refuse part for shame of the worlde.[3] This you were ashamed to inserte, because you were not able to answere. Therfore in all this they but counterfeite, and you cavil.

What folly can you finde in this saying, that in using part they doe homage for the whole? Stand not all your ministers bownd to this Booke, sworne in their canonicall obedience to administer according to the order prescribed therin, and not to preach against anie

---

[1] *A Short Treatise*, p. 16.
[2] *Ibid.*
[3] Barrow, in the above five sentences, is quoting what he wrote in 1587 or 1588. See "A Brief Summe of the Causes of Our Seperation," in Carlson, *The Writings of Henry Barrow, 1587-1590*, pp. 131-2.

A Plaine Refutation

thing by publique authoritie established?[1] Stand not the church-wardens and sidemen bownde to present the defaults, and the arch-deacon and commissarie, to censure the same? How then (seing all your ministers stand in this subjection unto it) would you have us thincke that the part they use is not in respect of their homage to the whole? Or howe woulde you have us thincke that they condemne anie part therof, when they speake not against it and cast it not out by the power of the worde, nether with-drawe themselves, nor the people from it, but joyne in prayers and sacramentes with them that use it? Is this to condemne it, or to condemne themselves rather in the things they do? Can you with your fleshly reason put this away? Might they not by your reason stand sworne to the masse-booke, joyne to such idolatrous priests and people as use it, yet if in their owne conscience or secretly they dislike some faultes therof, be as cleare as these ministers you speake of are of the corruptions they condemne? There are some truthes and some good things in the masse-booke also? You use no good reason to persuade us by your schismes and divisions in your church, unto your church. We know that Christ is not divided, and that there is but one spirit, one baptisme. Christ is not yea and nay; yea in one place, naye in an other. Though Christians may through the ignorance and darcknes that is in them, dissent in some things, yet ar they to walke by one rule, and not to teach divers doctrines. Who so teach otherwise, or causeth anie dissention or offences besides the doctrine which we have [48] learned, is to be avoyded, to be cast out. If either of these factions you speake of had bene of Christ, they would yer [ere, before] this Rom. 16:17 have proceded according to the rule of Christ against Gal. 1:8 the offenders: and not have remayned in this contention and division.

To your next vehement exclamation of frensie, in

---

[1] See "Articles for Doctrine, and Preaching" and "Protestations to Be Made, Promised and Subscribed" in *Advertisements (Short-Title Catalogue*, no. 10026). Archbishop Parker's *Advertisements* were first *published* in 1566, not 1564 or 1565, as is often stated. See Albert Peel, *Essays Congregational and Catholic* [1931], pp. 261-6.

that we terme the best part of your portesse [portas] but a piece of swine's-fleshe, etc. Wherin you saye we strike at God and blaspheame that which is most holy, because therin are sondrie portions of Scripture: as the Lorde's Prayer, the tenne commandementes, the articles of your faith, etc.[1] We beseech you (when you shall be a little come to your self), are not all these with your pistles and gospells in the masse-booke also? Yet you wil hold no part of that execrable idoll, good. The papistes hange the first wordes of the gospel after John about their necke for manie purposes; shall we not saye that this or their *Agnus Dei* are abhominable idolls therfore? Conjurers use divers psalmes and Scriptures in their magical incantations and divers collects, with as little evill as most of yours; shall we nowe allowe anie part of their conjurations? Are they not altogether accursed?

The Scriptures then we see may be abused, yet no way justifie anie part of the wicked action or naughty thing to which they are applyed. The Scriptures are holy and good of themselves, yet when they are thus violently rent, dismembred, constrayned, perverted, abused, joyned to these idolatries, they no way justifie any part of the worship, but make the whole more execrable. We can saye then that those Scriptures which you thus prophane and abuse to your idolatries above-said (as your idoll feastes and all your idol worship and ministration) are in their due place and true use, holie, reverend, gratious; but when they are abused, perverted, and joyned to patch up this idolatrie, they make the whole the more execrable. All the Scriptures then of God are holy and pure, and all the whole masse-booke, the English service-booke and everie part therof are detestable idolls. All which idoll and every part therof we can condemne, and yet preserve the sacred majestie and aucthoritie of the Scriptures.

All this your festered conscience and blasphemous mouth could to your furder judgement confesse in our

---

[1] *A Short Treatise*, p. 16.

name, though Sathan that speaketh in you, by and by sought to quench it, by deriding our holie suffrings.[1] Our bandes unto us are comfortable, glorious unto God, and shal rise up and be produced in judgment with this idolatrous murderous generation of your horned cleargy. But now to the Scriptures be [by] you alledged. If you were demaunded where you learned to mumble over that Scripture (by you falsely called the Lord's Prayer) five times in your morowe-masse, and to use it at all assaies, to saye it over the sick, over the deade, over the weomen in churching, over the marryed, etc., should not your holie father the pope be founde the aucthor of all this ? Also if we should aske you where you reade, and how you could prove that blasphemous article of your faith, that Christ discended into hel, what scripture could you shew or alleadge for it?[2] Thus are even those thinges wherof you glorie, [49] tourned to your shame, if so be that you could be ashamed of anie thing. Yet howsoever you maye

---

[1] Gifford had written : " then take you heede, least being in prison, and fettred with heretikes, ye be turned also into heretikes," *ibid.*

[2] The doctrine of Christ's descent into hell is the third of the Thirty-Nine Articles. See E. Tyrrell Green, *The Thirty-Nine Articles and the Age of the Reformation*, pp. 36-38. See also Edgar C. S. Gibson, *The Thirty-Nine Articles of the Church of England*, fifth edition, pp. 159-180. The Scriptural bases for the doctrine are found in Luke 23 : 43 ; Acts 2 : 24-31 ; Ephesians 4 : 9, 10 ; I Peter 3 : 18-20 and 4 : 6 ; Psalms 16 : 10. Hugh Broughton wrote *An Explication of the Article* (see *Short-Title Catalogue*, (no. 3863). William Perkins discusses four interpretations : 1. Christ's soul did descend into the place of the damned ; 2. Christ descended into the grave ; 3. The assertion really means that Christ suffered inwardly, in his soul or spirit, and felt God's wrath upon him, as distinct from the physical suffering expressed in the words, " was crucified, dead, and buried " ; 4. Christ was held captive in the grave, in bondage to death, from the time of his death to the hour of his resurrection. Perkins regards these views as follows : the first, improbable ; the second, possible ; the third, permissible and good ; the fourth, true and best. See *An Exposition of the Symbole or Creed of the Apostles, according to the Tenour of the Scriptures, and the Consent of Orthodoxe Fathers of the Church* (1595), pp. 296-304. See a criticism of Perkins' views by William Barrett in John Strype, *Whitgift*, II (1822), pp. 236-37 ; also pp. 220-22, 320-27, 355-67. Henry Jacob and Bishop Thomas Bilson treat of the subject of Christ's sufferings ; Jacob in *A Treatise* (1598), and *A Defence* (1600) ; Bilson in *The Survey* (1604). See also the work of John Higgins, *An Answere* (1602) ; Adam Hill, *The Defence* (1592) ; Thomas Rogers, *The English Creede*, 2 vols. (1585-1587) ; Christopher Carlile, *A Discourse concerning Two Divine Positions* (1582).

harden your heart and your face against the manifest truth, by this sleight discussing of your worship, doctrines, and administration, even by this litle which is alreadie said, all men may discerne what kinde of ministers and blinde guides you be. Also anie that had but once seene the Church of Rome, might easilie by the flea-spotts and freakes you speake of, knowe her

Ezech. 16:44 daughter of England at the first blush. For as the mother such the daughter is[1] in al her limbes, features, and proportions.

Hetherto we have spoken of some odious fowle faultes and errors in perticular founde in this their worship or leitourgie: the furder examination wherof and searche of the rest that remaine, we leave to the furder diligence of others.[2]

And nowe touching this their service-booke and leitourgie in general, this we saye.

1. In that they presume to give and enjoyne their prescript wordes in praier, they take the office of the Holie Ghost awaie, quench the spirit of the ministrie, and of the whole church, stop and keepe out the graces of God, thrust their owne idle devises upon the whole church, yea, upon God himselfe, whether he wil or no.

2. In that bie their leitourgie they prescribe what and how much to reade, at morne to their mattens, at eaven, etc., teachinge the church and ministrie to pray by nomber, stint, and proportion, it is not onely popish, but most frivolous and vayne, disgracing and not instructing the church and ministerie.

3. In that by this their leitourgie they prescribe unto the church what Scriptures publiquelie to reade and when to reade them, as these chapters and psalmes at their mattens before noone, those at afternoone, etc. On all the dayes that they have publique meetings

---

[1] Ezekiel 16 : 44. This verse is on the title-page of Barrow's *A Brief Discoverie of the False Church*, in reference to the Church of Rome and the Church of England.
[2] That is, to John Greenwood.

A Plaine Refutation

and service through the yeere, and soe from yeere to yeere. They therebie take from the church the holie and free use both of the Scriptures and spirit of God. They therbie conceale and shut out of the church a great part of God's holie worde which they reade not. As also abuse without order those Scriptures they enjoyne to be reade.

4. In that they shread, rend, and dismember the Scriptures from the holie order and natural sense of their context, [50] to make them epistles, gospels, lessons, select psalmes, to their festivals, and idol worship above-said, they most heinouslie pervert and abuse the Scriptures to the high dishonor of God and their owne feareful judgment.

5. In that they bring in and commaunde the apocrypha writings to be publiquelie read in the church. They both mainetaine and publiquelie teach the dangerous errors therin contayned, to the poysoning and subverting of the faith of the church. They thrust these devises of men into the place of God's worde, causing the people therbie to reverence and esteeme them as the holie oracles of God, of like aucthoritie, dignitie, and truth, and to resorte unto them to builde their faith therupon, and therbie they bring in an other foundation into the church: besides the high injurie donne unto God therbie.

6. Finallie in that by this their leitourgie they bring in, erect and enjoyne a new and strange kinde of administration, as is above proved in the perticulars. They make and erect a new gospel, and so must needes also erect unto it a new ministrie. For the ministrie of Christ is only bounde unto, and wil onlie administer by Christe's Testament wherein they have a most perfect leitourgie for the whole administration of his church. Therfore this present leitourgie and ministrie of England are by al these reasons in general and perticular founde and proved at once to be counterfeite, ungodlie, and antichristian.

His wide frivolous parenthesis from the 17th page of his booke unto the 47th, touching read prayer and prescript leitourgie, we leave to be discussed and refuted by

Henry Barrow

Esay 50:11

an other, to whose writinges we referr the reader.[1] Leaving Mr. Giffard and the whole Church of England touching this first pointe of their worship, to be compassed about with the sparckes, and to walke on in the light of the fire that they have kindled. Yet this to them of our hand, they shal lye in sorrowe. [51]

THE SECOND PRINCIPAL TRANSGRESSION, IS:

That the prophane ungodlie multitudes without the exception of anie one person, are with them received into, and retayned in the bozome and bodie of their church.

In Mr. Giffard his former answere unto this transgression, he then not being past al shame, confessed, that the most churches in England want [lack] godlie pastors, and there al are admitted, he that admitteth them being the worst in the companie.[2] These assemblies as openlie guiltie of this confusion, sacriledge, and wilful prophanation of the holie things of God, he would not then defend. But now upon better advise (the world being greatly changed with the reforming priests since that tyme, and no hope left for that sect to prevaile against the bisshops)[3] he hath changed his copie

---

[1] Pages 17-46 of *A Short Treatise* relate to prayer. Greenwood replied in a book of forty-two pages, entitled, *An Answere to George Gifford's Pretended Defence of Read Praiers and Devised Litourgies*, and published about August, 1590.

[2] Gifford's reply is printed in *A Short Treatise*, p. 47, but not in black letters, as it should be, probably because of the printer's error. Gifford admits that "manye churches in England want godly pastours, and there all are admitted. It may be, he that admitteth is the worst in the company." Barrow may have strengthened Gifford's statement, or the latter may have softened his own statement. In Gifford's second reply, "manye churches" becomes "very manye assemblies in England."

[3] This is an indictment of the Presbyterians, and of the classical movement, which collapsed in 1590 with the arrest of Thomas Cartwright, and other Presbyterian leaders. See A. F. Scott Pearson, *Thomas Cartwright and Elizabethan Puritanism*, pp. 316-358; Patrick Collinson, "The Puritan Classical Movement in the Reign of Elizabeth I," a dissertation (1957) at the University of London; Marshall M. Knappen, *Tudor Puritanism*, chapter XIV; R. G. Usher, *The Presbyterian Movement in the Reign of Queen Elizabeth as Illustrated by the Minute Book of the Dedham Classis, 1582-1589*.

A Plaine Refutation

quite, building againe those Romish abhominations he had before destroyed, as in the transgression above handled appeareth.

And nowe in this transgression, as one greatly greived that such large wordes had escaped him, he seeketh to retract them in the best maner he may, and to salve al againe by saying, " that the Church of England doth neither approve such admission of prophane men to the sacrament, nor yet suffer it in practize wholie," howsoever they are admitted through the negligence of the ministers, etc.[1] Where this high sacriledge is wittingly and wilfully committed by the most of the ministers, seene and suffred by al the governours of the church who have made, and doe maineteine such wicked ministers, where most of the people of the land consent and joyne in this sinne, where that lesser part of ministers and people (he speaketh of) that doe not the like have made no separation from these wicked governours, ministers, and people, that thus wilfully contynue in this presumptuous sinne and sacriledge, but joyne unto them in the communion of their prayers and sacraments, etc. Here we would knowe whether the Church of England may not justly be reproved for I Corinth. 5 suffring and approving this sinne. Ells the Apostle faulted for reproving the whole church of Corinth for suffring and not casting out the incestuous person, although no doubt there were in the church of Corinth [those] that utterly disliked and condemned the offence. That all the governours of your church thus approve and maineteine these wicked ministers whom they have made, is manifest, in that they doe not censure them for their heinous offences. That these ministers commit this sacriledge, your self hath in your former answer confessed, terming them ungodlie, and judging them the worst of the companie.[2] Where by the waye (not to hinder the matter in hand) we must advertise you that you have highly broken the rules of christian [52] order and charitie towards these your brethren and

[1] *A Short Treatise*, p. 47.
[2] *Ibid.*

fellowe ministers, thus to publish and condemne them (and that [moreover] to such as you hold hereticks and schismaticks from your church) before your church had censured them, or you for the churches' wilful default had forsaken either the church or them. If they be to be esteamed the true ministers of Christ (which office they professe to beare in your church), then great is your sinne thus disorderlie to blaspheme, judge, and publish them. If they be not to be esteamed the true ministers of Christ, then as great is your sinne in joyning unto them in communion of prayers and sacraments, etc., and in not separating from them and from that church which thus presumptuouslie doth make, impose, and maintaine such an antichristian ungoldly ministrie. Thus your disorderlie and unchristian behaviour towardes your bretheren, yea, the ministers of your church (wherof your self by profession standeth as yet a minister and member) might be greatly agravate and more justly charged with those faults you lay upon us of accusing, condemning whole assemblies of Christ, of rending and tearing up the tender plants in most desperate and savage maner, and al this before the Church of England hath censured these ministers and assemblies. If we would be so frivolous, we could throughly wound you with your owne weapons. But we remitt you to the judgment and vengeance of the Lord for all your blasphemie and cursed speaking: stil witnessing against the sinnes of your church, proving if God at any tyme wil give you repentance.

Furder in your former answeare you affirmed, that you knewe manie congregations in England where the pastor repelled the unworthie from the sacraments, etc.[1] We replyed, that even in those special congregations all the prophane and their seede were at the first receyved, as in all your other congregations. And that this suspension of the pastor, wherbie he repelled, was popish and antichristian, even the instru-

---

[1] Gifford's "former answeare" was a manuscript, and Barrow's reply was also in manuscript. See "A Brief Summe of the Causes of Our Seperation," in Carlson, *The Writings of Henry Barrow, 1587-1590*, p. 133.

A Plaine Refutation

ment of that idol shephearde, rebated, without edge or poynte, of no value, or power, etc., and therfore this could be no separation, seing the suspended stil remayned of and in your church. That al without exception were received in these congregations we proved, because all without exception of anie were baptized. That none were or could be there put out we proved, because the parson and his whole flocke, or al these special pastors or flockes together, have not that power which our Lorde Jesus Christ hath given unto his church unto the worlde's end, to caste out the wicked by excommunication; and the other congregations by his owne confession did not caste them out. All this notwithstanding, Mr. Giffard (before he hath either proved the orderly gathering and communion of these congregations at the restoring from apostasy, or that they nowe had the power of Christ amongst them to excommunicate the wicked) wil needes by this idol popish suspension justifie these congregations, and convince us of false accusation. And thus everie where he administreth weapons unto us to wound and beate [53] himself with his owne wordes, Prov. 14:3 according to the proverbe, "in the mouth of the foole the staffe of pride."

But at length to reconcile himself againe with those most part of congregations and ministers which he before condemned, he hath changed, perverted and subtilely sullected [subjected, selected, sullied?][1] our reason which we brought against those speciall assemblies which he endevoured to justifie, and turned it against the whole Church of England thus.

Where all are received in by baptisme, and no power to cast forth anie by excommunication, there all the prophane multitudes are without exception of anie one person received into and retained in the bozome and bodie of the church.
But in the Church of England all are received in by baptisme, and there is no power to cast forth anie by excommunication.

---

[1] "Sullected" is not in the *New English Dictionary*. If this is a printer's error, we may conjecture that the word intended was "subjected" or "collected" — that is, inferred. Perhaps "deflected" was intended.

Therfore in the Church of England all the prophane multitudes without the exception of anie one person are received into and reteined in the bozome and bodie of the church.[1]

Thus after he hath manifestly falsified our wordes and changed our whole reason, framing it in his owne conceipt as he might best deale withall, he then procedeth with all might and mayne to refute this argument, and to convince us. Which being donne, he followeth the chace so whotely, spending and opening his mouth freely into all maner blasphemie, as he driveth us into sondrie heresies, etc.

But now if we might be so bolde to awaken the man out of his cholerick dreame, and to call him backe againe to our former reason after all this conflicte, pursute, and triumph, he shalbe founde to have skirmished all this while but with his owne shadowe, and never to have comen [*sic*] neare our argument, and so all his reproches and heresies must be fayne to returne back againe into his owne heart, where they were forged and whence they proceded.

Our former argument being reduced into forme, was to this effect.

> Into what congregations all are received as members, and the said congregations have not the power of our Lord Jesus Christ to caste out anie by excommunication, there all the prophane multitudes without the exception of any one person, are received into and retayned in the bozome and bodie of that church, or of those churches.
>
> But in those special congregations he spake of, where the pastor doth repell from the sacrament, al are received as members, and the parson and whole parish, or all those pastors and their flockes have not the power of our Lord Jesus Christ to cast forth anie by excom-[54]munication.
>
> Therfore even in those speciall parishes where the

---

[1] *A Short Treatise*, p. 48. This represents Gifford's formulation of Barrow's argument.

A Plaine Refutation

priest by their service-booke repelleth from their sacrament, are all the prophane multitudes without the exception of anie one person received into and reteined in the bozome and bodie, etc.

Here Mr. Giffard finding the major or first proposition irrefragable, the minor thus proved unto him, because al in these parishes are baptized, and the parson's suspension is not Christ's excommunication, hath sought to escape by changing and falsifiing our reason, which otherwise he was never able to answeare. He hath quite chaunged it by putting in a newe minor proposition. Namely, for these peciliar congregations wherof he made instance, he hath put the whole Church of England as they stand one bodie altogether. And is now driven to mingle these his select congregations with the other " most parte of churches and ministers," whom erewhile he condemned and graunted guiltie of this transgression, and also to praye in ayde and appeale unto the popish excommunication of that antichristian hierarchie of their church governours. And this by furder falsifiing our wordes in both his propositions; *vizt.*, where we said, " have not Christe's power to cast forth anie by excommunication," he saith " have no power to cast forth anie by excommunication." We never doubted but the Church of England, as also her mother of Rome, hath a false kinde of excommunication exercised in the power of the dragon and of the beaste; but we stil denie that they have that true excommunication which is exercised in the name and power of Christ, which only belongeth to the church of Christ. Thus if the man had taken his worcke before him and proved as he had gonne, happely his triumphant conclusions would not so fast have followed; then should he have had lesse to feare, and more to rejoyce of his doings, wheras now his reckonyng and judgment are yet behinde. But if Mr. Giffard would vouchsalf to take his adversaries into the field with him before the fight, and give them leave to bring and use their owne weapons, then (seing he will needes have the question now generall of the whole Church of England, and our argument after a scholastical maner) let it be thus touching this second transgression.

> Where all the prophane and ungodly are received into and reteined in the church as members therof, there cannot be said the true established church of Christ.
> But in the Church of England all the prophane multitudes and ungodly of the land were received into and are reteined in their church as members therof.
> Therefore the Church of England in this estate cannot be saide the true established church of Christ.

Exod. 19:5, 6
I Pet. 2:9
John 15:19
Acts 2:41

The first proposition is confirmed through the whole Bible from the beginning to the end; the church of God having alwaies con-[55]sisted of a select peculiar people, caled and separated from the prophane of the worlde; none entring into Christ's church but by a voluntarie profession of their true faith and obedience; or standing longer there, than they keepe the same faith and obedience.

The second proposition may be proved by way of argument thus. Where all were received into the church without any separation at the first gathering therof, and they have not the power of Christ to caste forth any by orderly excommunication, there all the prophane multitudes may justly be said to be received into and reteined in the bozome and bodie of the church. But in the Church of England al the prophane multitudes of the land were together without difference or separation received into the church, neither have they the power of Christ orderly to cast forth any by true excommunication. Therfore al the prophane multitudes are truly said to be received into, and to be reteined in, the bozome and bodie of their church.

This aucthor his two exceptions to the first proposition of the [persons] repelled from the sacraments, and such as depart of them-selves, no waye diminish the truth, or hynder the course therof. For the suspended, they still remaine members of their church. For such papists, hereticks, and schismaticks as depart of themselves, though they ought also to be cast out by orderly excommunication, yet are they not nor can be in this their

A Plaine Refutation

church so cast out, howe infectious and wicked soever they be, because they have not the power and excommunication of Christ amongst them. So that nowe all the controversie wil be about the second proposition, whether the Church of England have received in al the prophane, and whether it have the power of our Lord Jesus Christ to cast forth any by true excommunication. Thus far forth it is manifest and cannot be denyed, that the whole land, even al the Queene's subjects at the beginning of ouer [our] Queene Elisabethe's reigne, were all at one instant receyved as members into this church,[1] this ministrie, worship, sacraments, ordinance, etc., set over them indifferently. Since, al their seede without exception of any, whether papiste, heretick, atheist, witch, conjurer, etc., are baptized in this their church. What then should let [hinder] us to affirme and conclude, that all the prophane of the lande are receyved into the bodie or bozome of this church, if so be that there then were at the beginning of her Majestie's reigne, or now are, anie prophane in the land? Wherfore he must either mainetayne that there have not beene since this our Queene's reigne, and now presently are not any prophane and open ungodly in the land; or ells confesse his church guiltie of this transgression, for receyving in al the wicked and prophane into their church. Neither wil all the devil's sophistrie, his rayling, accusing, blaspheming of Christ's faithful servantes and witnesses of heresie, intrusion into God's judgment seat, savadge and desperate rending up the Lorde's tender plantes, yea, of whole christian assemblies,[2] help the matter, excuse him, or chardge us.

We hold al such prophane, as either are not yet come

---

[1] That is, by the Act of Supremacy and the Act of Uniformity, both assented to by Queen Elizabeth on May 8, 1559. For the latter Act, episcopal authority "to reform, correct and punish by censures of the Church" went into effect after the Feast of the Nativity of St. John the Baptist (June 24, 1559). See J. E. Neale, "The Elizabethan Acts of Supremacy and Uniformity," *English Historical Review*, LXV, no. 256 (July, 1950); F. W. Maitland, "Elizabethan Gleanings, V. Supremacy and Uniformity," *English Historical Review*, XVIII, no. 71 (July, 1903); Carl S. Meyer, *Elizabeth I and the Religious Settlement of 1559* (1960), Chapters II, III.

[2] *A Short Treatise*, pp. 49-50.

to the true faith and obedience of Christ by outward profession, or are departed from the [56] true faith and obedience of Christ, remayning obstinate and hardned in transgression or error. And this second sort, although the church should neglect or refuse, to cast them out by excommunication. We hold, that only such as voluntarily make a true profession of faith, and vowe of their obedience, and as in the same faith and obedience seek the communion and fellowship of the faithful, are to be receaved as members into the church. And that only the children of such by the one parent are to be baptized. We hold furder, that howsoever the dearest children of God doe and may fal, yet are they still renued by repentance. And that all such as continue obstinate in their sinne after due admonition, are not by us to be esteemed faithful, but to be held wicked and prophane, although the church should refuse to cast them out. This we hope in anie christian or sober judgment wil not be founde, to call all suche prophane and to condemne them as infidells which professe the faith truly, and continue outwardly obedient, although in some weaknes and infirmities, as this malitious accuser falsly sclandereth us.

Neither shall we be founde "to intrude into God's judgment seate," "to rend and teare up the weake plantes in desperate and savadge maner,"[1] whilest we affirme those rowtes and multitudes of atheistes, papists, idolators, heretickes, blasphemers, extortioners, wrongedoers, covetous, proude, vayne, and light persons, glottons, dronckardes, adulterers, bawdes, whores, and whoremasters, theives, murderers, and other such like flagitious ungodly persons, which were received into and are retayned in their church as members, to be esteamed amongst the wicked and prophane of the world, and not as the right plants and true members of the church in this estate. We are taught to knowe and judge the tree by the fruictes, and easily can discerne these vines of Sodome from the Lorde's vines, these stincking weedes, these nettles, thornes, thistles, from the Lorde's pleasant

---

[1] *Ibid.*, pp. 3, 4, 49, 50.

A Plaine Refutation

plantes, the sweet incense trees, olive, pome-granate, figge trees of the Lorde's walled orcharde of his church. We cannot mistake the mountaines of these leopardes and wolves, for Christe's sheepfold; the cages of these uncleane and hateful birdes, for the holie assemblie of sainctes. Neither may we nowe flatter and dissemble contrarie to the evident truth of God, and our owne conscience, to justifie and blesse the wicked, to call the churle liberall, to saye to the wicked they are righteous, and to them that despise the Lorde, they shall have peace, as this wretched man doth for his bellye. Who being in league with his Ordinarie,[1] and in covenante with hell, is not ashamed to stand a priest of all these abhominations to the most abhominable, seeking to pleade for and justifie both; terming these rowtes of all sortes of wicked ungodly persons, the sainctes; the assemblies of them, the church and sheepfold of Christ; calling the most hateful and horrible sinnes they daylie commit, but their infirmities and weaknes; the most execrable blasphemies and idolatries, but the spotts and bleamishes of their church. What then shall we judge of their sinners and [57] sinnes, if these be their sainctes, infirmities, bleamishes? Cant. 4:13, 14 Esay 60:21 Cant. 4:8 Revel. 18:2 Esay 32:5 Prov. 24:24 Ezech. 13:18 Jerem. 18

But there are none so bad as we that speake against these holie assemblies of these sainctes, and that for these their bleamishes, infirmities, etc. All that feare God may tremble at our intollerable wickednes (Mr. Giffard saith) that teare up these weake plantes, yea, whole assemblies that unfeinedly sorrowe and mourne for their sinnes, and studie to please God. We are they that " take upon us to plucke up al the darnel, though we be commaunded the contrarie, lest we plucke up the wheate,"[2] Mathew 13. What spirit leadeth us, and possesseth him and his church, as also how they sorrowe and mourne for their sinnes, let the ocasions of these controversies betwixt us, their tyrannie, our sufferings, and this his present writing declare. Wee blame, and witnesse against manie most heynous and horrible sinnes.

---

[1] John Aylmer, Bishop of London.
[2] *Ibid.*, p. 50.

So far are they from acknowledging the same, that they wil not be confessed amongst the bleamishes of his church. Yea, insteade of repentance they persecute, he blasphemeth, and in everie sentence of his booke casteth at us in his furie these his firebrandes, poysoned arrowes, and deadly dartes, wherwith his whole booke is seasoned insteade of better grace, and al for shewing and admonishing them of their sinnes.

Unto this place, Mathew 13, which he bringeth against us for plucking up the tares, he must acknowledge these his weake plantes, even al the prophane multitudes and deluge of people, to be those tares, or ells he cannot use it against us, or blame us for plucking them up. This if he confesse, then can they not be held in this estate the children of the kingdome, that tender wheate, that blossomed and made fruite. Then hath he granted us as much concerning this poynte as we require, yea, and judged them as far as we judge; which is not concerning their future, but their present estate. Their election or reprobation we leave to that great hous-holder, the maker and judge of all, conteyning our selves within the rules of his revealed worde, whose judgments we cannot lighten, or pronownce the wicked innocent; against whose judgments who so spurne or resist, but stomble at that rocke which wil grind them to powder. If Mr. Giffard understand the field in this place to be the church, he choseth rather to insist in the errour of others, than in the exposition of our Saviour himself; who saith, [Matthew 13] verse 38, " that the field is the worlde, the good seede are those children of the kingdome, but the tares are the children of the wicked one." If it should be understoode of the planted church, then were al the rules, ordinances, censures, and government of the church utterly abolished. Then might al be received in, and none at anie tyme for anie offence cast out of the church, etc. Then also could not the civile majestrate put anie offendor to death, for that were to roote out the tares. Neither can these tares be understoode of those hypocrites whose sinnes appeare not; for then could not the disciples discerne, judge, and seeke to roote them up. Or being

A Plaine Refutation

so understoode, be compared to those multitudes of prophane, whose heynous sinnes are manifest. Let the tares then be the children of the wicked one, and not the sainctes of Christ. Let the tares be in the worlde, and not in the [58] church, seing our Saviour himself so pronounceth them, and instructeth his disciples so to thinck of them. Yet let not his disciples in anie inordinate zeale seeke to roote them up, seing they have nothing to doe to judge them that are without. But let them rather by al meanes seeke their ingrafting, in in- structing them in al gentlenes, if so be that God at anie tyme wil give them repentance to the acknowleging of the truth, that they also may be partakers of the like mercie and grace with them. I Cor. 5:12, 13
II Tim. 2:25

What then hath Mr. Giffard gayned by this place? That the open prophane and such as never made true voluntarie profession of their owne faith (other than that prescript verbal confession which is enjoyned to them al in their service booke,[1] which a childe of four yeeres olde may say after the priest as wel as they) may be receaved into the church. Or that al sortes of open wicked grosse impenitent offendors may be reteyned in the church as members. This he must prove, or ells all that he saith is nothing to the purpose, seing we chardge their church as heynously guilty of, and wilfully obstinate in, these transgressions. But insteade of proving, he slilie seeketh to change the question, by turning it from these open prophane and wicked, to hypocrites and wicked persons which remaine in the church, whose children he saith ought to be baptized. Wherin, besides that he beggeth the question, assuming in a stronge imagination that which he shal never be able to prove, that these parish assemblies are the true planted and established churches of Christ, and these ungodly multitudes true members therof, he furder so doubleth and windeth betwixt these two starting holes, the hypocrites, and the prophane, as one cannot knowe where to find him, or wherof he affirmeth.

---

[1] See "A General Confession," "The Apostles' Creed," and "The Creed of Saint Athanasius," in *The Book of Common Prayer*, sections or divisions 10-12.

It being graunted that the children of hypocrites ought to be baptized, he wil therupon conclude, that the children of the prophane also. Which if it be denied, then he wil make no conscience to give out, that we denie baptisme to the seede of hypocrites in the church. Thus standing upon no grounde, he flitcheth and fleeteth up and downe, seeking in an evil conscience to shifte off the truth wherwith he is pressed. First presupposing that al these multitudes of prophane and wicked are within the church. Then endevouring to prove that al the children of such prophane and wicked as he termeth within the church and to professe Christ, ought to be baptized. Wherin, before we come to the consideration of his reasons, we must note unto the reader in his proposition expresse contrarietie, error and sacriledge: contrariety, in that he with the same mouth in the same sentence pronounceth them as prophane and wicked, and also as faithful and members of the church, such to whom the covenante and the seales therof belonge. Error, in that he thus judgeth and blasphemeth them, if they be faithful and members of the church. As on the contrarie, if they be prophane and wicked, to justifie their profession whilest they are obstinate in such sinnes. Yea, furder to harden them therin, to give the seale of the covenante unto their children in [59] respect of their profession, which cannot be donne without open and wilful sacriledge; for if they be to be judged prophane and wicked, then are their children also (until they make profession of their owne faith) to be held of us as prophane; the devised written profession of their church cannot sanctifie or justifie either the one or the other unto us. Moreover, the church cannot denie to receave those parents or that parent unto the communion of the Supper, whose infantes they baptize in that estate.[1] And thus by Mr. Giffard's divinitie may the bodie and bloude of Christ be prostitute to the open prophane and wicked, whom he thus proveth within the covenant.

[1] For a more detailed and extended presentation of Barrow's views on baptism, see Carlson, *The Writings of Henry Barrow, 1587-1590*, pp. 31-34, 134, 205, 206, 419-453.

A Plaine Refutation

" The interest of God's covenant " (saith he) " doth not depend upon their next parents, but upon the antient Christians their forefathers."[1] For when God saith, " I wilbe thie God and the God of thie seede," the promise is made to a thousand generations. Exodus 20.[2] So Levi paied tithes unto Melchi-sedec because he was the loynes of Abraham: Yea, al the whole nation of the Jewes were in the loynes of Abraham, and therfore holie and within the covenant. " For if the first fruictes be holy, so is the lumpe; if the roote be holy, so are the boughes," Romans 11: [16]. Yea, though manie of them were wicked, idolatro[u]s [idolators?], reprobates, yet even in the worst tymes were they circumcised, and it was not disalowed. But the Lorde caleth the children of those wicked idolators his children. " Thou hast taken thie sonnes and thie daughters which thou broughtest fourth unto me and [these hast thou] sacrificed unto them to be consumed: thou hast slaine my sonnes and given them, by causing them to passe through unto them." Ezechiel 16 : [20], 21.

Behold into how manie errors, mischieves, and blasphemies they fal, which in this maner spurne and strive against the truth, everie worde becomming a snare unto them to hold and drawe them unto their greater judgments. If the interest in God's covenant (as being the seed of the faithful unto the sight of the church) depend not upon the faith of the next parents, but upon the antient Christians their fore-fathers within a thowsand generations, etc.,[3] then ought al to be receaved, and none to be kept or caste out of the church. Then is the whole world within the covenant, of the church, holie, al being spronge within far lesse than a thowsand generations of manie faithful, and lineallie come from the patriarck Noah. Then ought by this rule the Israelites under the lawe to have circumcised all their captive Canaanites and heathen that came into their power.

---

[1] *A Short Treatise*, p. 50.
[2] This Scriptural reference is wrong. The best reference is Genesis 17 : 7, 8. See also Deuteronomy 7 : 9; I Chronicles 16 : 15; Psalms 105 : 7, 8.
[3] *A Short Treatise*, p. 50.

Then ought the church nowe also to baptize all the seede even of the most wicked and ungodlie, whether Turcks, papists, idolators, etc., because they are all spronge of faithful parents within lesse than a thousand generations.

But because we reade in the Scriptures that God's covenant only belongeth unto the faithful, and the seales of his covenant are nowe only committed to his true established church; seing lawes and rules are given by God unto the church, to whom, and how to administer the said seales; seing none can enter into this church, but by this true outward profession of faith and obedience, neither anie remaine longer there, than they [60] keepe the said faith and obedience outwardly; seing baptisme only belongeth and is given to the members of this church and unto their seede, and can to none other be given without heynous sinne and sacriledge: we doubt not to pronownce and reject these doctrines of this false prophet, as most blasphemous and divelish, as tending to the open breach of al God's lawes and ordinances, to the utter abolishing of the truth and feare of God's judgments, to the taking away of al faith and godlines out of the earth, to the bringing in of al atheisme and confusion, to the prostituting and prophaning of the holie things of God. And therfore al true Christians by the commandment of God are to avoide and hold accursed the aucthor and bringer of such doctrines, and so much the rather, in that he so wretchedly and bouldly falsifieth, dismembreth, perverteth, and abuseth the holie Scriptures therunto.

Gal. 1:8
II John 10

As to prove that the covenant dependeth not upon the outward faith of the parents, but upon the faith of their godly ancestors, he voucheth, Exodus 20. "I wil be thy God and the God of thy seede," the promise is made (saith he) to a thousand generations.[1] But he wittingly suppresseth the next wordes of the sentence [" of them that love me and keepe mie commande-

---

[1] In Exodus 20 : 6 the reference is to " thousands of those who love me and keep my commandments." But in Deuteronomy 7 : 9 the promise is made " to a thousand generations."

A Plaine Refutation

ments "]¹ which shewe to whom this covenant is made and belongeth, and the condition on our part. As the former part of this sentence, verse 5, sheweth, howe we may forfeite this covenant, namelie, by breaking and contemning the lawe of God, in whose love we cannot remaine, except we remaine in his obedience. John 14 : 21 and 15 : 10. So that the Lorde most plainely in this, Exodus 20 : 5 and 6 verses, declareth who and whose seede are within his covenant of love and protection: namely, the faithful and their offspring to the thousand generation, so long as they contynue in his faith and obedience. But if they breake his lawe and wil not be reduced to his obedience, then are they and their children caste out of his favour, then as a jealous God wil he visit their sinnes upon their children upon the thirdes and fourthes, etc. [generations].

How boldly and presumptuously then hath this wicked man without al conscience and feare, falsified this Scripture in suppressing what parts therof he list, dismembring and rending what he alleadgeth from the natural context, perverting and abusing these wordes " to a thousand generations " quite against the expresse sense of God himselfe, receiving the children of the open wicked and ungodly (which the Lord rejecteth together with their rebellious parents) into the outward covenant of his grace, and delivering the seale therof unto them by vertue of this place, because some of their fore-fathers have bene faithful, and the covenant is made to a thousand generations. As though the Lord plighteth his love to us, and requireth not agayne our faith and obedience unto him in the same covenant. Let Mr. Giffard shewe one place of Scripture through the whole Bible where the Lorde his covenant is made unto us without this condition, and then peradventure he may cleare himself and his Ordinarie for the publishing of this wicked and divelish heresie, so directly con-[61] trarie to the whole Scriptures in more than a thousand places. For to what end should the Lorde have given unto us his holy word, if he had not required of us our

¹ The square brackets are in the text.

heartie obedience unto the same? But because the Lorde is never founde contrarie unto himself, neither anie contradiction in his worde, we may by the direct warrant hereof hold Mr. Giffard and his Ordinarie[1] most heynouse falsifiers and corrupters of the whole lawe and worde of God, most blasphemous and pernitious false prophets, that receive into the covenant and justifie all sortes of prophane, wicked, and ungodly persons, and so open the doores to all atheisme and impietie. His starting hole and subterfuge of undiscovered hypocrites will not hide or help him herein, seing we complayne, "*that the open prophane and all sortes of the most wicked and their seede without exception of anie are received amongst them as members of their church*," and seing he endevoureth to approve the same by manie other Scriptures.[2]

Al Israel (saith he) was in the loynes of Abraham, all in the covenant, and holy with him, as the boughes with the roote, all within the church by outward profession, and esteemed members therof, because the seedes of Abraham. Yea, though multitudes of them were infidells and idolators, yet even of them sprang the right holie seede, and therfore, as also because of their outwarde profession, were all of them held members, al holie; and all their children (in the tymes when idolatrie was openly mainetayned) were circumcised, and that was not disalowed, etc.[3]

Exod. 19:5, 6
Rom. 9

We doubt not, speaking of al Israel in generall without anie perticular reference unto this or that tyme or estate, but that nation was a peculiar, chosen, adopted people above all other nations unto the Lorde, that they might be an holie nation unto him, a kingdome of priestes, etc., of whom the adoption, the glorie, the covenantes, the giving of the lawe, the service, and the promises. We acknowledge also that the Israel of God according to the election of grace are all of them holy

---

[1] Gifford's Ordinary was John Aylmer, Bishop of London.
[2] *A Short Treatise*, p. 47. Carlson, *The Writings of Henry Barrow, 1587-1590*, pp. 54, 56, 84, 120, 132-4.
[3] *A Short Treatise*, p. 51.

A Plaine Refutation

with their fore-fathers Abraham, Isaac, and Jacob, as the lumpe with the first fruictes, the boughes with the roote. But yet we acknowledge not all to be that Israel which are of Israel, neither all the children of the covenant which are the seede of Abraham. But they are the children of Abraham and of his covenant which doe the worckes, and remayne in the faith of Abraham. Otherwise their circumcision is made unto them uncircumcision; neither doe their literall titles and prerogatives any whit availe them, but rather agravate their judgments whilest they are found transgressors of the lawe. The covenant doubtles was not otherwise made unto them than it was unto their father Abraham. To whom it was said, " be thou upright, and walke streight before me." How often doth the Lord at the giving of his lawe, and the entring covenant with the whole people stipulate and require their faith and obedience, when he promiseth to be their God and the God of [62] their seede? How oft doth he pronownce the covenant broken and disanulled on their partes, when they transgresse and reject his lawe, and denownce of his part all plagues and fearefull judgments for the same everie where through the lawe and prophets, but most plentifully in the booke of Deutronomie? Protesting plagues against such as when they heare the wordes of this oath, blesse themselves in their heart, saying they shal have peace, although they walke according to the stobbornnes of their owne heart. John 8 Rom. 4 Rom. 2:25 Genes. 17:[1] Deut. 29:19

How then should these frivolous reasons of this ignorant caviller stand? That because the Lorde, speaking generally and indefinitely of his first chosing and receiving that people, sometimes caleth all Israel his people, a holy nation, etc. Therfore all Israel in all tymes and estates of that kingdome should alwaies be his true visible church, within the covenant, etc. This we see were directly contrary to the whole lawe and prophetts. Should it followe that because the Lorde reserveth in and draweth out of the loynes of the wicked his right holy seede, that therfore the parents are within God his covenant? Thus might the Turckes, Jewes, and most wicked of the world be justified, because the

Lorde his secret election is not restreyned towardes them. Should it followe that because all the Israelites were alwaies circumcised, that therfore they were within the covenant, or were not blamed, or did not amisse in prophaning God his holy ordinance? So might the Ismaelites, Ammonites, Edomites, and Moabites be said within the covenant, because their ancestours and they were circumcised. We see outward circumcision availeth not, when the condicion of the covenant is broken. And how could this bolde blinde guide saye, " that it was not disalowed when all their children were circumcised in the tymes when idolatrie was generally and publiquely maineteyned?"[1] Are such idolators within the covenant of the Lord, or doth the seale of his covenant belonge to them? Are not the children of the wicked excepted and rejected out of the covenant by the commandement of God, Exodus 20:5, as the seede of the faithfull are received into the covenante? Then must it needes be high presumption and sacriledge thus to abuse circumcision, and therfore it could not be allowed in those times to such persons. Moreover, when these wicked are forbidden so much as to name the name of God, to bring any offrings or worship unto him, or to meddle with anie of his holy ordinances, are they not forbidden circumcision?

Psal. 50:16
Esay 1 and 66

Should we also collect and conclude, because the Lorde, Ezechiel 16:20, 21, caleth the children of those idolators whom they offred to Molech, his sonnes and daughters, that therfore the kingdomes of Israel and Juda whilest they remayned in these horrible sinnes, were outwardly in that estate the true church of God? Or is this great prophet so inconversant in the Scripture, that he yet understandeth not this usuall kinde of phrase and maner of speaking, where the Lord in sondrie places caleth them his sonnes, daughters, and people in respect of their first caling, whom in regard of their present evill life he pronownceth [63] not to be his. As Deutronomie 32: the 19 and 5 verse; Micha 2:7, 8, 9; Amos 8:2, and no where more plainely than in this Ezechiel 16, as

[1] *Ibid.*

A Plaine Refutation

were easie to demonstrate by the least touching of the argument of that chapter. The Lorde there setting before their face by sondry allegories their estate, even from their original unto that present time. Of what parents they by nature sprange, in what plight he founde them at the first, all embrued [stained] in their mothers' and their owne guiltines, their navel uncut, unwashed, unsalted, unswad[l]ed, caste out into the open field, no hand to help, no eye to pitie, unable to help themselves untill the Lord shewed mercye, tooke them up, chearished, nourished them, entred into covenant and sware unto them, so that they grewe up into riper yeeres, then he spredd his garment over them, washed and anoynted them, clothed them with broydred garmentes, fyne lynnen, silck, skarlet, adorned them with gold, silver, pretious stones, fed them with meale, wyne, oyle, set a beautifull crowne upon their heade, and maried them openly unto himself, and spredd their name amongest the heathen. But now Israel waxed proude of her owne beautie, plaid the harlot, built high places, and decked them with her garments, and plaid the whoore upon them, made images of the instruments and of the Lorde's gold and silver which he gave them, and committed fornication with them, offring the Lorde's meate, flower, oyle unto them as a sweet savour, yea, sacrified their owne sonnes and daughters unto them, committed fornication with the Egiptians, Assirians, Caldeans, and that in most shamefull sort, and vilely hyring them with the Lord's gold and silver of his temple, etc. Wherfore the Lord doth pronownce and repudiate them as an harlot, as a most filthie, poysonous, monstruous whore, and denownceth judgments against them as against murtherers and adulterers, and these judgments to be executed by these their lovers, who should breake downe their cities and high places, and slay them with the sworde, the Lorde not only comparing them, but shewinge them to excede Sodome and Samaria in sinne and iniquitie, etc. ^{Gen. 9 16 ?] Deut. 22:22}

Who then but this perverse fellowe could thus stomble and cavill at these wordes " my sonnes and my daughters," and wrest them not onely against the whole scope of that chapter, but even of the whole Bible ? Whether these wordes be to be understoode of all their seede which were at the first together with them received into the Lorde's covenant, or of their first borne only, which by a peculiar right and lawe were reserved unto the Lorde, Exodus 13 : 2 (which first borne they are blamed in the twentieth chapter of the same prophecie, verse the 26 and 31, to have offred unto idolls) may be some question. Yet with no sense or truth they may be understood as of the Lorde's elect and adopted childeren, or pronownced that holie seede, being the children of such rebellious obstinate idolators. How often doth the Lord call them by his prophets " rebellious children, an adulterous nation ? " Should we therefore conclude, that they were the Lorde's children, the Lorde's spouse ? Or rather pronownce from the just lawes of the [64] Lorde, that rebellious children, and the adulterous wife, ought to be produced, repudiat, and put to death. Deuteronomy 20 : 18, Leviticus 20 : 10. Furder we reade the Lorde to denownce extraordinarie and speedie judgments not only against them that offer of their seede unto Molech, but against that whole nation that dissembleth or suffreth that sinne amongst them. Leviticus 20. How then could this ignorant priest collect and conclude from these wordes " my sonnes and my daughters " (which were spoken but to convince and agravate their sinne and judgment, to stimulate and wounde their conscience) that these children of these idolators, thus offred to Molech, were of us to be judged the holy seede of the Lorde, within his covenant, or these idolators in this estate to be judged the true church of God ? Can they together serve God and idols ? Together breake and keepe the covenant ? If Mr. Giffard can by his learning prove this true, then peradventure we shal beli[e]ve him that the kingdome of Israel in their schisme and defection, having erected new temples, priests, altars, lawes, were defyled with all the abhominations of the heathen, despised and persequuted the Lorde his prophets which were sent to them, etc., were to be held of us the true church of God. Then peradventure he might persuade us that the kingdome of Juda in this

A Plaine Refutation

apostasye, having as this prophet Ezechiel sheweth in his eighth chapter brought al maner abhomination into the temple and defiled the whole land as we reade in the rest of his prophecie, was also by us to be esteemed the true church of God. Is it a good reason for Mr. Giffard to say, because the whole land was so throughly defiled, that it could neither by ecclesiasticall censures, nor by civile judgmentes, be purged, that therfore it remayned still the church in that estate? Is not this to say they had not thus sinned, because their sinnes were incurable? That they had not committed adulterie, murder, idolatrie, because they were not presently stoned, slayne by the sworde, burned? But howsoever they and their false prophets blessed themselves in these sinns, boasting of vaine titles of the temple and people of the Lord, etc., yet the Lorde for those sinnes did in his due tymes exe- Jer. 9:13, 14, 15 cute these judgmentes upon the whole land; and in the Jer. 7:4 meane tyme his lawe and prophetes spake plainely, that Jer. 28:8, 9 these judgmentes were due unto them in this estate.[1]

And as wel might this false prophet justifie the Jewes nowe to be the true church of God in this time of their apostasy (wherof he speaketh) because the Lorde nowe amongst and in the loynes of these wicked ones reserveth to himself an holy seede, a remnant. It wil not help him to say that the vyne-yarde was not then utterly taken from the Jewes, as it is now. For though the Lorde's time to abolish that material Jerusalem that he might bring in and erect the spirituall, was not as then accomplished, though the Lord in his wisedome, mercy, and patience, and for causes knowen to himself, doe oft deferr his judgmentes: yet may not we therby flatter our selves, or justifie our estate whilest we remaine under the condemnation of his written lawe, and in open wilfull breach of his covenant. Yet howsoever the Lorde nowe hath utterly broken off the [64][2] Jewes for their sinnes Rom. 11 and infidelitie, that the Gentiles might be gathered and grafted in by faith, yet is the Lord in his greatest wrath

---

[1] For a good summary of the vicissitudes of the Jews, see William O. E. Oesterley and Theodore H. Robinson, *A History of Israel*, 2 vols. (1932).
[2] Page 65 is erroneously given as page 64.

alwaies mindeful of his mercy, and hath set a tyme when to cal and ingraff againe the Jewes, that al Israel might be saved, and brought into one shepefold, as it is written. But in the meane tyme it is no reason to say, that because the Lorde even in the worst tymes alwaies reserveth a remnant in his mercy, therfore these wicked people in those evil tymes are his visible church. Or because the Lorde in the loynes af [of] the most wicked hath a holie seede according to his secret election, that therfore these wicked parents are in the visible church, or their offspring under the outward covenant.

Yet are these Mr. Giffard's best arguments to prove Israel in their open schisme and idolatrye, and Juda in their open apostasy and idolatrie, to be the true outward church, wherunto the seales of the outward covenant belonged and were given even to the seede of the greatest idolator. Yea, the schisme, apostasy, idolatry, prophanation of the holie things of God amongst these Jewes and Israelites, are the best and onlie groundes he hath, or bringeth to approve and justifie the corrupt estate of the Church of England, and that the seed of their prophane idolators ought to be baptized.

Save that at length he hath founde out a merveylous knot in a rush, and of the same made such a snare for his Brownistes, as they must needes either confesse the baptisme of their church to be a signe of the covenant, and so they all from their ancestors and their whole church are within the covenant, or ells if they denie it, fal into the heresie of the Catabaptistes,[1] and make themselves also without the covenant, or ells to have a covenant without seales.

---

[1] Catabaptism, or Anabaptism, was taught by Thomas Münzer and Nicholas Storch, by John Denck and Balthasar Hübmaier, by Melchior Hoffman and Bernard Rothmann, by Bernhard Knipperdolling and John of Leyden The teaching was that infant baptism was not valid. Hence, re-baptism or anabaptism was necessary when accompanied by intellectual maturity and assent. Since the first baptism was invalid, the second baptism was really the first true baptism. Therefore, Baptists regard " Anabaptism " as a misnomer. One may consult the works of well-known Baptists such as H. W. Robinson and E. A. Payne. See Franklin H. Littell, *The Anabaptist View of the Church*, 2nd ed. (1958) and also his work, *The Free Church* (1957); George H. Williams, *Spiritual and Anabaptist Writers* (1957) and *The Radical Reformation* (1962).

A Plaine Refutation

But now if he wil give us leave to unlose this knot, we must desire him to learne to put a difference betwixt false sacraments and true sacraments, and againe betwixt false sacraments and no sacraments. The false church hath her hyd bread and stollen waters, her false sacraments. The Israelites in their schisme, and the Jewes in their apostasie, stil had and used circumcision. This circumcision was no true sacrament unto them, neither sealed the Lorde's covenant unto them in that estate. Yet was this circumcision true circumcision concerning the outward cutting, and was upon their repentance and retourne neither defaced nor reiterat, but they were restored againe to the temple and received to the passover, as wee reade in Ezeckia's [Hezekiah's] and Josiah's tymes, as also after the retourne out of Babilon.[1] In like maner in this general apostasie and defection from the gospel (so much fore-told in Christe's Testament) the baptisme contynued and used in these apostatical and false churches cannot in this estate thus administered, etc., be said a true sacrament, or seale of God's covenant unto them. Yet concerning the outward washing it is true baptisme, and upon their repentance and restoring to the church, the outward action need not and ought not to be againe repeated after the abuse therof in the false church is purged away by true repentance. Yet justifie we not hereby anie thing donne in the false church, but cal all men by all [65] meanes from the same, willing their whole worship to be repented of and left, and forbidding al men upon incurring the Lord's heavie indignation to offer and bring their children unto the false church to be baptized, exhorting them rather patiently to expect, and diligently to seeke out and repair unto the true church of Christ, where at the handes of Christe's true ministers they may receive the true seales of his covenant unto their comfortes.

Prov. 9:[17]

II Cron. 30

---

[1] Hezekiah was king of Judah from 716/15—687/86. Josiah was king of Judah from 640/39 to 608. The return from Babylon occurred after 538 B.C. See Edwin R. Thiele, *The Mysterious Numbers of the Hebrew Kings* — an excellent work on Hebrew chronology. Another helpful work is Jack Finegan, *Handbook of Biblical Chronology* (Princeton University Press, 1964).

Yea, assuring them, that whilest they refreyne from that which they knowe to be evil, and with true heartes sprinckled from an evil conscience, diligently seeke to doe the wil of God as he offreth meanes, they and their seede are within the covenant of God, although through the iniquitie of the tymes they be stil restreyned for a ceason from having outward baptisme, so that they neither neglect or contemne, much lesse abuse and prophane so heavenly an ordinance.[1]

Joshua 5

Thus this learned divine having (as you have heard) bestowed all his labour and long studie to prove the kingdomes of Israel and of Juda in their schisme and apostasy to be the true church, yet to make the matter more cleare and the more easie for the Church of England, he wil also prove her mother of Rome to be the true church of Christ, because the Brownistes hold that this land in the tyme of poperie was not the true church of Christ, and that nowe they are but confuse multitudes not rightly entred into covenant with God. This that he may doe, he holdeth it not enough to affirme with other learned divines, that the invisible church of God is in the papacye, as in all other places of the world: because God hath his elect there and in al other places. But he (to be singular) inverteth the proposition and saith, that the papacy with the whole apostasie, and all their abhominations, and al that receive the beaste's marcke, and worship his image, are in the church, because Antichrist doth sit in the temple of God.[2]

Thus whilest he without al understanding or feare (after his accustomed presumption) perverteth and wresteth the Scriptures from their holie sense accord-

---

[1] A more detailed statement of Barrow's views on baptism and rebaptism, on the question of the Queen's baptism in the Roman Catholic Church, and on the arguments of the clerk of Oxenford against Dr. Robert Some, is given in Barrow's main work, *A Brief Discoverie of the False Church*, pp. 99-122; see Carlson, *The Writings of Henry Barrow, 1587-1590*, pp. 418-453. See also Barrow's "Letter to an Honorable Lady and Countesse of His Kin[d]red Yet Living," pages 91-92. The letter was first printed in Henry Ainsworth and Francis Johnson, *An Apologie or Defence of Such True Christians as Are Commonly (But Unjustly) Called Brownists* ([Amsterdam ?], 1604), pp. 89-95. It will be printed in volume VI.

[2] *A Short Treatise*, pp. 53-54.

A Plaine Refutation

ing to his owne lust, no merveile though God give him up into a reprobate sense, and suffer him to drawe these heretical doctrines and damnable conclusions from the same, to the destruction of himself and of as manie as receive his doctrines. If Antichrist may be said to sitt, reigne, and remaine in the church of God, the Christ is not made heire and Lorde of all, and set as Kinge upon Mount Sion. Then Christ is either cast out of his house, or made subject unto Antichrist, or divideth with him. Then the church of Christ maie remaine subject unto, and be governed by Antichrist. Then the church of Christ may stand under and be subject unto two heades, Christ and Antichrist. Then Christ is not the onlie head of the church. If Antichrist's ministers and marcked servants maie be brought into and set over the church of God, then is not Christ's ministrie which he hath instituted to his gospel and his church, permanent unto the worlde's end, but variable at the wil of [66] man. Then may the church of God caste out Christe's ministrie, and receive Antichriste's. If Antichriste's doctrines and lawes may be brought, set up, and remaine in the church, then Christ is not the onlie prophet and lawe-giver, then may the church be builte upon an other foundation than upon God's worde. If al Antichriste's abhominations, heresies, idolatries, may be brought into and remaine in the church of God, then no blasphemie, heresie, apostasie, or anie thing that man can commit or devise, can breake the covenant, then may the church of God and idols be placed together. If they that worship the beast and his image may be said to be in the church of God, and their seede outwardly within the covenant, then the most abhominable and execrable may be said in this estate members of Christ, washed and purged with Christ his bloude, sanctified and led by his spirit in assurance of salvation. For none can be said to be within the church, but the members of the church. And whomsoever we may affirme to be within the church, those (so longe as they contynue in that estate) we are also to judge assuredly saved, for anie thing to us revealed or knowen to the contrarie. But if al these

_{Hebr. 1}
_{Psal. 2}
_{I Cor. 6:15}
_{Eph. 1:21}
_{Eph. 4}
_{Rom. 12}
_{Heb. 12:28}
_{Deut. 18}
_{Eph. 2:20}
_{Esa. 57:21}
_{I Cor. 10:20}
_{Rev. 14:9, 10}
_{Reve. 21:8}
_{Rev. 22:15}
_{Rom. 8}

be most divelish heresies directly contrarie to the whole truth of God, if they be most execrable blasphemies, such as Christians abhor but to heare, then let the aucthors and spreaders of these doctrines tremble, for fearful judgments remayne them.

His slie distinction or evasion rather wherby he divideth the Church of Rome into two parts, the pope and his adherents, and the nations under the tyrannie of the pope,[1] doth rather bewray the thick darckness of his heart (wherin he is held with chaynes unto judgment) and his giddye amazednes, than anie way cleare him of these heresies and blasphemies aforesaid. His first understanding of the Church of Rome is " the pope, his lawes, his worship, which hath bene devised by himself, his adherents and al that worship him or receive his marcke." These (he saith) " are the apostasie seduced to damnation, and not the church of Christ, otherwise than thus, that the pope, the cardinals, and al that worship the beast be false Christians by profession, bredd in the church and contynuing in it, their seede not excluded from the covenant."[2]

What a Delphick orakle is this? What strange repugnancie and contradiction is here betwixt everie worde of this his cleare proposition? How can the pope and his adherents be said to be that apostasy seduced to damnation, not the church of Christ, and yet by the same mouth in the same sentence at one and the same instant be pronownced to contynue in the church, and their seede not be excluded from the outward covenant? Can they be said to be utterly departed from the faith, from Christ, from his church (which is meant by this word apostasy) and yet to remaine in the church? How hangs this together? May they be pronounced " seduced to damnation, and not the church of Christ," and yet both they remayne in the church, and their seede not to be excluded from the seale of the covenant? There ought none to remayne in the church but such as are by outward profession and

I Cor. 7:14

[1] *Ibid.*, p. 54.
[2] *Ibid.*

A Plaine Refutation

obedience members [67] of the church. Neither ought the children of anie be baptized in their infancie, except one of their parents be a member of the church. The pope then, his cardinals and adherents remayning in the church, their seede thus baptized as members, seing none ells may either remayne in the church or be baptized, how may they thus be pronounced seduced to damnation and not to be the church, seing they are confessed to be outward members of the church?

The second understanding of the church of Rome, is, " of al those companies of people over whom the tyranie of the pope hath hertofore extended [it selfe], and doth at this daye. Or those things which were given by Christ which remaine in the same." This (he saith) " is not the church of Rome but the church of God."[1]

If by the people and tyrannie he here meane such persons, as though their bodies were under the cruel handes of the pope, his bishops, or prelates, yet they kept their bodies and soules undefiled with their idolatries and abhominations, and free from their antichristian yoke, counterfeite ministrie, and ministration, and have on the other side faithfully kept and practized the things which are given by our Saviour Christ in his Testament, these people indeed can at no hand be said the church of Rome, these are the true church and servants of Christ, witnessing and fighting through the faith of the gospel against the pope, the church of Rome and al their antichristian cleargie and religion. But what is this to prove the kingedome of England or other nations which have beene and are defiled with the idolatries and abhominations of the church of Rome, in that estate to be the true church of God, but rather the quite contrarie; seing these faithful witnesse against them, and have no fellowship or communion with them.

The church of Rome, we reade, Revelation 17, to be caled that " great whore that sitteth upon manie waters; " that " great Babylon, the mother of whoredomes and abhominations of the earth," " with whom the kings of the earth have committed fornication, and

[1] *Ibid.*

the inhabitants of the earth have bene droncke with the wyne of her fornications " mingled unto them in her golden cup.¹ We reade there, verse 15, that " the waters [which thou sawest] where the whore sitteth, are people and multitudes and nations and tongues." We reade also that the beast and the false prophet shal deceave the people of the earth, and cause them to set up and worship the image of the beast, and to slaye al that wil not so doe; "and cause al, both smale and Rev. 13:[14-17] great, riche and poore, free and bonde, to receave a marcke in their right handes or in their fore-heades; and that no man might buy or sel, save he that had the marcke of the beast." Wee reade furder more that all that receave the beaste's marcke, that worship him or Rev. 14:[10] his image, " shal drincke of the wyne of the wrath of God." With what shame then can this marcked priest goe about to prove the church of Rome to be the true church of God? Or those nations which have committed fornication with her, receaved her ministrie, wares, abhominations, that have receaved the marcke and erected the image of the beast, and worshipped the beast and his image, in this time of their poperie, to be esteemed the true [68] church of Christ? His three stowte reasons wil not al prove this poynte. Though they held many poyntes of true and sounde doctrine, yet the many heresies they held, and those (as this man himself in an other place of his booke confesseth) fundamental, doe poyson and leaven the whole lumpe. Ther is no heretick that holdeth not some truth.

As to their holy sacrament of baptisme, it being delivered by a false ministrie, after a false maner, with new adulterate elements of salt, oyle, chreame, etc., with their magical incantations and signes, etc., and that to open idolators, can no waye give them Christendome, as this popish priest supposeth. Or if this baptisme in the popish church be an holy sacrament and

---

¹ " The great whore " of Revelation 17 : 1 is usually identified with the city of Rome, or the Roman Empire, or the goddess *Dea Roma*. See R. H. Charles, *A Critical and Exegetical Commentary on the Revelation of St. John* (2 vols.; Edinburgh, 1920), II, 54-75. See also *The Interpreter's Bible*, vol. XII (New York, 1957), pp. 489-97.

A Plaine Refutation

true seale of the covenant, then would we knowe of Mr. Giffard or his learned abettors, whie their other sacrament of the Supper or Altare should not also be held in the same accompt? Or how the church may be said to have one true, holy, and availeable sacrament to be receaved, an other so blasphemous and execrable as is to be abhorred, at the same instant? Or what kinde of covenant this is that hath one true authenticke seale, an other forged and adulterate annexed unto it? Furder also we would knowe, if the baptisme of the church of Rome be a true and holy sacrament, whie they should inhibit any from fetching the same there, and how they dare schisme from that church that hath the covenant sealed and confirmed unto them. His second reason of some in all kingdomes that hold the faith,[1] is above shewed not to justifie, but to condemne the church of Rome. But all those that had any communion with them in their worship, etc., in the tyme of poperie, cannot in this estate be said to hold the true faith, or to be members of the church of Christ. His third reason concerning the infantes is yet as false and as fond [foolish] as the rest. For neither are the infants of these idolators by us to be judged holy, or to receave baptisme, as he himself, page 49, confesseth. Neither can these infantes anie waie justifie their wicked parents, or the open idolatries, etc., of the Romish church.

Againe, although it be most true that the truth was before error and apostasie, yet hereupon it followeth not that error and apostasie are of [or] in the truth, as this man would conclude of Antichrist; that because he is said to rise in the church of God, and to sit in the temple of God, therfore the place where he now raigneth and rageth is the church of God.[2] But by all these rules of the word of God we finde the sinagogues that Antichrist hath erected to be of the false and malignant church, and the church of Rome pronownced by God himself to be that great whore. Howsoever then Anti- II Thes. 2:7

---

[1] *A Short Treatise*, p. 54.
[2] *Ibid.*

christ might have his original and worcke in his mysterie in the visible church, yet as soone as his wickednes brake out and was apparent, he forfeited his place and was to be caste fourth, as the angells that sinned were precipitate out of heaven, and cast headlong into hel. Yea, those churches that neglected thus to doe, and spared him, in the just judgment of God lost their happie estate, became guiltie of his sinne, and partakers of his judgment, and fel away with him. [69] So then this phrase of Antichrist his sitting in the temple of God might be much better understoode, than thus grosly to affirme ther upon that Antichrist now sitteth in the church of God.

^(margin: Revel. 9:1; Rev. 12:10, 11, 12; Revel. 12:4)

Whether we understand this his sitting in the temple of God, as in regarde of his original before he was reve[a]led; or in that he should sit where sometimes the true churches of Christ had bene, which he should so destroy and waste, as there should be no shape or steppes of any of them left upon the earth, as it was foretold, Mathew 24:29, Revelation 6:14. Or ells of those counterfeight names and titles of the temple and church of God, which the false church should arrogate and take unto her self. Howsoever, nothing is more sure than that all these abhominations cannot remaine in the church of God. And in that it is in the same verse [II Thessalonians 2:4] said that Antichrist shalbe lifted up above all caled God or hath that veneration, this cannot be donne by any minister in the church, seing everie soule must be subject [unto the higher powers]. Furder, also, that he should shewe himself that he is God. If this also should be literally understoode, what blasphemie wil not ensue. And aswel might it from the same verse be enforced, that Antichrist is God, as that the place where he raigneth is the temple of God.

^(margin: Revel. 18:7; Rom. 13:[1])

Thus having finished his three cardinal reasons of Israel in their schisme, Juda in their apostasie, and this universal falling away and corruption in the time of poperie, to prove the Church of England aswell as these the true church of God, he at length addeth a conclusion in this authenticall assertion of his owne. The Church

A Plaine Refutation

of England in the tyme of poperie was a member of the universal church, and had not the being of a church of Christ from Rome, nor tooke not her beginning of being a church by separating herself from that Romish sinagogue, etc.[1] If he here meane that the Lord had his secret ones chosen and knowen unto himself in England in the tyme of poperie, which were members of the universall church, we graunt wel. But what were this to approve the generall estate of England in the tyme of poperie when they were th[o]roughly infected with the apostasie and idolatrie of the church of Rome, to be a visible member of the universal church? So that albeit they had not their being a church from Rome, yet they had their not being a church from Rome, when they were defiled with their apostasie and idolatrie. Wherfore to have this conclusion passe, it had beene needfull that Mr. Giffard had approved and made evident demonstration by the Scriptures that the Church of England was rightly gathered unto and established in that holy faith and order which Christ hath left unto his church in universall and particular according to the rules and examples in his Testament. Then, that in tyme of poperie they fel not away from this holy faith and order. And that nowe they contynue and faithfully walke in the same faith and order. This if he had donne, then had he proved that which now he beggeth and assumeth. Then had he powerfully convinced [70] and stopped the mouthes of al schismaticks and gaynesayers for ever. But with al his learning and labour he hath not enterprised, neither ever is able to prove this by Christe's Testament. The tyme past and estate present of their Church of England witnesse the contrarie unto his face, and shew unto all men how dieplie it hath bene and still is infected with the Romish idolatries and apostasie from the Testament of Christ, and in what sort they have at this daye caste forth the tyrannie and yoak of Antichrist with his abhominations, idolatries, heresies, false worship, false ministrie, and false governement, etc. He

[1] *Ibid.*, p. 55.

therfore in steade of approving his church by the rules of Christ's Testament, striveth to prove it a true church though it consist of prophane multitudes never as yet rightly gathered unto, or established in, the faith and order of Christ, though it have not Christ's ministrie and officers which he hath appoynted unto the church, but that false and antichristian ministrie, which the pope erected, used, and left, though it be governed not by the rules of Christe's Testament, but by the pope's courtes, canons, etc., and such lawes as these Romish bishopps doe devise, though it worship God after a popish and most idolatrous maner, though it reject the truth of God and persecute all such as call them unto or stand for the same. And this most barbarous and divelish assertion he striveth to confirme by the schisme of Israel, the apostasie of Juda, and the universall defection and corruption of poperie. Unto which our finall answere is, that if anie of these three be justified and finde mercie before the Lorde, then hath their Church of England also occasion to rejoyce. But if the prophets everie where have denownced the fearefull judgments of God against them, then will not their false prophets' untempered plaisters, and lying divinations of peace, help them in that daye.

But nowe Mr. Giffard procedeth to the second part of the assumption which he first forged, and now refuteth in our name. Wherin he wil needs make us to say (though it never entred into our thought) that their Church of England hath no power to caste forth anie by excommunication: and herein he saith we speake verie falslie: for the Church of England hath some power to excommunicate.[1] We have alreadie shewed how he hath chaunged and falsified our reason, leaving out and altering what he liste, and taking no more of it than he thought himself able to deale withal. But if he had made his answere to our wordes as he receaved them, then he should have proved that the Church of England (especially those select congregations whose pastors used to repel the unworthy from the sacra-

---

[1] *Ibid.*

A Plaine Refutation

ments) had the power of our Lord Jesus Christ to caste forth by true excommunication, before he had chardged us with lyes or absurdities.

For us we never doubted or denied that their Church of England had power to excommunicate, even that power, throne, and great authority [71] which the dragon gave the beast. We take their excommunication to be the self same which was usualy exercised in this land in the tyme of poperie, donne by the same officers and courtes, as the bishop, the archdeacon, or commissarie, in Latine, in maner of a write [writ],[1] in the bishop's sole name, and that not for anie offence, transgression of God's lawe, or heresie, how pernitious, damnable, and detestable soever; but only for contumacye or contempt of their courts, as for not appearing, or not paying such mulctes and exactions as those birdes with fingers enjoyne and exact. Unto al this busines is neither the parish-priest, questmen, sidemen, or anie of the parish caled, it nothing concerneth them. The priest he must of force pronownce it, and the parish allowe of it, how unjust soever it be or disorderly donne. This is the only excommunication of the Church of England, other than this they have not.[2] Revel. 13:2

This popish thunderbolt cannot be defended or mistaken for that holie reverend excommunication given by God and used in the church of Christ against everie obstinate offender unpartially and orderly, according to the rules therunto prescribed, the whole church with one consent in the name and " power of our Lord Jesus Christ giving up such a one unto Sathan for the destruction of the flesh, that the spirit might be saved in the day of the Lord; " and this publiquely in the open church when the whole congregation is gathered together. Neither may such excommunicat be receaved I Cor. 5:[4, 5]

---

[1] The writ *de excommunicato capiendo* or the writ *de contumace capiendo*. See Edward Cardwell, *Synodalia*, I, 118, 130, 138; II, 530, 548-552. See also Felix Makower, *The Constitutional History and Constitution of the Church of England*. The index for " excommunication " and " writs " is to sections, not pages.

[2] See F. Douglas Price, " The Abuses of Excommunication and the Decline of Ecclesiastical Discipline under Queen Elizabeth," *English Historical Review*, LVII, no. 225 (January, 1942), 106-115.

againe but of the whole congregation upon his publique repentance in the assemblie.

It were needles to demonstrate the monstrous abuses of this their popish excommunication in perticular, and how contrarie it is in every pointe unto the ordinance of Christ, seing this may readily be donne of the reader by comparing their descriptions together: especially seing this adversarie himself dare not undertake the defence therof. But [he] saith, " that though their excommunication doth not binde in heaven, yet it is of force to remove from the societie of their assemblies: which proveth our accusation false, because we reason about this outward removinge."[1] Verie good, but may this outward removing or casting out of the church be without the power of our Lord Jesus Christ, or by any other power? Or are not such as are caste out by the power of Christ, bownde in heaven? Can any other power in heaven or in hel separate any of God his children from the love of Christ, and cut off any of Christ's members from his bodie? Or may the church be subject touching these spirituall judgmentes and censures to anie other power or voyce, than unto the power and voyce of Christ, execute or confirme anie other judgments than the judgmentes of Christ? Or may any mortal man thus presume into the verie throne and office of Christ? Doe not al the elders in the church of God caste downe their crownes before the throne of the Lambe? Do not all the sainctes execute and ratifie all the judgments of God that are written? How then dare these Lucifers, these popes, rather than popish bishopps, thus [72] presume to bring in this popish excommunication in place of Christe's, and thereby in their owne Romish courtes, name, and power, without due order or cause, without the consent or privity of the congregation or anie of the congregation, to cut off and caste out of the church at their pleasure? Or how dare these wicked priestes pronownce these accursed antichristian excommunications, and expel from their publique exercises,

Rev. 4:10
Psal. 149:[9]

---

[1] *A Short Treatise*, p. 56.

A Plaine Refutation

prayers, and sacraments such excommunicate? Or the parrish thus receave and ratifie this divelish proceding? Is it to be thought that that man which either taketh this for Christ's or christian excommunication, knoweth what christian excommunication is? And what it is to cut off anie member of Christ? Or thincketh he to hide the horrible tyrannie and blasphemie of the bishops, or his owne fellow priests' perfidie and treason, in yeilding his flocke unto these greivous wolves, or the miserable servitude and spiritual bondage of their whole church, that thus are held and wittingly stand under Antichrist's yoke, by caling it an outward removing? Is it not all the ex[c]ommunication their church hath? Doth it not remove from the publique exercises, prayers, and sacraments of their church, etc.? And would he make us believe that this is but an outwarde removing? Hath the church of Christ anie other or furder power than outwardly to remove from their fellowship and communion? Or may their church outwardly remove anie by publique censure from their prayers, sacraments, etc., and yet the partie excommunicate be in this estate esteemed a member of Christ, or they have anie communion with him? Then, this excommunication of theirs being founde a meere popish forgerie, and presumptuous blasphemie, directlie contrarie in everie poynte to the rules and institution of Christ, cannot be saide to binde in heaven, because God ratifieth nothing there, whether it be donne by man or angel, but what he here commaundeth, and we doe according to the rules of his worde.

This then being so contrarie to the worde of God, cannot be ratified in heaven, and so it is apparant not to be donne in the power of our Lorde Jesus Christ, but in the power of Antichrist and Sathan. Their church therfore having none other excommunication than this, cannot be said to have the power of Christ to caste out anie by true and orderly excommunication. And seing they do exercise this popish blasphemous excommunication, which is not donne in the power of Christ, we may justlie conclude, that their church doth caste forth Sathan in the power of Sathan, to which power their whole ministerie and people stand and contynue in subjection.

And now this aucthor not being able to justifie the publique excommunication of their Church of England, seketh to withdrawe us from the present question, by moving two newe questions, and from those (after his accustomed maner) laboureth to confute us. Because the assumption, even as he himself with longe studie had changed, contrived, and framed it, could not yet serve his tourne. His first question is this. " If the bishop with sondrie other ministers of the gospel do dulie ex-com-[73]municate an obstinate wicked man, is he not excommunicate before God."[1] We first answeare, that the bishop or the Church of England doth not excommunicat for anie wickednes or crime whatsoever, be it never so heynous, though obstinacie be joyned therunto, as for adulterie, murder, witchcraft, etc., but only for contempt of their courtes, for not appearing, or not paying their exactions. Then we answeare, that the bishop never caleth anie other ministers to this action of excommunication. Furder we answeare, that this lorde bishop is no minster of the gospel or church of Christ, and therfore he hath nothing to do with the excommunication of anie member of the visible church; neither may or wil anie true ministers of the gospel joyne unto the bishop in this busines. But if they should, we say that such excommunication is not allowed before God, because it is founde contrary unto his worde. Yet this we say, that the obstinate wicked are bounde and excommunicate before God, whilest they continue in that estate, albeit the church here should neglect or refuse to cast them out. For the judgments of God do neither take effect by man, neither depend upon man, or stay of man, but the judgments decreed are accomplished, and the wrath of God is reve[a]led from heaven against al impietie and unrighteousness of men that are contentious and disobey the truth.

Finally, though it were admitted (which can never be proved) that the bishop and these priestes were true

John 9:31
Esa. 57:21
Deut. 29:19, 20, 21
Esa. 34:1b
Rom. 1:18
Rom. 2:8, 9

---

[1] *Ibid.*

A Plaine Refutation

ministers of the gospel, yet wee say, that this excommunication donne by them in their private assemblie or consistorie (as they cal it) is contrarie to the rules of Christ's Testament, and unlawful. For there we finde this power committed and given unto the whole church by our Saviour Christ, who sendeth al men to " tel the church," Mathew 18 : 17. There we finde the execution and publishing of this, performed in and by the church, I Corinthians 5. We find also the remitting and receaving in againe of such excommunicate to belong and to be referred unto the whole church, II Corinthians 2 : 6, 7, 8. Furder, we there finde the judgments of God denownced against the whole church, and everie member of that church, where this censure of excommunicating the wicked is neglected and rejected, I Corinthians 5 : 26. To these if we add the peculiar interest that everie member hath in the worde, doctrine, and faith of Christ, and in al the publique actions of the church, as also the perticular dueties that everie member oweth unto the whole church, together with the sondrie charges and exhortations everie where in the Scriptures given them to watch, to admonish, to exhorte, and that not onlie the private members, but even the greatest officers of the church; to marcke them diligently that cause divisions and offences contrarie to the doctrine that they have learned, and to avoide them, Romans 16 : 17. II John 10. To take heed what and whom they heare, to hold such accursed (be they men or angels) that preach unto them besides that [other than] they have receaved, Galatians 1 : 9. To admonish Archippus, Colossians 4 : 17. To withdrawe themselves from everie brother that walketh inordinately, and not according to the tradition they have receaved. II Thessalonians 3 : 6. To note such as abey [obey] not [74] the worde, and not to be commingled with them that they may be ashamed. II Thessalonians 3 : 14. If their brethren sinne, to rebuke them; if they repent, to forgive them; if not, to retaine their sinne, Luke 17 : 3, 4. And to procede according to the rule, Matthew 18 : 15, 16, 17. [I Thes. 5:14 Mark 13:34, 37 Heb. 10:24, 25 I Pet. 4:10, 11]

These perticular dueties and chardges dulie considered, there can be no doubt but everie Christian is a king and priest unto God to spie out, censure, and cut downe sinne as it ariseth, with that two-edged sworde that proceedeth out of Christ's mouth. As also that the excommunication of anie member belongeth to the whole congregation, the whole bodie together, seing al the members have like interest each in other, etc. Albeit the church thus assembled be to use the help or ministerie of the most fit member for the pronowncing of this excommunication, etc.

Rev. 1:6
Psal. 149:[6]

Here then fal to the grounde those four interpretations of Mathew 18 : 17. *Tel the Church.* 1. Some understanding by the [word] " church " [that it means] the pope, who they say is Christe's vicare general and supreame head of the church. 2. Others would understand it of the lord arch-bishops' grace, or of the lord bishops, who apart may excommunicate and absolve for the whole church. 3. Some others there are that understand by this word " church " the companie of elders apart, from, and without the people, which companie they cal the consistorie, and this ought to excommunicate, etc. 4. The last sorte are in a quite contrarie extremitie, and these would have the people without the elders to excommunicate, elect, etc., and that by pluralitie of voyces.[1]

The two first sortes depend of one lyne, and builde their preheminence upon the promise made to the Apostle Peter, Matthew 16 : 18, 19, where the keyes of the kingdom of heaven are given him. And upon the Apostle Paul his example, who delivered Hymeneus and Alexander unto Sathan. I Timothy 1 : 20. They

---

[1] These four expositions of Matthew 18 : 17 are respectively the Roman Catholic, the Anglican, the Presbyterian, and the Congregational interpretations. Francis Johnson, who embraced Presbyterian and Congregational ideas, wrote a book, entitled, *A Short Treatise concerning the Words of Christ*, " Tell the Church " ([Amsterdam ?], 1611). Some of the writers who published their views on the vexed problem of church government and ecclesiastical polity are Henry Ainsworth, Robert Baillie, Richard Bancroft, Théodore de Bèze, Thomas Bilson, Thomas Cartwright, Richard Cosin, John Cotton, John Dove, George Downame, John Field, Richard Field, Richard Hooker, Francis Johnson, Richard Mather, Philippe de Mornay, John Paget, Hadrian Saravia, Matthew Sutcliffe, Walter Travers, John Udall, and John Whitgift.

A Plaine Refutation

bring also the commandement of Paule unto Timothy, to rebuke the elders that sinne openly. I Timothy 5 : 20, and the commandement unto Titus to reject an heretike, Titus 3 : 10.

Touching the power of the keyes, we have above in the handling of the priestes' absolution shewed it, not to depend upon the dignitie of men's persons or offices, but upon the vertue and truth of God his worde : from which when Peter or the pope himself departeth, his worde not onlie bindeth not, but is lyable unto reprofe, and bownd by the worde. Which worde is given not to Peter onlie, but to the whole church that is builte upon that rocke, and to everie member therof, and hath like power to binde or to loose in the mouth of the least, as in the mouth of the greatest. For it is impossible that the word of God should be made of none effect. As to Paule's example, we suppose they can evil shewe any such authentike warrant for their apostolike auctority over al churches and persons, or such measure of grace as Paule had : and therfore we thinck they ought quietly to remaine within such lawes and limits in their calings as Paule hath left order. For the commaundments given to Timothy and Titus, they can neither prove that they executed them in such pontifical maner as they do, or in their owne names alone. The contrarie appeareth in the verie words of the [75] commandements. Neither if this were so, can they shewe themselves to have an evangeliste's office, as they had.

The other two sortes, the one wherof giveth this power of excommunication unto the consistorie of elders without the people, the other unto the people by pluralitie of voyces without the elders,[1] fal into these errors and confusion in that they knowe not, or at the least doe not

---

[1] It is clear that Barrow by this sharp contrast disagrees with those who wish to exclude the elders from voting. He believes that the congregation assembled, not the eldership or consistory exclusively, should possess the power of excommunication. But Barrow specifically says : "They [elders] are members of the whole bodie, and not the whole body." Therefore, any plan of depriving the governors and guides of the right to vote with the congregation is " a most monstruous confusion and high rebellion."

dulie consider, what either the communion of sainctes, or the holie order of Christ, is in his church. For if they did, they would never thus unnaturallie separate the members from the bodie, or divide the bodie into partes.

The first sorte of these interpret these wordes *eipe te ecclesia*[1] [to mean] *Tel the consistory*, building it upon the Jewes' Sanhedrin or Sunedrion,[2] that as the Jewes in those tymes complayned unto their elders in this councel, and the councel cast out of the synagogue such as they judged offenders, as John 9 : 22 and 12 : 42. So our Savior, Mathew 18 : 17, sendeth to his newe consistory, who have like power to caste out of the church. We may here as in a mirrour behold how far the wisest whilest they followe their owne devises, do erre from the truth. Is it likelie or possible that our Saviour Christ would fetch his patterne for the elders of his church and the executing these high judgments from that corrupt degenerat Sunedrion of the Jewes, which by the institution of God was merelie civile, and not ordeined for causes ecclesiasticall, as appeareth Exodus 18, Numbers 11, Deuteronomy 1, the priestes bearing the chardge and having the deciding of al ecclesiasticall causes, Numbers 18, Deuteronomy 17. But this councel of theirs was now mixed of the elders, of the people, and the priestes, and handled al causes both civile and ecclesiastical indifferently, Matthew 26 : 3, Acts 4 : 5. How unjustlie and ungodlie they dealt, may appeare by their handling our Saviour and his apostles from tyme to tyme. Now as

---

[1] Eipon tēi εκκλēsiai — tell the church. Matthew 18 : 17.
[2] The Sanhedrin (sunedrion) was the highest court of justice among the Jews. It consisted of seventy-one members, including the president. See " Sanhedrin," in *The Jewish Encyclopaedia*; see also " Synedrium " in the *Encyclopaedia Biblica*, ed. T. K. Cheyne and J. S. Black. Much information on this court may also be found in the works of Josephus; in Heinrich Graetz, *History of the Jews*, 6 vols. (1940); Emil Schürer, *A History of the Jewish People in the Time of Christ*, 6 vols. (1885-91); Theodor Keim, *The History of Jesus of Nazara*, 6 vols. (1876-83); Sidney B. Hoenig, *The Great Sanhedrin* (1953); George Foot Moore, *Judaism in the First Centuries of the Christian Era*; *The Age of the Tannaim*, 3 vols. (1927-30); Alfred Edersheim, *The Life and Times of Jesus the Messiah*, 4th ed., 2 vols. (1887).

A Plaine Refutation

there is no likenes to collect these surmises from that place, so is ther no one circumstance in that Scripture to leade therunto, there being taught how al Christians ought to reprove and prosecute offences one towards an other, as being generallie comprised within this rule, to admonish and be admonished, aswel elders as others. There is no mention of anie sending unto such consistory of elders as they feigne unto themselves, and would erect. The heathen and publicane there spoken of have no reference unto, neither give anie occasion to speake of the Jewish Sunedrion. The heathen al men knowe were not excommunicate or caste out, but kept out of the temple: they might not enter, Deuteronomy 23. The publicanes, though in civile conversation they were abhorred of the precise Pharasies, yet were they not caste out of the temple, being Jewes or proselites, Luke 18:10. So that our Saviour there rather teacheth his disciples by the present estate and estimation of the heathen and the publicane how to walke towards the excommunicate, by the example of the one to avoide al spiritual communion with them as with heathens, as also by the example of the publicane [to avoid] al civile conversation as much as may be, than anie way there sendeth to this consistory, wherof through the whole Testament of Christ they can shew no warrant. But directlie con-[76]trarie it were to the order, power, and libertie of the whole church, to the duties of everie member, and to the duties of these elders in their offices, that they should in this maner draw all the actions and affaires of the whole church into their private consistory before themselves only.

Elders were appointed for the preservation of the order of the church, and not for the subvertion therof: for the defence of the libertie of the least, and not to plucke away the libertie of all. Elders were appointed to instruct and to guide the church in the worde and wayes of God, and not to plucke the worde of God from them into their owne handes only, and to debarre them from walking in the waies that God hath prescribed and commanded.

Though elders be governours and overseers of the

I Tim. 3
Tit. 1:5
III John 9
II Cor. 11:20

church, yet are they servantes of the church, and not lordes over Gode's heretage. They are members of the whole bodie, and not [but they do not constitute] the whole body. If al [the body] were one or some fewe members, where were the bodie? The bodie is not one member but manie. And as it consisteth of manie members, so hath it use of al, and may be separate from none. How unnaturall then are those members which thus separate and seclude themselves from the whole, yea, rather sequester and seclude the whole from them, and arrogate and assume the publick duties and power of the whole into their owne handes, as though God had given al giftes unto them, and they had no neede of others. And thus puffed up with pre-eminence of their owne place and excellencie of their owne giftes, despise all the rest as base, ignorant, unworthie to be in their consistory, to have anie voyce of consent or dissent there, alleadging them to be tumultuous, contentious, factious, ungoverned, ignorant, inclined to the worst, etc. Thus abuse they their owne giftes and deprave others.[1] These are evill speaches and harde reportes to be gyven out upon the people of God, the chosen of Christ, partakers of the same pretious faith and glorious inheritance with themselves, members of the same bodie, even members of Christ with them, sanctified with the same spirit, and abhorring these evils wherwith they are chardged, humble and easie to be ledd, ordered, and governed by the worde of God in all thinges. Not presuming to speake beyonde the proportion of their faith and knowledge, or without necessitie, or due order; which who so transgresseth is publickly reproved; so that these fitlier agree to these tumultuous assemblies where all the prophane are receaved as members, than unto the holie churches of Christ where none but the faithfull are admitted or

Marginal references: I Pet. 5:3; I Cor. 12:19; Ephes. 4:7, 10; Rom. 12:3

---

[1] This may be an unfair indictment of a theoretical and power-hungry eldership. Barrow seems to forget that elders are elected by the people, derive their delegated powers therefrom, and serve that group. Far from being secluded from the whole, they constituted and represented the choicer spirits. A small committee is usually more judicious and efficacious than a large group.

A Plaine Refutation

remayne. Wherfore these accusations which are caste upon the people are rather caste upon the church, yea, upon Christ himself, who is the aucthor of this lawe and commandement; who sendeth to the whole church, and commandeth the whole church and not the con- I Cor. 14:33
sistory to excommunicate: yet is not Christ the aucthor I Cor. 11:16
of disorder but of peace, neither have the churches of God custome to be contentious. For the avoyding of which disorder and contention are elders appointed of God to instruct and guide the church in doing the wil of God, and not to withdrawe those actions which God hath com-[77]maunded to be donne in and by his I Cor. 14:24, 25
church publickely, into a private consistory, into the handes of a fewe. Wherin they made themselves transgressours of the wil of God, disturbers, and violaters of that holy order which Christ hath established in his church, and of that heavenly symphony wherin Christ hath contempered the whole bodie together.[1]

And now as the fault and pride of these elders is great and intollerable of the one side, so were it againe a most monstruous confusion and high rebellion on the other side, if the people should thus expulse and shut out their governours and guides, those most fit members that God hath given them to these actions, from amongst them, and then decide and determine causes by pluralitye of voyces. What can be devised more barbarous and unworthie the church of Christ than this? Were not this as if the bodie should offer violence unto or laye aside the eyes, and then divide itself into factions and

---

[1] For the general subject of church government and discipline at Geneva, see *Calvin: Theological Treatises*, trans. J. K. S. Reid, "The Library of Christian Classics," XII (Philadelphia: Westminster Press, 1954), pp. 48-72; James Mackinnon, *Calvin and the Reformation* (London, 1936), pp. 76-92; R. N. Carew Hunt, *Calvin* (London, 1933), pp. 141-152. See also James L. Ainslie, *The Doctrines of Ministerial Order in the Reformed Churches of the 16th and 17th Centuries* (Edinburgh, 1940); A. Mitchell Hunter, *The Teaching of Calvin* (2nd ed.; London, 1950), chapters VIII, X, XI, XII. See William D. Maxwell, *John Knox's Genevan Service Book, 1556* (1931), not for discipline but for liturgical procedures, ministerial dress, election, and ordination. See especially pp. 58-60, 165-174, 210-231. Cartwright, de Bèze, Farel, and Travers were contemporary writers on the subject of church government. For two recent works, see John T. McNeill, *The History and Character of Calvinism* (1954) and François Wendel, *Calvin* (1963; French ed. 1950).

partes for the busines it hath to doe ? This balloting by suffrage or plurality of voyces might well be a custome amongst the heathen in their popular governmentes, but it is unhearde of and unsufferable in the church of Christ, whatsoever some dreame unto themselves therof.

<small>Esay 8:19
Phil. 3:16
Phil. 2:2, 3</small>

There all from the highest to the lowest in all actions enquire the will of God : which being knowen, they all then walke by the same rule, and with one consent doe the will of God accordingly. There is no division in that bodie, neither anie thing donne according to the will of man, but according to the will of God only, all having received of and being guided by one and the same spirit, even as God is one, and Christ not yea and

<small>I Cor. 12
Rom. 12:4, 5, 6</small>

naye. Now though all the members have received of this spirit of God, yet have not all received in like measure. Though all the bodie be light, yet is not all the bodie an eye. But God that hath made the bodie to consist of divers members, hath distributed divers giftes in divers measure unto them. Some he hath given pastors, some teachers, etc., for the helpe and service of the whole, which members the whole bodie useth according to their gifts, office, and function. The whole bodie asketh instruction of their teachers, councel

<small>I Thes. 5:12, 13
Hebr. 13:17
II Tim. 4:1, 2
Acts 20:28</small>

of their elders, etc. The people are commanded to obey their leaders, and to submit, to acknowledge, to honor them, and to have them in super-aboundant love. These are of God set over the flocke, to watch, to instruct, admonish, exhort, rebuke, etc. ; yet not to plucke awaye the power and liberty of the whole church, or to

<small>III John 9
Rom. 16:17
Gal. 1:8, 9
Col. 4:17
Tit. 3:10
II Thes. 3:14</small>

translate and assume the publicke actions of the whole church into their owne handes alone. They are men and may erre. They themselves even for al their doctrines and actions are subject to the censure of the church, or of the least members of the church, if in any thing they be founde to erre or transgresse. Yea, if they remaine obstinate, that congregation wherof they remaine ministers and members is to procede against them and to excommunicate them as any other member. For (as it hath bene said) the judgments of the church are not the judgments of men but of God, to

A Plaine Refutation

which al the members of the [78] church must alike be subject. Which judgmentes, as they are committed to the whole church with perfect rules for their maner of proceding in everie circumstance, so is the church hereunto to use such members as God hath given and made most fit. For Paule, Apollo, and Cephas are theirs. I Cor. 3:22, 23 And this doth no way diminish the power and interest of the church in this action, or translate these publick affaires from the whole unto these elders, whose councel, direction, and service the church useth herein, no more than a prince or state may be said not to doe those thinges whereunto they use the advise and service of their councel.

By the church then here we understand everie perticular congregation subsisting of al the members. Everie of which congregations hath equall interest in the worde, promises, judgments, and power of Christ. Christ hath given unto al churches the same Testament, ministrie, lawes, and ordinances, with like chardge and aucthoritie to observe the same. He hath given them the same order and communion in all places, one and the same rule to walke by towardes them within the faith, as also to avoide and cast out such as depart from the faith or walke inordinatly. Neither hath Christ given unto anie one church more power or prerogative than unto al other, or set one church above and over an other, otherwise than to wish and seke the good each of other and of al, to admonish, exhort, stirr up each other as occasion requireth. And unto this everie member of Christ is also bounde in his caling, but not to intrude and encroach upon the publicke actions and duties of the whole church, or the perticular functions and offices of others.

As to pastors and elders, their office extendeth but unto those flockes wherof the Holy Ghost hath set them overseers, and not unto all churches in this maner, to which their ministrie neither doth nor can extend. Agayne, excommunication is no part of their ministrie. Neither hath God tyed it unto the office of any, but left it a publick dutie of the whole congregation to be donne of al with one consent. How presumptuous then is he

Acts 20:28
I Pet. 5:2

that usurpeth this power over, yea, of other congregations to excommunicate, absolve, elect, depose, etc., for them, yea, that thus plucketh from them that power and chardge which Christ hath given unto them?[1] But how monstruous and intollerable were the pride of that consistory, which consisting but of a few perticular members, shal assume the power and duties of so many churches into their owne handes?[2] We are of minde that the best and learnedst of them shall finde their owne perticular offices in their owne perticular flockes as much as they can well performe and dischardge, though they should not thus encroach upon and assume the public duties of the whole church, much lesse of manie churches. And sure if this consistory should duely intend [consider, attend to] all the several occasions, complaintes, and matters of offence that howrely arise in so manie sondrie congregations, especially where all the multitudes are received in as members, they should doe nothing ells through their whole life but sit in this consistory, yea, their whole lives would not suffice to a litle part of this chardge, where al the offences of these multitudes, both publick and private, were duly admonished and [79] prosecuted according to the commandement of God. And so should these pastors and elders never be able to exercise their owne ministri and officers [offices?] in those peculiar congregations where they are chosen to serve.

Againe, if everie congregation should be thus posted over and sent to this consistory for the censuring of everie perticular offence and offender howe manifest soever, etc., manifold inconveniences and mischieves would therupon ensue. As that they must be driven oft-tymes to receave and joyne unto the most wicked and abhominable in their prayers and sacraments; yea, if the pastor himself should fal into some sinne and heresie, they must of force suffer him to administer untill this consistory had caste him out. Many were the

---

[1] Barrow is denouncing the bishop and episcopal jurisdiction.
[2] Barrow is criticizing the Presbyterian classis or presbytery, as well as the Anglican synods or convocations.

A Plaine Refutation

reasons and more the inconveniences that might be alleadged against this presumptious irregular consistory, which hath no grownde in the worde of God, but utterly subverteth, destroyeth, and corrupteth the whole order and communion of the churches, openeth a wide gap to al licentiousnes and prophanenes of maners and conversation, wherin if the thowsand part of the heynouse faultes of these wicked multitudes, these Sodomitical Christians of these tymes should be noted, prosecuted, censured, they should then in one weeke have as few Christians as now they have many; but nowe by this rejecting God's ordinance and erecting their owne devises, al sinne aboundeth and over-floweth, and no sinne (though obstinatly held and persisted in) is judged to deserve this censure, especially here in England where they excommunicate for no sinne; but as the faultes above alleadged are held but bleamishes in their worship, so the greatest sinnes and wickednes are held but infirmities in their life by the prophets of these dayes.

But unto this their consistory againe. They that thus shall erect and advance one perticular congregation as a judge and a mother over others their sisters, must also erect in the same congregation or consistorie, one perticular pastor that must be a judge and a father over other pastors his brethren. And then let them duly consider how far this differeth from, or at leaste how then they can condemne that apostatical sea [see] of Rome, and that unholy father that sitteth therin. And let Mr. Giffard that is so wel skilled in discipline and so derideth our ignorance, now at length consider better of this reason, seing every perticular congregation of Christ hath the power of our Lord Jesus Christ against all sinne and transgression to censure the sinne, and to excommunicate the obstinate offenders, etc. And seing these parishes have not this power of Christ, neither in themselves in perticular, nor yet in their consistories, as hath bene proved, whether this conclusion, which he termeth so absurde, will not followe, that they are not therfore the true churches of Christ. And let him the next time frame a better answere than the Geneva consistory, which though for the reasons abovesaid it can yeild him no help, yet may it not be compared with the popish courtes of these antichristian bishops.

Neither will his other kindes of excommunication in their English Romish synodes prove better. Our answeare then unto his second question is,[1] that the excommunication of an hereticke after he [80] is dulie convinced and founde obstinate, belongeth not to anie bishops or elders of other churches, but unto that congregation wherof this heretick stood a joyned member. Although we graunt that for the discussing of matters in doubt, and the convincing of some notorious subtile heretick, the ayde of other churches is verie necessarie. But the bloudie procedings of these popish bishops that in their consistory not onlie convince the heretike after their scholastical and unchristian maner, but deliver him to the secular powers to be burned with fire (whether the qualitie of the heresie deserve death or no by the lawe of God, wherbie they make the magistrates together with themselves guiltie of murder) declare unto al men how unlike their popish consistories are to the holie, free, wel ordered synodes of christian churches. But blessed be God that hath somewhat restrayned their crueltie and hewen their antichristian hornes by statute[2] heere in this land that they cannot in that maner procede unto bloode: howsoever, their tongues are not restrayned therbie from pronowncing that truth of Christe's gospel (which they cannot and dare not undertake to convince) heresie: and those Christians which yeild not to their antichristian yoke and enormities, hereticks.

Unto the convocation also of these Romish priests and horned cleargie, we answeare, that it carieth no shew of a christian synode or councel, and so their excommuni-

_{Acts 15}

---

[1] Gifford has asked: "if there be an hereticke convinced, and found obstinate, and the bishops and ministers of the Church of England assembled, or some competent number of them, as in the convocation, or such synod doe duely exccommunicate him, is it no excommunication?" *A Short Treatise*, p. 56.

[2] The Act of Supremacy, I Elizabeth, *caput* 1, section XX. Great Britain, Parliament, *The Statutes of the Realm*, IV, Part I (London, 1819), p. 354. See G. W. Prothero, *Select Statutes and Other Constitutional Documents Illustrative of the Reigns of Elizabeth and James I*, 4th edition, p. 12. The taking of life for heresy is made very difficult by the statute.

A Plaine Refutation

cation of as litle value as their sire the pope's is. Furder we answeare, that synodes and councels were not instituted to plucke away the power or to execute the publicke dueties of the church, but to instructe, stir up, and confirme them in their duties, to help them to decide controversies, to shew them the rules of God's worde, and not to breake them or to make newe. Moreover, we saye, that in a christian synode no Christian ought to be shut out, but hath equal power and freedome to speake in assent or dissent of anie thing there handled, as occasion requireth. Yet ought everie Christian to use this power and libertie aright, not disturbing the holie order of the church, presuming to speake before their auntients, or against anie thing by them said, without shewing just cause, etc., alwaies keping themselves within the compasse of faith and sobrietie. Who so doth otherwise is reproved of al, and judged of al as a disturber. Acts 15

Next commeth the suspension or half communication [excommunication] of the Church of England, namely, the prieste's repelling notorious offenders and the open wicked from the sacrament. Mr. Giffard being demaunded of us simple Christians what warrant he could shew for this strange censure in the Testament of Christ, and what auctoritie the priest there hath to excommunicate anie member of the church, if so be this suspension were in nature of excommunication, answeareth, that it is " in nature of excommunication to such as have bene before admitted, yet not to be compared or anie thing neere so great as excommunication," and for the minister, that " he is to take heed to himself that he give not holie things to doggs; to beware of that which may give publick offence [81] and bring the holie mysteries into contempt."[1] Because these his answeres doe no way shew or prove that [which] we demaund, it is needful that we make a litle furder search to seeke out the nature of this suspension, and how neere it commeth to excommunication. We finde that such as before were partakers of, are now openlie

[1] *A Short Treatise*, p. 57.

repelled from, the table of the Lord for notorious sinne and wickednes by the priest alone. Now, touching this sacrament, doth not the Apostle say, " the cup of blessing which we bless, is it not the communion of the blood of Christ? The breade which we breake, is it not the communion of the bodie of Christ? Because we manie are one breade, one bodie; for we all partake of one breade," I Corinthians 10 : 16, 17? We see here this sacrament of the Supper to denote that communion which all that partake therof have with Christ as his members. And againe that communion which they have one with an other in Christ as one an other's members. This their suspension, then, being a publick removing of notorious offenders from the communion of Christ, and from al benefite of his death; from the communion of the church, and from al interest of the sainctes, we would knowe of him what it lacketh of excommunication, and what excommunication is more? If he say that the suspended are not repelled from the ministerie of the word, and prayers of the church, as the excommunicate are, we would then know of him where he hath learned to receive such to the communion of the ministrie or anie actions of the church, that are repelled from al communion and fellowship with Christ and his church. Or how dare he undertake to offer up their prayers in this estate unto God, whom for their notorious sinne and impenitencie he hath repelled from the communion of Christe's bodie and bloode? Thincketh he that Christ can be a priest for anie at the golden altare to offer or receive the incense and odoures of their prayers, unto whom he refuseth to be a sacrifice at the brazen altare? Or hath he not some popish conceipt of more holines in the outward elements of the breade and wyne in this sacrament, than there is in the fellowship of the holie prayers and administration of God's worde in the church? Els whie should he more repel for notorious sinne and wickednes from this sacrament, than from the communion of the prayers and ministrie of the church?

Math. 18:17   Our Saviour Christ doth commaund that when the sinne is publick and brought unto the church, then if

A Plaine Refutation

the offender heare not the church but remain impeni- ^{I Cor. 5}
tent, he should without delaye or partialitie be cut off ^{I Tim. 5:21} ^{John 15:6}
and caste out as a withered branche, and be delivered
"unto Sathan for the humbling of his flesh, that the
spirit might be saved in the daye of the Lord." The
parish priest in the Church of England insteade of excommunication doth suspend such notorious wicked
and impenitent from the table of the Lorde, yet admitteth he them stil to the prayers and ministrie of the
church in this estate, and holdeth them stil members
as before. The Lord saith that excommunication when
the sinne is publicke and the offender obstinate, is the
only remedie that we can administer for the salvation
of the partie, and the preservation of the whole church.
The Church of England saith that excommunication is
to[o] rough and severe to cut [82] him quite off, and
caste him quite out at once, and therfore hath devised
this temperate and middle course to cut him half off,
and caste him half out. Is not this to judge their owne
wayes equal, and the Lord's wayes unequal? Is it not
to esteeme themselves more merciful, just, and wise
than the Lord himself? Ells would they not say that
excommunication were to[o] rough when the sinne is
notorious, and the offender obstinate. Ells would they
not in place of excommunication bring in their owne
devised popish suspension. Wherby, besides that they ^{Lev. 20:4, 5}
controle God and breake his commandement in sparing, ^{Nomb. 35:33, 34}
where they should smite and cut off, and in suffring, ^{Jer. 3:1} ^{I Corin. 5:6}
when they should caste out, they furder bring the whole
church into the contagion of these sinnes, and into the
judgment and wrath of God for the same; if so be it
be true that that is written, "that a litle of such leaven
maketh sower the whole lumpe," or that the wrath of
God for such offences burneth against the whole church.

Moreover, it would be knowen of this discipliner,
this suspender, in what estate we might esteeme and
hold this notorious wicked person thus suspended,
whether as a brother, or as an heathen. If a brother,
how may he then be repelled from the communion with
Christ and his church? Whie should he being a member, having made profession of his faith, and not yet

excommunicate, be denied those heavenly comforts and helpers of his faith ? If he be not to be held a member, whie is he not then according to the commandement of God publickely caste out, that al men might know how to esteeme of him, and how to walke towards him ? For surely except it were the pope's purgatorie, we never hearde of such a middle meane estate as this. Neither ever in Christe's Testament have we read of such a sensure as this idole suspension they use. Neither, for anie by him alleadged, can we perceive anie warrant that the priest may in this maner by his sole aucthoritie reject anie from the communion table. It followeth not, because he is to looke that he give not holie things to doggs, to beware of publick offence, and that he bring not the holie mysteries into contempt, that therfore of his sole aucthoritie he may repel anie from the sacrament, that hath before received it. The meanes for him to avoyde offences, to preserve his ministerie from contempt, is to kepe the commandements of God. The Lorde hath commanded that when anie, that is caled a brother, faleth into open sinne, and remaineth obstinate and hardened therin, so that he refuseth to heare the church, that such an offender in open congregation by the whole church be caste out, delivered to Sathan in the name of our Lorde Jesus Christ. No where is there in all Christe's Testament anie commandement that the minister of his sole authoritie should reject anie from the communion of Christ and of the church, especially in this conterfeite maner. The way then for the ministrie to avoyde offence, to preserve the holy mysteries from contempt, is to cause the church according to the commandement of God to reject and caste out such offenders and wicked persons : so shal he be sure not to deliver the holy things of God unto doggs. Yea, if the church should [83] refuse to caste them out, then ought he to staye his ministerie, and not to communicate with other men's sinnes, or in this estate to execute the ministerie of Christ unto them whilest they refuse to obey Christ's voyce. But instead hereof this sacrilegious priest and his compaignions are not afraide to prostitute and sel the bodie and bloude of Christ to the open prophane,

I Corin. 4:2
Hebr. 5:2

A Plaine Refutation

notoriously wicked, skorners, and contemners, for their wage, offrings, tithes, etc.; thus trampling the Sonne of God under their feete, and compting the bloode of the Testament a common thing. What florish soever they may seeme to make with this their wooden dagger of suspension (which rather manifesteth their follie and presumption, than anie waye cleareth them of this sacriledge), great is their presumption in that they take upon them this absolute power over the whole church and over the table of the Lord, to repel whom they liste of their owne sole aucthoritie from the communion of Christ and of his church, wherof they are but ministers and particular members in the best accompt, and not lords and sole rulers. And yet greater is their presumption in that they dare thrust out the whole ordinance of God (namelie, publick excommunication), and in place therof set up their owne devised idole suspension; which what kinde of censure it is, may appeare by that which hath bene said. It hath no foundation or warrant in Christ's Testament, but possesseth the place of that [which] it is not, namely, of true excommunication, therfore it must needes be that idole instrument of that Zach. 11:[15] foolish shephearde, which the Lord setteth over those sheepe with whom he hath disannulled the covenant.

The aucthoritie of their portesse [breviary, portas], their service-booke, wil no way justifie either them or it. The abhominations of that booke have bene a little touched, yet is not this wretched man ashamed to stand under that monstruous idole, and to professe that all the ministerie of England use that booke in the publick prayers, and administration of and prohibition from the sacraments. The vanitie and follie of this idole suspension most plainely appeareth unto al men by the litle good it doth in anie of these parishes where al prophanenes and iniquitie still aboundeth. The bishop, his chauncelor, or commissary, may with one worde of their mouth heale the greatest wounde the parish-priest can make with this suspension, whatsoever Mr. Parson saye. They have power to absolve anie that he bindeth; and how cheape their absolutions are, is not unknowen to anie whore-master in al the parrish. The bishop hath power to make and to depose ministers at his pleasure; he hath power over the whole ministration; he prescribeth how, when, to whom they shal administer. What truth then is in these wordes that the bishop cannot take away that power which their service-booke giveth them, when he may absolve the partie, disanul the suspension, depose the minister, etc. In that he saith the bishop is but a minister and no lord over their faith and conscience.[1] The same will everie popish priest say of their soveraigne lorde the pope, to preserve the dignitie of their ministerie. The pope writeth himself but the servant of the servants [84] of God. What lordlie authoritie the bishop hath and exerciseth, and in what servile subjection the priestes and all the parishes stand unto their courtes and jurisdiction, shal hereafter more apeare when we come to the discussing of those poyntes. In the meane while we willingly assent unto Mr. Giffard, that the christian reader shall judge whether their service-booke be not a " fit portesse [breviary] for such priestes," and this suspension " a fit toole for such worckmen." Still affirming even with wonder that " if the judgmentes of God were not upon their right eye and upon their right arme, they might perceave how their lordes and bishops dresse them, and how this weapon they allowe them wanteth both edge and poynt, etc."

Thus having finished his answeare to our assumption, he procedeth to a former answeare where he denied the consequence. " That where wicked prophane men are received into and reteyned in the bozome of the church, there [therefore] the covenant is disanulled with them, and they are no longer Gode's people, but a false antichristian sinagogue."[2]

To disprove this, he alleadged " that there were but fewe true worshippers that frequented the temple amongst multitudes of prophane and ungodly men."[3] To this he now addeth the examples of the church at

---
[1] *Ibid.*, p. 58.
[2] *Ibid.*, p. 59.
[3] *Ibid.*

A Plaine Refutation

Corinth and of the seven churches in Asia, etc.[1] We before answeared and stil answeare, that there is no comparison betwixt, or argument to be drawen from, those churches which were rightly gathered and established, and these confused Bibilonish [sic] synagogues of theirs. The Israelites were a peculiar separated people unto the Lorde from the worlde. The people of these other churches were wonne, caled, and gathered unto Christ by the preaching of the gospel, every one entred into the church by the voluntarie profession of his owne faith. No uncircumcised or Gentile might enter into the temple to offer any gift there. All, nor yet the greatest part of the citie of Corinth, nor of these other parts of Asia, were not received into the church as members. But here in their Church of England al the whole land is received in, and that immediatly from open idolatrie without any voluntarie profession of their owne faith by the people in perticular, yea, without the preaching of the gospel going before to call them unto the faith. Therfore, in these reasons he but beggeth the question, and assumeth that which he ought to prove, namely, that these multitudes of all the prophane and al sorts of wicked persons, were somtymes rightly gathered unto and entred covenant with the Lorde, having the true ministrie and governement of Christ set over them, and nowe being fallen into some sinnes are not cast out but stil retayned in their church. This if he had donne, then had there bene some cause that he might have brought against us the examples of these churches. Then should not we have needed to have shewed him his follie twise.[2] Yet this if he had donne (the contrarie wherof is manifest to al that remember the beginning of her Majestie's raigne, or but behold the present estate in the same, or rather in more confusion, sinne being more encreased), yet then we should easily have [85] put difference betwixt those

---

[1] *Ibid.*, p. 62.
[2] Barrow's first manuscript reply to Gifford's manuscript answer is in "A Brief Summe of the Causes of Our Seperation." His second reply is the present work, *A Plaine Refutation*.

churches that amended at the Apostle's admonition, and these which reject all the rules and ordinances ecclesiastical of Christ's Testament as pernitious and intollerable to the estate of this land, and persecute al such as admonish them of, and will not partake with them in, their idolatrie and sacriledge.

We also in our former writing[1] shewed him how the faithful servants of God in the idolatrous dayes of Kinge Achas, [Hezekiah], Menasse, Amon, Jehoiakim, etc.,[2] refrayned from the temple, being so polluted and defiled, and mixed not themselves with the wicked in idolatrous worship. This Mr. Giffard confesseth to be true, and that it was their duetie so to doe. But he saieth we do not argue whether the godly did joyne with the wicked in idolatrie, but whether the wicked were suffred and did joyne with the godlie in true worship.[3] To the question we have above spoken. Only this by the waye we drawe from his own confession, that if the godly in those dayes did wel in separating from and not communicating with the wicked in those tymes of publick idolatrie, then cannot we be blamed which separate and withdrawe our selves from these prophane assemblies, where such abhominable idolatrie and sacriledge is publickly used and enforced, as we have above proved; and thus are we by him cleared and justified.

Againe we convince him of his owne mouth thus. If the faithfull did well in those tymes to withdraw and

---

[1] Barrow's manuscript reply to Gifford's manuscript answer to the Barrowists' manifesto — "A Breefe Sum of Our Profession." See "A Brief Summe of the Causes of Our Seperation," p. 12 [11], which is printed in Carlson, *The Writings of Henry Barrow, 1587-1590*, pp. 118-150.

[2] King Achas, or Ahaz, son of Jotham, was twenty years old when he became king of Judah. He reigned from 732/31 to 716/15. His son, Hezekiah, was king of Judah from 716/15 to 687/86. Manasseh, son of Hezekiah, was king of Judah from 687/86 to 642/41. He was only twenty-one years old when he began his long reign of forty-five years, after serving from the age of twelve as co-regent (696/95—687/86). Amon, son of Manasseh, ruled only two years, 642/41—640/39, and then was assassinated by his own servants. His son Josiah, only eight years old, succeeded him, and reigned until 608. Jehoahaz was crowned, but was deposed in favour of his brother, Jehoiakim, who was king of Judah for eleven years, from 608 to 597 B.C. See II Kings, chapters 16-21. See also Edwin R. Thiele, *The Mysterious Numbers of the Hebrew Kings*, pp. 281-285.

[3] *A Short Treatise*, p. 60.

A Plaine Refutation

separate themselves from the wicked in their idolatrie, which then was publickly set up, then was not the publick estate of the Jewes in those tymes of us to be held the true church of God. For the godly maie at no tyme separate from the true church of God, nor repayre unto the false church. And thus by himself is an end put at once to all his cavils wherbie he hath endevored to proove the Jewes in these most corrupt tymes to be the true outwarde church of God, and to accuse us of heresie that affirme, where such heynous transgressions are obstinatly defended and persisted in by the whole church, there the covenant (unto the judgment of the faithful) is disanulled, there the faithful may not communicate. And verie ignorant is Mr. Giffard if he thinck that the wicked and prophane may either be received into the church, or retayned in the church as members. The wicked and prophane which were never entred into the church, may and ought to be caled to heare the ministrie of the worde of God in the church, as the meanes wherbie they may be caled unto the faith, and so upon their profession be received as members into the fellowship and communion of the church. But until they make open and voluntarie profession of their owne faith and obedience, they cannot be received as members, or have communion with the church. Then until Mr. Giffard prove that the prophane multitudes and open wicked which never made anie voluntarie profession of theire owne faith and obedience, may be received as members into the church, he cannot justifie these parish assemblies of England, or convince us. Furder we graunt, that wicked men, such as fal away from their profession and [86] obedience, shal daylie arise in the church, ells there should be no cause of excommunication. But when their sinne is publicke, then ought the church to censure it, and if they be found obstinate, to caste them out; ells were there no use of excommunication. We graunt also, that the church sometymes of negligence, delaying in due tyme to caste out such wicked, is notwithstanding (if they amend upon admonition), to be held the true church of God. And this our adversarye himselfe, page 56, acknowledgeth that we confesse, although now forgetting himself (his heart being fraught with malice), he bursteth foorth in the gall therof, accusing and sclandering us to hold these heresies, that where any wicked and open sinners worship together with the church as members of the church, there the covenant is disanulled with the whole church.[1] Again, that where corrupt maners breake forth in those that professe the gospell, they be not only utterly voyde of faith which offende, but also all they that worship together with them (though never so much grieved at their sinnes) are fallen from the covenant.[2] Thirdlie, that we make the stablenes of God's covenant to depend upon the worckes of men, and not of the free grace and mercie of God.[3] How could this accuser drawe these heresies from this assertion: it is the church of Christ which hath the power to excommunicate, though it fault much by negligence in executing the same?[4] Doth not the expresse contrarie herein appeare? How can he then reconcile these chardges of his unto this proposition of ours? Or can he produce any one sentence that ever we wrote or spake conteyning such odious doctrines as these? If not, these heresies must stil retourne to his owne throate, as to the sepulchre from whence the[y] sprange; these chardges must remayne upon his reckoning and not upon ours.

We hold that the open prophane and wicked, such as were never caled unto the faith, canot be received into the church as members, before they make open and voluntarie profession of their owne faith and obedience. He that hath from the beginning distinguished light from darcknes, hath alwaies made difference and separation betwixt the world and the church, caling the one the sonnes of God, the other the daughters of men; preserving the one in his arcke, drowning the other in

---

[1] *Ibid.*, p. 63.
[2] *Ibid.*, p. 64.
[3] *Ibid.*, p. 65.
[4] " A Brief Summe of the Causes of Our Seperation," *A Plaine Refutation*, p. 12 [11]; printed in Carlson, *The Writings of Henry Barrow, 1587-1590*, pp. 118-150.

A Plaine Refutation

the floode: he chose and separated to himself out of the whole world one peculiar nation and people to be his visible church, to whom no prophane which made not profession of the same faith might be admitted or joyned in their worship. The worde *ecclesia*, or church, we knowe to be a companie caled from the world, as were Christ's disciples, and the faithfull in all places at the first gathering of the church. Againe, we hold that such as are dulie entred into the church, falling from their profession, and after due admonition remaine obstinate and hardened in their sinne, ought by the church to be excommunicate. And if the church, being admonished and stirred up unto their duetie, refuse to obey and execute the commandement of God, that then unto the faithfull it ceaseth to be the [87] true church of God, and ought to be avoyded until they repent.

The church of Christ must ever be obedient unto Christ's voyce, which voyce when they openlie despise and wilfully resist, they are a companie of rebells and not a companie of sainctes. When they fal away from the faith, they fal away from the covenant of God; when they obstinatelie persist in sinne and wilfully despise God's voyce, they fal away from the faith. Faith beleiveth, reverenceth, and obeyeth God's worde so far as it is reve[a]led unto them, and never wilfully despiseth or rejecteth anie part of the same. God can never be severed from his worde; they that despise and reject God's worde, despise and reject God himself. Christ ruleth and reigneth by the scepter of his owne worde, they that are not subject unto, but wilfully disobey, that word, are not subject unto Christ, have not him a kinge, but a judge over them. Severe lawes and judgments are set downe in God his worde against presumptuous sinne, yea, against al sinne wherof they denie to repent. God hath executed these judgments upon the angels that sinned, upon the original world, upon the nation of the Jewes. Neither wil anie vayne titles of church, covenant, etc., excuse or deliver them (being founde in the like transgressions) from the like judgments. God is just, and his judgments are alike pronounced and executed against al, as against one, being founde and wilfully remayning in the transgression of his lawe.

Nowe then, whilest we conclude, that where the people were never rightlie caled unto the faith or gathered unto Christ, and orderly joyned together in Christ, but multitudes of prophane and al sortes of wicked persons, idolaters, atheists, etc., even the whole land without any choice, any separation, received into their church as members, without any voluntarie profession of their own faith, that in this estate they cannot be esteemed the true planted churches of Christ. With what conscience or truth can this ungodly man hereupon defame and divulge us to hold this heresie, "that where corrupt maners breake forth in those that professe the gospell, they be not only [utterly] voyde of fayth which offend, but all they also which worship together with them (though never so much grieved at their sinnes) are falen from the covenant."[1] How can he liken these rowtes of prophane atheists and wicked persons of the world to the faithful servantes of Christ in his church, or compare their open wickednes (which they commit even with greedines) to the faultes and eskapes [mistakes, peccadilloes] of frailety or negligence in the sainctes?

Againe, whilest we affirme, that where open obstinacie is joyned unto publick sinne, whether it be in the whole congregation or in any perticular member, there that congregation or that member cannot by us be judged faithfull or within the outward covenant untill they repent, with what feare of God or shame of men can this man publish us to hold, that where any open grosse sinne is committed by anie, and they stil through ignorance or negligence are suffred in the church, there the covenant to be disanulled with the whole church.[2] And so we to fall into this heresie. "To make the stablenes of God his [88] covenant not to depend upon mercie and free grace promised and bownde with an

---

[1] *A Short Treatise*, p. 64.
[2] *Ibid.*, pp. 63, 66.

oathe, but upon our worckes, yea, upon the worckes of other whom we must judge."¹

This heresie, after he himself hath devised in our name, he procedeth to confute it with manie wordes, shewing the stability of God's promises, the greatnes of God's mercie, that remembreth his covenant in his greatest indignation and wrath, as also the smale beginnings and daylie growth and proceadings of our sanctification in this life. As though we ever doubted or denied that the Lord our God his covenant was made, established, and preserved unto us in his Christ only without any worckes or merite in us, present or to come, to deserve or to retaine his favour the least minute. Alas, our miserable and forlorne estate even from our mother's wombe before we knowe the Lorde, yea, our contynual transgressions and defections ever since we knewe the Lorde (when we behold our lives in that sparckling glasse of his lawe) do shew us that we are not saved by worckes, but by the free grace and mercie of God through faith in Christ, and that not of our selves, but by the gift of God whose worcke we are, created in Christ Jesus unto good worckes which God hath fore-ordayned that we should walke in them.

But now whilest we acknowledge the whole worcke of our salvation, from the beginninge to the end, to be of God and not of our selves, to procede from and to be established upon his free grace, mere mercy, and love, and not from or upon any goodnes in us fore-seene or subsequent; yet make we not therby the grace of God and his Holy Spirit which he hath given to al his elect, to be idle, vayne, or fruictlesse in any of them, but to regenerate, chaunge, enlighten and sanctifie them, to bring all their affections into, and to keepe them in the love and obedience of the truth. By the profession of which truth they are knowen and received as members of the visible church, made partakers of the commune comfortes and covenant of the sainctes. From which profession when they fall away, and will not be reduced by the voyce of the church or renued by repentance, but remaine obstinate and hardned in their sinnes, then

¹ *Ibid.*, p. 66.

Henry Barrow

are they by the commandement and power of Christ to be cut off as withered branches, to be cast out from the fellowship of the sainctes, and all interest in Christ, to be delivered unto Sathan, etc. The same rules, faith, salvation, judgments, we have above shewed to belong unto al and unto everie one, unto al as unto one being founde in the same faith, or in the same transgressions.

Now then whilest the whole congregation or anie member therof shall remaine hardened in sinne, deniing to obey Christe's voyce, refusing to repent, who can say that this church or man in this estate, can by us (which judge and see but according to the rules of the worde) be affirmed and held the true church of Christ within the outward covenant, when Christ himself commandeth us to deliver them up to Sathan in his name, to have no fellowship with them? This cannot be donne of us unto any, whom we may affirme within the outward covenant. God his secret election and councels wherin he [89] hath determined from before al worlds who shalbe saved, how far the faithful shalbe tryed and fal[l], *Deu 29:29* and when he wil raise them againe, belonge not unto us to judge of. Onely this is most sure, they that thus fal away and are hardened, are not of us to be held and esteemed within the outwarde covenant, or received until they as publickly repent.

How then can this wicked sclanderer drawe this gracelesse collection and damnable conclusion from this holie doctrine, that where obstinacie is joyned unto publick sinne, there the outward covenant is broken, no communion to be held until repentance be made; therfore we holde that the stablenes of God's covenant with his church dependeth upon the worckes of men? Because we say that God sanctifieth al that he saveth, therefore we hold salvation by workes; because we hold that faith which is without fruictes to be deade and worthles, therefore we hold salvation by workes. Because God requireth obedience of al his servants that enter into or remaine in his house, and commandeth them to have no fellowship with anie, longer than they contynue in the same fayth and obedience, therfore we make the stablenes of Gode's covenant to depende upon

A Plaine Refutation

our worcks, " yea, upon the workes of others whom we must judge."[1] What heretick or perverted spirit could more highlie abuse and deface the holy doctrines of Christ? Is Mr. Giffard a teacher of the Church of England, and cannot yet put difference betwixt the worcke of our salvation by Christ for us, and the worke of God's Holy Spirit, the fruicts of God's grace in us? That cannot put difference betwixt obedience and merite, but that he wil make the worck of God's grace to abrogate God's grace? That cannot discerne betwixt the secret election of God and Christe's visible church? Betwixt the temporarie judgments of Christe's church according to the rule of God's word, and the final doome of God in his determinate councel? Thus not knowing what either God's covenant, Christe's church, the communion, or excommunion therof meaneth, this impious man upon these dotages [stupidities, follies], seeketh to convince us of his surmized heresies, because we blame and forsake these Babilonish confuse assemblies, where al sortes of prophane and wicked are gathered together without faith or order, bownde, fed, and suffred together in al impietie, mischief, and licentiousnes, without censure or controlement, unto whome he for the wage of Balaam is powred forth, and most sacrilegiously selleth them his pretended sacraments for their two pennie shot or offring.

He laboureth to defend this sacriledge and confusion by the examples of other churches under the law and under the gospel. He beginneth with the estate of the church under Moses, where the rebellious Israelites whose carkases fel in the wildernes, of whom the Lorde sware " that they should not see his rest; yet were not cast out of the assemblie nor separated, so longe as they lived, nor their seed rejected."[2] So that he stil beare in minde that he but beggeth the question so ofte as he compareth these confuse prophane assemblies (that were never rightly gathered unto nor established in the faith) unto true churches, unto this [90] place we answeare. That he most ignorantlie and boldlie affirmeth an un-

[1] *Ibid.*
[2] *Ibid.*, p. 60. See Numbers 14 : 26-33.

truth. We reade, Exodus 33, after the Israelites had made their calf and committed idolatrie, that Moses both did execution upon the chief idolators, and withdrewe his tent, and separated from the rest until they were reconciled unto the Lorde. Furder we reade, that upon publick notorious transgressions the Lorde executed publick judgments sondrie tymes, wherby the chief were taken away, the rest brought to repentance, Numbers 12 and 14 : 39 and 25 and 21 : 6, 7. We reade of separation from those of Corathe's [Korah's] conspiracie, etc., Numbers 16 : 21, 24, 26 verses. We reade also, Numbers 12, that Miriam was separated out of the hosts until she was healed. Likewise we reade of sondrie perticular judgments for perticular transgressions. As for breaking the Sabaoth, for blaspheming, etc., Numbers 15. Whereby his impudencie is convinced. But nowe if it were graunted him (than which nothing can be more untrue) that these multitudes of prophane rebells were not separated out of the hoste, yet except he can prove that they were received during these sinnes unto the tabernacle of the congregation (which he can never shew, because it were so directlie against those lawes prescribed unto and by Moses), it can help him nothing. The wicked may remaine in the common wealth, which yet ought to be caste out of the church. In that he alleadgeth the seed of the wicked were not rejected; we first answeare, that we find an outwarde repentance made by the offenders in the places above recited. Furder we find that circumcision ceased al the tyme they traveyled in the wildernes untill they came to Gilgal, forty yeares. Joshua 5. Wherfore this example nothing helpeth their wilful sacriledge in the Church of England.

As to the other tymes when idolatrie was publickly set up by the kinges of Juda; Ahas, Manasses, Amon, Jehoiachim, Zedeckiah,[1] we have alreadie proved that they were not in that estate the true visible church of God, and that those faithful amongst whom the Lord preserved his church, neither might, neither did, com-

Isa. 59
Ezek. 8

---

[1] Ahaz, Manasseh, Amon, Jehoiakim, and Zedekiah.

A Plaine Refutation

municate with them in their publick worship and _{Jer. 7} idolatrie. Which those places of Isay, Jeremias, and Ezechiel doe evidently prove both in manifesting the sinnes of those tymes, and taking awaye all vaine titles and pretextes; shewing that the name of temple, covenant, Jerusalem, etc., could no more avayle them, than the arck at Shilo and the like titles did them in the tyme of the judges. The prophet Jeremiah in his lamentations[1] doth no where justifie their publick estate so much as everie where lament the desolation of Sion, which name may much rather be understoode of the former prerogatives and dignity of that nation, place, and people, which were chosen and separated to the Lorde's service and worship, than of that most corrupt estate of that sinful generation. As to the tymes after their returne out of captivitie when they mixed themselves with the heathen and brake the Sabaoth, we reade they made notable repentance when they were admonished, Ezra 10, Nehemiah 9 and 13. So that these tymes verie evil fit Mr. Giffard.

[91] Furder if we come to the tyme that our Saviour was exhibited in the fleshe, we reade in the tyme of his birth of sundrie just and holie men, both priestes and others, and how al thinges were performed by them according to the lawe of the Lorde. But afterwardes when they would not be instructed nor reformed by our Saviour Christ, but with one consent despised, blasphemed, rejected, and persecuted him, and all that believed on him; then were they not the true church of God, but the persecuting and malignant synagogue; except Mr. Giffard hold not our Saviour Christ and his disciples the true church: or that there may be two true churches one opposite unto an other, ledd by two divers and contrary spirites: or that God may be divided from Christ: or the church in covenant with him without Christ. Also in that he affirmeth, that our Saviour Christ commanded his disciples to worship together with them in this estate, to heare the Scribes and Phara- _{Luke 1:6 and 2:25}

---

[1] The reference seems to be to the book of Jeremiah, where there are fourteen verses which speak of desolation. In the Lamentations of Jeremiah, there is only one reference (3 : 47) to desolation.

sies teach and expounde the lawe, although they taught corruptly and leavened the doctrines therof, though they were hypocrites, blinde guides, covetous, and ambitious, and verie reprobates, yea, though some of them were not of the tribe of Levi, only because they were ministers and sate in Moses' chayre. What execrable heresies and horrible blasphemies doth this wretched man runne into, whilest he seeketh to justifie their heynous sacriledge, open idolatrie, and confusion by our Saviour Christe's example ? Doth he not hereby make our Saviour Christ guiltie of the open breach of God's lawes, and the destruction of al the people ? Doth not God in as manie places as he commandeth to heare true prophets, forbid to heare false prophets, as he commandeth to obey his lawe and commandements, forbid all humane devises and traditions ? Is there not a prescript lawe, Deuteronomy 13, that they ought not to herken to the wordes of that prophet that teacheth other doctrine, and seeketh to seduce, though he had the power to do miracles and worke wonders ? Doth not Salomon by the Holie Ghost command all the children of the truth not to hearken to the instruction that causeth to erre from the wordes of knowledge, Proverbs 19:27? And againe in the first chapter of his Song, is not the church councelled by Christ himself not to staye in the steps of that flocke, but to feede her kiddes above the tentes of those shepheardes ?[1] How plentifull are all the prophets in this argument, Jeremie 23, Ezechiel 13, Zechariah 13. To which concorde all the doctrines of the New Testament, Mathew 7:15 and 15:14 and 16:6, John 10:5, Romans 16:17, Galatians 1:8, I Timothy 6:3, II John 10, II Peter 2. Was there not

Levit. 21

also expresse lawes that the priestes which drawe neare unto the Lorde should be holie, and not such open reprobates as he now acknowledgeth these to be ? And

Num. 3 and 18

also that the Lorde had only separated and chosen to himself the tribe of Levi to serve and administer before him in the tabernacle of the congregation, and that no stranger might presume into that office ? Yet is not

[1] Verse 8.

A Plaine Refutation

this blinde guide afraide to affirme, that the Pharasies not being of the tribe of Levi were ministers, and sate in the chaire of Moses, and therfore our Saviour commandeth his disciples to heare them, were they never so wicked [92] of life or corrupt teachers, Mathew 23. In which place our Saviour, having to deale with the persons of the corrupt teachers, first seketh to reserve the dignitie of his Father's lawe and ministrie; then sheweth these present teachers to be degenerate from both, being fallen into all maner of vice, pride, vayneglorie, hypocricie, sectes, schismes, calling them false teachers and corruptours of the lawe, blinde guides, such as shut up the kingdome of heaven before men, neither entring in themselves, nor suffring them that would; devowring widdowes' houses, cunning seducers, making their proselytes the children of hel like themselves; killers and murderers of the servants of God that are sent unto them; so that in conclusion he there leaveth sondrie woes, all the bloode of the righteous, and even the *Maranatha*[1] upon them.

Now, is it likely, or may it without blasphemie be thought, that our blessed Saviour Christ would commit his Father's lawe and ministrie unto these wretches, or the soules of his deare disciples to be instructed and kept by these murderous blinde guides? Yet these blasphemies doth this wicked man publish, his Ordinarie and all the cleargie of England allowe and suffer to passe in print. Againe, if the disciples in that place be commanded to heare the ministerie of the Pharasies, then are they there commanded to observe all the humane devices and traditions so contrarie to the lawe of God, which they most zealouslie taught and enjoyned, which our Saviour himself openly brake and rejected; and gave often warning unto his disciples of them, and

---

[1] The word "Maranatha" or "maran atha" is found in I Corinthians 16 : 22. Barrow uses the word in its later imprecatory sense, making it synonymous with "anathema." But the real meaning of the term "maranatha" may be, "Our Lord, come." Therefore, in using the term as a formula of excommunication, both Calvin and Barrow are exegetically in error. The revised edition of Liddell and Scott, *A Greek-English Lexicon*, has "maran atha," from a Syriac expression, with the meaning — the Lord is come.

such like false prophets, commanding them to take heede of them, teaching them howe to knowe them by their fruictes, Mathew 7 : 15, 16, willing them to let them alone as the blinde leaders of the blinde, using an argument of the inevitable peril, "if the blinde leade the blinde, both shall fal into the ditch," Mathew 15 : 12, 13, 14, chardging them to "beware of the leaven of the Pharasies," Mathew 16 : 6, which leaven, verse 12, they found to be the doctrine of the Pharasies. To these if sondrie other places of his conflictes with these Scribes and Pharasies be added, it will evidently appeare that he withdrewe his disciples from their doctrines, pronouncing everie where woes and judgmentes against them.

That he made also a separation and especiall choise of his disciples from the wicked people of the Jewes, evidently appeareth by the office and ministerie of John the Baptist, whom he sent as an heralde before him to prepare his waye, to proclaime his kingdome, to call the people to repentance, and to make readie a people to receive him, lest when he came he should smite the earth with cursing. Mightely did John refute all these vayne arguments and allegations that Giffard alleadgeth of the seede of Abraham, the outward covenant, nation, temple, etc. Shewing them that God was able of stones to raise up children unto Abraham; calling those boasting Pharasies the generation of vipers, shewing them that only those trees that bring forth good fruicte are the plantes that shall stand and growe in the Lorde's orchard, that the other shalbe hewn down and caste into the fire, and that the Lorde's axe is nowe laide to the roote: shewing them that the Messiah of [93] whom they boasted and whom they looked for, should come with his fanne in his hand to clense his barne floore, to preserve his wheat in his granarie, and to burne the chaffe with unquenchable fire, baptising none but such as confessed their sinnes. The same course toke our Saviour Christ, sending forth his disciples to preach the gospel of the kingdome, who received and baptized none but such as repented of their evill life, and gave obedience to their doctrine : these our Saviour acknowledged, received, taught, instructed, guided as his owne peculiar flocke. But al the other (as the sheepe of Zech. 11 distruction) he gave over to be spoyled and devoured of their owne rulers, and one of an other, to be guided by those wicked and idoll sheepheardes whose soule abhorred him, and his soule loathed them. Yea, how ful a separation there was betwixt these sheepheardes and these flockes, the hostilitie they shewed unto our Saviour and his disciples by excommunicating, persecuting, blaspheming him, and his rounde reproving them, everie where in the historie of his life doth appeare. Furder, that he communicated not with them in their feastes, offrings, and worship in this their sinne and obstinacie, appeareth as plentifully. He a longe season when the Jewes laid wayte to kill him refrayned Judea and Jerusalem. At other tymes when he came thither, it was not to keepe the feastes together with them, so much as to take occasion upon such conc[o]urse of people to instruct them, and to call them unto himself. He sometimes went not at all, sometimes went at the mid-feast. And when he was there he kept not the Paschal together with them before the temple according to the lawe, Deutronomie 12 : 5, Leviticus 17. But he kept it apart with his disciples in a private chamber. As when there was no publicke assemblies, as in Egipt, or when the temple was shut or polluted, and the worship corrupted, Exodus 12, II Chronicles 35. Yea, he kept it upon an other daye, namely, upon the fourteenth of the first moneth[1] according to the lawe, and

---

[1] The month of Abid. See Exodus 12 : 2 and 13 : 4. It is also called Nisan, a Babylonian equivalent. The Jewish Passover should have been observed on the fourteenth day of Nisan. See Exodus 12 : 18, Leviticus 23 : 5, and Numbers 28 : 16. The Festival of Unleavened Bread was appointed to begin on the fifteenth day of Nisan. See Leviticus 23 : 6 and Numbers 28 : 17. In Matthew 26 : 17 and Luke 22 : 1, 7, the two feasts seem to be regarded as one festival. There is a thorough investigation of this problem in Daniel A. Chwolson [Khvol'son], *Das letze Passamahl Christi und der Tag seines Todes* (Leipzig, 1908), pp. 36-43 ; Joachim Jeremias, *The Eucharistic Words of Jesus*, trans. Arnold Ehrhardt (Oxford: Basil Blackwell, 1955), with a selected bibliography (pp. 177-183). See also Roland H. Bainton, " Basilidian Chronology and New Testament Interpretation," *Journal of Biblical Literature*, XLII (1923), 81-134; Philip Schaff, *History of the Christian Church*, II (1887), 206-220, and III (1886), 386-409. A recent work is J. B. Segal, *The Hebrew Passover from the Earliest Times to 70 A.D.*

not upon that daye the Jewes kept theirs, which was a daye after, as appeareth evidently by the historie, Mathew 26. For the Jewes' solemne feast or cessation ought by the lawe to have bene upon the fifteenth day, the next day after the Paschal, upon which daye they crucified our Saviour, and kept their feasts upon the Sabaoth, deferring the Paschal by their tradition one daye longer than the lawe commanded: Leviticus 2:4, 5, 6 [23:4, 5, 6?]; Numbers 28:17, by all which reasons, circumstances, and places, it is evident that our Saviour and his disciples did not communicate with, but withdrewe from the Jewes and their worship in this their sinne and obstinacie.

By whose example this great clearke, Mr. Giffard, hath endevoured to confute the Brownistes of heresie, and to proove that the open wicked and prophane may be kept in the church and communicated with, and yet neither the church therefore cease to be a true church, nor the faithfull which together with these prophane joyne in the worship of God and the sacraments, be defiled therebie. [94]

Yet to make the matter more sure, he bringeth certaine churches planted by the apostles, as the church at Corinth, and the churches of Asia. In the church of Corinth were factions and schismes, corruption in the teachers, negligence in the governours, the incestuous person suffred, contentions among the people and that under heathen judges. They feasted in idoll temples, they prophaned the Supper of the Lorde, they abused spiritual giftes, some denied the resurrection of the deade; yet the Holie Ghoste vouchsaveth them the name of the church of God. Well, what of all this? Therfore the wicked prophane multitudes, which were never rightly gathered to the faith, may be received as members into the church. We see no such consequent. The church of Corinth was orderly gathered by the apostle unto the faith, none received but such as believed and made open profession of their faith and obedience, sainctes by calling. Agayne, the church of Corinth was rightly established into that order, and had such ministers, officers, and ordinances, as Christ

A Plaine Refutation

in his Testament had assigned and the apostle instituted: so hath not the Church of England, but popish and antichristian. Therfore no comparison thus far foorth betwixt the church of Corinth and the Church of England.

Neither can these faults wherein he compareth the Church of England to the church of Corinth, and wherein it is founde like unto, or rather far without all comparison to exceede them, make the Church of England the true church of God. What is it then this learned man would conclude from thence? That the open prophane and obstinate wicked may be retained in and by the church, wittingly and willingly after admonition, and yet that congregation not cease to be the church of Christ. This he striveth to prove. And therfore where it is alleadged that the church of Corinth repented at the Apostle his admonition, and is by the Apostle himself said to have shewed themselves pure in that busines, II Corinthians 7, he maketh unto this a double answeare. One, " that they were Gode's true church before they repented; " the other, that all did not shewe repentance, as appeareth,[1] II Corinthians 12 : 20, 21. To the first we answeare and never denied, that they being rightly gathered unto the fayth and orderly established in the faith (notwithstanding that grievous sinnes brake out amongst them), so long as they despised not admonition and refused not to repent, were to be still held and esteemed as the true church of Christ, who " if we confesse our sinnes is faithfull and juste to forgive us our sinnes, and to clense us from all iniquitie."[2] But as we have often said, this maketh against Mr. Giffard, because the Church of England was no such true church before that and wherein these faultes were and are committed. Unto his second allegation, that all shewed not repentance for the uncleannes, fornication, and wantonnes, which they had committed;[3] we acknowledge it as the Apostle recordeth it to be a great fault in the whole church, that they did

---

[1] *A Short Treatise*, p. 62.
[2] I John 1 : 9.
[3] *A Short Treatise*, p. 62. II Corinthians 12 : 21.

not more diligently search out the sinne, and speedely caste out the sinners that remayned impenitent. Yet was this [95] in the church but a fault of negligence, and not of anie obstinacie; they neither contemned admonition, neither spurned against their admonishers. Yet even this slacknes and negligence the Apostle thus sharplie and severely reproveth, threatning (if they amend not) to come with a rodde, and with the power of Christ against them. He neither justified nor flattered them in their sinnes, as this false prophet doth, who hath no better argumentes to pleade for or justifie this apostasie and obstinacie of the Church of England, than the greatest sinnes and odious faultes of other churches. But to such a height and measure is their wickednes encreased, as all the sinnes of all churches in all ages are too narrowe to cover the bedd of their fornications, etc.; neither can those fearful breaches and lamentable ruins in the churches of Asia heale the wounde of the Church of England. If God so threatned or menaced those churches to come and fight against them, to remove their candle-sticks, etc., what shalbe the judgmentes of the Church of England? What can she expect, whose sinnes so far exceede, which taketh boldnes to contynue in sinne, and pleade for the same from these examples which the Lord hath lefte as monumentes of terror to all posterities? Yet in all these desolations of these churches can there be no comparison betwixt these barbarous confuse assemblies, and those churches which somtymes were rightly gathered and established unto the faith, and into the order of Christ; and so all Mr. Giffard's labour and paynes herein is lost.

Neither will this conclusion followe, that because it ceaseth not to be a church by and by where the open wicked are not separated (because the church sometimes may fall into such sinnes of ignorance or of negligence), therefore the godly are not defiled which communicate with these open wicked in prayers, sacramentes, and other spirituall exercises.[1] Might he not

[1] *A Short Treatise*, p. 63.

A Plaine Refutation

aswel conclude, that because it ceaseth not to be a church hereupon, therfore it is no sinne? But if it be a sinne in the whole church, then is the whole church guiltie of and defiled with that sinne.

Nowe as Mr. Giffard laboureth to drawe this conclusion, so striveth he to prove this proposition, that the admission of the open wicked and impenitent to the table of the Lorde doth not defile either the sacrament or the faithfull receivers. Hereunto he hath gathered a fewe stale reasons.

1. As that the wickednes of the minister doth not defile the holy things of God: Judas, Ely his sonnes, the Scribes and Pharasies were wicked men, yet were the thinges they administred holie.[1]
2. Then that the godly communicant toucheth not the sinnes of others, but the holie thinges of God; because there cannot be a separation from the wicked in bodie or bodily thinges alwaies: but they which touche not their sinnes obey the commandement.[2] " Come out from amonge them, separate your selves, and touche none uncleane thinge."[3]
[3]. That the blame of receiving such wicked resteth only upon such as have the power of the discipline in their handes, and not upon private members which mourne and lament to see such fowle matters wincked at, which mourners are cleared.[4] Ezechiel 9.

[96] To discusse these pointes in perticular would make this discourse over long, brieflie therfore this we say. To the first, that difference must be put betwixt hypocrites (whose wickednes is onlie knowen unto the Lorde) and such wicked, whose sinne is knowen unto the church. The publicke ministerie of secret hypocrits that are rightly caled to a lawful office, and execute their office without fault or blame, is holie, blessed, and profitable to the whole church (which can but looke upon and

[1] *Ibid.*, p. 67.
[2] *Ibid.*, pp. 67-69.
[3] II Corinthians 6 : 17.
[4] *A Short Treatise*, p. 67.

judge the outwarde action and estate, and not the hearte and conscience of anie), yet this their ministerie is unavayleable to themselves, and maketh to their owne greater condemnation. But where the minister is detected of, and remayneth obstinate in any transgression, his ministration is not acceptable to the Lord, neither ought to be suffred or joyned unto of the church. The Lord will be sanctified of all that come neare unto him. Under the lawe he required an holie ministerie to serve in the prieste's office without outward mayne [mayme?] or bleamish, lest he defiled the holie thinges of the Lorde; the offringes of anie other were not acceptable to the Lorde. It is also written that the sacrifice of the wicked is an abhomination to the Lorde, as if they cut off a dogge's heade, or offred swyne's bloode. They have nought to doe to declare the Lord's ordinances that hate to be reformed, and caste his worde behinde them. The church ought not onlie to forbid such to administer, but to cast them out of the fellowship, which if the church neglect and refuse to doe, then are they guiltie of the open or wilful breach of God's holie ordinances in suffring his holie name and ministerie to be prophaned, yea, in joyning therunto and rejoycing therin. The examples by him alleaged no waye help him. Judas whilest he remayned with our Saviour was an hypocrite, his sinnes undiscovered, yea, uncommitted; so longe in that estate his publicke ministerie was lawful, holie and acceptable unto others. The ministerie of the sonnes of Eli (after their wickednes was publick) was abhominable unto God, to be detested of all the faithfull; yet was the sinne of the people verie great, who upon and for the sinnes of these wicked prestes abhorred the offringes of the Lorde, which were ever to be esteemed most holie, being lawfullie administred, otherwise they are not the offrings of the Lord. The people then (as nowe) grewe into atheisme and all impietie, abhorring all God's worship, and refusing to be at anie chardge, loving the creatures better than the Creator, by seing the great insolency and inreverence of the prestes. Touching the Scribes and Pharasies we have alreadie said enoughe.

A Plaine Refutation

To his other allegations, that the faithfull are not defiled by communicating with the open and obstinate wicked in the Supper of the Lorde and other spirituall exercises, because they touche not the sinne of the wicked but the holy thinges of God, etc.[1] Surelie this is verie odd divinitie, contrarie to al groundes of Scripture that we have read of. We had thought that all the communicantes at the Lorde's table had bene joyned and commingled together into one spirituall body, even [97] into Christ, as manie grapes are there bruzed [bruised, crushed] into one cup, manie graynes into one loafe. Furder we had thought that no obstinate offender whose sinne is publicklie knowen, might have beene admitted to that holie table without wilful sacriledge and high prophanation of those holie mysteries, both in all the communicantes and in the minister. We reade in the lawe plentifullie that the leprous or polluted person defiled whatsoever touched him, whether parson, vessel, holie or civile, etc., and that such person or vessel, etc., remayned unholie therebie, until they were clensed according to the lawe. The prophet Haggai confirmeth the same and saith, that whatsoever holie thing, bread, wyne, or oyle, a polluted person toucheth, it is made therebie uncleane. The Apostle also sheweth in expresse wordes, that as a little leaven leaveneth the whole lumpe, so one open unworthie received to the Supper of the Lorde maketh all the communicantes guiltie, and their rejoycing or feast not good before the Lord, likening the whole church to the lumpe, the wicked person and sinnes kept amongst them to the leaven, their rejoycing to the eating of the Paschal, etc. Which most direct place this ignorant sacrilegious priest would put away and falsifie by likening this rejoycing here spoken of to a glorying in the sinne of the incestuous, as though the Church of Corinth had ever bene so beastlie. And by endevouring to separate the elements of the breade and wine in this sacrament from their mystical sense, the communicantes that receive the same together, from their spirituall communion they

Marginal references: Lev. 11, 12, 13, 14, 15, 21, 22 chapters; Hag. 2:12, 13, 14, 15 verses; I Corinth. 5:6, 7, 8

[1] *Ibid.*, pp. 63, 67, 69.

have one with an another, the whole church from the preparation and care they ought to have both generally and perticularly in administring and receiving the sacraments.

And having thus royled [stirred up] the pure fountaynes, he confowndeth the sense and distinct doctrines of the Apostle, by bringing in certaine instances where the wife, servant, passenger, upon some especial dueties and necessities, may by occasion eate ordinarie bread with the excommunicate. Wherupon he concludeth, that the faithful also may upon necessitie (as if the church will not caste out the open wicked and impenitent) communicate with them in the supper of the Lorde. And if so be these faithfull mourne and are grieved for this wilful sacriledge of the minister and the rest of the church, then they touche not their sinne, but the holie thinges of God, and are cleare, Ezech[i]ell 9, because the separation from the wicked cannot alwaies be in bodie,[1] as in the cases by him alleadged of eating common breade with them. But let this caviller knowe that there is no comparison, much-lesse anie consequence, betwixt the eating common breade, and the eating of the Supper of the Lorde, with the open wicked and impenitent. There is no such spiritual mysterie, communion, or commixture in the first, as in the second. Common bread is not forbidden the wicked, but these holie pledges utterlie are, they ought not to be caste to hogges and dogges. Neither are we forbidden al civile conversation so absolutelie with them, as we are all spirituall communion. In the one we see [98] provision and exception made for duetie and necessitie. In the other there is no such duetie or necessitie, neither anie such provision and exception mentioned in the Scripture, until these priestes to defend their port-sale [public sale] and open sacriledge devised these shiftes. The Scripture utterlie forbiddeth and repulseth the open wicked and impenitent from this holie banquet by more than the Cherubims' shaking the edge of a sworde. So far are the open wicked from being ad-

[1] *Ibid.*, p. 69.

A Plaine Refutation

mitted to this feaste, as they are to be caste out, to be delivered unto Sathan, so far are they to bee kept from all communion with Christ and with his church. But none are to be admitted to this sacrament, but such as outwardly stand in the faith, and therby (unto the judgment of the church) have fellowship with Christ and his members. The verie action or symbole it self sheweth this communion with Christ, and one with an other, I Corinthians 10 : 16 and 12 : 13. No sophistrie can disjoyne the mysterie or signification from the outward elements and action, neither the com- I Cor. 11 munion from the participation in this action, so far as we may judge. As the unworthie receivers are guiltie of the bodie and bloode of the Lorde, so the church in admitting, administring unto, and communicating with them, is guiltie of most high sacriledge and prophanation of the holie thinges of God, especially they doing it wilfullie and wittinglie. Now then if they all communicate in this action, and this action delivered in this maner be sacriledge, how should they not all be guiltie. Can anie man here say that anie of the communicantes in this case toucheth not the sinne, but the holie thinges of God, when first in this action they are all spirituallie commingled and joyned together, then the verie action which they all doe (as they doe it) is most highe sacriledge, not a touching but an open (if not a wilfull) prophanation of the holie thinges of God ? Can the aucthoritie of the church excuse them before God ? Or wil it here excuse them to say they cannot doe with it, because the power of the discipline is not in their handes ?

We have above shewed that everie member hath interest in the power of the church ; and that the power to receive in and to caste out belongeth to the whole church, and not to the presbiterie or anie perticular member of the church onlie. Neither yet these matters referred to the wil or choise of the church, but rules prescribed them whom and when to receive, whom and when to caste out. As upon publick profession of faith and obedience with desire of joyning, the church cannot refuse but must receive, so upon publicke sinne and obstinacie joyned to the same, the church must then caste out, and cannot retaine without sinne. Which sinne becommeth so much the more heynous when they doe it wittinglie and willinglie, but most of al when obstinacie is added, when the church wil not be admonished, neither amend. Though every private member cannot excommunicate or reforme the publike actions of the church, which are donne contrarie to the worde, yet [99] everie private member may and ought to refraine such publick actions, as they see to be contrary to the worde, and to admonish the church, etc. And in so doing they depart not from the church, neither withdrawe from the communion, so much as preserve the church and the communion. Our fellowship must alwaies be in the faith, out of the faith we maie have no communion with man or angel in knowen sinne. They that depart from the faith depart from the church, and breake the communion. We may not followe a multitude or the mighty in evil. It behoveth everie Christian that receiveth to knowe what the action is he doeth, to knowe what he receiveth and howe he receiveth, to knowe by whom and with whom he receiveth.

We say not now (as some in the idlenes of their conceipt conjecture) that we ought to examine and judge everie one that communicateth. No, it sufficeth us if they by outward profession stand stil members, and remaine not convict and impenitent in anie open sinne knowen to them and to the congregation. They must knowe that the minister that delivereth is according to the outwarde rules (so far as they maie judge) a lawful minister of the gospel, and that the communicantes by outward profession (so far as they can judge) stand in the faith. Ells can they not discerne what the communion of the church or the action they doe, is. It wil not suffice or excuse them to saye they mourne and are grieved for the sinnes of the wicked with whom they communicate, and for the sinne of them that should put them from the sacrament, yea, caste them out of the church, and deliver them over unto Sathan, for the humbling their flesh, and the preservation of others

A Plaine Refutation

from the contagion of their sinne, yea, of the whole church from the wrath of God. How should they be said to mourne for the sinne of these wicked, with whom they feast and rejoyce in this heavenly banquet? From whence al sorrowe, and grief, and feare, and despaire or doubt are banished, al teares wiped from their eyes, they being by this symbole received to the communion of Christe's bodie and of al the joyes which he possesseth, hath prepared and reserved for al those for whom he died, etc., against whom layeth no accusation, no condemnation, no imputation of sinne. Againe, the mourners he speaketh of which were marked by the angel, Ezechiel 9, did not onlie mourne but crye out against the sinne of the tyme, yea, they refrayned the publick worship and the temple, which was so wholy polluted and prophaned, as is described in the eighth chapter of the same prophecie, the fierce wrath of God powred forth upon the whole citie and sanctuarie, [Ezechiel] chapter 9. The glorie of God utterlie departed from the temple and citie, chapter 11. But how should these that communicate and are commingled with these open wicked and unworthie, and participate and joyne in the sinne and sacriledge of the ministrie which they see and acknowledge, be said of those marked mourners which refrayned and cried out against the abhominations of the tyme? Or how should these eskap[e] the vengeance of the destroyer? The seale of God, wherwith al Christe's servants are marked and knowen, is, that they [100] " that name the name God depart from iniquitie." II Timothy 2:19, Revelation 14. They may not communicate with the sinnes of others, nor be drawn into the transgression of any of God's commaundementes by an angel from heaven. Galatians 1. No traditional writings of any man whatsoever, can defende these errors which tend to the open and wilful prophanation of the holy things of God, to the most dangerous contagion and infection of the whole church, and to the high provocation of God's wrath against them all.

What then hath this great clarck gayned by this traditional divinitie, save bewrayed his corrupt judgment and great ignorance of the truth of God, yea, even of those principal actions wherof he professeth himself a minister. What hath he obtayned or endevoured by al this discourse to proove, if not that all these prophane multitudes and rowtes of all sortes of wicked may be received into and nourished in the church as members, even with the holie pledges of Christ's bodie and bloode by this idolatrous and sacrilegious ministrie (for so having alreadie proved them we may pronownce them) made by themselves, labouring to justifie and approve their church, ministrie, and ministration in this estate, and most severely to censure, blaspheme, and condemne all such as by the word of God reprove them, and for their obstinacie forsake them for the same, thus opening a wide doore to all atheisme, wickednes, impietie, sacriledge, and bloodie persecution, as by his next argument which he bringeth for a conclusion of this discourse appeareth; which before we come unto, this for conclusion we insert and rest upon, that our Saviour Christ hath instituted, that of necessitie there must be at the celebration of his Last Supper a lawful minister of the gospel according to the rules of Christ's Testament to deliver, a faithful people by outward profession to receive, the pure elementes commanded, used, and that forme of administration which he and his Apostles prescribed; that except al these concur, there is not the sacrament rightly delivered, neither maie any Christian communicate where he seeth any of these rules broken.

So then if Mr. Giffard had thus approved his ministerie, people, ministration, by the rules of Christe's Testament, and by the evidence of God's worde, he should more have persuaded and convinced us, than by al this opprobrie [reproach], blasphemie, and rage which he breatheth forth out of the mouth of that dragon, al which nowe add unto his owne, and not unto our judgments that feare not the curse causeles;[1] neither yet the false prophets' threates, whose custome it is to curse them that God blesseth, and to blesse

Rev. 16:13
Prov. 26:2
Deut. 18:22
Pro. 24:24

---

[1] Proverbs 26 : 2.

them that God curseth, to justifie the wicked, and to condemne the just. Therfore shall he be an abhomination both to God and men, as the Lorde himself hath spoken.

As to his bloodie argument drawn from the execution of certaine of Saul his progenie, because Kinge Saul in his hypocritish and bloodie zeale murdered the Gibeonites, which were yeilded and made slaves unto them, contrarie to the will and commandement of God. Joshua 8, Deutronomie 20 : 10. Our innocencie shalbe our defence, and his refutation. If we have committed or when we shall commit or con-[101]sent unto any such crime, we refuse not the like judgment. In the meane time let all men judge with what equitie or conscience this Cainite could thus applie and enforce this example against us. ^{Josh. 4 I Kings 9:20, 21}

And for conclusion, let anie man by the worde of God judge, whether we that reproove these their confuse parish assemblies consisting of all sortes of ignorant, prophane, ungodlie people, worshipping God after an idolatrous maner, and living in all disorder and ungodlines, etc., or this mercenarie sacrilegious priest, that standeth a minister to all these wicked, delivering the sacraments unto them and blessing them with the peace of God, etc., doe destroy and murder their soules.[1] The Scripture is plentiful in this poinct.

THE THIRD PRINCIPAL TRANSGRESSION OR CAUSE OF OUR SEPARATION FROM THEIR ASSEMBLIES, IS:

For that they have a false antichristian ministrie imposed upon them, retained with them, and maintained by them.

As we have already shewed that the house of God which is his church cannot be built or consiste of any other

---

[1] In this summary Barrow repeats the oft mentioned causes of separation — false membership, false worship, and false ministry. False discipline is discussed in the "Fourth Principal Transgression."

than such chosen, pretious, living stones as God hath therunto caled, separated, appointed, namely, such faithfull obedient willing people as come under Christ's conduct, and willingly submit to his government, and cannot consiste of prophane, wicked, ungodly, headstrong, disobedient multitudes, whereon the whore is said to sit as upon manie waters; so in like maner can this house, this church, this people of Christ, be built into none other order, receive none other ministrie and ordinances, than Christ, the owner and builder of the house, hath instituted and prescribed in his last wil and Testament. We may boldly affirme and conclude that flocke which consisteth of all sortes of wilde and uncleane beastes, not to be the flocke or shepefolde of Christ, in asmuch as these in this estate cannot of us be judged to be the shepe of Christ. We may also by the same undoubted reason affirme, that they which stande hierdes [shepherds] to these wilde and uncleane beastes, cannot be saide the Lorde's shepeherds of his shepe and lambes. Of what sortes of people these their parish assemblies generally consiste, how they have bene gathered, builte, stand, and walke in the faith and order of Christ, by that which is above written may partly appeare, but much more shall to everie single eye and heart (wherein is any light) upon the furder examination of their present estate and life. That this aucthor and all the priestes of the tyme stand hierds, administring the sacraments, etc., to these prophane multitudes in this ignorance, confusion, and sinne, after that idolatrous superstitious maner above-said for their hire or tithes, cannot be denied. [102] What defence this champion hath made for their publique administration and worship, and how by never a worde of God he hath justified any one of those manifold enormities and idolatries reckoned up unto him. As also how he hath approved the gathering and present estate of their church, by the greatest apostasies, defections and sinnes of other churches in other ages, and with what blasphemous doctrines tending to all atheisme and impietie, we are content to refer to the judgment of the godly readers.

Hebr. 3
Ephes. 4

A Plaine Refutation

And now being come to the proofe and defence of his owne ministrie which he exerciseth, and of the whole ministrie of their church, instead of Christe's Testament he bringeth us forth a fable out of Aesope of the asse in the lyon's skinne,[1] and at the first entrance into this discourse in the first page within the space of twenty-four lynes[2] he convinceth us with these arguments. That we are prompt and plentiful in false accusations and hereticall opinions which must be admitted for reasons against their church, worship, ministrie. That we are desirous of glorie, presumptuous, bold, rash, ignorant, not to be encountred with great learning; [that] sophisters, nay, poore artificers and husbandmen, are the eavenest matches to dispute with us. We have put on the lion's skinne and imagine that all learned men tremble at us, but they have espied our long eares. That we impudently sclander and belye the learned, who disdaine to deale with mad frensie. That we are without all care what we speake, etc.[3]

Is it likely that this man hath either care or conscience what he saith, that through his whole booke from the first to the laste worde, thus rayleth, inveieth, accuseth, blasphemeth? Are these the sweetest waters in his fountaine, the best salt he can season us with? Or do the ministers of the Church of England thus use to improve, rebuke, exhort with al longe suffring and doctrine? Is this Mr. Giffard's countrie divinitie[4] or universitie learning, or courtly chaplen-like behaviour? He hath a president [precedent] what a

---

[1] Aesop's fable is available in *The Fables of Aesop as First Printed by William Caxton in 1484 with Those of Avian, Alfonso, and Poggio, Now Again Edited and Induced by Joseph Jacobs*, 2 volumes (London, 1889), II, 219-220. Gifford had written: "You have put on the lion's skinne, and so imagine, that all the learned doo tremble at yee, and the truth is, they have espied your long eares."

[2] Actually, twenty-eight lines, but there are thirty-four lines in all, on page 71. Perhaps 24 was a misprint for 34.

[3] *A Short Treatise*, p. 71.

[4] Gifford had written a book, *A Briefe Discourse of Certaine Points of the Religion, Which Is among the Common Sort of Christians, Which May Bee Termed the Countrie Divinitie* (1581). This religion, which Gifford seeks to refute, is one of indifferent secularism.

goodly viewe Mr. Some makes in his colours.[1] If he lighted into some men's handes that would take pleasure to laye open his shame, Mr. Some and his paynter might give place in al rayling and vituperie where this man should appeare.

But our purpose is not to meddle with his raylinges so much as his reasons, leaving him to answeare for the one, and endevouring ourselves to answeare the other. Yet this we saye, that if this be the course of those greate learned he speaketh of, we had much rather be matched with such poore artificers and husbandmen as feare God (whome he despiseth) than with these greate clarckes. Yea, we had much rather that they should in disdaine of our ignorance breake their promise in deniing and refusing to conferre with us, than in this maner grieve the spirite of God in us by such hellish writinges as this booke of Giffard, perverting the Scriptures, pleading for, defending, and justifiing the throne of iniquitie, together with all the enormities, idolatrie, and abhominations which flowe from the same, railing, blaspheming, and accusing the truth, and the poore persecuted professors therof, as he doth. Yet to satisfie the reader in this matter which he so confidently denieth, and urgeth us so vehemently to make some colourable shewe of, that if he had consulted with his learned [103] bretheren, the forewarde preachers, they would have councelled him rather to have used his discretion in the pulpit (where he might feigne what error he liste, and then with the same breath confute it in our names), then [than] by conference, but especially [they would have warned against] thus by writing to meddle with the defense of these defaults and exceptions taken against their church, ministrie, worship, etc., knowing

---

[1] This is a reference to the book, *Master Some Laid Open in His Coulers,* issued about 1589-1590. This work is listed in the *Short-Title Catalogue* (12342) as one by John Greenwood. This is clearly an error in ascription by Henry M. Dexter. The probable author is Job Throkmorton. Dr. Some had issued *A Godly Treatise* (37 pages) in May, 1588; about September, 1588, he issued *A Godly Treatise Whereunto One Proposition More Is Added* (200 pages). The new material was a refutation of John Penry, whom Throkmorton defended.

A Plaine Refutation

that the more they are discussed and raved in [opened up, pried into, examined], the more apparant and odious they wil appeare unto all men; especially when they are brought unto and examined by the light, which will foorth-with shew of what sorte they are. That these preachers had taken this course amongst themselves we knowe certainly by a letter that two of the cheif of them sent unto us, denying that conference which they had before promised, because we denyed their church and ministrie.[1] After that, two of them, being procured to our prison,[2] denyed to deale with us concerning those exceptions we made against their church and ministrie, alleadging that they were forbidden by their bretheren to deale with us in those matters. To be shorte, what ells can with any probabilitie be conjectured to be the hindrance of the first companie of preachers that at the first sent unto us to knowe the causes of our dislike, promising either to assent, or to shew unto us the causes whie they could not, that they upon the sight of that litle paper (wherin we set downe unto them the causes of our separation from these parish assemblies, as also what we purposed in our owne assemblies),[3] never as yet could be drawen to make any answeare in writing or conference, if not that they perceived that they were neither able to defend their estate, neither yet had faith to leave it for feare of persecution and danger. And whatsoever this bold champion may pretend, we cannot be persuaded that ever the forwarde sort of preachers (that sometime laboured reformation) ever gave their consentes to this

---

[1] A marginal printed note reads: "These two were Mr. Floud (William Fludd or Floyd) and Mr. Chatterton" (Laurence Chaderton?). See "The True Church and the False Church," in Leland H. Carlson, *The Writings of John Greenwood, 1587-1590*, pp. 97-102.

[2] A marginal printed note reads: "These two were Mr. (Humphrey) Fenne and Mr. (Stephen) Egerton."

[3] See "The True Church and the False Church," in Carlson, *The Writings of John Greenwood, 1587-1590*, pp. 97-102; also see "A Breefe Sum of Our Profession." This is printed in Carlson, *The Writings of Henry Barrow, 1587-1590*, pp. 81-85. See also "A Brief Summe of the Causes of Our Seperation, and of Our Purposes in Practise," *ibid.*, pp. 118-150.

blasphemous booke of his,[1] except also together with the aucthor therof, they have made shipwracke of faith and good conscience, and be wholy apostatate and fallen from that smale measure of grace and light they sometime made shew of. Neither shal those pontifical prelates his lordes, their horned cleargie, or Romish associates, the civilianes and canonistes,[2] to whom he is yeilded and joyned, give him any thanckes in the end for all the paynes he hath taken to defend their apostatical throne and procedings: which these his writings are so far from defending and justifying as they manifest unto al men that they cannot be defended or justified.

To our present purpose in this third principal transgression, it remayneth that we nowe proove this ministrie of the Church of England to be false and antichristian. Which that it may the sooner be donne, we are to enquire what kinde of ministrie Christ hath instituted and left unto his church? Of which sort if we finde not these, then may we with assurance from God's owne worde pronownce them false and antichristian. For as there is but one God, one Christ, one Spirite, so is there but one true church, ministrie, ministration. Christ being [104] ascended gave unto his church apostels, prophets, evangelistes, pastors, teachers, elders, deacons,

Eph. 4
Rom. 12
I Corinth. 3
Hebr. 2
II Pet. 1
II Timothy 3
Acts 20:33

widdowes. The three first, apos[t]les, prophets, evangelistes, being instituted but for a time, having finished their ministerie, ceased. For the foundation being now fullie laide, the worde perfectlie exhibited, the gospel throughlie and sufficientlie confirmed and ratified, the whole frame of the building set up and erect, and now a most perfect and absolute patterne left unto all churches, to what purpose should there nowe be Apostles to lay

---

[1] Barrow had challenged the Presbyterian leaders, but Gifford had entered the fray. The Separatists "take it greevously, and reprehend me [Gifford], as having intercepted this businesse, and taken it from the hands of the learned" (*A Short Treatise*, a 2).

[2] Archbishop John Whitgift, Bishop John Aylmer, Bishop Thomas Cooper, Dr. Edward Stanhope, Dr. Richard Cosin, Dr. William Gravett, Dr. Robert Some, and Dr. William Hutchinson are some of the persons whom Barrow has in mind.

A Plaine Refutation

the foundation, to give the worde againe, prophets to ratifie and confirme the same? Evangelistes to deliver and shew the Apostles' rules unto the Church? Besides that, the Lorde hath evidently shewed (by the ceasing of the extraordinarie calings and giftes unto these offices) that they are nowe perimplished [completed] and ceased, as might also by soundrie other testimonies and direct Scriptures be proved if it were needful in so playne a poynte.

Nowe then, there remaine by a perpetual decree these offices to the ministrie, governement, and service of the church: pastors, teachers, elders, deacons, relievers. Unto these distinct offices, are fit and distinct members dulie chosen and ordayned by each several congregation, upon due proofe according to the manifestation of the spirit in each member so elect, according unto the rules prescribed in Christe's Testament; in which offices is required of them that they diligently and faithfully administer, which whilest they doe, they are honored, obeyed, provided for of the flock with al reverence, care, and love. Nowe let the ministrie of the Church of England be compared unto and examined by these rules of Christe's Testament, in their office, entrance, administration, maintenance. In al which we before affirmed them to varie from the Testament of Christ, and to have no place or mention there, requiring of this aucthor some proofe of his ministrie in these pointes by the worde of God. In steade whereof wee have his bare affirmations to approve their ministrie, and his most bitter raylings to convince and perswade us after his accustomed maner, which evil either satisfie us, or approve themselves to all men's consciences such as they woulde be thought to be.

I Corinth. 12
Acts 14:23
I Timothy 3
Titus 3
I Corin. 4:2
I Thes. 5:12, 13
I Timo. 5:17

We had thought our demaunde herein had bene so just and reasonable, as no true church or minister could or would have denied. And wonder that in this flourishing estate of their church which over-floweth with so great learning, aboundeth with so manie writers, that not one of them should undertake to approve the ministrie of their church directlie, by the rules of God's word in their office, entrance, administration, maintenance. Wherbie they might justifie themselves of such crimes wherof they are chardged, convince their adversaries and al gaine-sayers, and put an end to these controversies and debates after a most christian and peaceable maner, much better beseeming the gospel and the ministers therof, than prisons, judgment seates, sclaunders, accusations, blasphemie, which hitherto have bene theire only argumentes. But now howsoever they be loth and will by no meanes be entreated or urged to this sober course and direct proof by writing, or unto anie christian free conference where these matters [105] might be discussed and decided by the worde of God peaceably, let us yet (seing occasion is here administred, and as our present purpose wil permit) shew some causes of our dislike whie we judge them not the true ministrie of the gospel, by shewing such apparant discrepance, as may declare unto all men that they were never cast in that moulde. And this but by a cursorie and briefe examination, leaving the more exact discussing and perfect demonstration of the forgerie, abuses, and enormities of this antichristian ministrie, to the furder diligence of others endued with greater measure of giftes and judgment.

We finde the permanent offices which Christ hath instituted for the ministrie of his church few in number, easilie recited, divided, and distinguished. The offices (as hath bene said) are these, of the pastor, teacher, elder, deacon, reliever. These are divided into overseers (whom wee call bishops, episcopai) and into deacons. The overseers are againe divided into teaching and governing elders: and into such elders as only by office attend unto governement. Of the first sort are the pastor and teacher. Of the second [are] such elders as are elect to the oversight and government of the churche. These offices are distinguished one from an other in their several functions by the apostle, Romans 12, and in sondrie other places of Scripture. The pastor to attend to exhortation. The teacher to doctrine. The elder to governement. The deacon to collect and distribute the benevolence and contribution of the

Phil. 1:1
Acts 20
Rom. 12:8
I Tim. 5:17

A Plaine Refutation

sainctes. The relievers to attend to the sicke, impotent, etc.¹   Acts 6 / I Timothy 5

But the offices of the ministerie of the Church of England wee finde so manie and intricate, as are harde to be recited, divided, or distinguished, and require greater skil than I have thereunto. Yet (so my simple conceipt prejudize not others of better judgment) for memorie sake and to avoide prolixitie, they may thus bee divided and recited at once. First, more generallie into [1] reigning [or] governing; 2. collegiate or idle;[2] and 3. servile or mercenary. The reigning or governing may be divided into 1. bishops, their assistants and substitutes. 2. certaine commissioners and 3. certaine delegate doctors etc. These bishops may be divided in 1. archbishops, 2. palatine bishops, and 3. ordinarie lord bishops. Nowe the arch-bishops may be divided againe into the 1. primate metropolitane of al England, and the 2. metropolitane of the north-partes. The raining [reigning] ministerie then of the Church of England, as I suppose under correction and better information, may be summed into these offices of archbishops, lord bishops, chauncelors, comissaries, arch deacons, high commissioners, civile doctors, with their courtes and attendants, advocates, proctors, registers, notaries, pursevants, somoners. The idle or collegiate ministrie, as I take it, are partlie in the colleges of the universities, as masters of houses, presidents, bowsers,[3] fellowes; or more generallie according to their degrees, doctors of divinity, bachelers of divinity, masters of arte, bachelors of arte, clarkes. These hitherto without certaine office, place, or chardge in the church. And partlie

---

[1] A simpler division would be that of elder (presbuteros) and deacon (diakonos). The former includes the preaching, teaching, and governing elder; the latter includes the deacon and deaconess, widow and reliever.

[2] Barrow's jibe at the idle collegiate ministry in the sixteenth century is reminiscent of Edward Gibbon's statement in his *Autobiography*, " Everyman's Library " (London, 1932), p. 40: " To the university of Oxford I acknowledge no obligation; and she will as cheerfully renounce me for a son, as I am willing to disclaim her for a mother. I spent fourteen months at Magdalen College; they proved the fourteen months the most idle and unprofitable of my whole life."

[3] Bursars, treasurers.

in their cathedral churches. As lord bishop, deane, sub-deane, prebendaries, cannons, peticannons, gospellers, pistelers, singing men, singing boyes, vergiers, sextines. The servile ministrie is divided into these several offices. Of parson, [106] vicare, curate, deacon, or half priest, church-warden, side-men, questmen, parish-clarck. But now to distinguish or describe all these offices according to their several orders and cannons, to shewe their original, processe, and contynuance in their several tymes, occasions, and circumstances, were not onlie a labor to me intricate and unachiveable, but to the reader tedious and unprofitable, as withdrawing them from the certaine and unvariable rules of God's worde, to the uncertaine and variable reportes of men.

Sufficeth it therefore that we finde not in al the booke of God anie such titles, names, dignities, offices, given or to be given to the ministrie of Christe's gospel; but we finde them rather those names of blasphemie written upon those heades of the beast. For if it be blasphemy for anie mortal man to receive, assume, or challenge those names, titles, dignities, or offices which are peculier and proper to Christe's sacred person alone, then are these chief ministers of the Church of England, these arch-bishops, and lord bishops, highlie guilty of blasphemie, that chalenge and assume unto themselves, some one of them to be the primate of al the bishops in England and Ireland, an other to be an arch-bishop, a metropolitane, others to be lord bishops, the leaste of these Anakims[1] to reigne over I knowe not how manie hundreth churches and bishops. That Christ is the onlie primate and arch-chiefe bishop and prince of pastors, the Apostle Peter giveth evident testimonie, I Epistle 5 *caput*, 4 verse, as also the Holie Ghost, Hebrews 13 : 20. That Christ is the onlie lorde-bishop every where appeareth in the Scriptures, and that al other christian bishops are but servants and fellowes, is fownd,

Rev. 13:1 and 17:3

---

[1] A people great and tall and many, sometimes accounted as giants. Joshua destroyed them with their cities in the hill country of Judah. See Joshua 11 : 21, 22; Deuteronomy 2 : 10, 11; 9 : 2.

A Plaine Refutation

John 13, Luke 22, Matthew 20, Mark 10, where Christ himself in expresse words with vehement chardges forbiddeth even his Apostles, I say not such blasphemous titles onlie, but all other wordlie titles of honor, all civile jurisdiction and secular power over others; and such arrogancie and presumption one over an other, as these pontificall prelates and lordlie bishops usurpe most directly wittingly and willingly against the commandment of Christ. Which they thinke to put away and abrogate by a second lawe of the prince and parlament, who (they saye) have cast these honors and titles upon them, and therfore neither can they refuse, neither may others blame them for this, except they shew themselves disobedient to her majestie and enemies to the state.

We wil answeare these their criminations of state matters at anie tyme before competent judges. In the meane while let them answere us in good conscience, whether they judge it lawful for princes to give, or at anie hand for themselves to receive such titles, dignities, etc. as Christ hath so expresly and often forbidden them. And whether their holy father the pope might not so justifie his exaltation and supremacie by the emperor's donation,[1] the confirmation of manie nations, states and councels through manie ages. If it be here alleadged that these titles, which we so stand upon, are but civile accomplements given them by the prince, but trifles, no matters of substance to prejudice their ministrie, they being preachers of the worde; yet must they acknowledge them inhibited verie severely and often by Christe's owne mouth. And therfore they by this [107] allegation laye the blame upon Christ that forbad them, and not upon us that hold them unlawful and intoller-

---

[1] Probably a reference to the Donation of Constantine, which is a forged document from about 752-850 A.D. Supposedly, Constantine " yielded his crown, and all his royal prerogatives in the city of Rome, and in Italy, and in western parts " to the Apostolic See — Pope Sylvester I (314-335). Lorenzo Valla proved the document a forgery in his book, *De falso credita et ementita Constantini donatione declamatio*, written in 1440, first printed in 1517. See Christopher B. Coleman, *The Treatise of Lorenzo Valla on the Donation of Constantine. Text and Translation into English* (New Haven, 1922).

able in the ministrie. Furder, if they be merely civile, let them then answere why they are and how they may be thus joyned to ecclesiastical persons and offices. And if they be such trifles, whie then [do] these grave fathers, these holy men, so violently contend with, and bloodely persecute their bretheren for them ? And this also let them consider and acknowledge, that these trifles, or titles they usurpe ar prooved most execrable blasphemies, names written upon the heades of the beast, and not upon the members or minister of Christ. And in their best allegation, that they are directly contrarie to the commaundement of Christ, who prohibiteth his ministers all such titles, howsoever Mr. Giffard alleadge against al conscience and truth that they exercise no lordship over the faith and consciences of men : the untruth wherof shal hereafter appeare ; yet this lordship they receive and exercise, even in the best consideration, is expresly contrarie to the commandement of Christ, and such as no true minister of the gospel, either wil or may receive, plead for, or justifie.

And now that we may come a litle nearer their ministrie, it would be knowen what office these lordlie prelates, these primates, metropolitanes, arch and lord bishops, exercise in the church of Christ. For everie minister must be of necessitie in som perticular office. I speake not nowe of the offices they beare in the commonwealth : as to be peres of the realme, lordes of the Parlament, judges of civile causes in courtes, justices of the peace, etc., but of their ecclesiastical offices, as being bishops, whither they have anie of the ordinarie and permanent offices, as pastors, teachers, elders ; or of those extraordinarie temporarie offices which are nowe ceased, of apostles, prophets, evangelistes. And sure by their magnificent stile, glorious titles, extraordinarie power, irregular aucthoritie, and inordinate rule, I should rather judge them of these extraordinarie offices, save that I finde those wholie nowe ceased, not expedient or to be loked for, and also that the estate, behavioure, and doings of these bishops accorde not to those offices.

First, Apostles these bishops are not, in that they have no immediate caling from God, or confirmed by God

A Plaine Refutation

unto that office. Neither doe they execute it as Christ's Apostles did, they goe not from place to place, from countrie to countrie, to preach the gospel, to call the people to the faith, to gather and plant churches; neither have they received such measure of grace, or can ratifie and approve by such evident testimonie, power, and wonders the doctrines, rules, and ordinances which they deliver unto and impose upon their churches, to be of God. Yet seing they lay a newe and an other foundation than the Apostles have laide, deliver other doctrines, rules, and ordinances, as appeareth by the whole ministrie, worship, ministration, ordinances, and governement of their church, than the Apostles have taught and left; seing also they usurpe a greater power and preeminence one over an other, one being a primate, an other an arch-bishop, etc., than the apostles did: Wee never reading of [108] anie primate, arch or lord apostle: (Peter's chayre now not standing in England). They had neede to confirme their offices, calings, doings, power by no lesse miracles and testimonies than the apostles did, if they wil have their ministrie and doings allowed and received; which if they should doe and draw fire from heaven, yet ought we to believe and hold fast that perfect foundation which Christe's apostles have layde, that authenticke al-sufficient worde which they have left as an absolute patterne for al actions of the church unto the world's end; and to hold them accursed, men or angels, that teach any thing besides that, or to varie from the same. Neither what signes or miracles soever they shall doe, may we hold them prophets, seing they persuade, yea, enforce to idolatrie and apostasie, as by their publick worship appeareth. And as to evangelistes, that office is too meane and base for these fellowes. The evangelistes take their caling, sending, and whole direction from the apostles, neither swarved from the same in any thing, but faithfully delivered to the churches those rules they received, and assisted them in the practize therof. These men in that they have no such caling to their office, neither doe so execute it, not caling the church unto or helping them in, but drawing them from

Mat. 28:19
Acts 1
John 20:21, 22
Math. 10
Acts 4:30
and 5:12
I Cor. 3:11
II Cor. 11:13

II Thes. 2:9, 10
Rev. 13:14

Gal. 1

Deut. 13

I Tim. 1:2
Tit. 1:4
I Cor. 4:17
Phil. 2:22
I Tim. 4:5

and utterly forbidding them the practize of those rules and ordinances the apostles left; teaching, bringing in, setting up, and inforcing their owne or other humane devises and ordinances upon the church in stead therof, and that in such high and waightie matters as the bringing in a new and strange ministrie, ministration, worship and governement. For all which causes and reasons and many other, which might be drawn from the rules of Christe's Testament, and their whole worke and doings which in nothing accordeth to the true patterne, we must hold them false apostles and prophets, counterfeite evangelistes, deceiptful worckmen and builders.

Neither yet, if we but as sleightly examine them by and compare them unto the rules of Christe's Testament, shall we finde them to execute any of the ordinarie permanent offices of the bishops belonging unto Christe's church, as the pastor's, teacher's, elder's office. A true christian pastor ought to be chosen of some one peculiar flocke, where after due proofe he is to be publickly ordeined and received. Unto which peculiar flocke he is bownde by covenant to administer and attend. Neither doth his pastorall dutie, ministrie, and chardge extend to more flockes or churches at one tyme than that one, wherof he is chosen pastor. Neither may a true pastor advance himself either in titles or power above or over other christian pastors, his fellowe bretheren; howsoever he have received a greater measure of giftes, by so much he ought to behave himself the more lowly, and to apply himself the more carefully and diligently to serve the Lord with the same, according to his pleasure and appoinctment within the limites of his caling; wherin if he behave himself faithfully he receiveth praise, if not, reproofe and censure of the whole flock accordingly. But now these arch and lord bishops neither have any certaine ministrie over or in any one peculiar flocke, neither [109] anie such choise, probation, ordination, by or in any one congregation, but are elected either by the convent and colledge of the deane and chapter, or ells by the prince, consecrate, invested, inthronised, or instawled,

<small>Acts 14:23
Tit. 1:5
Acts 20:21</small>

A Plaine Refutation

with I know not how manie popish rites, trincketes, ceremonies, belonging therunto, whose verie ordinarie attire is so popish, ridiculous, and fonde [foolish], as they passe not in the streates without the wonderment and skorne of young and olde.

Their ministerie also is not limited and tyed to one certaine office, or to one certaine flocke, but as they exercise sondrie offices, so doe they it over and in sondrie churches, preaching, administring the sacraments, where and when they list of their pontifical aucthoritie, and ceasing againe from preaching, etc., at their owne pleasures when and how longe they list. Againe, some of them exerciseth absolute aucthoritie over al, no, one of them put over many hundreth churches and ministers, over all causes and doctrines, to cite, sommon, suspend, silence, excommunicate, absolve, emprison, sequester, confiscate, at their pleasure whom and wherfore they list without accompt or controlement, no, not by the prince's royall writts and courtes to which every soule ought to be subject.[1] They impose upon all churches and ministers their owne devises for the publicke worship and administration, stinting and limiting the pastor what wordes to reade and say, what Scriptures to reade on this and that daye through the yeere. They limite and restraine the doctrine of the pastor from speaking against anie thing by publick aucthoritie commanded.[2] They determine and dispose of all the doctrines and causes of all churches at their owne will, no man so

---

[1] Archbishop Whitgift, supported by Queen Elizabeth, infused new strength into the spiritual courts, especially the Court of High Commission. But after Whitgift's death in 1604, Archbishop Bancroft encountered growing and effective opposition to the jurisdiction of the ecclesiastical courts. Despite the aid of Attorney-General Sir Henry Hobart, of Solicitor-General Sir Francis Bacon, and of King James, Archbishop Bancroft was unable to stop the issuance of writs of prohibition by the common law judges. The Lord Chief Justice, Sir Edward Coke, aided by the Puritans, the House of Commons, and the common law barristers and judges, effectively limited the jurisdiction of the Court of High Commission by issuance of writs which stopped, delayed, and transferred cases before the high commissioners. See Stuart Barton Babbage, *Puritanism and Richard Bancroft* (1962), chapters 8, 9.

[2] *Advertisements* (1584), A 3 recto and B 3 verso; *A Booke of Certaine Canons concernyng Some Parte of the Discipline of the Churche of England* (1571), pp. 22-24.

hardie to gainesay or to cal in question anie thing they affirme, or to denie anie thing they commande or forbid. There is nothing judged error in the Church of England, but what they judge to be error, be it never so grosse, popish, blasphemouse, nor anie thing compted truth which they pronounce error, be it never so holy, sounde, and warranted by God's word. The whole ministrie, doctrine, publick administration, causes and censures of the Church of England, are wholie in their handes, to commande, restraine, or execute upon al persons, and they themselves subject to no reproofe, liable to no censure. Now let any judge that knoweth what belongeth to the office, entrance, and administration of the pastor's office, whether these bishops possesse this office, be rightly caled and entered to the same, and faithfully administer and execute the same.

The teacher's office, for the reasons above-said, they cannot hold or chalendge, both in regarde of the fastuous [haughty] titles and inordinate power and aucthoritie which they usurpe and exercise over all the ministerie, even such as they cal pastors, and over all churches, causes, censures, etc., which can at no hand be joyned or agree unto the christian teacher's office. As also for that they, their ministrie, and office, belongeth not to any one peculiar congregation. The like reasons maie be drawn from their popish entrance and administration, seing they take upon them to deliver the sacraments, and attend not unto doctrine only or diligently, giving over and [110] ceasing to preach when they list, neither submit the doctrines they teach to the censure and tryal of other prophets by the Scriptures.[1]

---

[1] The trial by other prophets, called exercises, or prophesyings, were meetings of ministers held for edification, expounding of Scripture, and spiritual growth. They were favoured by Bishop Parkhurst of Norwich, Bishop Chaderton of Chester, Bishop Scambler of Peterborough, Bishop Grindal of London, and others. Originating in Northamptonshire and Norfolk, they spread to various counties, attracted laymen to the services, but sometimes became occasions for acrimonious debates on church government, episcopacy, and doctrine. Queen Elizabeth ordered Archbishop Grindal to suppress them, and Grindal defended them in his famous letter to the Queen, December 20, 1576. On May 8, 1577, the Queen issued her letter to the bishops, ordering them to suppress the prophesyings. See John Strype, *Edmund Grindal* (1821), pp. 260-2, 325-33, 558-76; *Annals*,

A Plaine Refutation

For al which reasons and sondrie other, they cannot be said to have or exercise the christian teacher's office.

Last of al, the office of governing elders they have not, for al the same reasons; in that they are not chosen of and belong not unto any perticular congregation to which they should be bownde by duetie to attend. Neither ever did we reade in al Christe's Testament of any bishops or ministers (setting aside those temporarie offices of apostles, prophets, evangelists) that were chosen, did attend, or minister unto divers or more than one congregation or office at one time. Certaine rules being there given for their election, ordination, and administration of and in one congregation, with manifold admonitions and exhortations to sture [stir] them up unto diligence, labour, and watchfulnes in that office and place they are caled unto, as a worcke enough for him that thinketh himself most able to dischardge it. And sure most monstruous and impossible it were for one man faithfully to attend divers congregations, except they can also shew that one sheepheard at one and the same time can diligently feed and guide two or many flockes far distant in place, or that one candle may be put into two candlesticks, and give light unto two several houses far distant asunder at one and the same instant. If the one be impossible, so is the other. Yet stand these men bishops or overseers not only to manie churches, each one of them, but their primate giveth, or rather selleth, licences to other inferior priestes, some one of them to stand a minister to two, yea, peradventure to three several flockes. This is an usual matter and passeth by way of statute law amongst the chapleins and doctors of the Church of England, who may have and be non resident, some of them from two, some from three, congregations or bene-

Vol. II, Part I (1824), pp. 133-140, 325-6, 472-481; *Annals*, Vol. II, Part II (1824), pp. 113-115, 494-5, 544-49, 612-13; *Annals*, Vol. III, Part I (1824), pp. 476-80; *Matthew Parker*, II (1821), pp. 358-62; *John Whitgift*, I (1822), pp. 163-4. See also Patrick Collinson, "The Puritan Classical Movement in the Reign of Elizabeth I," pp. 175-214 (London University Thesis, 1957), and Edward Cardwell, *Documentary Annals of the Reformed Church of England*, I, 367-69, 373-80.

fices, especially all his gracelesse chaplaines,¹ by a singular prerogative.

But to retourne againe to our purpose, these arch and lord bishops cannot be said to have this office of governing elders, for that they professe to be ministers of the worde and sacramentes, which duetie belongeth to the pastor's office. And because they exercise absolute power over pastors, churches, and causes, to depose, excommunicate, absolve, and determine in their owne sole name and power, which no true elder, minister, or member of Christ may do.²

Reasons also might be drawen from their sitting, chandging, aspiring to the richer and higher roomes. From their princely lordly state, pompe, trayne, revenues, pallaces wherin they live in all worldly excesse, pleasure, idlenes, to which thinges whilest they attend, it is impossible they should faithfully execute and dischardge any ministrie in the church. From the apparant and odious sinnes of their persons and lives, that appeare and breake out in their conversation, which is most unchristian, fleshly, and unholy. As coveteousnes, oppression, extortion, open wrong doing, usurie, ambition, pride, idlenes, lovers of pleasure, such as cannot governe their wives,³ children, and families, in the feare of God, sobrietie, or common honestie, but nourish and bring them up in pride, vanitie, [111] idlenes, superfluitie, voluptuousnes, gaming, chambering, and wantonnes, yea, peradventure in unchastity, and that not unknowen to themselves, who also themselves are not all of them of the most chaste and temperate life, some of them being given to wyne, strikers, sorcerers, blasphemers, skorners, and deriders of the most holie exercise of the preaching of God's worde, causing their counterfeight and natural fooles openly in their owne

I Tim. 3
Titus 1

---

¹ Chaplains of His Grace, Archbishop Whitgift.
² For a defence of the bishops, see the works of Thomas Bilson, John Bridges, Thomas Cooper, Richard Hooker, Thomas Rogers, and Matthew Sutcliffe.
³ Possibly a reference to Thomas Cooper, Bishop of Winchester, whose wife was ungovernable. She is held up to derision by Martin Marprelate in *Hay Any Work For Cooper*, p. 37. See William Pierce, *The Marprelate Tracts, 1588, 1589*, pp. 234, 235, 268.

A Plaine Refutation

house at the time of their solemne idolatrous feastes to make a sermon of ribaudrie or follie in the most high despight of God, and of his blessed ordinance. Not here to perticulate the sondrie heresies contrarie to the truth and blasphemies of the truth holden amongst them; the least of which faultes publickly knowen, are enough to disable the best of them from exercising any publicke ministrie to the Lorde in his church, if we may believe the Apostle.[1]

To conclude, this one reason (if there were no more) might shew and prove them to be no christian bishopps, in that they exercise some civile office or offices together with this their pretended ministrie. Which is not only expresly forbidden and utterly unlawful by the worde of God, but also impossible for any man to performe both, or either of both faythfully whilest he keepeth both. God himself hath made two distinct and several offices, and appointed unto them two distinct and several persons for ministers; it being no more lawfull for a bishop to execute the civile magistrate's office, than for the civile magistrate to administer the sacraments. What monstrous parsons then are they which thus confounde and commingle in their owne persons these two divers and distinct offices and powers.[2] Might not they that assume both the swordes into their handes, carry them acrosse also in their cote armour [coat of arms, heraldic insignia], aswell as their holie father the pope? What a monstrous confusion and perturbation make they both in church and commonwealth herebie? Disturbing the holy order that God himself hath set for the governement both of the church and common wealth in this worlde, removing, yea, utterly breaking downe therbie all the limites and bowndes which God hath set and established for all estates, degrees, offices, caleinges, actions, so that no man by this meanes either knoweth his duetie, or orderly walketh within the bowndes of

Math. 20:25, 26
Luke 12:14

---

[1] See William Pierce, *An Historical Introduction to the Marprelate Tracts,* pp. 99-134. See also Francis O. White, *Lives of the Elizabethan Bishops of the Anglican Church* (1898), *passim.*

[2] For a detailed study, see William P. M. Kennedy, *Elizabethan Episcopal Administration,* 3 vols. (1924), "Alcuin Club Collections," Nos. 25-27.

his calling, wherbie it is come to passe that the whole land over-floweth with all impietie, violence, crueltie, and iniquitie, as in the dayes of Noe [Noah].

Thus by al these reasons have we proved, and al that have not utterly made shipwrack of faith and good conscience, or that stand not vowed bond servantes to their apostaticall throne, must confesse, that these arch and lord bishops are no true christian bishops according to the gospel of Christ, neither have or exercise any lawful office or ministri of or in the church of Christ. If then they be not members of that body belonging to that heade Christ Jesus, it must needes followe that they, their offices, and ministrie, are false and antichristian, belonging to an other head, an other bodie, even antichrist, and that whoore, the false church [112] his spouse. If their inordinate power and irregular ministrie be found contrarie to al the rules and ordinances of Christe's Testament, then can it not be of God, belong unto, or [be] used in Christe's church, or be blessed to the governement or salvation of his people. Then must it needes be the power and throne of Sathan given to the beast, accursed, given to seduce, and to drawe all the children of wrath to distruction. Neither shal Mr. Giffard or all the false prophets belonging to their throne, be able to tourne away or withstand those judgments and plagues which are powred out of the Lorde's viall upon the throne of the beaste, or with their softe tongues to licke whole the woundes of the beast, that are given with that two-edged sworde that procedeth out of Christe's mouth. It shal not help them though they raile and blaspheme and gnawe their tongues for grief. For their kingdom shal wax darke, and Antichrist shal consume and be abolished as he is

II Thes. 2:8 reveiled [revealed], even by the same light; the Lord himself hath spoken it.

How weake nowe and sclender are Mr. Giffard's defences for these his lordes the bishops. That the bishops have not their caling, consecration, or power from the pope, but from their church. That they have by oath renownced the pope's usurped power and tyrannie. That they do not maintaine or defend the

A Plaine Refutation

religion and lawes of Antichrist, but professe and advance the gospel of Christ, and by the lively word cut downe all idolatrie, heresies, abhominations. That they usurpe not a lordship over the faith and consciences of men, but their peculiar power is onlie in the administration of external discipline. Therfore we with manifest and wicked sclander call the bishops antichristian.[1] If you demande the proofe of al this, we refer you to Mr. Giffard's bare affirmation without anie one reason in his learned answeare to the Brownistes,[2] page 75. If he were himself sometime of an other minde,[3] you must thinke it was before he had so neere friendship with, or was imployed in such trustie services by, his Lord of London [Bishop Aylmer]. Who, as also his lord's grace, must not be driven to prove everie thing they affirme, that were enough to put young divines unto, their pontifical mouth is sufficient warrant to all the churches in England. Yet I would of their curtesie they would give us their schismatiks that cannot be so satisfied, leave to doubt (though we wil not contend) whether their caling, consecration, and this their power first came not from the pope.

For albeit we have heard that the offices of provincial bishops, arch bishops, metropolitanes where [were] almost [completed, existed virtually] when this general defection from the gospel so much foretold of began to

---

[1] *A Short Treatise*, p. 75.
[2] It is interesting to see this phrase " answeare to the Brownistes," which is the running title throughout *A Short Treatise*. In the *Stationers' Register* for May 4, 1590, there is entered a work, entitled *An Aunswere to the Brownenistes*. The editors of the *Short-Title Catalogue* have equated this with Gifford's *A Plaine Declaration That Our Brownists Be Full Donatists*. This is a mistake, because the latter book is a reply to Greenwood's *An Answere to George Gifford's Pretended Defense of Read Praiers*, which had been published about mid-summer, 1590. Therefore, *A Plaine Declaration* could not have been published in May, 1590. It is much more likely that *A Plaine Declaration* is the book entered February 25, 1590-1, under the title *An Aunswere to Certen of Master Barrowe's Ascertions and His Adherentes*. A possible objection to this suggestion is that the *Stationers' Register* lists John Wolf as the printer, whereas the *Short-Title Catalogue* lists [T. Orwin ?] f. [for] T. Cooke.
[3] Gifford had been a person of Presbyterian views in the 1580's, and had participated in the Essex classis movement. He had also been suspended from his ministry in Maldon, Essex, by John Aylmer, Bishop of London.

breake out and appeare, longe before the pope obtayned his supremacie over all other churches and ministers; yet might it be that this maner of their caling, solemne consecration, and lardge irregular power of his lord's grace and lord bishops sprong from their unholie father the pope. Who when he was inthronized by Sathan, had received the dragon's high commission, to be his vicare general in earth, could not of his fatherhoode but provide for these his natural children, and bestowe them in his garrison cities, as his tetrarches, lieutenants and tribunes, with magnificent titles, priviledges, power, and authoritie to rule in his name and absence, even as his owne engraven image over all realmes, countries, and territories within their father's dominions. For [113] (as we have also crediblie hearde) there was never a lord arch-bishop or lord bishop with such titles, priviledges, power hearde of before the pope created them. Notwithstanding, because wee have these thinges but bie [by] hearesay, and would be lothe to affirme of things so unsure, we wil content our selves to have proved and shewed the arch lord bishops to be no true ministers of the gospel and church of Christ, and therfore of themselves antichristian, from whom, or howsoever they rise, it skilleth us not [it mattereth not, it is not important]. Neither shall it availe them though they have broken their faith and schismed from the pope, cast off his yoke, renownced his usurped power and tyrannie, when they themselves are founde to usurpe, retaine, and exercise, if not the same, yet as antichristian and enormous a power as the pope, retayning the same courts, officers, cannons, constitutions, privileges, over all churches, ministers, causes, doctrines, censures, they themselves not being subject to the censure of anie church, exercising their aucthoritie and commandementes contrarie unto and above all lawes both of God and of their prince; whose royal courts and writts are not of power to baile anie one committed by the leaste of their hierarchie, assuming unto themselves both the swordes, exercising together and at once both civile and ecclesiasticall offices, etc.

How well they advance the gospel of Christ, that

A Plaine Refutation

blaspheme the same, and pronounce the rules, ordinances, and ministrie therof intollerable, and persecute all such as either speake against them, or for it, let the tyrannous havocke they make in the common wealth of poore Christians in the prisons of the land, shewe.[1] How wel by the livelie worde they cut downe al idolatrie, heresies, and popish abhominations, let the service-booke and publicke worship of their churche, shewe. Which, whilest with a stronge hande they obtrude upon everie conscience, as also impose upon the church, is not this to tyrannize and exercise a lordship over the faith and conscience? Or (to speake as he doth) is this nothing but to execute the external discipline, to make and impose a newe leitourgie for the whole administration of the church? Or is it likelie that this marcked minister of Antichrist knewe what the outward government of Christ in his church meaneth, that saith it concerneth not the conscience? Is there anie more dreadful or reverend action on earth amongst men, than the judgmentes of Christ in his church, which are al most holie and true? Or doe not these concerne the conscience? Doth not everie action of which there are such certaine lawes set by Christ himself, nearlie concerne the conscience to doe it according to the same? When the least abuse, neglect, or swarving from the rule even in the least circumstance that is enjoyned in the least censure doth so deface the action, is so offensive and prejudicial, do not those actions which are donne for the salvation of soules, that are saide to binde in heaven, not concerne the conscience? Or doe not those rules which are given for the direction and preservation of the publick communion of the whole church, and private [114] conversation of everie member therof (without the

Math. 18
I Corinth. 5

---

[1] In 1590 there were fifty-nine Separatists in the various jails of the London area, and ten more had died in prison. In his letter to Mr. Fisher, in December, 1590, Barrow mentioned that more than eighty had been committed (Lansdowne MSS. 65, f. 182). See Carlson, *The Writings of Henry Barrow, 1587-1590*, p. 253. For the names of the prisoners, see Carlson, *The Writings of John Greenwood, 1587-1590*, pp. 285-88, 305-344. See also Albert Peel, *The Noble Army of Congregational Martyrs*, pp. 17, 18, 23-48.

Henry Barrow

observation of which rules there can be no order, no dutie either publick or private, no holie walking in anie caling kept) concerne the conscience? Except Mr. Giffard can imagine such a congregation and such members therof, as either never sinne, and so need no watching over, admonition, reproof, or ells such a church and members therof as make no conscience of anie thing, as when they sinne will not amend, wil not heare admonition, or suffer reproof, which is the meanes given of God to bring them to amendement. Yet Mr. Giffard maketh this holie outward government of Christ over and in his church not to concerne the conscience;[1] the miserable divines of this age, not to be of necessitie to the being and preservation of a church; the blasphemous bishops of this land, not to be a thing tollerable, with manie other reprochfull blasphemies of the same, which are not of anie Christian almost to be hearde or repeated, much lesse pronounced and defended.

Math 21
Luke 19:14

These husbandmen are they that caste the sonne and heyre out of the vineyarde, that wil not have him reigne over them, but take the regiment into their owne hands, devising and erecting a newe forme of governement unto the church, as these their popish courtes, cannons, customes, officers, declare, and persecuting with al hostility and tyranny all such as pleade for Christe's governement, and wil not subject their bodies and soules unto their antichristian yoke. But yet for all this they exercise no lordship over the faith and conscience, though they usurpe, exercise, and impose this strange ministrie, ministration, and governement in and over the church. All this, saith Mr. Giffard, is but the administration of

---

[1] For material on the general subject of conscience, see William Perkins, *The Whole Treatise of the Cases of Conscience* (1606); Richard Bernard, *Christian See to Thy Conscience, or a Treatise of the Nature, the Kinds and Manifold Differences of Conscience* (1631); John Cotton, *The Controversie concerning Liberty of Conscience in Matters of Religion* (1646); see also George L. Mosse, *The Holy Pretence* (1957); Wallace St. John, *The Contest for Liberty of Conscience in England* (1900); Edward B. Underhill, *Sruggles and Triumphs of Religious Liberty. An Historical Survey of Controversies Pertaining to the Rights of Conscience* (1858); Joseph Lecler, *Toleration and the Reformation*, 2 vols. (1960); W. K. Jordan, *The Development of Religious Toleration in England*, 4 vols. (1932-1940).

A Plaine Refutation

externall discipline, and concerneth not the conscience (especiallie if it be seared with a whote iron, as Mr. Giffard is).[1] Wherfore we doe impudentlie and wickedlie sclander when wee therfore conclude that the bishops be antichristian, and whosoever is ordayned by them hath his ministrie from Antichrist and from the devil.

What kinde of ministrie your lord bishops exercise, and aucthoritie they usurpe, by that which is alreadie written, the reader may judge, or at leaste hath a direct way shewed furder to examine. What kinde of rule they keepe or (as you call it) discipline they execute, remaineth to be tryed in the fourth principal transgression.[2] Where if you make not a better defence for it than you have donne for their ministrie and ministration,[3] they are all like to prove (as wee have affirmed them) strange, false, forged, antichristian, such as belong not unto and cannot be exercised in anie christian church; and then let Mr. Giffard see whether that grievous conclusion will follow and fal upon the men upon whom the marcke of the beast is fownde, that ministrie which is ordayned by, proceded from, and standeth under the throne of these antichristian bishops. In the meane while let us in a verie few wordes consider of the rest of the ministerie in the Church of England in their order. [115]

We would gladly learne of him what office in the church of God [the] chancelors and commissaries may be said to exercise, for we confesse that in Christe's Testament we never read of their names or offices; they are strangers there, and we in all the worlde knowe not from whence they came or who brought them into the church, if not their father the pope, or durste there retaine them, but these his children and successors the

---

[1] *A Short Treatise*, p. 75. I Timothy 4 : 2.
[2] See *infra*, p. [158], pp. 285-331.
[3] The third principal transgression pertains to the false ministry, pp. [101-158]; the first principal transgression pertains to false worship and ministration, pp. [25-50]; see *supra*, pp. 60-102 and *infra*, pp. 183-285.

bishopps.¹ A lardge power they have and exercise over all parrish churches their ministers and members, to keepe a judiciall courte, to cite, convent [convene or summon], trie, punish by mulct [fine], judge, imprison, absolve, purge, not only for ecclesiasticall causes, as the neglect of their ceremonies and trinckets, and for not duelie reading and observing their injunctions and service-booke, but also for civile causes, yea, criminatory and judicial causes, such as by the lawe of God deserve death, and only belong to the prince's royall aucthoritie, to whom therfore God hath committed his sworde. Whose judgment seate and aucthoritie for anie private person to usurpe, is judged rebellion both by the lawe of God and of his land. For all that take the sworde shall dye in the sworde, Mathew 26 : 52. Againe, these chauncelors and commissaries are civilians (laye men as they cal them) and not priestes, therfore we mervaile how they came to exercise such an high ministrie over and in the Church.²

The same we say of their other delegate civile doctors of their courts and trayne of advocates, proctors, registers, etc.³ We finde in the Testament of Christ no mention, in the church of Christ no use, of such offices, officers, courtes, to decide their controversies, to execute their censures and judgments. These handle both ecclesiastical and civile causes mixtlie, after a most

---

¹ There are scattered references to chancellors and commissaries in W. H. Frere and W. M. Kennedy, *Visitation Articles and Injunctions of the Period of the Reformation*, 3 vols. (London, 1910). See II, 103, 133, 134, 356, 362, 404-408; III, 53, 138, 199, 207, 233, 234, 268-272, 280, 298, 319, 334, 336, 384. See also W. P. M. Kennedy, *Elizabethan Episcopal Administration*, 3 vols., *passim*; Irene Josephine Churchill, *Canterbury Administration*, 2 vols. These two volumes are especially helpful for the medieval period, but see volume I, 486-488, 573-615.
² Barrow is probably referring to Edward Stanhope, chancellor of the diocese of London. Dr. William Bingham was an Official and John Walker was Archdeacon of Essex. Dr. William Aubrey and Dr. William Lewin were civilians.
³ A delegate was a commissioner and a layman member of the Court of Delegates, which served as a court of appeal from ecclesiastical courts. Advocates and proctors were lawyers or counsel, either barristers or serjeants, who handled cases involving civil or canon law. Charles Dickens described a proctor as " a sort of monkish attorney." A register was a registrer, or registrar, an official recorder.

A Plaine Refutation

corrupt and litigious maner, amongst whom al things are venal in their courtes, etc., wherof in due place; sufficeth it here to finde them in name, office, and use counterfeit, forged, false, without mention or warrant in God's worde, such as not Christ but antichrist devised and brought in.

As to the persons in their High Commission, they are of two sortes, chieflie ecclesiastical, and partlie (for countenance and fashion sake) civile;[1] of the ecclesiastical we have above entreated. Neither finde we that anie civile person may exercise anie ecclesiastical office or function: as to over-see so manie churches, to decide and determine ecclesiastical causes, or to execute the censures of the church, as by way of office or by vertue of anie humane commission, especially after that ungodlie maner, which is in al things so contrarie to the order Christ hath instituted, so contrary to the faith, power and libertie of Christe's church, as were not hard to shewe if we should examine their procedings by the rules of God's worde. And great ruth [pity] it is that so noble and honorable personages should be so highly abused by these wicked bishops. The Lorde in mercie shew them their deceipts, the error and daunger of their wayes.

Yet of this governing ministrie remayneth the arch head deacon of the Church of England to be considered of, who is no smale officer of this [116] church, having and keeping his solemne judiciall court, synode, and procedings in such ecclesiastical causes as fal within his consideration, with absolute power in his owne name also to cite, sommon, judge, and punish all such parish churches with their parsons and ministers as fal within his limites. To impose taskes upon pastors, what Scriptures to reade privately everie daye, what to conne by

---

[1] See Roland G. Usher, *The Rise and Fall of the High Commission* (Oxford, 1913). Of the civil members of the Court, we may mention Dr. William Aubrey, John Clark, Richard Cosin, Dr. Valentine Dale, William Fleetwood, Dr. William Lewin, Edward Stanhope, and Sir Owen Hopton. For the Court of High Commission at York, see Ronald A. Marchant, *The Puritans and the Church Courts in the Diocese of York, 1560-1642* (1960), pp. ix-xii, 1-10.

heart, and to take accompt of them at his synodes accordingly. This arch-deacon also (if such be his learning that he can) may administer the worde and sacramentes, and have a benefice or two for neede. Howsoever, he may pleade and boaste of his antiquitie aswel as the arch-bishop,[1] and of the great cause of his erection and necessarie use of his office, etc. Yet seing we finde no mention of his name, or use of his office, in all the Testament of Christ, seing we find there no such heade arch-deacons with such stately courts and absolute jurisdiction, and that not over many deacons but manie of their pastors, yea, manie whole churches, we must, or rather the Lorde hath given the same sentence of them, that is given of their fellowes above-said, that they are not the ordinance or ministrie of Christ, but of Antichrist, even the heades and limbes of that beaste, that wilbe held within no limites or boundes, in no order or callings, but breake, corrupt, and confounde all lawes, boundes, order, and offices as they luste. Christ himself is the only heade of all his ministers, whether pastors, teachers, deacons, etc., and they againe his members of their part. The christian deacon is to attend to the faithful collection and distribution of the benevolence of the sainctes, and not to such court-keeping over the church, ministrie, and sainctes. He is to attend in his function to that peculiar flocke wherof he is chosen a deacon, and not in this maner to intrude and incroach upon manie churches. A christian deacon is to kepe himself within the boundes of his owne office in sobrietie, and not to intermeddle with the pastor's office also, with the ministration of the worde and sacraments; yea, [he

Collos. 1:18
I Cor. 12:27
Acts 6
Rom. 12:8
I Tim. 3

---

[1] John Molyns, or Mullins, was archdeacon of London from 1559 to 1591. He was born about 1523, was about sixty-seven years old in 1590, and therefore was about eight or ten years older than Archbishop Whitgift. He died in June, 1591.

The reference to "his antiquitie" is interesting. When Barrow was examined on November 19, 1587, he said that he knew John Whitgift at Cambridge University. The Archbishop replied that he was there before Barrow was born. "Then he entred into discourse of his antiquititie" [sic]. See "Barrow's First Examination, November 19, 1587," in Carlson, *The Writings of Henry Barrow, 1587-1590*, p. 96.

is not] to exalt himself and usurpe power and jurisdiction over his superiors, not only over many pastors, but over manie whole churches.[1]

Thus have we taken a superficiall veiwe [sic], or rather as it were a sodaine blush of the reigning ministerie of the Church of England, leaving the furder investigation and demonstration of the manifold deformities therof to their furder diligence, to whom God hath given greater knowledge and opportunitie, leaving place also unto Mr. Giffard or anie of that false hierarchie to make defence and justification of these poyntes wherin they are here chardged by the worde of God. Which if they can doe, then let them be held excused, and us justly chardged with impudent and wicked sclander. In the meane while I haste to the second sort of their ministrie.

The next sorte of the ministrie of the Church of England is the collegiat or idle ministrie, which may be divided, or rather distinguished (because sometimes they are mixed and joyned, one man being a master of [117] a colledge and a deane, a fellowe of a house and a prebend,[2] and each of them have a parsonage or two for a neede) into these two kindes, academical, and cathedral, the third sorte, the monastical, being by the hand of God and the magistrate's sworde cut off and suppressed. These academical divines live, have their education and degrees in the colleges, halles, and celles of the two universities. The originall corrupt customes and use of which places, it is not mie purpose here to discourse; neither indeed have I skill aright to discusse whither and how they sprange from the

---

[1] For archdeacons and rural deans, see Samuel Brewster, *Collectanea Ecclesiastica* (1752), pp. 329-399. See also Congregational Union of England and Wales, The Moderators, *The Deacon, His Ministry in Our Churches* [1957]. A recent work is J. G. Davies, " Deacons, Deaconesses and the Minor Orders of the Patristic Period," *Journal of Ecclesiastical History*, April, 1963, pp. 1-15.

[2] A prebendary, one who holds a prebend. The two words are sometimes used interchangeably. Barrow may be referring to Dr. Robert Some, who was master of Peterhouse. Or he may have thought of Matthew Sutcliffe, who was dean of Exeter, prebendary of Exeter, and vicar of West Alvington, Devonshire.

heathens, or from the papistes. Only this I dare affirme, that from the booke of God they never dirived these their colleges, scholes, hal[l]es, orders, degrees, vowes, customes, ceremonies, attires, that I say not their artes, aucthors, exercise, and use of their learnings, disputations, commencements, etc. But as they have received them ells where, so have they ever belonged to an other heade and kingdome, and can by no meanes (in this estate they now stand and have tyme out of minde continued) be made to accorde to the gospel and kingdome of Christ, wherof these universitie divines have ever bene the professed and most bitter enemies, furnishing Antichrist's hoste in all the roomes and places, even from the pope's chayre, to the parish prieste's pulpit or pue, with fresh servitors continually, corrupting the pure fountaines, and perverting the text it self with their gloses, paraphrases, notes, figures, etc., fighting with their schole learning, vayne artes, philosophie, rethoricke, and logique against the truth and servantes of God,[1] striving hereby to uphold Antichriste's ruynous kingdome and abhominable wares, which these marchantmen set to sale for gaines, as we by present experience see (nowe their portion and idle monasticall life, beginneth but even a litle to be reproved by the light and power of the gospel) how these craftes-men, these universitie clarkes, rage and take on, and with their schole learning seeke to tourne away the evident truth of God, to colour and plead for all the abhomination and sinne of the tymes, to heale the wounde and uphold the throne of the beaste, to rend, reproch, and blaspheme such as speake and witnes against it, as their vituperious, unchristian, and erroneous bookes, which they daily publish, declare.

Neither is their education and learning (if they be duelie examined) such as is required in the holy ministerie of Christ; all of them (as is said) being nourished

---

[1] See Wilbur S. Howell, *Logic and Rhetoric in England, 1500-1700*, Chapter 2, Part III; Chapters 3, 5. See also Peel and Carlson, *The Writings of Robert Harrison and Robert Browne*, pp. 173-193, 210, 223.

A Plaine Refutation

even from their cradles with the milke of superstition, instructed in the scholes of heathen vanitie, brought up in the colleges of more tha[n] monkish idlenes, and disorder, exercised in the vaine and curious artes, whose divinitie is by tradition, etc.[1] The truth of these things Mr. Giffarde not being able to gainesay, seeketh to shoffle off with a bold boasting chalendg[e] against men unto himself unknowen, upon the dispence of bearing the shame, if he find not in the universities many bachelours of arte far exceeding in the knowledge of the liberall artes, the three tongues, Hebrew, Greek, and Latine, or in sounde judgment of divinitie, even the principall masters of Brownisme; which if it could in so fewe yeeres be obtayned with more than monkish idlenes, then may the Brownistes in [118] some thing be believed.[2]

First we give him to weite [know] that there are, of those he calleth Brownistes, sondrie of greater contynuance, and that have as high degree in those scholes, with as high commendation as himself, although they boaste not of such thinges wherof they ought to be ashamed. Then that there are as manie of his bretheren, the monckes, that thinck themselves as skilfull as himself, or the greatest clarke in the universitie.

But nowe in all this what will our ignorance helpe him, or their store of learning shewe, that they have not bene and are not thus initiate and brought up. In their grammer scholes it cannot be denied, but they learned and learne the Latine tongue from the most heathenish and prophane aucthors, lascivious poets, etc., which are allowed with the priviledge of the

---

[1] "A Brief Summe of the Causes of Our Seperation," printed in Carlson, *The Writings of Henry Barrow, 1587-1590*, pp. 118-150.
[2] *A Short Treatise*, p. 77. The Brownists have no claim to special intellectual eminence, but they are not uneducated men. Robert Browne, Robert Harrison, Henry Barrow, John Greenwood, John Penry, Nicholas Crane, Thomas Settle, and Arthur Bellot were all university men. Later, Francis Johnson, Henry Ainsworth, John Robinson, John Smyth, Richard Clifton, Henry Jacob, John Canne, William Bridge, Jeremiah Burroughes, John Goodwin, Thomas Goodwin, Philip Nye, John Owen, and Sidrach Simpson were all men of university education. Henry Ainsworth was a very able Hebraist and a voluminous writer.

Church of England as most christian rudiments to be taught the youth in the publicke scholes. When they have passed all these formes, and can both say much of those aucthors by heart and use their phrase, then are they sent to the universitie to learne the artes, and to be instructed in philosophie, etc. Hitherto it cannot be denied but heathenisme and such execrable idolatrie, as is found in those aucthors, is wrytten and engraven upon the tables of their hearte, and filed [defiled, polluted] upon their tongue even from their infancie. Wel, and when they are come to the universitie, there are they first salted,[1] as they call it, in their college, and matriculate in the publick scholes, solemnely sworne upon the proctor's booke to keepe their mother's statutes and secretes, and not to reveile [reveal] her mysteries or teach her artes aniewhere but in the universitie. Then are they instructed both publickly and privately in logique and rethorick, in the elenches and topickes,[2] in the tropes and figures of all kindes; wherein they must be perfect, for these artes are of speciall use unto them, and to serve at all assaies. Then procede they to philosophie, and there Aristotle is *autos eipe*[3] amongst them, out of whose mouth and writings they fetch their positions and axiomes, definitions, aphorismes, distinctions, etc.; out of his *Ethickes*, *Economickes*, and *Pollitickes* they fetch the order and governement of their maners, private estates, and common wealth. He yet furder instructeth them of the Soule and of the worlde in lardge and special bookes, of the heaven, of natural and supernatural thinges, of Nature, Fortune, the eternitie of the worlde, and perpetuitie of all the creatures in their kinde *in specie*, of the regions of the ayre and several thinges in

---

[1] Admitted as freshmen with burlesque ceremonies, such as drinking salted water.
[2] See "Categoriae," "De Interpretatione," "Analytica Priora," "Analytica Posteriora," "Topica," and "De Sophisticis Elenchis" in W. D. Ross, *The Works of Aristotle*, volume I; see also "Rhetorica" in volume XI.
[3] Autos eipe, ipse dixit and ipse dixitism imply a mere dictum, an assertiveness that seems dogmatic.

A Plaine Refutation

them contayned, the meteores, etc.;[1] there learne they the causes of the raine-bowe, the making of the windes, cloudes, and of the whole skye, far otherwise than is set downe in the Genesis. Yet leadeth he them higher and sheweth them the celestial spheares, planets, starres, quintessences, even from the mone to their *caelum crystallinam* and their *Primum Mobile*, with their severall places, dimensurations, motions, and motors [movers, forces]:[2] yea, yet learne they more secret thinges with their constellations, radiations, influence, and predomination according to their signes, houses, oppositions, aspects, eclipses, etc., wherbie most strange and wonderfull thinges are prognosticate and foretold concerning the [119] weather and ceasons [*sic*] of the yeere, the estate of kingdomes, the diseases and dangers to come, etc.; concerning nativities and tymes of death (commonly caled fortunes), concerning things to come or things past, stolen, lost, found, etc.

These thinges it were frensie if not blasphemie to call vayne and curious artes. Mr. Giffard would never beare it at the handes of such blinde schismatickes (whose bane such deipe learning is), seeing these sciences are vulgarely taught, studied, practized, allowed, and maintained not only in the universities, but of the whole Church of England, as by their yeerely prognostications everie where to be sold, is to be seene.[3]

---

[1] "Ethica Nicomachea," "Magna Moralia," and "Ethica Eudemia" are in W. D. Ross, *The Works of Aristotle*, volume IX. See volume X for "Oeconomica" and "Politica." Discussions on the soul and the world are in "De Anima" and "De Mundo" in volume III. For a treatment of heaven, nature, and fortune (or chance), see "De Caelo" and "Physica" in volume II. "Meteorologica" is in volume III.

[2] See Francis R. Johnson, *Astronomical Thought in Renaissance England; A Study of the English Scientific Writings from 1500 to 1645* (Baltimore, 1937). See also Aristotle's "De Caelo," "Physica" and "Meteorologica." See further Lynn Thorndike, *The* SPHERE *of Sacrobosco and Its Commentators*, and also his *A History of Magic and Experimental Science*, volume VI, chapter XLII, "For and against Aristotle."

[3] The almanacs and prognostications were popular. See *Short-Title Catalogue*, nos. 386–532, 20414—20430. See Thomas Buckminster, *An Almanack and Prognostication for the Year 1598*. Introduction by Eustace F. Bosanquet. "Shakespeare Association Facsimiles No. 8." (London: Oxford University Press, 1935). See Paul H. Kocher, *Science and Learning in Elizabethan England* (San Marino, California: Huntington Library,

Henry Barrow

These studies and artes we may not call perierga,[1] curious, because Mr. Giffard saith Luke speaketh only of conjuration, Acts 19. But let him approve these [to be] lawfull by the Scriptures, and surely I wil gladly confesse mine ignorance and sinne in caling these studies and artes prophane, curious, unfit for a Christian, much more for a minister of the church. Otherwise let not any through mine unskilfulnes (who peradventure repeate not aright or in due place the tearmes of these artes, as having either forgotten them through longe discontynuance, or may be, never learned them aright) take occasion either to carpe at me therfore, or especially to thincke the better of these vaine and curious, yea, unlawfull and unchristian, artes and studies, which have not only no warrant in God's worde, but are directly contrarie unto and expresly forbidden in the same, as were not harde to shewe and proove, if the subject were not to[o] lardge, and should not make to[o] wide a parenthesis in this treatise, and drawe it out to a greater length than I would.

I wil not therfore stand here to discusse their philosophicall probleames, paradoxes, axiomes, or severall sentences and opinions, which are authenticall and currant amongst them, how evil they agree to the worde of God. Or to shewe how far these curious inquisitors, these starr-gazers, astrologians, calcars [diviners], wisardes, devines, exceede the boundes of faith and sobrietie, and passe the limites of God's reveiled [revealed] wil. Or whether they maie wander by these heathenish or divelish opinions of the heavens, starres, and their revolutions, influence, etc., motors,[2] demones, or spirits, and howe neare this approcheth to conjuration. Or to shewe howe far they are suffred to procede, yea, professe and practise in these divelish artes. Let the

---

1953), pp. 205, 208, 209. See especially Eustace F. Bosanquet, *English Printed Almanacks and Prognostications. A Bibliographical History to the Year 1600* (London: Bibliographical Society, 1917).
[1] Periergos, curious, futile, superfluous.
[2] In medieval astronomy, the primus motor (mover) was the outermost of the terrestrial spheres, which though fixed caused motion by attracting the other spheres.

A Plaine Refutation

bookes (that I chardge no persons) which are commonlie bought and studied in the universities, and in all other partes of the realme, without controlement, shewe. Neither will I here proceede to repeate their other vaine, curious, fonde [foolish], trifiling and vile artes, and studies, which were endlesse. Onlie in this place I must here add unto those publicke professed artes above recited, the studie of all heathen and prophane histories, of all ages, nations, persons, wherin they must of necessitie be prompt and expert; as from those fountaines to drawe their examples and platformes of maners and the governement of states, as from whence to fetch the chiefe ornamentes of their stile, orations, sermons, bookes, to exemplifie, illustrate, proove or [120] improve; yea, as wherby to open and expounde the Scriptures both of the Old and Newe Testament, chieflie the old prophets, without which they cannot be understoode, but especialy Esai and Daniel.[1] As to rethorick and logique, they are so necessarie, as without which it is impossible to understand or divide anie part of the Scripture aright; as without which they cannot understand or declare to the people by what trope or figure, by what forme of argument or syllogisme the Holie Ghoste speaketh.[2]

In these artes and studies are these academical divines or rather peripateticke philosophers trayned and exercised. In these they must needs spend seven of their first yeeres at the least, els should they be unfit to take those degrees of Bachelour and Master of Arte, or to make that publick profession they doe of the artes at their commencements. In these artes and studies when they are once a litle exercised and instructed that they beginne to perceive the groundes and methode therof, then are they trayned both publicklie and privatlie to defend or oppose against some of these axiomes or positions, both by waye of oration and argument in

---

[1] The books of Isaiah and Daniel lend themselves to historical treatment.
[2] These satirical remarks are reminiscent of Robert Browne's scornful denunciations in his work, "A Treatise upon the 23. of Matthewe," in Peel and Carlson, *The Writings of Robert Harrison and Robert Browne*, pp. 171-193.

their sophismes and disputations, and therin being approved (or at the least allowed), they then take the first degree of the scholes, and commence Bachelours of Arte, and have as ensignes of their degree and knowledge, special attire and furniture assigned them to be knowen from other common schollers; as the square cap, the troncke gowne, the hoode of one shoulder, the habite, etc., which they must weare. Afterward having spent more than th[r]ee yeeres in studie on these artes, and having donne their publicke actes *pro gradu* [for the B.A. degree], then they commence Masters of the said Artes; and are againe solemnly sworne and made regents and lectorers of their scholes, and sit, reade, and dispute of the same artes publickly in a solemne high seate, pulpit, or chaire for orations, as also reade private lectures therof in their colleges.

Now I would here by the way know of Mr. Giffard what tyme and leisure a Bachelour of Arte that contynueth in the universitie and procedeth in those orders and degrees can have, to studie divinitie, or to growe so prompt in the knowledge, judgment, and exercise therof, as he dare ingage his credite [so that] he shalbe fownde far to passe therin such as in their university have bene allowed publickly to preach, and of the bishops bene made ful ministers.

But to our purpose, when these clarkes are thus instituted and furnished with these liberal sciences, and this groundworck throughly laid, then maie they in good tyme proceede to the studie of divinity[1] (as they

---

[1] There is an interesting letter of Thomas Cartwright to Arthur Hildersham, "For Direction in the Study of Divinity," in Albert Peel and Leland H. Carlson, *Cartwrightiana*, pp. 108-115. Cartwright especially recommends Deuteronomy, Joshua, Chronicles, Daniel, Ezekiel, Hosea, Psalms, Proverbs, Romans, Revelation. He recommends the study of Commentaries and Commonplaces, of Councils and Canons. Of the Greek Fathers he urges the reading of Chrysostom and Gregory of Nazianzus. Of the Latin Fathers, he recommends Tertullian, Cyprian, Hilary of Poitiers, Ambrose, Jerome, and Augustine. For modern writers he finds Luther, Oecolampadius, Calvin, Beza, Peter Martyr, and Martin Bucer most helpful. Of the adversaries he lists four: Peter Lombard, Thomas Aquinas, Stanislaus Hosius, and Peter Canisius. There is an interesting inaugural lecture by S. L. Greenslade, *The English Reformers and the Fathers of the Church* (Oxford, 1960).

A Plaine Refutation

cal it), which is set out unto them in great volumes and infinite bookes of men's writinges both old and newe, where they have such varietie of paraphrases, commentaries, common places, catachises,[1] etc., (not to trouble them at the first with the primative histories, doctors, councels) as they may in shorte space (if they studie harde) become pretie divines, and be able to shewe their aucthors' judgment, yea, (through the helpe of rethoricke and a good memorie), to make a sermon an howre longe; alwaies carefully provided that they utter no more, than that they have read in some allowed aucthor, having the priviledge of the Church of [121] England, and presume not either to understand the text otherwise than their aucthors interpret it, or to add one note of their owne observation, for that (how consonant soever to the truth) were great presumption and rashnes. Neither may they over-far applie or inforce the judgment of their aucthors against anie present enormitie established by aucthoritie in the Church of England, for that were intollerable against the peace of the church, yea, seditious against the magistrate's aucthoritie, etc.

Thus whilest these divines are helde within these limites of modestie and sobrietie, and contynue with their mother the university, they maie in due time set up their bills of chalenge upon the schole doores, that they meane to dispute upon such and such questions of divinity, and to doe their actes *pro gradu*. Which being dispatched either *in taenebris* [*tenebris*] or *in luce*, then are they fit for the comencement to be made Bachelours of Divinity. In like maner against that daye must such of them as have before passed all these degrees, and nowe are fit to proceede Doctors of Divinity, do their actes in the publick scholes accordinglie in these divinity disputations, sermons *ad clarum* [*clerum*], etc. And against this sollemne commencement must especial choice be made of those that are to commence Bachelours

---

[1] Catechesis, catechisms. Books of Commonplaces were collections of useful passages, of reference material, and of texts and quotations worth remembering.

and Doctors of Divinitie to keepe the publicke actes that daie. And these for their furder credites often tymes wil undertake to defend against all commers such propositions as are most odious to all men in whom is anie light, conscience, knowledge, or feare of God. As that it is lawfull for one man to have more beneficies and flockes to attend than one at one time. That it is lawfull to be a non resident, to live from his flocke wherof he taketh chardge. That the unpreaching ministers are true and lawfull pastors, and the sacraments by them delivered true and holie sacramentes. That Christe's outwarde government in his church, practized and set downe by his Apostles, is not of necessitie or perpetuall, but variable and arbitrable at the wil of men, according to times, estates, etc.[1] These and suche like, these graduates publish and defende, the vice-chancelour and whole senate of the universitie conclude and confirme, as catholicke, orthodoxe, and most sounde, rejecting whatsoever Scriptures or reasons shall by these comical disputers, either universitie doctors and divines, be brought against them.

Wel, unto this famous act are these commencers solemnelie brought in their several attyres and arrayes, in their ska[r]let gownes, hoodes, habites, caps, tippitts, etc., with the bedells [beadles] proclayminge and carying staves and maces before them, with a greate troupe of graduates and clarkes following them. And thus they martch thorowe the streates to the place appoincted and prepared for these prizes, where they have their sticklers [reconcilers] and moderators readie to rescue, when they are in anie distresse, and where their adversaries sight bootie, beeing of their owne confederacie. Where it is not lawefull for anie that will to oppose, or to speake for the truth of God.

---

[1] The Anglican position is given by Thomas Cooper, Bishop of Winchester, in his *An Admonition to the People of England*, pp. 73-84 (in the edition of 252 pages [1589]). Thomas Bilson and Richard Hooker represent this same position in the 1590's. See Bilson, *The Perpetual Government of Christe's Church* (1593) and Richard Hooker, *Of the Lawes of Ecclesiasticall Politie* (1593).

A Plaine Refutation

Neither are these questions discussed in the English tongue before those multitudes of people and strangers, but in the Latine tongue [122] after their syllogistical and Romish maner, lest the follie of these prophets should be laied open unto all men, and these gamsters be hissed off the stage by the people. Thus, though with manie other trifling ceremonies and circumstances than I either can or care to recite, are these academical divines advanced to their degrees. Which degrees, titles, ceremonies, orders, oathes, vowes, maner of disputations, etc., how consonant they are to the ministrie of Christ by the Apostle's rules, let Mr. Giffard or those learned divines approve by Christe's Testament, as it standeth them upon, that bring them in and exercise them in the church.

For ourselves wee protest we never there read or heard of anie such; and therfore cannot but thincke them fond [foolish or silly], strange, and antichristian, such as no waye belonge to, or beseeme the ministrie of Christ, neither are necessarie or tollerable in Christe's churche. Thus even by this verie brief and insufficient recital of but some of their artes, studies, orders, degrees, etc., I hope this assertion wil not prove so false or incredible. That the learned ministrie of the Church of England is nourished even from their cradles "with the milke of superstition, instructed in the scholes of heathen vanitie, brought up in the colleges of more than monckish idlenes and disorder."[1]

For of such kinde of societies and colleges of ministers and clarks, to live together after this monastical maner, wee never read in the whole Booke of God. Howe like they are to the scholes of the prophets at Naioth, Rama, Jericho,[2] let their artes, studies, vowes, customes, orders, ceremonies, degrees, disputations, exercises, etc., declare. And as to the holie exercise of prophecie spoken in the New Testament; it belonged unto and

---

[1] "A Brief Summe of the Causes of Our Seperation," *A Plaine Refutation*, D recto, p. 13, in Carlson, *The Writings of Henry Barrow, 1587-1590*, p. 139.
[2] See I Samuel 19 : 18-24 ; 10 : 10.

alwaies was exercised in some christian congregation, in a more holy, reverent, and free maner, and not after those heathenish popish customes abovesaid. We in Christe's Testament never read of such a monasticall ministrie so withdrawen and sequestred from anie perticular congregation, office, chardge, and function, as these universitie divines and ministers are in their colleges, halles, celles. Where they must needes live in idlenes and disorder, that are thus licentiate [unrestrained, licentious] and dissolute, that wilbe held within no christian bondes or order. Wee never read in Christe's Testament of anie such societies or ministers, that lived in no perticular congregation, that were caled to no perticular office, or flocke, that live idlelie, professing to be ministers and yet execute no certaine ministrie or function. When Mr. Giffard shall directlie prove by the Scriptures these thinges to be lawful, then so farre foorth we shall allowe of these universitie divines, these collegiat ministers. And the rather if he also approve by God's worde their worship in their servicebooke. And last of all (not to comber [encumber] him with their manifold other superstitious customes, commemorations, etc.,), if he can shew it to be lawfull for anie minister or Christian to joyne unto and live in anie such college, societie, or fellowship, where God's holie ordinance of honest mariage is by expresse lawe forbidden all the fellowes and schollers of these colleges, they being no longer to [123] remaine in that societie than they live unmaried, I say not now chastely. For howe possible or likelie that is, for so manie yonge men in the flower of their youth and prime of their strength, especialy being noseled in such heathen vanitie, prophan[e]nes, vaine-glorie, curiositie, superstition, disorder, dissolutenes, and (as is said) contempt of God's ordinances, let anie judge; yea, let the Scripture itself judge: where God sheweth the reward of these sinnes, how he therfore giveth them up to the lustes of their owne heartes, unto uncleannes, to shamefull lustes contrarie to nature, to worke filthines, and to dishonor their own bodies amongst themselves, etc. And so until some of them can justifie this their life, orders,

Rom. 1:24

A Plaine Refutation

customes, vowes, and procedings of these academical divines in their scholes and colleges, wee must nomber and leave them with their bretheren and sisters, the monkes, friars, nunnes, etc., under God's feareful judgmentes, utterly in this estate unfit for the ministrie or church of Christ.

Yet would I not here, that anie should deeme or suppose that wee condemne anie lawful artes or necessarie sciences, anie holie exercises, or scholes of institution. And so doe labour to bring in barbarisme, as Mr. Giffard, Mr. Some, and others have given out.[1] No, wee are so far from it, as we blame these universities, colleges, and scholes for their heathen, prophane, superstitious, unchristian societies, disorders, customes, ceremonies, for the vaine, curious, unlawfull artes and studies, and their maner of teaching and exercising them, etc. We desire with our whole hearts, that the tongues and other godlie artes were taught, not in the universities or a fewe places onlie, but in all places where an established church is, at the least in everie citie of the land. Yet this indeede wee hold, that everie christian man ought to have his abiding and dwelling, and to bring up his children, in some such place where a christian congregation is, and that all scholes of learning ought to be kept in such places where both teachers and schollers may be under the holie government and censures of Christ in his church, and may live and be kept in holie order. Then, that the artes and sciences which are thus taught or studied, be not vayne, curious, or unlawful, but necessarie and godlie. Thirdlie, that they be not taught, exercised, or practized after anie prophane, vaineglorious, or superstitious maner, but in al sobrietie, modestie, and in the feare of God. To these fewe rules if their universities, colledges, scholes, were reformed, then should they not be, as they nowe are, the seminaries of Antichrist, the bane of the churche, the corruption of all youth in the lande. But then should they be (that which they nowe pretend) the scholes of

---

[1] *A Short Treatise*, p. 77, and Robert Some, *A Godly Treatise, Wherein Are Examined and Confuted Many Execrable Fancies*, pp. 1-4.

all godlie learning to garnish the church, to furnish the commonwealth with fit and vertuous men for everie place, office, and estate.[1]

Let us now procede to the other sorte of this collegiate idle ministrie of the Church of England, which are these cathedral abbay lubbers [louts, stupid fellows], these lord bishops, deanes, subdeanes, prebendes, cannons, etc., as in their cataloge; who live together like monkes in their cloisters and celles, adjoyned [123][2] and annexed unto some cathedral church, within which precincts they are fedd and stalled up to intend [attend, minister to] the divine service of the said cathedral, at certaine howers of the day limited, everie one in his severall array, ministerial vestures, surplices, copes, vestimentes, hoodes, tippets, cappes, rochets, etc., according to their severall office, place and degree, some singing, some piping, some reading, some praiing, some pisteling, some gospeling, some preaching, some administring the sacraments, etc. Of whose offices, ceremonies, rites, orders, customes, severally to entreate, is not mie purpose; it sufficeth me that I finde not any such cathedrals, cloisters, societies, offices, orders, ceremonies, worship, etc., in all the booke of God, and therfore I dare pronounce them antichristian, such as God wil not be pleased or served with in his church.

Let not Mr. Deane under the visarde of a christian

---

[1] Five of the recent works on university education are: M. L. Clarke, *Classical Education in Britain, 1500-1900* (1959); William T. Costello, *The Scholastic Curriculum at Early Seventeenth-Century Cambridge* (1958); Mark H. Curtis, *Oxford and Cambridge in Transition, 1558-1642* (1959); H. C. Porter, *Reformation and Reaction in Tudor Cambridge* (1958); Craig R. Thompson, *Universities in Tudor England* (1959). There is much useful information in the older work of James Heywood and Thomas Wright, *Cambridge University Transactions during the Puritan Controversies of the 16th and 17th Centuries*, 2 vols. (1854). The second volume of Charles Henry Cooper, *Annals of Cambridge* (1843) and J. B. Mullinger, *The University of Cambridge from the Royal Injunctions of 1535 to the Accession of Charles the First* (1884) are useful for studying university history and developments.

[2] This is a printer's error for [124]. The same mistake was made for page [64]. Henceforth the pagination is two pages behind the correct number, but it remains the same as in the 1591 edition.

A Plaine Refutation

name and office thincke to escape,¹ for when we bring him to the light, we finde him but a counterfeight, having neither the office nor ministration of a christian deacon. The christian deacon's office is faithfully to collect and distribute the almes and contribution of the church. But these cathedral deanes feede themselves and their troupes, I say not of the weekely almes of their church (for that they neither gather, neither woulde it suffice the tenth part of their pompe), but of the lordships, landes, and fees of their church; lying loitering in their stately pallaces, and not distributing to the poore of that congregation according to the appointment of the elders and the church. A christian deacon keepeth himself within the limites of the office he is called unto, and doth not intermeddle with the execution of their offices which belong not unto him, as the administration of the worde and sacraments, etc. But these cathedral deacons take upon them the ministrie of the worde and sacraments, manie of them having personages beside their deanerie; and having bene pastors before, yet for living and promotion's sake, are not ashamed to goe back to the deacon's office, or to retaine both offices. Neither doth the christian deacon usurpe such place, preeminence, and dignitie in the church to sit in one of the chiefe roomes with his velvet quishon [cushion], cloth of estate, or be brought to his place with a silver mace before him.

To conclude, these cathedral popish deanes have nothing common or like to a christian deacon, either in office, caling to their office, administration of their office, or place where they administer. Therfore what titles soever they carie, or pretextes they make, we may affirme them to be impes of Antichrist, to belong to his spouse and throne, the false church; and not to be those

---

¹ The New Testament pattern includes a dean or deacon — diakonos. But this pristine office, Barrow avers, has been perverted by the Church of England. He may have been thinking of Gabriel Goodman, dean of Westminster, or William Hutchinson, dean of St. Albans, or John Molyns, archdeacon of London, or Alexander Nowell, dean of St. Paul's, or Matthew Sutcliffe, dean of Exeter, or Richard Cosin, dean of Arches, or John Bridges, dean of Salisbury.

holy ministers, those christian deacons which Christ hath instituted to his church.

Of subdeanes or their office we reade not in Christ's Testament.[1] And as to those idle bellies, those prebendes [prebendaries], we knowe not what to make of them. Ministers of this church, yea, ful priests they should be, in that they are bownde to make four sermons in the yeare in their cathedral; yet are some of them civilians (as they terme them), lay parsons. But it is no noveltie in the Church of England, for ecclesiastical ministers to ex-[124]ercise civile offices, and likewise for civile persons to usurpe and possesse offices in the church, both of governement, as in their courtes above-said, and of the ministrie of the worde and sacraments, as prebendes, parsonages, and those not impropriate, etc.[2] Of such monkish secluding and gathering the ministers of their church into these colleges, halles, cloisters, we have alreadie spoken. As also of their idolatrous and false worship which they exercise. Of the several rites and ceremonies that these stalled bulles use therin, here to discourse, were long and tedious; or to stand to refute the unlawfulnes of these mother cathedral churches, where Sathan's throne is, wherin sit his lieutenants, these arch and lord bishops, wherin are the colleges of these idolatrous priests and loyterers, whose verie names being but recited, and the light of the gospel being but brought to their college and cloister doores, is enough to discover them of what stampe and broode they are. Yea, let this light of the gospell be brought to the tryal of their ministrie and ministration, though nothing be said to them, but they only put to approve themselves by God's worde, you shall see them discover themselves of what kingdome and spirit they are, defending themselves with their nailes and tongues, smiting al such as thus call their doings into this question with the fist of wickednes, and with the tongue of reproch, as by their

---

[1] Anthony Anderson, vicar of Stepney, became subdean of the Chapel Royal in 1592. See Walter H. Frere, *Two Centuries of Stepney History, 1480-1680* (1892).

[2] A prebend not impropriate would be one that had not been transferred to lay control or ownership.

A Plaine Refutation

prisons and bookes is to be seen; the one being ful of poore persecuted Christians in great distresse and miserie, without any judgment or help by lawe,[1] without any equity, mercie, or compassion shewed; the other being ful even in everie leafe, yea, almost in everie line of wicked sclanders, accusations, suggestions, blasphemies, against these faithful servantes of Christ, their adversaries. Not approving their ministrie, worship, and procedings directly by any one place of Scripture, though they be never so much urged therunto. But if they have no better defence, their kingdome shalbe left unto them desolate, as their brethren the lord abbots, monckes, fryars and nonnes are. Al which might aswel (for any thing I can see, or they can say) have bene reserved, reformed, and tyed to the saiing over this service book as these, all being alike without warrant in God's Worde, and therfore detestable and accursed.

It now remayneth that we take like sodaine viewe of the third sorte, the servile ministrie of the Church of England; namely, these parsons, vicars, curates, hirelings, preachers, deacons. These were blamed to Mr. Giffard to carye strange and antichristian names and offices, also to have as strange and antichristian an entrance unto their office, and administration in their office, as also that their support and maintenance is not such, as belongeth to the ministrie of the gospell.

In these poinctes we desired Mr. Giffard to approve the ministrie of England, or his owne ministrie, by the rules of Christ's Testament. This if he had done, all controversie had ceased, and we yeilded. Al this by his owne bare worde of affirmation and never a place of Scripture, he proveth in lesse than one page of his booke.[2] He affirmeth their names to be ministers of the gospell, pastors, and teachers. That the names of parsons and vicares are not to make any distinc-[125]tion

---

[1] There were about eighty Separatists who had been imprisoned in the period 1587-1590. Of these, about fifty were still in prison in 1590-91. See Barrow's "Letter to Mr. Fisher," in Carlson, *The Writings of Henry Barrow, 1587-1590*, volume III, p. 253.

[2] *A Short Treatise*, p. 73.

of the ministrie, but of the maintenance annexed to the same. That the offices they beare, " are to teach and instruct their flockes by the wholesome worde of God, to administer the sacramentes, and to make publick prayers." These he is sure are prescribed in Christ's Testament, and if our eye were not malignant we might espie them there.

That these names and offices of pastors and teachers, with this administration spoken of, are in Christ's Testament, we never doubted or made question, but now whether these parsons, vicares, curates, hired preachers, carie, truly have, and execute the names, offices, and functions of these christian pastors and teachers, all the doubt is. And more than Mr. Giffard his bare worde, we as yet have not to assure us therof: although we have even with importunitie begged and urged him, or any of his fellowes, either directly to approve their ministrie by the rules of Christe's Testament in their office, entrance and administration, or els to approove unto us by the worde of God that such offices, entrance unto and administration in their offices, is not now necessarie and of necessitie in the church of Christ:[1] but that the prince (whose honorable name they over much abuse to the patronizing of all their abhominations) or rather the pope (to whose kingdome this antichristian ministrie served) hath power to erect a newe and other ministrie in office, entrance, and administration unto the church, than that of Christe's Testament.

---

[1] In his *An Admonition to the People of England*, pp. 82, 84, 141 (the edition used (1589) has 245 pages, not 244 or 252), Bishop Thomas Cooper had argued that " one forme of church government is not necessarie in all times and places of the church." Furthermore, he contended that christian princes " may have that outwarde forme of jurisdiction, and deciding of ecclesiastical causes, as to the state of the countrey and people shall be most convenient." Barrow, as a strict-constructionist, supports the point of view expressed by Walter Travers, in *A Full and Plaine Declaration of Ecclesiasticall Discipline*. Bishop Cooper, as a loose-constructionist, supports the point of view which permits liberty of action by the church and magistrates in matters of discipline. Richard Hooker defends this position in his *Of the Laws of Ecclesiastical Polity*.

There is an interesting observation by Thomas Arnold, in *Sermons*, II (1834), p. 427: A divine " command given to one man, or to one generation of men, is, and can be, binding upon other men and generations, only so far forth as the circumstances in which both are placed are similar."

A Plaine Refutation

In al which if this ministrie of England cannot by the expresse rules of the word be justified, al the powers in earth or hel cannot make them the true ministers of the gospel. For other ministrie and offices of the gospel is not given or to be given unto the church, than those Christ hath instituted in his Testament. Neither may any other entrance or administration be joyned to that ministrie and those offices, than is in Christ's Testament appoynted. If therfore we shew that these ministers have not those offices, that entrance, or administration mentioned in Christe's Testament, it shal be enough to shew them conterfeite, strange, and antichristian.

First then by Mr. Giffard his leave, we must a litle insiste even upon these strange names of parson and vicare, which were given by their first founders and creators at the erection of their ministrie and offices, and are not read of in all the booke of God. Neither are any of those names which our Saviour Christ hath given and knyt unto his ministrie, for the distinguishing and expressing of their several offices, and therfore can at no hand belong unto the ministri of the gospel. Neither may any mortal man be so presumptious to give other names and denominations unto his reverend ministrie and holie offices, than the Lord of the house himself hath given. Neither may or will the true ministers of Christ carye any other names or titles (as in regarde of their ministri or office) than Christ hath given to their ministrie and office. But Mr. Giffard denieth these names to make any distinction of their ministri, but only of the state of maintenance annexed unto the same. Let us then aske him one question; what difference is there betwixt the arch and lord bishops, and the parish parsons and vicares of the Church of England in respect of their ministrie, if these [126] names be not given to put difference betwixt, and distinction of their office and ministrie? I trust he will not say these lord bishops and parsons have al one office and ministrie in their church. I believe his Ordinarie wil hardly agree to him in this poynte. Let him finde therfore a newe distinction to help this matter,

Againe, we could say to Mr. Giffard, that these names of parsons and vicares do not only distinguish their ministrie from their lord bishops, arch-deacons, deanes, etc., but yet maketh a distinction even amongst themselves, betwixt them and such of their other roving ministers, which have no certaine flocke or chardge, but as sone as they are made ministers unto and of any one certaine flock, then take they forthwith their denomination of that flocke or towne, as the bishops doe of the greate cities, and are then and not before called parsons or vicares of such a towne.

To conclude, these names of parson and vicare being distinct names, and having distinct livings appropriate unto them, belonging also to one and the same church or towne, and being given to two divers men and so possessed at one and the same tyme, cannot but belong to two divers offices of their church, except two men may also have and execute one and the same office at the same instant, as wel as one man may execute two or mo[r]e divers offices of their church at one instant. But sure these paradoxes are so inaudible and incredible, yea, so impossible in the church of Christ, as I see not how all Mr. Giffard his logique and learning can reconcile them to the Testament of Christ.

But to come to the offices of these parsons and vicars, Mr. Giffard saith (if we may believe him) they are pastors and teachers, yet setteth us not downe who be the pastors, and who be the teachers of their church. It should seeme by his speach that these two, the parson and vicare, are one office, namely, pastors, and that such hireling predicantes as himself [1] are the teachers of this Church of England. Let us first consider of their pastors, by comparing them to the pastor's office. The true christian pastor is placed of God in his house, his church, as a steward both to divide the portion, and to oversee, take chardge, and looke to the order and governement of that church, wherof he is chosen and made a minister, and of al the publicke actions therof,

Tit. 1:7
Math. 24:45
Mark 13:34
I Tim. 5:17
Heb. 13:17

---

[1] Gifford was deprived of his position as vicar, but he continued as " preacher of God's Word " at Maldon Essex.

A Plaine Refutation

togither with the other elders. But these parsons by vertue of their office and ministrie, are not bounde to labour in the worde, otherwise, than to preach four sermons in the yeere, either by himself or by his substitute, and that not by law, except his benefice exceede a certaine annuall somme in the queene's booke.[1] Otherwise they are but bounde to reade the service prescribed in the Common Booke, at such tymes and tides [hours] as is there injoyned, to weare the prieste's attire, to reade injunctions and homelies, etc. Neither are they permitted, or by vertue of their office may intermeddle, with the oversight, order, and governement of that flocke wherof they are parsons. Christ nowe in his church hath instituted no ecclesiasticall office above the pastor's office. Neither may anie true christian pastor stand, or exercise his office under anie such false ecclesiasticall office, as Christ hath [127] not instituted. But there are sondrie offices in the Church of England above the parson's office. Unto which superior offices al these parsons stand subject, havinge sworne their canonical obedience to their courtes, cannons, commandements, to their sommance [summons], censure, controlement, for al their actions, ministrie, conversation, to be made ministers, deposed from their ministrie, silenced, sequestred, suspended by them. _{Rom. 12} Gal. 2:4, 5 John 10:12 Acts 20:29 III John 9, 10

The true christian pastor (as by vertue of his office) intangleth not himself, neither intermedleth with civile actions and affayres, but these parrish parsons (especialie these of the countrie) are busied, and almost wholly entangled, with renting, tithing, prowling their parrish-[io]ners, whether faithfull or unfaithfull, rich or poore, widowes or orphanes, they marrie, they burie, etc. by vertue of their office, and are to all outwarde seeming and judgment rather rieves [reeves, magistrates] and bayliffes, than ministers of the gospel. Yea, if it be II Tim. 2:4 Acts 6:2 I Pet. 4:15 I Tim. 3:3 Ezek. 13 Mat. 23:14 Phil. 3:18, 19

---

[1] See Great Britain. Record Commission. *Valor Ecclesiasticus Temp. Henr. VIII Auctoritate Regia Institutus.* Edited by John Caley and Joseph Hunter; 6 volumes (London, 1810-34). See also *Valor Beneficiorum: or, a Valuation of All Ecclesiastical Preferments in England and Wales* (London, 1695).

true which some writers of no smale accompt both olde and new have written of them, these parrish parsons were at first devised and brought in to serve the metropolitanes in the offices of rieves and bayliffs to gather up their rents, etc. Againe the true christian pastor's office cannot be possessed by anie civille person. But the parrish parson's office may be, and often is, bestowed upon *civilians, phisitions,* who, if they weare [wear] the prieste's weekes [apparel, dress] injoyned, it sufficeth. Not here meaning or speaking of impropriations which have no office and chardge of anie ministrie, it being transferred to a vicare endowed. Moreover, the christian pastor's office cannot be kept or executed by a man absent, or by anie other in that congregation wherof he is chosen, than by the elect of that congregation. But the parish parson's office may be kept by a man absent, executed by an attourney [deputy] or curate. Finaly, everie true christian pastor is by that his officie, a bishop.[1] But no parrish parson is by vertue of that his office a bishop. Therfore, and for al these reasons abovesaid, the parrish parson's office can in no juste intendement [view, interpretation] be held the true christian pastor's office.

Acts 20
I Tim. 3
Tit. 1

Nowe let us procede to their entrance, this being first a position perpetual, that everie true minister of the churche must not onlie be caled to a true office, but must have a true and right caling unto that his office: otherwise he is no true minister, but an usurper, an intruder, a theife, a murderer. Everie true minister then, by the rules of the Worde ought to be thus caled.

Heb. 5:4
John 10:[?]
Numb. 16:5, 40

---

[1] Barrow's view is that the New Testament teaches the identity of presbuteros and episkopos, of presbyters (priests, elders, pastors) and bishops (overseers, superintendents). Therefore, the Anglican bishop is a usurper of power not rightfully belonging to him. At best he is a *primus inter pares.* For an introduction to this complicated subject, see Roswell D. Hitchcock, " Origin and Growth of Episcopacy," *American Presbyterian and Theological Review,* New Series, Vol. V, No. 17 (January, 1867), pp. 133-159. See also J. B. Lightfoot, " The Christian Ministry," *Saint Paul's Epistle to the Philippians* (London, 1913), pp. 181-269. See further, Edwin Hatch, *The Organization of the Early Christian Churches* (London, 1918); *Cambridge Medieval History,* I (1924), Chapter VI; Eduard Schweizer, *Church Order in the New Testament* (Naperville, Illinois: Allenson, 1961).

A Plaine Refutation

Everie perticular congregation, being a faithfull flocke, destitute of some minister (for example of a pastor), ought to make choice of some one faithful Christian, of whose vertues, knowledge, judgment, fitnes, and conversation (according to the rules in that behalf prescribed) they have assured proofe and experience in some christian congregation or other, where he hath lived. Such a one, the whole congregation being gathered together in the name of God with fasting and prayer for the special assistance of his Holy Spirite, to be directed to that person whom the Lorde hath made meete and [128] appointed unto them for that high chardge and ministrie. In which election everie perticular member of the said congregation hath his peculiar interest of assent or dissent, shewing his reasons of dissent in reverent maner, not disturbing the holie and peaceable order of the church. Whose exceptions and reasons are to be considered of, and compared to the rules of the Worde, if they be founde peremptorie and true. As the partie to be of no sounde judgment in the faith, of no sufficient knowledge in the Scripture, a drunckarde, a smiter, coveteous, one that ruleth not wel his owne house, wife, children, etc., then yeildeth the whole church to their reasons, or rather to the Word of God. [I Tim. 3; Tit. 1; Acts 14]

But if their exceptions be unsufficient or untrue, then procedeth and standeth their election, and the persons that take them are publicklie reproved, according to their offence.

This choice thus made, accepted, and determined, the elect is to be publicklie ordayned and received in and of the same congregation, wherof and wherunto he is chosen. If there be an eldership in that congregation, by them, as the most meete instruments, with fasting, prayer, exhortation, etc., if not, then by the help of the elders of some other faithful congregation, one churche being to help and assist an other in these affaires.

But if the defection and apostasie be so generall as there be not anie where anie true elders to be founde, or conveniently to be had, yet then hath the church that hath power and commandement to chuse and to use ministers, yea, that only hath that most high and great spirituall power of our Lorde Jesus Christ upon earth committed unto their handes, power also to ordaine their ministers by the most fit members and meanes they have. For the eldership doth not add more power, but more helpe and service to the church in this action. Neither doth this action (which is but a publishing of that former contract and agreement betwixt the whole church and these elect, the church giving and the elect receiving these offices as by the commandement of God with mutuall covenant and vowe each to other in al dueties) belonge to the elders onlie as separate from the church, but to the elders as the most fit members and instruments of the church, to doe it for and in the churche. Otherwise, when the true ministrie ceased, as in the generall apostasie, they could never againe be recovered in the church: because they cannot have this ordination of true christian elders, and so must the ministrie, sacraments, and ordinances of Christe's Testament cease for ever, and the true established churche never be seene againe upon earth. Unlesse with the papistes they wil make a personal succession of ministers in som place ever since the Apostles' tyme. Or with Mr. Giffard make a true publick ministrie, sacrament, etc., in the church of Rome in the diepest apostasie. Which yet of al other is the most absurd proposition that ever I suppose was uttered by anie man, or published and allowed by anie churche, contrarie to al the rules of God's Worde, and even to it self. For how can there be by anie reasonable man immagined or seene publicke apostasie, and publick faith in the same estate, at one and the same instant? [129] Likewise, if of necessitie the ordination must alwayes be donne by a christian presbutrie [*sic*] or eldership, we woulde then knowe of them by what elders Mr. Luther, Mr. Calvine, or our Englishe bishopps in King Edward's daies, were ordayned. Other elders than of the popish church there were not then to be founde.

Nowe these are sure groundes that cannot be doubted of. The true ministrie of Christ doth not belonge unto, and may execute no ministrie in the false churche.

A Plaine Refutation

Neither yet hath the execrable ministrie of the false church anie thing to doe to ordaine the true ministrie of Christe's churche, neither is their ordination availeable. If then the Church of Rome and the ministrie therof were false and antichristian, then cannot the ministrie of these men which was then in that estate given and received, be esteamed the true ministrie of Christ belonging to his church. But now if they hold the Church of Rome the true churche, and her elders true ministers of Christ, then is it utterly unlawfull to with-drawe, depart, or separate from the true church at anie tyme. And then were al these, and are al they in a most deadlie schisme. Mr. Calvin's distinction, that he separated from the corruptions of the church of Rome, and not from the churche of Rome, wil not here stand.[1] For therby they confesse the Churche of Rome the true church, and that they for the corruptions of the church departe. Which corruptions if they be not such and so incurable as to make the Church of Rome no churche, then is it not lawfull for [because of] anie such corruptions to depart from, and to forsake the true church, and then are they all stil in schisme, by their owne doctrine, and so no true ministers.

This I have thus lardglie written of the true election and ordination of ministers, because I finde so great ignorance and error amongst the divines of the Churche of England therin. Some of them (as the most reformed) that seeme to seeke Christe's discipline (as they cal it), holde, that elections and ordinations ought to be donne by the presbutrie, at the least the ordination alwaies of necessitie. Others of them, the more grosse of the common sorte, that holde with the time, give the election to the patrone, the ordination to the bishop onlie.

Let us now come to the election, probation, ordination of this parte of the ministery of the Church of

---

[1] Calvin, *Institutes of the Christian Religion*, translated by Henry Beveridge, volume II, book IV, chapter II, pp. 304-314. See also Calvin's "Reply to Cardinal Sadolet's Letter," and his treatise, "The Necessity of Reforming the Church," in John Calvin, *Tracts and Treatises on the Reformation of the Church*, ed. T. F. Torrance, volume I (Grand Rapids, Michigan: William B. Eerdmans Publishing Co., 1958).

England, which exactly to set downe in everie perticularlie [sic] circumstance, I cannot, not having their booke of consecration, election of their ministrie (for anie thing that ever I could heare),[1] they have none, only the bishop appoynteth a certaine day and place when he will give (or rather sel) orders. Thither then repaire unto him all such as want other meanes to geate their living, poore, idle, inordinate walkers, to whom the ministrie is *ultimum refugium*.[2] None here staying for the caling of God in his church, but running before they be sent. Hither to this market these hungrie foxes flocke. There they are by certaine of the bishopp's substitutes, examined, if so be that they be under the degree of Masters of their Artes, [130] for al double graduates neede no probation, their hoodes of both shoulders shewe that they have learning and divinitie enough. And as for proofe of their honestie and vertue, that is not material, that is not required or looked after in this busines, except they be so evill beloved as some come to crye shame of them at that verie tyme. Which if they doe, yet must the matters be too badd and broade, that wilbe received there.

And as to this probation that is there made, it is but to know whether they have the Latine tongue, and how they can construe some sentence of some aucthor. If they be not prompt they shall be holpen, or have more easie questions, or tyme given them, if so be they have anie favour with Mr. Examiners, they are verie meane clarkes which are there refused or sent away if they bring money in their purse, without which there is no ministrie to be had in the Church of England. Such other as yet cannot endure this severe tryal, having only their mother tongue, are to resorte to their lord bishop

---

[1] Perhaps the parenthesis should follow the word "none." The book referred to is *The Form and Manner of Making and Consecrating Bishops, Priests, and Deacons*, which was first issued in 1549 and 1552, as part of *The Book of Common Prayer*, and as separate publications. See *A Short-Title Catalogue*, under "Liturgies," 16462—16478. See also *A Book of Certaine Canons concernyng Some Parte of the Discipline of the Church of England. In the Yeare of Our Lord, 1571* (*A Short-Title Catalogue*, 10063).

[2] A last recourse or place of refuge.

A Plaine Refutation

at his house more secretly; where if they can make any friend unto him, they shal not misse of their desire; for the bishop maie, or at least doth, make ministers, as wel privatlie in his owne house, as publickly at this sollemne tyme and place.[1] But these approved, they are brought arayed in their white ministeriall vesture, unto the bishop's chayre, where he solemnelie sitteth in his *pontificalibus* [vestments and insignia]. At whose feete these ministers that woulde be, are caused to kneele down; where having certaine articles read unto them, unto which they are sworne and subscribe, then are they by the bishop's owne mouth made and pronounced ministers, *vzt.*, deacons, certaine chapters of the Bible enjoyned them as a taske to reade everie daye, as also certaine bookes to studie diligently: his orders also with the bishop's great seale at them in a boxe, are delivered them; for which they must paye full sweetlie. Thus is he made half priest, to reade the booke and serve a cure, but not to enterprise to preach without the bishop's special licence written, sealed, and wel paied for, therunto; neither may he administer the sacraments, until he have his ful orders, and be made ful priest. Yet nowe is he a fit curate for anie parish, a fit clark for anie benefice, come by it where he can. For here is he made minister of the Church of England in general, without certaine flock or chardge, and is sent into the wide worlde with his licence to geat him a living where he may. Wherebie sondrie of them (by reason of the multitudes that are dailie made) are driven to make verie harde shift, to teach young children, or to become house-priests (I meane not nowe chaplains, for they are rufflers [vagabonds, swaggerers] for verie meane wage. Yet must I needes saye, the bishop taketh an

---

[1] William Overton, Bishop of Lichfield and Coventry, was accused by Lord Burghley of making "seventy ministers in one day for money, some taylors, some shoemakers and others craftsmen." See Public Record Office, State Papers Domestic, Elizabeth, vol. CLXXVI, nos. 68, 69, 72, 75. See William Pierce, *The Marprelate Tracts*, 1588, 1589, pp. 24, 155-7; John Strype, *Annals*, III, Part I, 131-9; III, Part 2, 207-18; *Edmund Grindal*, 404-10; *John Whitgift*, I, 199-213; Francis O. White, *Lives of the Elizabethan Bishops in the Anglican Church* (1898), 271-6.

especial care to prevent this, for he hath certaine of their sufficient friendes to be bounde, I thincke, or ells to testifie, that they have five poundes by yeere to live upon; lest indeede the bishop himself shoulde be after chardged to finde them, by an especiall cannon made in the behalf of poore priests and ministers.

Wel, being nowe stepped into the ministrie, it is not longe for the most part (especiallie if anie benefice befal them) before they be made [131] full priestes either by the bishop privately, or publickly at such day and place above-said.[1] Where they are againe examined how they have performed their taske enjoyned, and how they have profited in the studie of divinitie. Wherein being approved, they are in maner and attire abovesaid, placed at the bishop's feete; who now layeth his handes upon them, delivereth them the Bible, and breathing his unholy spirit upon them giveth them the Holy Ghost (as he blasphemously saith)[2] and sendeth them foorth unto all people to preach and deliver the sacraments, for as yet there is no certaine chardge or flocke mentioned. Where these priestes having sworne their canonical obedience, and againe subscribed, paying for his orders and al other fees, are now made ful priestes in any ground in England.[3]

This common sort thus priestified, either serve cures, or by some meanes or other geat a benefice by presentation or resignation, etc. And here must the patrone that ow[n]eth the advowson present him to the bishop,

---

[1] According to the *Book of Common Prayer* for 1552, a deacon must be twenty-one years old at the least before admission to the order; a priest must be twenty-four years of age, and a bishop thirty years of age. According to the *Book of Common Prayer* for 1662 and later editions, a deacon must be twenty-three years of age, " unless he have a faculty " [special permission, dispensation, license].

[2] In the ordination service the bishop placed his hands upon the candidate and said: " Receive the Holy Ghost; whose sins thou dost forgive, they are forgiven; and whose sins thou dost retain, they are retained." Then the bishop delivered the Bible, saying: " Take thou authority to preach the Word of God, and to minister the holy sacraments in this congregation, where thou shalt be so appointed."

[3] A marginal printed comment reads: " These men by this office, ordination, and sending should be apostles. Matthew 28 : 18, 19. John 20 : 21, 22. And what high office then exerciseth the bishop that maketh and sendeth foorth apostles and giveth them the Holie Ghost."

A Plaine Refutation

as his clarke; to whom this priest must yet againe subscribe, and then receiveth the bishopp's institution in writing, with his seale thereat, which must be well paied for also. This priest thus instituted, cometh with his letters and seales to his parish, and taketh possession of his parsonage; where he must be inducted, an other priest delivering him the key of the church doore, which he must open, and enter; where he hath a bell-rope put into his hand, and must knole [toll] a bell. After which a peale is ronge, and he caried to some feaste-house or other, insteade of fasting and prayer. And thus have you hearde the maner of the election, probation, and ordination of these pastors and teachers of the Church of England. Which if it can by any learning or conning be prooved that holie caling which is prescribed in Christe's Testament, and which may not be severed from the ministrie of the gospell, then have they the more to rejoyce, and we to repent, before the Lorde.

And now whether we have lyed (as Mr. Giffard verie boldly chardgeth us) in saying that their ministrie is imposed upon these churches, let the indifferent reader judge. Yea, let him also consider, what kinde of interest, freedome, and power these parishes have to chuse and ordaine their owne ministers, the people never seeing or knowing their minister, until he come with his letters of institution, or having any thing to doe at his ordination; he being made ful priest, yea, and their priest, and that whether they will or no, before he come at them. And let Mr. Giffard himself looke what power any parish in England hath to disanull the patrone's presentation, the bishop's ordination and institution. The bishop, he ordayneth them ministers, though he or his examiners never sawe or knewe the men before that present howre. He maketh them ministers to no certaine flocke or chardge, therfore can no peculiar flocke have interest in their election and ordination. The patrone whatsoever he be, whether woman, childe, foole, wicked person, papist (yea, worse, if worse may be), he presenteth his clark to that benefice, though he be an hundred miles off from the bishop; and the [132] bishop, though he knowe neither parish nor minister, must admit, or ells lyeth a *quare impedit* to compel him.¹ The priest thus instituted, he cometh to the parish, taketh possession of the parsonage, and theire minister he will be, whether the people will or not; they must receive him, and may not keep him out, how bad soever he be.

And whereas Mr. Giffard bringeth instance to proove that the ministrie is not imposed, because that sondrie flockes have those pastors and ministers of the gospel that they have desired and made choice of by sute unto the patrones, and to the parties whom they desire to have.² This yet more sheweth their bondage, in that they are driven to make sute unto their patrones, and to receive from him their ministrie; which I believe Mr. Giffard shal never be able to shew that any christian congregation did or might doe. And to the choice he speaketh of, I weene they were ministers, yea, pastors, before they chose them; and being so, they then by the rules of Christ's Testament ought to belonge unto some certaine and peculiar flockes; which if they do, how then may they chuse the pastor of an other flocke to make him their pastor? What kinde of choice will Mr. Giffard make his? Whilest he goeth about to stop the gap, he maketh it wider.

But now to their chopping, chaunging, and leaving of their benefices at their owne pleasures as more gaynful are offred, without the people's privitie or consent (which is an usual trade amongst them all, not one amongst a thousand that doth not thus flitt up and downe, and Mr. Giffard none of those odd ones) for this he had not one excuse coyned, we must stay until the minte go the third tyme.³ And then let him also consider, how these parish parsons may without the

---

[1] The writ " why he impedes " was used in disputed cases of presentation to a benefice. If the person who had been appointed by a patron to the benefice was refused by the bishop, then that person had recourse to his patron, who sued for a writ, making the bishop a defendant, and requesting him to answer why he refused to admit the appointee of the plaintiff.

[2] *A Short Treatise*, p. 73.

[3] We must wait until Mr. Gifford produces his next (third) answer. Gifford's *A Short Reply* appeared about December, 1591.

A Plaine Refutation

people's consent or liking be absent and live away from the flock as longe as they liste, even al the dayes of their life if they will, finding them a curate, a journey man to reade them their service, marrie, burie, etc., and four sermons in the yeere, which they may also do by their attorney.[1] These thinges if Mr. Giffard can shew that a christian pastor may lawfully doe, then at length shal he shew them like a christian pastor in some thing.

Now to the teacher's office of their Church of England; except they make their bishopps and parsons to be both pastors and teachers, and to execute both offices, we know not what he should meane; for we finde no such office in their church. Their universitie doctors have this title rather in ostentation of their learning, than by vertue of any office ecclesiasticall. This title is given aswell to other sciences, as phisick, civile lawe, etc., as to divinitie. Their civile doctors execute other offices of their church, as to be judges of courtes, commissaries, chaunsclours, comissioners, neither are busied in teaching, therfore they cannot be said to have a teacher's office. Their doctors of divinity are either bishops, deanes, arch-deacons, parsons, vicares, or ful priests, al which meddle with the administration of the sacraments, and are distinct offices from the teacher's office and therfor not the same. Neither may two distinct or divers[e] offices of the church be possessed or executed by one and the same per-[133]son at once, except they can prove it possible for one member to be both an eye and an eare or hand, and to execute their functions at once. These officers are caled members of Christ's bodie, his church; these offices are distinct and several. Men with several giftes and graces by the distribution of God himself are appointed therunto: whose holie order they breake, besides all other inconveniences and im- Rom. 12:5 I Cor. 12

---

[1] See *Injunctions Given by the Queene's Majestie. Anno Dom. 1559.* The fourth injunction required one sermon in every quarter of the year at least, "unlesse some other preacher sufficiently licenced, as hereafter chaunce to come to the parish for the same purpose of preaching." See also [Church of England], *Advertisements*, A 3 recto, (1584). In the first edition of 1566, see "Articles for Doctrine, and Preaching," A iii *recto* — A iv *recto*.

possibilities that insue therof, which thus presume in their owne person to execute sondrie offices of the church at one tyme.

Furder, the churches of England have allowed them by lawe but one priest each of them (which roome possessed, they are said to be full) except some few which have parson and vicar, or two parsons in a towne, both which meddle with the administration of their sacraments, and therfore cannot be said to have the teacher's office. As to these curates and stipendarie preachers, they are either full priestes, or but half priestes or deacons. The ful priestes all of them by office may administer the sacraments. The half priestes none of them by office may preach or expounde the word, without especial licence. Therfore neither the one or the other of these have the christian teacher's office.

And now to the stipendarie preachers, let us for example insiste upon Mr. Giffarde's own ministrie; he writeth himself "minister of God's holie worde in Maldon."[1] We would know of him in what office he doth administer unto this church. We reade in Christ's Testament but of two ministers of the worde now belonging to his church, the pastor and the teacher. Pastor of that church he is not; because they have an other allowed by lawe, which is also his pastor, (and that to his furder shame a double beneficed man).[2]

---

[1] This description is on the title page of Gifford's book, *A Short Treatise*. Maldon is in Essex, in Dengie Hundred, about ten miles east of Chelmsford.

[2] Mark Wiersdale (or Wirsdale, or Wyersdale) was instituted to the living of All Saints' with St. Peter's on June 18, 1584. Gifford had been presented by Richard Franck to this church in August, 1582. For non-subscription to the second of Archbishop Whitgift's three articles, he was suspended about May, 1584, but he remained as a lecturer. In 1586, Wiersdale wished to resign in favour of Gifford, but Bishop Aylmer refused this request. Gifford was also summoned before the Court of High Commission, about 1585 or 1586, perhaps twice, on charges of holding conventicles and advocating only a limited obedience to civil magistrates, but he was acquitted. See John Strype, *Annals*, III, Part I, 354, 691; *Aylmer*, 71-73. Albert Peel, *The Seconde Parte of a Register*, II, 260; T. W. Davids, *Annals of Evangelical Nonconformity in the County of Essex*, pp. 78, 84, 109, 117, 126. Robert Palmer was the vicar of All Saints' with St. Peter's after the departure of Mark Wiersdale for Cambridge, in 1586 or 1587. Palmer served as vicar from 1587 to his death in 1600.

A Plaine Refutation

Teacher there he [Giffard] is not; because that church hath no such office, and is full; as also because this man is ful priest, and (as I have heard) was sometime a vicare (a pastor he saith) from which his ministrie and place he is now deprived, departed, and apostatate, as also from all grace and feeling.¹ Neither hath he [Giffard] in Maldon the credite or roome so much as of a curate, the pastor there supplying his owne office, but is brought in by such of the parish as having itching eares, geat unto themselves an heape of newe fangled teachers after their owne lustes, disliking and lothing the ministrie that is set over them, to which not-withstanding in hypocrisie and for feare of the world they joyne in prayers and sacramentes, paye tythes and maintenance, as to their proper minister.   II Tim. 4:3

To such people being riche and able to pay them well, these sectorie precise preachers runne for their hire and wages, but chiefly for vaine-glorie and worldlie estimation. And there teache and preach [to] this people for the most parte, under some dumbe or plurified pastor: from whom as from unsufficient and blinde guides they withdraw not the people, shewing them the will of God in that or in anie other poynct, be it never so odious and abhominable, that might bring perill. Yet for their owne estimation, advantage, and entertainment, they will by all subtile meanes under hand   Rom. 16:18
Phil. 3:18, 19
Acts 20:27
Gal. 5:11
Gal. 4:17

During the vicarship of Wiersdale and Palmer, from 1584 to 1600, Gifford held a lectureship and designated himself as minister of God's Word at Maldon. Wiersdale was sympathetic with Gifford's views, but Palmer was not.

¹ Wiersdale resigned in 1586 or 1586/7, probably because of his sympathy with Gifford, and possibly because he had been suspended by Bishop Aylmer. He then went to live in Cambridge. Barrow may be speaking of Wiersdale's successor, in the following sentence. Wiersdale served as minister at Gaddesby, Leicestershire, 1588-1590, and as rector of Costock, Nottinghamshire, 1595-1639. He was frequently cited before the spiritual courts for not wearing the surplice, refusing to subscribe to the Three Articles, omitting services on week-days, failing to announce Holy days and fasts, not reading the canons, not using the sign of the cross in baptism, not catechizing in the manner prescribed by the *Book of Common Prayer*, not using the prescribed service, and sharply rebuking the character of clergymen. See Ronald A. Marchant, *The Puritans and the Church Courts in the Diocese of York, 1560-1642* (1960), pp. 316, 317.

seek to abalienate the heartes and mindes of this forewarde and best inclyned people from these their pastors, [134] and slily to drawe them unto themselves. Long it were to relate their artes and engines, wherebie they hunte and entangle poore soules: their counterfeit shewes of holines, gravitie, austerenes of maners, precisenes in trifles, lardge conscience in matters of greatest waight, especially of any danger; strayning a gnat and swallowing a camel; hatred and thundring against some sinne, tollerating, yea, colouring some other in some speciall persons; cunning insinuating into, and never offending the riche, nor regarding the poore; holding and with-holding the knowen truth of God in respect of tymes, places and persons; dissembling, hiding, withholding it in their publick ministrie and doctrines, where it may draw them into any trouble or tryall; yea, balking, if not perverting, the evident Scriptures as they arise against any publicke enormitie of the tyme, under the coloure of peace, christian policie, and wisedome. Wherebie these scorpions to poyson and sting every good conscience, so leaven them with hypocrisie, and teach them to halt with the times, dissembling with God and their owne conscience, that such proselytes as are wonne unto them, become two-fold more the children of hel than they were before. Yea, so is their whole auditorie entangled with their snares, as skarce any of them (without the especial mercie of God) are ever recovered, brought to any soundnes, stability, or upright walking, to any conscience, true faith, or feare of God. Herehence ariseth these schismes and sectes in the Church of England, some holding with these preachers, which make shewe as though they sought a sinceare reformation of all thinges according to the gospell of Christ, and yet both execute a false ministrie themselves, and they, together with all their hearers and followers, stand under that throne of Antichrist, the bishops their courtes, and accomplices, and all those detestable enormities which they would have utterly removed and not reformed. And these are hereupon called Precisians, or Puritanes, and nowe lately Martin-

A Plaine Refutation

istes.[1] The other opposite side are the Pontificales, that in al thinges hold and jumpe with the tyme, and are readie to justifie whatsoever is or shalbe by publick authoritie established. And with these hold al the rabble of atheists, dissembling papists, old [cold?] and luke-warm Protestants, libertines, dissolute and facinorous [wicked, vile] persons, and such as have no knowledge or feare of God. Even that antient sect of the Pharasies and Saduces, the one in precisenes, outward shewe of holines, hypocrisie, vaine-glorie, covetousnes, resembling or rather exceeding the Pharasies: the other in their whole religion, and dissolute conversation like unto the Saduces, looking for no resurrection, judgment, or life to come, confessing God with their lippes, and serving him after their careles maner, but denying him in their hearte, yea, openly in their deedes, as their whole life and all their worckes declare. Longe it were, and not my purpose in this place, to shewe howe these Pharasie sectorie teachers, these stipendarie roving predicantes [preachers], that have no certaine office or place assigned them in their church, but like wandring starres remoove from place to place [135] for their greatest advantage and best intertainement, in the error of Balaam powred out for wage, seduce and distracte the people of the lande, drawing them from their owne churches and ministers, some to this, some to that preacher by heapes, each one as he standeth affected to him that best fitteth his humore. *Jude 11:13 verse*

Mie desire rather here is to shewe the forgerie of this whole ministrie of the Church of England in their false office and entrance, aswel these precise esteemed preach-

---

[1] There is an interesting manuscript in St. John's College, Cambridge, (M9, No. 392), entitled " Certain Slanderous Speeches against the Present Estate of the Church of England, Published to the People by the Precisians " (M. R. James, *A Descriptive Catalogue of the Manuscripts in the Library of St. John's College, Cambridge*, p. 346). This manuscript was edited by Albert Peel and published posthumously as *Tracts Ascribed to Richard Bancroft* (Cambridge University Press, 1953).

The term " Puritan " began to be widely used about 1564-1567, and the term " Martinist " began in October and November, 1588, with the appearance of the first two Martin Marprelate tracts, the *Epistle* and the *Epitome*.

ers, as the parrish parsons and curates: which I hope by this which is said either is or may be donne. Nowe it remaineth that wee proceede to their administration and maintenance.

Of their administration we have above in the discovery of their publicke worship more perticularlie intreated, finding it wholly according to that erroneous apocripha popish leitourgie, that idolatrous abhominable booke of their service, wherunto they are bounde, whereby they are stinted and nourtered in al thinges, upon what dayes, eaves and houres through the yeere to come to church, what garmentes to weare in the church, where and when to sit, stand, and kneele, what and howe much to reade at this and that tyme, at this and that lesson, pistle, gospel. When to reade, when to singe, when to praye, where to verse, when to collect: with all other circumstances, ceremonies, trincketts in their sacraments, marriages, purifications, visitations, burialls, etc., as is in that parte of the treatise (though sommarily, yet more playnely) declared, whereunto I refer the reader. Here only affirming, that this their devised, abhominable idolatrous worship, miserable abuse and high prophanation of Scriptures, open portsale [public sale], and wilful sacrilege of their ministerie and sacraments, to the most prophane and ungodly, doe sufficiently declare what kinde of ministerie they execute, and ministers they are. Howe possible it is to joyne or to make the holy gospel and ministrie of Christ accorde unto this people in this confusion, ignorance, and sinne, or to these devises and tromperiers [*sic*], let anie in whom is anie light judge, when light and darcknes can be mingled togeather, or the stubble and strawe remaine in the flambing fire unconsumed, then shal this be.

Jer. 23:29

Yet furder to manifest what kinde of preachers of the gospel they are, and preaching of the gospel they make, let their most heynous and open professed perfidie in betraying their whole ministrie, gospell, church, Christ, and al into the handes of their lords these antichristian bishops, shewe, from whose apostatical chaire they have received their ministrie, to whose orders and injunctions

Gal. 1:10, 11

A Plaine Refutation

they have subscribed, to whose courtes and power they have sworne their canonical obedience: from whom they have received their licence and aucthority to preach, with condition not to preach against any thing by publick aucthority established, how ungodly and enormous soever they be:[1] And also have submitted their whole doctrines and persons to these their ordinances, not to preach anie truth, or against anie error that they inhibit, to preach, or cease to preach, to administer or cease to administer, at their direction and inhi-[136]bition. And for their private estate, by them to be enjoyned what kind of apparel to weare when they ride, walke abroade, or administer. Not to marrie without their knowledge, consent, or licence even to this or that perticular woman, etc.[2] Must not this needes be an excellent ministrie and ministration of the gospel that is thus mancipate [made subject] to and by these slaves, that is thus bought and solde, limited, prescribed, restrayned? When they can prove that the gospel may be in this maner used in the true churche of Christ, or preached by the true ministrie of Christ, we wil then yeild to their whole ministration, and acknowledg them the true ministers of Christ. But in the meane while because this is impossible, and cannot without blasphemie be enterprised, without sinne be thought; because also we finde upon this present ministrie of theirs, even al the markes of the false prophet, that are written in the booke, and al the markes of the beast, we must hold them as they are, except we wil with them condemne the truth of God, and call Christ execrable.

Gal. 2:4, 5

Neither yet is this their preaching (considered even in it self) set apart from all the abuses and enormities above recited, such, as they glorie of, abounding with such great learning, excellent giftes, and rare graces of

---

[1] [Church of England], *Advertisements Partely for Due Order in the Publique Administration of Common Prayers* (1584), B 3 *verso*. Barrow has in mind the article which reads: "First, that al they which shalbe admitted to preache, shalbe diligentlie examined for their conformytie in unitie of doctrine, established by publique authoritie." *Advertisements* (no date but first edition 1566, not 1564 or 1565), A iii *recto*.

[2] [Church of England]. *Injunctions Given by the Queene's Majestie*, number 29.

the spirit, or answearable to that heavenly exercise of prophecie in Christ's church. Of their education and learning even from the grammer schole to the pulpit, you have alreadie heard: as also their divinity to be traditional, wholly derived from other men's writinges and books, both for the understanding, dividing, and interpretation of al Scriptures, as also for all doctrines, questions, and doubtes that arise, and not springing from the fountaine of God's spirit in themselves, according to the measure of knowledge, faith, and grace given them. So that these dumbe blinde guides and watchmen doe but see with other men's eyes, but speake with other men's mouthes, and (as one of their chief aucthors saith of them) without these bookes they are as blinde as molles, as mute as fishes,[1] not able of themselves to decide, open, and interprete almost anie Scripture, or to discusse, judge, or decide anie doubt, or controversie with assurance. And therfore when anie newe question unwritten of before ariseth, they are either al at a full poynct, not knowing what to saye to the matter, or ells when they speake, so manie opinions and sentences, as speakers. Yea, even in the thinges they reade and teache (there being so great diversitie and contrarietie amongst these writers their aucthors) there also ensueth great difference and contrarietie in their doctrines which they publicklie deliver, one teaching one thing in one place, an other the quite contrarie in an other. And this not onlie in interpretation and understanding of sondrie, yea, almost all places of Scripture, but even in most waightie (and as they call them) fundamentall poynctes of doctrine. As whether the Church of Rome be to be esteemed a true churche or no, the sacraments there delivered, and the ministrie there ordayned, be to be held true sacraments, and a true ministrie or no.[2] Also if the ordi-[137]nances, order, and outward government of Christe's church left in Christe's Testament be perpetual and of necessitie to be observed,

---

[1] Morris Palmer Tilley, *A Dictionary of the Proverbs in England in the Sixteenth and Seventeenth Centuries* (Ann Arbor, 1950), pp. 217, 467.
[2] [Job Throkmorton ?], M[aster] *Some Laid Open in His Coulers*, pp. 39, 94, 100, 101, 102. Gifford, *A Short Treatise*, pp. 53-55.

A Plaine Refutation

etc.¹ And al this diversitie and contrarietie of judgment publickly taught in their church, must be coloured and passed over with this sweete sentence of Mr. Giffard, that they are but brotherly dissentions, they agree in al fundamentall doctrines.² A happie tourne it were, that those fundamental doctrines were once agreed upon and set downe, that wee might then knowe which part of Christe's Testament is fundamentall and of necessity, and which is accidental and not necessarie, but variable and at man's wil. In the meane while wee must stil II Cor. 1:19 believe that Christ is not yea and naye, of one minde in one place, of an other ells where. Neither that the spirite of God can rule in both places, where such contrarie doctrines are taught and maintayned. We also are taught, that howsoever bretheren through ignorance maie doubt and differ in judgment for a ceason, yet are they not hereupon to teach such thinges as they are not assured of, lest they publish and sowe errors: Which who so doth, be he man or angel that teacheth any other thing or otherwise than Christ and his Apostles have Gal. 1:8 taught and delivered, or causeth division and dissen- Rom. 16:17 / I Tim. 6:3 tion contrarie to their doctrine, or commeth [consenteth] not to the wholesom wordes of our Lord Jesus Christ, etc., wee are to hold them accursed, to watch, and avoide them.

Likewise, the maner of their pulpit preaching nothing I Cor. 14:29, 30, 31, 32 accordeth to the order of Christe's church, where the Rom. 12:6 prophets (I meane such as are knowen to have the gift I Pet. 4:10, 11 of interpretation of Scriptures) have al of them libertie to speake, what God reveileth [revealeth] unto them besides that which hath bene delivered, so that they neither hinder, disturbe, or interrupte the publick ministerie of the churche, but use their libertie opportunely and holily to edification. They have libertie also, yea, their especial dutie it is, to observe and publickly to reprove anie false interpretation, or false doc-

---

¹ *Ibid.*, p. 74. Robert Some, *A Godly Treatise, Wherein Are Examined and Confuted Many Execrable Fancies*, pp. 13, 34, 35. Thomas Cooper, *An Admonition to the People of England*, pp. 79-94 in the 1589 edition of 245 pages; in the 1589 edition of 252 pages, see pp. 73-84.
² *A Short Treatise*, pp. 89, 90.

trine delivered publicklie in the church, by whom soever. Yea, this power hath the least member of the church in due order and place, if the prophets and elders should oversee, omit, neglect, or refuse. The whole church also, even everie peculiar christian congregation, hath power in it self to censure not onlie anie doctrine delivered, but the person of anie member or minister of the same congregation. But here in these Babilonish synagogues one priest climbeth up into their pulpits for orations, and possesseth the place alone, where he declameth, delivereth his studied tale to the howre-glasse, which being runne out, he must make an end for troubling of his auditory, and leave no place or tyme of addition, assent or dissent, to anie other, al the people hasting awaye. In his pulpit, after he hath read his text, he may divide, teache, or ha[n]dle it, leave or take it, corrupt, falsifie, wrest or pervert it at his pleasure. In that his priviledged tubbe [pulpit] he may deliver what doctrines he liste, be they never so corrupt, false, blasphemous. None of his auditor[i]e, whatsoever they be, hath power to cal them into question, correct, or refute the same presently and pub-[138]lickly, for that is by laweforbidden.[1] But the church is driven to their Lord Ordinarie to complaine, and except or until he redresse, they must hold and use him stil as their minister. In that priviledged tubbe he may inveighe, accuse, sclander, denounce against anie truth or person that witnesseth against their kingdome, or against anie publicke sinne or enormitie of the tyme, without censure or controlement. Nay, these men are praysed, incited, and commended for this, as the most faithful and godly, which maketh both the sectes, as well Reformistes as Pontificall, yearne [for] praise by

---

[1] "If any preacher or parson, vicar or curat so lycensed shall fortune to preach any matter tending to dissention, or to the derogation of the religion and doctrine received, that the hearers denounce the same to the Ordinaries, or the next byshop of the same place; but no man openlye to contrary or to impugne the same speache so disorderly uttered," *Advertisements Partely for Due Order in the Publique Administration of Common Prayers* (1584), A 3 *verso*. For the first edition of *Advertisements* (1566), see the fifth article, A iii *verso*.

A Plaine Refutation

this vayne,[1] and fight with one accorde for their kingdome against Christe's faithful servants, whom they cal Brownistes, as against a common enimie; yea, more bitterly than they doe against anie other enimie, heretick, or wicked person. Onlie here in this tubbe if they can keepe their tongues from speaking against their lords the bishops and their procedings, or against anie publicke enormitie in the church or commonwealth, they maie then ease their stomackes against anie meane person, or one priest against an other, and rayle their fil. These perticular congregations have neither power to reprove their doctrines, or to censure their persons, be the one never so hereticall, the other never so obstinate; and needes then must here be a cleane church, I trowe.

And now how sincerely and purely these learned priests and divines al the rable of them preach God's lawe and Christe's gospel, to set downe their several defaultes, ignorances, corruptions, and unfaithfulnes, were infinite. Let the high open wilful breach of al God's laws by al degrees, suffered, and unreproved, declare and witnesse to their faces. Let their execrable idolls, and idolatries, their abhominable worship and innumerable devises, their taking the Lorde's name in vayne, their common swearing in everie matter, and tryal for everie cause and triffle, yea, without anie cause, their common and open blaspheming, and cursing, yea, transfiging [insulting?] the holy and dreadfull name of God in their anger and mirth; their impietie, prophannes, pride, vanitie, glottonie, excesse, idlenes, riote, playing, sporting, dauncing, etc., on the Lorde's day openly seene, suffered, unpunished, shew how well they keep and teach the first table of God's lawe in the Church of England. And for the second, let the evil nourture and bringing up of their youth, their dissolutenesse, irreverence, head strong and incorrigible nature, yea, their open disobedience and contempt of parents and superiours, the inordinate walking of all degrees helde within the compasse of no

[1] Vein, or habit, practice, procedure.

lawes, limites, callings, in the feare and obedience of no person, magistrate, parent, master; let the common quarles, frayes, foodes [feuds], tumults, blood-shed, murder, manslaughter, the jarres, hatreds, contentions, debates, wrath, anger, envying, cursing, reviling, nicknaming, etc.; let the common and open whoredoms, adulteries, fornications, chambering, wantonnes, daliance, lightnes, delicacie and softnes of apparle, diet, maners, to deck, provoke, allure, their courting intertainement, open and secret lust (otherwise caled love) most rife as in Sodome; let their [139] open robberies, their secret theftes, kickings, pilferinges, their open oppression, violence, wronge, extortion, usurie, their usual deceipt and coven [covet] in all bargayning, buying, selling; let their common and customable open and secret lying, blaspheming, sclandering, accusing, reproching, defaming, bringing up, carying, and receiving evil reportes one of an other, their false swearing in testimonie, their swearing and foreswearing to deceive even in everie trifle.

And as for coveting of wife, virgine, servant, house, land, cattle, goodes, insatiable coveteousnes and greedines, heaping and hourding up treasures, contynual purchasing and adding field unto field, yea, towne unto towne, till they have gotten whole countreyes into their possession, never satiate till their mouth be full of moulde. These are the best and only esteemed Christians of the Church of England; where coveteousnes is no sinne. They that should speake against it, pride, intemperance, etc., should judge the heart, and enter into God's judgment seate. Let these capital sinnes and transgressions against the lawe of God, which are committed without shame or feare, either not punished or wrongfully punished (murder only excepted, which how also it is wincked at or pardoned I wil not stand upon), let these, I say, stand up to the faces of these priestes and prophets, being thus commonly and openly comitted in their church, and witnesse how faithfully and sincerely they expounde and declare the lawes and judgmentes of God, how carefully they watch over the soules of men, and governe the church, that have not

A Plaine Refutation

against all or any one of these sinnes, any spirituall weapons, or ecclesiasticall censure in a readines; so that if the magistrate's sworde (which yet wanteth an eye to guide it) did not represse some sinnes, there should be no humane peace, as there now is no christian order in their church.

And now if I should here stand to dirive the several and speciall kindes of sinnes (which as rivers are divided and flowe forth from all these generall heads, and as a deluge cover the face of this whole land) it were infinite; but what then to divide these rivers againe into their perticular droppes? Namely, such perticular persons as commit the same, yea, such and so many perticular tymes as they commit the same, who then should nomber them? All these sinners and sinnes are in this church by these leaches, these prophets, healed with the plaister of peace, with the bloode and merites of Christ, though there be neither faith nor repentance, they are all good Christians.

Likewise if I should here stand to relate and recite the falshode, deceipt, and hypocrisie of these priestes (let me here be understoode even of those best esteamed forewarde learned preachers, commonly called good men) how conningly and craftily they teach the lawe, never touching or offending their auditorie (at least the mightie or rich of them), be their sinnes never so heynous and manifest; especially if they will countenance, esteeme, feaste, and heare these preachers, they are in them but infirmities, and imperfections, be they never so deiplie set and incurable. And againe how sharply they will inveigh against others [140], which thincke not so wel of them, especially if they be not of power to doe them hurte, nor of will to doe them good; howe they wil speake against such sinnes of the second table,[1] as their rich auditorie are not at al, or least addict unto, and beate them downe as with thunder from heaven, though they suffer as greate in

---

[1] The religious commandments, or the first table; the moral commandments, or second table; and the Yahwistic Decalogue, or ritualistic commandments; these are given in Exodus 20 : 1-17; Deuteronomy 5 : 6-21; and Exodus 34 : 14-28.

them and their houses before their face uncontrolled. Yea, what fine shiftes, excuses, and veales [veils, concealings] they will finde out to extenuate, excuse, or hide the sinnes of these greate rich persons, in whose houses all excesse, glotonie, ryot, pride, idlenes, gaming, shalbe but good hospitalitie answearable to their estates, honest recreation. And this veale [veil] of recreation must cover al their heathen sportes within doores and without, though it be all the day, yea, al their life longe, though they drawe never so many idle beholders, or idle assistantes to keepe them companie, to followe their dogges, hawkes, etc., as their only caling and profession. Yea, go these Esawites,[1] their wives, and children never so disguisedly in their strange prodigious shapes, newe fangled attires, with their infinite devises and curiosities, it is but according to their degree, sexe, age, calling, with infinite such like.

Also, if I should stand to relate the sondrie shiftes of these Reformist preachers, these sighers for reformation, these conscience botchers, these preachers of the gospell, to winne and keepe credit with the world; how zealous in some place, tyme, auditorie, where they may be wel backed they wil seeme against some triffles [trifles, trivialities], as though they were of most precise and unstayned conscience. And againe how luke-warme, colde, and backward they wilbe in the same poyntes at an other tyme, place, and auditorie. How strange to the poore that shal desire their judgment of some poynctes, especially of these. But cheiflie if any have espied more light than they would they should, and doe but make question of their ministrie, worship, church, etc., with what exquisite sleights they will seeke to draw them backe, as running too farre and too fast before their guides, with what poysoned cavills to quench their zeale and spirite, to pleade for and defend their sinne and apostasie. These thinges to discusse, or but to shew in perticular, with their due circumstances, would require a longe and lardge discourse, yea, no booke

---

[1] Esau was given to war and the chase. He is characterized as a profane person in Hebrews 12 : 16 — a materialist, one indifferent to things sacred.

A Plaine Refutation

were able to containe all their divelish devises and delusions, which even fill that flying volume the prophet speaketh of,[1] Sathan having his fordge of all mischeife continually going amongst them.

Al which their dealings evidently shew what kinde of ministers and preachers of the gospel they are, which drawe the people unto, and with their preaching keepe them in, this defection and apostasie from the gospell, which keep the people from, and will not leade them to, the sinceare practize of the gospell; but with their schole learning drawe a veale [veil] before Christ's face, that the people might not see to the end of his ministrie, neither discerne what Christe's will is for any action of the church, or to examine by the rules of Christe's Testament any thing by publick aucthoritie established. Yea, we see and have shewed, how they drawe the people unto, and themselves administer by an other leitourgie than Christ's [141] Testament, which prescribeth an other kinde of administration both to themselves and to the whole church in all thinges, than Christ hath prescribed. We see and have shewed, how they hold all the people under this more than Babilonish yoke of these antichristian prelates, their courtes, etc., and stand themselves the marcked ministers, sworne subjectes, and bond servantes of these their lordes, have fetched their ministrie, licence to preach, and their whole administration from them, how they are prescribed, stinted, limited, censured, silenced, deposed by them, how they have submitted and betrayed themselves, church, gospell, Christ, to these enemies. Also what merchandize they make of their prayers, gospel, preaching, sacraments, selling all and themselves to[o], for money. What trafique they make of their benefices, how they come by them and part from them, how they have in all thinges goone astray, forsaking the right waye, having followed the wage of Balaam of Bosor[2]

---

[1] Zechariah 5 : 1, 2.
[2] The reference to Balaam the son of Beor occurs eight times in the Old Testament, but in the New Testament there are three references to Balaam, one of which speaks of Balaam of Bosor (II Peter 2 : 15).

that loved the hire of unrighteousnes, and are in all thinges so throughly corrupted, as they are the most bitter and pestilent enimies of the kingdome of Christ, and of the sinceare practize of the gospel; devising to themselves and their miserable followers daily new errors and byepathes, as faste as the old (wherin they have walked) are discovered, as any that will take the paynes to examine by the rules of the Scriptures, their bookes of discipline and newe formes of reformation, or rather those antient primative defections which they seeke againe to revive, shall perceive.

For mie parte, I am even ircked to rave in this bottomlesse abysme of their iniquities, which the more they are looked into still offer more matter of reproofe, even without end. Wherfore, I even with wearines here cease furder to speake of their corrupt administration, hoping that by this alreadie saide, at the least upon due examination therof, it may appeare to al men, that this their whole administration and preaching of the worde is altogether as corrupt, and in all poynctes rightly fitteth unto their antichristian office and entrance.

It now remayneth that we hast to and over their maintenance.

The maintenance of the ministri[e] of the Church of England is of these fower sortes[:]

1. Either by lordly revenues, with their royal rightes, civill jurisdiction, courtes baron, tenancies, etc., belonging therunto.
2. Or by fees and pollages [extortions] raised and ravened in their spiritual courtes, for judging, pleading, solliciting, writing, fetching up, sommoning.
3. Or by gleabes and tithes.
4. Or ells by annual set stipendes.

The first sorte of these we have alreadie shewed to belong to princes, to civile lordes and persons, and to be utterly unlawful and forbidden to the ministrie of Christ. Mr. Giffard his liberall maintenance, or the ordinance of the church, cannot mainteine them. Neither will that worde *Philoxenos*, which they so lardgly

A Plaine Refutation

stretch and interpreat, carrie half this pompe.¹ [142]

To the second sort we affirme these courtes, officers, judges, advocates, proctors, registers, pursevantes, sommoners, together with all their functions, the orders of their courtes, maner of jurisdiction, pleading, etc., where all thinges are pleadable if not vendible for money, where al causes, even the most foule, finde their advocates, colours, defence, delayes, for mony, etc. Al these spiritual courtes, officers, judgments, pleadings, customes, we finde divelish and antichristian, and not to appertaine to the church and kingdome of Christ, but to belong to the kingdome and throne of Antichrist, and of the beaste. And therfore may conclude that they are the revenues of sinne, not to belong to the ministrie of Christ.

The third kinde, these tithes, we finde merely cere- Nomb. 18
moniall, to have bene ordayned for, and belonged unto, the Leviticall ministerie under the lawe. We finde them an inheritance of the Levites: an offering of the people. Therfore they cannot in this maner by lawe be tyed to the ministrie of Christ, be made an inheritance unto them, an offring of the people unto them. For if Heb. 7:12
there be a chandge of the priest-hoode, then of neces- Gal. 4 & 5 chapters
sitie must there be a chandge of the lawe. No part of Collos. 2:20
the ceremoniall lawe or of those shadowes can be joyned unto the gospell and ministrie of Christ, they or any part of them cannot now be revived or retayned without the denial and losse of Christ. And how is the ceremoniall lawe abrogate whilest these tithes are in this maner allotted by lawe unto the ministrie of the gospell, as an inheritance to them, as an oblation of the people, even as in former tyme unto the Levites? The prince's commandement, or the churche's decree, cannot alter the nature of these tithes, to make them either civille or lawfull. God was the aucthor of this law, he made it ecclesiastical. Man can neither chandge the propertie or the end therof, to make that civile that God hath make [made] ecclesiastical. Kinge Ezechia II Chron. 31
commanded and revived this lawe, it became not ther-

---

¹ A lover of hospitality to strangers. See I Timothy 3 : 2; Hebrews 13 : 2.

bie civile.¹ A godly prince commandeth al the lawes of the first table, all the ordinances of Christe's Testament, shall they therbie be made civile, and no longer ecclesiastical or God's lawes? The decree of the church also (alleadged by Mr. Giffard) sheweth it ecclesiastical, for the church maketh no civile decrees, it medleth not with the execution of civile governement.

Touching the power of the church to make lawes and decrees, we have in the first parte of this booke spoken. The church is bounde to the lawes of God, and may make or receive none other lawes than God hath made. Christ is the only law-giver and kinge of his church. Againe, this decree of the church to ordaine that the ministerie of the gospell should be maintayned by tithes, you see is directly contrarie to the wil, yea, to the being of Christ, receiving that lawe and maintenance which Christ hath abolished together with the Levitical ministrie. And aswel might they revive the Levitical ministrie, or any other Jewish ceremonie, with as great pretext and warrant, as this; except the Church of England have some speciall warrant from or together with her mother of Rome to revive and erect whatsoever [143] Christ hath abolished, be it never so contrarie unto him; yea, and to abrogate whatsoever Christ hath instituted, be it never so necessarie. How bold the Church of England is in these things, in their tithes, offrings, purification, suspension, their holy cimiteries, and cells, the shape of their church, with the porche, batlementes, isles, folding doores, lightes, ministerial vessels, ministerial garmentes, dayes, feastes, etc. As on the other side to abrogate Christe's ministrie and the ordinances of his Newe Testament, is above declared, and in this appeareth. For Christ having instituted an other maintenance for his ministrie, namely, the free contribution and benevolence of his sainctes in these congregations wherunto they belonge and administer. The Church of England, judging this al to[o] base for

I Cor. 9
Gal. 6:6

I Cor. 16:1, 2

---

¹ The law of tithes for crops, fruits, herds, and flocks is given in Leviticus 27 : 30-33. King Hezekiah revived this practice. See II Chronicles 31.: 4.

A Plaine Refutation

her ministerie, hath instituted or rather received of her mother of Rome lordly, yea, princely livings, courtly judicial sees, gleabes and tithes, sett and certaine stipendes. She wil not have the lowest of her ministrie to live thus beggerly, to depend upon the benevolence of the people, as our Saviour himself, his Apostles and ministers did: (which a certaine doctor of hers in disdaine caled the almouse basket).[1] But she wil have al her ministry sure of their maintenance before hand, they shal neither depend upon God nor the church. But she giveth them their lines and portion in the lande amongst the people, and also giveth them a lawe over the people, wherbie they may exact their duetie, if the fleese or flesh be worth so much. The priest here thrusteth his flesh-hooke into everie poore bodie's kettle, his sithe [scythe] and sickle into everie field, prying and prowling in everie place and corner, skratching and gathering up his tithes even to the chicken and egge, to the mynte and anise, without regarde to whom they belonge, whether to the faithful or prophane, papist, atheist, witch, or heretick, to the poore or fatherlesse, catching up al with the angle, they cetch it in their net and gather it in their yarne and burne incense to their yarne, because this their portion is fat and their meate plenteous, devowring widowes' houses under colour of longe prayer. Mich. 3 Ezek. 34 I Sam. 2

Mat. 23:23 Lev. 22:25 Hab. 1

Math. 23:14

Now how this tithing, prowling, extortion, may be made the christian minister's maintenance, I would faine learne, who, as the prophet saith, should be fed with cleane provander that is winowed with the shovel and with the fanne. Who themselves ought to be examples of pietie, equitie, meekenes, and not like greedy wolves thus to make a praye [prey] of the sheepe. Likewise how this tithe gathering and continuall prow- Esa. 30:24

Ezeck. 13:4, 19

---

[1] Dr. Robert Some, in seeking to refute Barrow's argument that the ministers should live by the voluntary contributions of the saints, *ex mera eleemosyna*, wrote: "If the teachers of religion in England were as singly [slightly] furnished with learning, and as strangely caried with fancies, as H. Barrowe and J. Greenwood are, the almes-basket were a little too good for them" (*A Godly Treatise, Wherein Are Examined and Confuted Many Execrable Fancies*, p. 6).

ling may be enjoyed or made to accord to a christian minister's office, or howe it is possible for the true minister of Christ diligently to attend his studie and office together with this his tith gathering, let anie that knoweth the worke of the ministrie judge. Yea, rather let the Holy Ghost judge, that expresly forbiddeth the ministrie of the worde to be entangled with such busines of this life. If it be here said these tithes may be gathered by an other, yet this sheweth they cannot be gathered by the minister. And so stil this reason holdeth, that therfore they are no fit maintenance for the ministrie. The other reasons above recited, prove the unlawfulnes of them.[1] [144]

II Tim. 2:4

To the set stipendes also and gleabes, I in like maner affirme them to be an other maintenance than that Christ hath instituted for his ministrie; yea, to take away that order, to the great detriment and manifold inconveniences of the church, and therfore likewise unlawfull. Holding this proposition firme, that where Christ hath instituted a maintenance for his ministrie, the church may not devise or receive anie newe or other lawes for the maintenance of their ministrie, than Christ

---

[1] For contemporary comment on tithes, see John Selden, *The Historie of Tithes* (1618); Richard Montagu, *Diatribae upon the First Part of the Late History of Tithes* (1621); Stephen Nettles, *An Answer to the Jewish Part of Mr. Selden's History of Tithes* (1625); Henry Spelman, *Tithes too Hot to Be Touched* (1646) or *The Larger Treatise concerning Tithes* (1647); Richard Tillesley, *Animadversions upon M. Selden's History of Tithes, and His Review Thereof* (1619); Lancelot Andrewes, *Of the Right of Tithes* [*Theologica determinatio de decimis*] (1647); (1842); [Anon.], *Tithes and Oblations according to the Lawes Established in the Church of England* (1595); William Prynne, *A Gospel Plea* (1653); Thomas Comber, *An Historical Vindication of the Divine Right of Tithes* (1682). Brian Walton's "Treatise concerning the Payment of Tythes and Oblations in London" is in Lambeth Palace Library, Codices Manuscripti Lambethani, No. 273, and is printed in Samuel Brewster, *Collectanea Ecclesiastica* (1752). For the general subject of tithes, see William Easterby, *The History of the Law of Tithes in England* (1888). William Bohun, *The Law of Tithes*, 3rd ed. (1744); 4th ed. (1760). Margaret James, "The Political Importance of the Tithes Controversy in the English Revolution, 1640-60," *History*, New Series, XXVI, No. 101 (June, 1941), pp. 1-18. One of the best recent treatments is chapter V of Christopher Hill, *Economic Problems of the Church from Archbishop Whitgift to the Long Parliament* (1956). See also F. Smith Fussner, *The Historical Revolution. English Writing and Thought 1580-1640*, Ch. XI, "John Selden and Problematic History."

hath given. Christ then hath ordayned that they that dresse the vineyard and feede the flock, should eate of the fruict of that vineyarde and of the milke of that flocke, to which they attend. This maintenance in other places is set downe to be the free contribution and benevolence of the sainctes from tyme to tyme, according to the present abilitie of the one, and necessities of the other. This the Lorde in wisedome hath thought moste meete for his church and ministerie unto the worlde's end, as wherby to knit the heartes of them together in the band of love, in al mutual dueties, to have each other in minde, to care, provide, and labour each for other as they ought. The minister according to his duety to seeke pasture for them, to thresh them out the corne out of the eares, yea, to grind, prepare, and divide yet [it?] to the nourishment and comfort of them al. And they againe on their parte to labour, to administer of their earthly goods to the necessities and wantes of their ministers and guides. Wherby the Phil. 4:10, etc. one is encouraged in their studies, laboures, and diligence, thus reaping the fruictes of the people's faith and love, and are assured that they doe their dueties to the approbation and good liking of the flocke; which when they shall faile and will not be drawn faithfully to doe, then is not the flocke any longer burdened with or bound unto such a minister. As one [on] the other side, if the people fal from the faith and refuse to walke orderly in the faith, then are the ministers no furder bounde, or to contynue to administer to such a people.

But now whilest the minister's maintenance is made certaine by law, or bargaine, by stint, rate, or proportion imposed upon the people, how much and when each one shal paye, how much the minister shall have yeerely; it first depriveth God of the glorie due to him for his blessing upon their labours and indevours, in restrayning the free contribution and willing benevolence of the people by this lawe or bargaine, making it of necessity, stinting, and apportioning it to this or that rate, which the Lorde hath left at the libertie, discretion, and will of each one, as God hath prospered, Hebr. 13:16
and according to that present ability God administreth. Phil. 4
II Cor. 9

With which contribution and sacrifice howe wel God is pleased, the Scripture everie where witnesseth. Then it taketh awaie or extinguisheth all those mutuall and contynuall dueties, benevolence, love, care, labour, etc., betwixt the flocke and the ministerie. The flocke therbie not knowing or having meanes to doe their duetie unto their ministerie. The ministers therbie so hindered, incombred, and with-drawen, as they either slack, or neglect their dutyes to the flocke. [145]

By this corrupt custome also sondrie intollerable inconveniences and grievous mischieves doe ensue. This setting out land or certaine rates by way of lawe or bargaine in everie parrish or congregation to the minister, doth hinder the church from the choice and use of such other ministers as Christ in his Testament hath ordained to the governement and service of his church, the parrish or congregation neither indevouring to have more, neither indeed suffred to have more, or by this meanes able or willing to keep more. This setting out landes, tithes, etc., to the minister by way of lawe, doth alwaies presuppose of necessity a true established church, and true minister in those parrishes unto the worlde's end; those landes and tithes being appropriate and bounde therunto, and having none other owners. Which confirmeth and establisheth those grosse popish errors of a personal and continuall succession of ministers, and local contynuance of a visible churche.

Againe when this living is thus by lawe given to a priest for terme of his life, be he never so unable, unworthie, or negligent, the parrish is so long bounde unto him, and can by no meanes get rid of him, yea, be he never so bad, his faultes and errors never so fowle, they cannot without or until their lord bishop wil, geat rid of him, they must mainetaine him and receive his ministry, whether they wil or no.

Furder, these annual livinges by lawe and set stipendes by rate, presuppose alwaies one permanent and certaine estate both of the parrishioners and ministers, the one, even everie person ever to be able to pay so much, the other never to need more or lesse. Yea, that alwaies to the worlde's end all the parsons and al the parrishioners of that towne shall never need or be able to give more or lesse, whether the Lorde send scarcity or plentie, dearth or cheapnes, sicknes or health, losse or advantage, children or no chardge, etc.

Againe, such unreasonable inequalitie is used in the distribution of these livinges, the parson of some one litle hamblet where are not twentie houses, having one hundreth or two hundreth pounds by yeere to live on, an other of a much greater towne not having twentie poundes, yea, peradventure ten poundes by yeare for that chardge he hath to live upon; and this for ever without regarde of the needes or laboure of them, it being alike to them and their successors whosoever.[1]

To conclude, the tithes and set stipendes of these parrish priestes being of the goods of the prophane, most wicked, and ungodly, even of al their parrish indifferently; yet are more odious and unmeet for anie christian ministers, who are not to stande hierdes [shepherds] to such dogges and swine to administer to them the gospel and sacramentes for their goods and hire. It was not lawfull for the priest under the lawe to receive the offring of anie stranger from the faith, such might not enter into or offer in the temple. Neither nowe under the gospel maie the unbelieving have anie fellowship with the church, or communicate in or intermeddle with anie actions of the church. But this contribution is an action of the church, a communion and dutie of the sainctes. How execrable then is this their sacriledg and covetousnes, that thus make marchandize of the [146] holie thinges of God, and let out themselves to hire, even to the prophane, for filthie lucre. The true ministers of Christ may not be suspected, much lesse openly taynted, of such peremptorie faultes as these, which disable him from all ministrie in the churche, and are everie where set downe as undoubted

---

[1] See Great Britain. Record Commission. *Valor Ecclesiasticus Temp. Henr. VIII Auctoritate Regia Institutus.* 6 vols. (1810-1834). This represents a survey made of ecclesiastical houses and livings in 1535, with the consequent returns made by the commissioners into the Exchequer.

markes of a false prophet. By al which then as by al other arguments of their antichristian office, entrance, and administration, we may still and yet more strongly conclude them not to be the ministers of Christ. Seing neither the office they execute, their entrance unto their office, their administration in their office, nor yet their maintenance, can be joyned unto the church, ministrie, or gospel of Christ.

There yet remaine a few base stragling offices of their church, *vzt.* [namely], their church-wardens, questmen, parish clark. These are al lay men (as they cal them), yet intermeddle they with ecclesiastical affaires. Their offices perticularly I can neither describe, nor yet wel distinguish. The church-wardens are (as it seemeth) an other kinde of deacons. They gather and keepe the church stocke and treasurie, and also the penalties of such as come not to their divine service, and also distribute the same unto the poore, the reparations of the church, etc.[1] They keep one of the keyes of the towne cheste. The quest-men are liker unto elders, these (I suppose) they looke to the order and governement of the church, as wel priest as people. That the priest use his ministerial vestures, vessels, and trincketts, reade his service, homelies, injunctions, orderlie. That the people do not bargaine, talke, or walcke in the church and church yarde during the tyme of divine service. They also must looke to the ale-houses that there be no tipling or playing, during the said tyme; and who be absent from their parrish church, and present such defaltes at masse commissaries' courte accordinglie.[2]

The parrish clarck, he is the prieste's accolouth[3] to help him to say his *mattens* and *even-songe*, with his due versicles and response, to help him at his sacraments,

---

[1] See *Advertisements Partely for Due Order in the Publique Administration of Common Prayers* (S.T.C., 10026). See also the section on "Churchewardens and syde men" in *A Book of Certaine Canons, concernyng Some Parte of the Discipline of the Churche of England* (S.T.C., 10063).

[2] Questmen, or sidesmen, held an inquest or inquiry in a parish or ward, and made presentments accordingly. In the church they served as churchwardens' assistants.

[3] Variant of acolyte, one who followed or attended the priests and deacons in divine service.

A Plaine Refutation

marriages, church-goings, visitations, dirges, rogations at all assayes. He ringeth their bells to and after their service, their knells and soule-peales; he keepeth the church doore keye; he sweepeth and trimmeth the church; he nurtureth the boyes and dogges that they be not to[o] lowde at service tyme; yea, he may doe yet manie things more, if he have the bishop's letter; as in tyme of neede to christen children, and to reade divine service in the absence of the priest, etc.[1]

To stand to shewe the forgerie, severall defaultes, or dissimilitude of these offices from the deacon or elders that God hath appoyneted, were tedious and needlesse, they having neither mention nor use in Christe's Testament and church.

Thus now have we summarily perused al this rable of the ministery of the Church of England, and have not founde anie one of them right, or almost in anie one poyncte according to the rules of Christe's Testament, they are all strangers there, they belonge not to Christe's bodie, his [147] church, neither are they knit as members unto that heade. But out of the smoke of the bottomlesse pit they came when that fallen starre Antichrist had the key thereof given him;[2] to his bodie, his kingdome, the false church, they have alwaies belonged, alwaies served; to him in his severall shapes they have alwaies bene knit, as the members to the heade; from him and not from Christ we all with our bodily eyes see the Church of England hath received them. We see they beare not Christ's but Antichrist's image, marcke, life, power. What then should hinder this assertion, that they together with Antichrist, their head, doe growe, live, raigne, stand and fal as the   Revel. 9 and 13 and 16 and 17 and 18 chapters

Luke 11:17

---

[1] See James Christie, *Parish Clerks* (London, 1893); Peter Hampson Ditchfield, *The Parish Clerk*, 3rd ed. (London, 1907); "An Essay concerning the Office and Duties of Parish-Clerks," in Samuel Brewster, *Collectanea Ecclesiastica* (1752). Cuthbert Atchley, *The Parish Clerk, and His Right to Read the Liturgical Epistle*, "Alcuin Club Tracts," IV (London, 1903, 1924); J. Wickham Legg, *The Clerk's Book of 1549*. "Henry Bradshaw Society," Vol. XXV (London, 1903); W. P. M. Kennedy, *Elizabethan Episcopal Administration*, I, Ch. VI.

[2] Revelation 9 : 1, 2. Barrow frequently uses the phrase, "the smoke of the bottomless pit."

branches with the tree. Should a revoult, division, and schisme [exist] in a kingdome within it selfe? No, this but hasteneth the Lorde's judgmentes the sooner to make it desolate. Can this revoulte and schisme either transforme or reforme this ministerie? Let their present estate judge.

^{II Thes. 2:7} [II Thes. 2:7 / Revel. 13] Should Antichriste's changing his shape from his mysterie to his exaltation, from his exaltation to his consumption [destruction], or his ministers' transforming and masking themselves under shewes and visardes of righteousnes, make them ever the better, or hide and defend them from the light? No, all thinges when they are reprooved of the light are manifest. The light of the gospel shall discover and abolish Antichrist. As he rose by degrees, so shall he by degrees vanish. As he and his trayne rose out of the smoke of the bottomlesse pit, Revelation 9, so shall they all goe into utter darcknes, even thether [thither] againe. The beast and the false prophet shalbe taken by him that rideth on the white horse and his holie armie, these both shal alive be cast into that lake of fire burning in brimstone. The Lord himself hath spoken it. Revelation 19.

[II Cor. 11:13, 14, 15 / Ephes. 5:13 / I Cor. 3:13, 14, 15]

[II Thes. 2:8 / Revel. 16]

Nowe let us see what arguments Mr. Giffard after more than two yeeres' studie[1] hath brought us to approove his ministrie by. He told us erewhile that they were true ministers of the gospel, pastors and teachers, had a true calling and ordination; nowe come his proves.

[I] The ministerie of the gospell which bringeth the worde of faith and reconciliation betwixt God and the world, is the true ministerie of Christ, for the divel and Antichrist ordaine no such ministerie. Nowe the ministerie of the Church of England doth bring no worde nor doctrine but the sacred Scriptures. It preacheth faith in God through Christ, and the doctrine of repentance, delivering the holie sacraments,

---

[1] Barrow's first reply to Gifford's answer was written about January, 1587/8. Gifford did not reply until about May, 1590. See "A Brief Summe of the Causes of Our Seperation," in Carlson, *The Writings of Henry Barrow, 1587-1590*, pp. 118-150.

A Plaine Refutation

as seales to confirme the same. Let all the schismaticks of the worlde barck, etc.[1] I am lothe to take Mr. Giffard in a paralogisme[2] at the first where reasons are so geason [unproductive], lest hereafter we have no more, especially lest we have more varyance about the forme than about the matter in this, yet when he shall have reduced it to right forme, he shal then but have begged that which we demanded, and still looke that he should proove, *vzt.*, [namely], that their ministrie is the true ministrie of the gospell. This, because everie true ministrie of the gospell is in some office, unto which office there must needes be a true and lawfull calling, therefore we desired him to proove their ministrie in the office, entrance, etc., by the Scriptures, Mr. Giffard giving us his [148] bare worde that they are pastors and teachers, making no proofe thereof, quite overskippeth their office and entrance, and prooveth them ministers because they doe administer. As if a private person should reason thus. I have knowledge of the lawe, I administer true justice and judgment, therfore I am a true judge, a lawfull magistrate. Doth he thinck that this reason wil excuse this usurper either before God or his prince? If he then wil have anie better speede, let him proove his ministerie directly and plainely by the Scriptures, first in the office he chalengeth, then in his caling unto his office, as al the Apostles and true ministers of Christ have donne, and ought to doe. And then if he can justifie his administration and be founde faithfull, he shall have praise with God and man.

Otherwise by this balcking and begging that he should, and hath bene so often urged to proove, he but manifesteth his weaknes and forgerie in those poynctes, and but to loseth [*sic*] as many of these preposterous argumentes, as he bringeth. Yet that he be not too far conceipted, or any other deceived with this argument, against his

---

[1] *A Short Treatise*, p. 79.
[2] A faulty syllogism, or an illogical argument. Frequently, a sophism implies conscious subtlety and deliberate fallacy, but a paralogism implies a reasoner who is unaware of his error.

next booke,[1] we give him to wiete [wit, know], that the second part of his argument is a false and impudent assumption. The Church of England bringeth and emposeth an other worde and other ordinances than the holie Scriptures, as that devised abhominable leitourgie, their idoll service-booke, the rule and foundation, yea, the verie matter and substance of their publick worship, and administration, their popish superstitious ceremonies and trincketts, their ungodly and antichristian ordinances, ministrie, and governement. To all these abhominations they joyne, or rather subject and abuse the gospell. And therfore preach not faith in God nor Christ, neither the doctrines of repentance truly and sincerely: but denie God in their workes and Christ in his offices. They beare the yoke of Antichrist, drawe all the people unto them, souder [solder, unite] them, even the most wicked and impenitent in their sinne and iniquitie, with their prayers, preaching, and sacraments. Not suffring any to forsake these seene sinnes and abhominations, or to come unto Christ, but drawing and holding all the land under the wrath of God, etc.

Next he by the way maketh a learned apologie for the dumb pastors of the Church of England, his bretheren, against whom if it be objected that their ministrie is not the ministrie of reconciliation, because they cannot preach the gospel, he here setteth downe a learned note by way of two rare distinctions. We must first, he saith, "distinguish betwixt the ministrie and the minister. The man may be of the divel, and yet his ministrie of God." Then we must distinguish betwixt the function it self, and the execution of the same. As "when the office is laide upon one that cannot preach, the function it self is entire, the defect only in the execution therof; therfore the ministrie of the Church of England is the ministrie of the gospell, though some doe not, and others cannot, preach."[2]

---

[1] Gifford's next book, *A Short Reply unto the Last Printed Books of Henry Barrow and John Greenwood*, was entered December 6, 1591. See Edward Arber, *A Transcript of the Registers of the Company of Stationers in London*, II, 599.

[2] *A Short Treatise*, pp. 79-80.

A Plaine Refutation

Sure this is so subtily contrived, as men of meane judgment and [149] capacitie shall never be able to perceive how it is or may be brought about. The first distinction is graunted, so the sinne of the minister be secrete, or not such as disableth him to the ministrie. But what of this, may any open, unworthie, or insufficient person be a minister? Or is the ministrie of such a one good and acceptable? Ther is no such consequence from hence to be gathered.[1] To the second in like maner it followeth not, because we may distinguish and put difference betwixt the office it self and the execution of the office, that therfore any office of the church may be given to anie open unsufficient, or unworthie person; or if it be, that the ministrie of such a one is good or acceptable. For the calling of the church cannot enhable such open insufficient [persons] to the ministrie, whom God refuseth, or make acceptable that ministration, which God disaloweth. Nowe then these dumbe pastors that cannot preach, are apparently insufficient and incapable of that office, therfore no calling of men can make them true and lawfull ministers. And being no true or lawfull ministers, their ministration is then unlawfull, accursed, abhominable to God and men. These then being allowed ministers, and their ministration publiquely by lawe approved, and received in the Church of England, we may conclude the publike ministrie and ministration of the Church of England to be unlawfull, accursed, and abhominable thus far foorth, notwithstanding Mr. Giffarde's payre of distinctions. Otherwise, if he laboured to proove the ministerie of the gospell to be in it self alwaies entire, holie, and blessed, notwithstanding the

---

[1] If the proof of the pudding is in the eating, then the test of the ministerial office is in the preaching. One can make a theoretical distinction between the office and the incumbent, but in practice men judge the office by its representative. For Barrow both the office and the incumbent are so closely allied that to distinguish them is caviling. The requirements *per se* in the Church of England for the ministerial office are unsound and unchristian. Hence all incumbents come short of the New Testament specifications. It is not the infirmities in men, which Barrow recognizes, but the defects in the calling to the office, which Barrow condemns.

infirmities and faultes of men, this all men will graunte, and needed not his learned distinctions to proove the same. But what is this to proove the ministrie of these dumbe pastors, or the other ministrie of the Church of England to be that ministerie of the gospell; which we for all the reasons above alleadged confidently denie? [II]. His second reason. " Such as have the caling and ordination of the church, have the ministrie of Christ. For it is given to the church to cal and ordaine ministers." In the next section his minor followeth. " In England the ministers have their caling and ordination by the church of God." Therfore, etc. To the major he addeth a clause, that it may be a true caling notwithstanding some faultes of ignorance or otherwise.[1] So he understand this " otherwise " to be of negligence, and not of anie wilful and obstinate transgressions, or not any of those peremptorie faultes excepted by the Holy Ghost, which disable the elect and disanul the election, then we thus far assent. But when we reason of the caling of the ministri of England, we speake not of a true caling, though unperfect with some faultes of ignorance or negligence, but of a false, counterfeit, and antichristian caling, which we have proved and affirme theirs to be. The caling of the church ought alwaies to be that caling of Christ prescribed in his Testament, which theirs is not. To his minor now, first, we denie the Churche of England to be the true established church of Christ. He prooveth it thus. " That people which hath forsaken heresies and false worship, and [150] imbraced the doctrine of the gospell, hath in it the true church which hath the power."[2] Wee observe much subtiltie and feare in this position. For whereas he ought to have affirmed, " are the true church, and have the power," he fearefullie and subtilly saith, " hath in it the true church, which hath the power," not daring to justifie or joyne issue of their outward estate, but leaving himself a starting hole to flee to such secret ones as God may call and have amongst them. We

[1] *A Short Treatise*, p. 80.
[2] *Ibid.*

A Plaine Refutation

doubt not but God hath in Turckye or Persia, yea, in the Church of Rome manie deare elect; but should we therfore say that Turcky, Persia, Rome, are the true church? We affirme also and will approve against al the false prophets of the world, that in this land the Lord hath such a people that have thus forsaken heresies and false worship, embraced the gospell, and have this power of Christ. But we denie this their church to consist of this people, to have forsaken heresies and false worship, to have truly embraced the gospel, or to have this power of Christ, to elect, ordaine, excommunicate, or to redresse anie enormitie; but are dryven to these antichristian bishopps for al these. Who receive not power of the church, but usurpe and exercise absolute power over the church, yea, the whole power of the church, as hath bene shewed. Which is unlawfull either for the church to give, or for any true Christian to receive or execute. Neither can the aucthoritie of anie mortall men of Parlament make that lawfull, which God in his Worde condemneth and forbiddeth.[1] And so even by this his owne allegation, all this ministrie made by and standing under this usurped inordinate antichristian power of the bishopps, are also unlawfull. To which if we add the unlawfulnes of the office these ministers are called unto and execute, the unlawfulnes of their calling in the whole maner therof unto, by, and in no flocke certaine, the unlawfulnes of the ordayners, as also of the ordayned, their open ambition, greedines, and insufficientcy, their false maner of probation and ordination, with all the ungodly and execrable ceremonies, vowes, othes, subscriptions, used to the same, none can mistake this caling and ordination of the ministers of England, for that true and holy election and ordination of the Church of Christ: without which true caling there can be no true minister. No true church may use or can justifie anie such false caling as

---

[1] Parliament can make laws even though they conflict with interpretations of Scripture by Puritans and Separatists. Those who regarded their own interpretation of Scripture as a higher law could refuse to obey the "lower" law — and could suffer the consequences of fines, imprisonment, or the death penalty.

theirs. And so still we must leave Mr. Giffard to prove the office and caling of his ministrie.

[III]. This clarke procedeth to an other reason. "That ministrie is of God, which is to bring men to the faith, and to build up the bodie of Christ. The ministrie of England is to none other end." Therfore, etc. The minor he proveth, because " the whole drift, scope, and burden laide upon them, is to feede with wholesome doctrine and to guide in the waies of godlines the sheepe of Christ, walking before them in godlie conversation."[1] Mr. Giffard said erewhile that the ministers of England were no intruders. But sure it seemeth they are verie nimble leapers which skippe over the hatch into the house, and wil not stay until the master of the house cal, until the porter of the house open, but without any lawful calling or entrance [151] wil needes thrust themselves ministers upon the Lord and his church, whether he and they wil or no. Yea, Mr. Giffard will prove himself and these his presumptuous companions true ministers without this caling or entrance, by the endes of their administration, although the Lorde of the house never caled them to be builders, or committed unto them the worcke and ministrie of his house. The deceiptfulnes and disorder of these kinde of arguments wee have above shewed, and with the same general answeare might dismisse this. Save that by the way wee must give him to understand, that his assumption is a shamelesse presumption. They build not upon but destroye the house of God, the bodie of Christ. This their worcke, the present estate of their church witnesseth to their face, and sheweth what maner of worckmen they are: where we finde not one pinne, nayle, or hooke in due order and proportion according to the true paterne. They feed not the Lorde's sheepe but the Lorde's goates, and that not with wholesome food, with sincere milke, that they might growe and be encreased therby, as the generall sinne, prophannes, and ignorance of al estates, both priestes and people, declare. Neither guide they in the way of godlines, but in the wayes of destruction

[1] Ibid.

A Plaine Refutation

and calamitie. They have al declined and bene made together unprofitable. And the way of peace they have not knowen. And as for the conversation of these priestes, it may wel be an example to the flock in al idolatry, superstition, impiety, unfaithfulnes, apostasie, halting and dissembling with God and man; worldlines, coveteousnes, deceipt, and what not. So that the saying of the prophet is come about, that there are like people like priest.[1] Al this Mr. Giffard in his festered conscience knewe before, and that his shamelesse assumption would not passe with his adversarie with whom he had to doe, and therfore he leaveth the proof of this assumption, as also of his office and entrance, and yet againe assayeth by a newe argument of the effectes, together with that which is properly adjoyned to the ministrie of Christ, to prove his ministerie.

[IV]. " That ministerie, with the execution wherof there is joyned the effectual grace, power, blessing and operation of the Holy Ghost, to the true convertion of men's soules, is not a ministerie of the Divel nor of Antichrist, nor cometh not in the life and power of the beaste, but is indeed the true ministerie of Christ." But such grace, power, blessing, operation, is founde in the ministerie of England. Therfore.[2]

First here stil must be oberved a begging and assuming of a true ministrie, which as yet is not proved. Neither doth this reason prove a ministrie, so much as shew the infallible effects of true doctrine and true preaching, whether it be by ministers, or by other faithful, which have the gift of prophecie, knowledge, interpretation, utterance, etc. For, far from the truth is it to thincke, that only ministers beget and winne to the faith (as some most shamelesse bishops, and sencelesse priestes of this age have published and mainetaine).[3] Then might they aswel with the papistes permit the worde of

---

[1] Hosea 4 : 9. Compare Isaiah 24 : 2.
[2] *A Short Treatise*, pp. 80-81.
[3] See Robert Some, *A Godly Treatise, Wherein Are Examined and Confuted Many Execrable Fancies, Given Out and Holden, Partly by Henry Barrow and John Greenwood*, pp. 19, 20, 23-26.

Henry Barrow

<small>Acts 20:32
Jam. 1:21
Rom. 11:16
Heb. 10:24, 25
I Thes. 5
I Cor. 14
Acts 8:4, and
11:19</small>

God only unto priestes: yea, suffer none but priests to speake of the worde or holie [152] doctrines, if this use and end of the Worde were taken away, if the blessing and power of God should not goe with his holy Word and truth in the mouth of all his servants, both to cal unto the faith, and to superedifie in the faith. Ells should al dueties in families, all mutual exhortations, admonitions, conferences, cease. But having the commandement of God to al these, the evidence and testimonie of the blessed and comfortable effects following the faithful testimonies of al Christe's disciples in all ages, and contynual experience hereof amongst our selves dayly, we dare affirme that others besides ministers may convert soules and begeate faith. So then this argument of the effectes proveth not so much a true ministry, as it doth prove true doctrine. For no false doctrine can beget true faith, though manie which be no ministers may beget true faith. Mr. Giffard then reasoneth verie corruptly and deceiptfully in attributing the convertion of soules as proper and peculiar to the ministrie, which is not so, and in bringing these effectes to prove a true ministrie, which only are to prove true doctrine. And nowe to Mr. Giffard his assumption. Wee denie that any false ministrie hath promise of blessing, or is sent of God for the conversion of soules, but on the contrarie we finde it accursed, and sent of God for the seducing of the reprobate. The ministrie then of the Church of England being proved false in office, entrance, and administration, can have no such promise or blessing of God as Mr. Giffard assumeth.

If it be demaunded then whether al under this ministrie be damned, I say it is a newe question, and kept secret to the Lorde, who onlie knoweth who be his, when and how to call them. It becometh not us to give anie such finall judgment of matters not knowen unto us. Yet this wee may by warrant of the whole Scripture saie, that the waies of the false churche and ministrie are the waies of death, and have no promise of salvation. But for the persons wee judge charitablie, even so longe and so far as wee may, measuring them by our selves, as wee sometymes were, hoping and not

A Plaine Refutation

doubting, but God hath manie thousandes deare elect there, yea, even in the popish churches, whom he in his due tyme by his appointed meanes wil cal. If Mr. Giffard here insist and say that many of those thousandes are converted by their ministrie, therfore their ministrie is not in the power of Antichrist, or of the Divel, but of God, having that sure seale, that worcke of the Holie Ghost, we have above answered that this rather approveth the doctrine than the ministrie, and is to be attributed to the Worde of God, rather than to the person of man. Furder, that the false ministrie hath no promise of blessing. Yet doe wee not herebie restraine the infinite power of God from savinge or calinge his elect even by the doctrine of the false churche: which though it be throughly leavened, corrupted, perverted, abused, yet can the Lorde bring that truth of his lawe and gospel which is there read, and after their maner preached in such sorte, to the eares and consciences of his chosen, as it shal both shew them their degenerate estate, how guiltie they are of the breache of God's lawe, howe lyable to his [153] wrath, and also shew them the true meanes of their restoring, redemption, reconciliation, salvation. Yet this doth neither justifie the false minister or his ministration, no more than when a young boye, dumbe minister, or unbelieving prophane person, reading the holie Scriptures, or some other booke of true doctrine, some of the hearers (God so opening their understanding) should therby be brought to the acknowledging and faith of Christ, the feare and love of God. This boy, reading priest, prophane person, by reading is proved a true minister, a true preacher, a true Christian; or these that are thus wonne, comforted, etc., to seeke no other minister or meanes of their salvation than thys reading by these persons.

Let the doctrine then in that poyncte wherby men are thus begotten to these beginninges of faith, or to anie encrease therof, be alwaies true and sounde so far foorth, the maner and tyme of apprehending, be the worcke and power of God, the meanes and instrumentes of convaying or bringing, variable at the will and appoynctment of God. Yet are we only to seeke, use, and rest in those meanes which the Lord hath ordayned for our instruction and leading foorth in the wil and wayes of God, which meanes only have warrant and promise of blessing unto us, howsoever the Lord by his infinite power and worcking can and no doubt doth save some in Turckey amongst the heathen, in the false church amongst the false worshippers, by what meanes it pleaseth him; yet may not we hereupon either resorte unto or remaine in these forbidden places in hope of these effectes, because God (if such be his will) can save us here, or if it be not his will to save us, then no true church or ministry can availe us. This were most highly and dangerously to tempt God, a reprobate kinde of reasoning. God his wil unto us is, that we alwaies obey and rest in his reveiled [revealed] wil, and not to presume upon his infinite will and power, which he keepeth secret unto himself. This caused the holy martyres and faithfull at all tymes, and us the Lorde's most unworthy witnesses at this tyme, after that God's spirit had wrought effectuallie in their and our heartes, and opened our eyes to see part of his holy truth, as also some of the heinouse abhominations committed, defended, and wilfullie persisted in, in the false church and ministrie, constantlie even to death and bandes to witnesse against the same, and to forsake the false church, notwithstanding al the pretextes, glos[s]es, and arguments the false prophet shal adorn the harlot with, or make for his ministry. So deare is the love of God and of his holy truth unto us, as we can suffer our selves neither by men or angels to be drawen into anie seene or willing transgression of his holy word.

And as for these arguments of Mr. Giffard, what other are they than the papistes have brought against the first faithfull witnesses, John Husse, Jerome of Prage, Luther, Calvine, Frith, Tindal, etc.[1] Or may bring

---

[1] Jerome of Prague was a friend of John Hus, an advocate of the teachings of Wycliffe, and a church-reformer. In 1415 he was arrested, and on May 30, 1416, was burned at Constance. John Frith (1503-1533), English martyr, was publicly burned at Smithfield on July 4 because of his views on transubstantiation and purgatory.

A Plaine Refutation

at this daye against al the churches that are departed from them? Unto the execution of our [Anglican] ministery is joyned the effectual grace, power, blessing and operation of the Holy Ghoste to the true convertion of some men's soules. Therfore our ministrie is not of the Divil or Anti-[154]christ, but indeed the true ministrie of Christ.[1] Ells al that have lived thus manie hundred yeeres before you in our church, and knew not these newe learninges you hold, are damned. Ells all that have died in our church are damned; yea, ells you must hold al the kinges and princes, nobles, pieres, and people in our church reprobates, etc. But let us come to your selves, ye that are the aucthors of this schisme. Where had you your faith, your first knowledge of God and of Christ, if not in this church by our ministrie? We have the true Scriptures amongst us, we teach truly concerning the Godhead and the three persons therof, God the Father, God the Sonne, and God the Holy Ghost, though distinct in persons, yet one God, etc. We preach Christ in his two natures verie God and verie man. That he came into the world for the salvation of al mankinde. "That God so loved the world that he gave his only begotten Sonne, that whosoever believeth in him should not perish, but have life everlasting."[2] Wee preach Christ crucified for our sinnes, dead, buried, risen againe, ascended, glorified. We preach him in his three offices to be our king, priest, and prophet. Wee preach al the fundamental articles of our christian faith; and as wee preach, so you believe al these. Yea, and we appeale to your consciences whether you have founde joy and comfort in your owne soules at the preaching of these doctrines. Againe, we preach the lawes of God in the tables, and beate downe such sinnes as wee see to bee contrarie to the same, in such sort as manie are drawen to repentance, to hatred, sorrowe, and remorce for sinne. And these againe wee raise up with comfort and hope of forgivenes, and with the promises of eternal

---

[1] *A Short Treatise*, p. 80.
[2] John 3 : 16.

life. These things if the schismaticks feele not, yet unto many others which by our preaching are converted unto the Lorde indeed, which unto feare and trembling doe feele the power and sweetnes of the lively worde, we may say as the Apostle unto the Corinthians in like case. "If I be not an apostle unto others, yet am I one unto you, ye are the seale of mine apostleship in the Lord."[1] And as for you Lutherans, if you continue not, that is not our default, if you fal from grace.[2] It is enough for us that you have felt this majestie of the worde, and it sufficeth to prove our ministrie that the power of the Holy Ghost goeth with it, when men have bene so moved, though they contynue not, seeing the reprobate may feele this power and taste this sweetnes for a tyme. Now then our ministry being thus proved by the law and the gospel, and by the testimony of the Holy Ghost in these powreful effectes, how can you thus separate from the meanes of your salvation, from that ministry which hath begotten in you, or at least doth begeat in others this knowledge, faith, comfort, etc. ? Our ministrie then being thus proved, our church must needes followe, for a true ministrie doth not belong, neither is at anie time found in a false church. Yea, you [Separatists] must graunt that whilest we hold the true foundation, wee are the true church, though we erre in

---

[1] I Corinthians 9 : 2.
[2] This reference to "Lutherans" is interesting and unexpected. There is not much evidence of Lutheran influence on the Separatists. But some such influence may have been mediated through the martyrs and continental writers. For the discussion of possible Lutheran influence on Tudor England, see Henry E. Jacobs, *A Study in Comparative Symbolics. The Lutheran Movement in England during the Reigns of Henry VIII and Edward VI, and Its Literary Monuments*, Revised Ed. (1892); Carl S. Meyer, *Elizabeth I and the Religious Settlement of 1559* (1960); E. Gordon Rupp, *Studies in the Making of the English Protestant Tradition* (1947); Rupp, *The Righteousness of God. Luther Studies* (1953); Rupp, *Six Makers of English Religion, 1500-1700* (1957). Dr. Meyer calls attention to such Lutheran influences as Melanchthon's *Loci Communes*, John Marshall's *Primers*, Anne Boleyn, Thomas Cranmer, Thomas Starkey, the Augsburg Confession, the Schmalkald Articles, the *Wuertemburg Confession*, Apology of the Augsburg Confession, op. cit., pp. 5, 12, 24, 90, 134, 151-167. Dr. Rupp especially mentions as a corrective to Jacobs the work by Georg Mentz, *Die Wittenberger Artikel von 1536* (Artickel der cristlichen Lahr, von welchen die Legatten aus Engelland mit dem Herrn Doctor Martino gehandelt Anno 1536) (Leipzig, 1905).

A Plaine Refutation

matters of circumstance and other doctrines, as you thincke: yet that taketh not away our beeing of a church. The churches at Corinth, Gallatia, Asia, abounded with many faults, errors, corruptions, as we reade, yet are [155] saluted by the Apostles, recorded by the Holy Ghost as true churches. Now that we hold the foundation, our confession of the articles of our christian faith, the ten commandementes, the Lorde's Prayer, etc. (which you also confesse and use) shewe. Therfore whilest you depart from us, you depart from the true church.[1]

Hereupon they might also use those rethoricall flowers of Mr. Giffard his divinitie to raile, reproach, and invaye. That they are ranck Donatistes, Lutherans, ignorant, furious, franctick, schismatickes, yea, damnable heretickes, forsaking the ministerie and truth of God, condemning the church of God, bringing the holie ministerie thereof into contempt, and so bring in flat atheisme, barbarisme, rebellion against magistrates, etc.[2] Howe thincketh Mr. Giffard, would not these argumentes fit the papistes aswell against them, as they do him against us? Is he not driven to hard shift, when he must borrowe weapons of them to defend himself, his church, ministrie, worship, government? They must needes stand fast when they are built uppon their groundes. Let him then first answeare the papistes to these reasons, before he bring them against us, and then if he be not satisfied, he shall heare what we can say to them. For sure if they be not of force to bring them home againe to their mother of Rome, they wil never perswade us to goe backe to them. In the meane time, Mr. Giffard, we signifie unto you concerning this reason which you

---

[1] This long paragraph is a series of conclusions by Gifford, and very likely includes direct quotations from Gifford's first manuscript reply to the Separatists. We do not have Gifford's manuscript, but some of his arguments and conclusions appear in Barrow's "Four Causes of Separation" and especially in his "A Brief Summe of the Causes of Our Seperation, and of Our Purposes in Practise," printed in Carlson, *The Writings of Henry Barrow, 1587-1590*, pp. 49-66, 118-150. See also Gifford, *A Short Treatise*, pp. 26, 81, 82.

[2] See "A Brief Summe of the Causes of Our Seperation," in Carlson, *The Writings of Henry Barrow, 1587-1590*, pp. 118-150.

urge and dilate, that it is a ground of Anabaptistrie to justifie open transgression by inwarde motions. It is a grounde of atheisme to pleade for or tollerate sinne, because of such good effectes as you imagine to procede therof.

[V.] Mr. Giffard, his next argument is drawen from our confession. " We confesse that they were blessed martyres that suffred in Queen Marie's daies." " But thei were converted by the same ministerie which we have now. They had the same motions at the preaching of Latimer, Ho[o]per, Taylor, Bradford, which our people have now at our preaching and sacraments touching faith, repentance, and resolution to die for the testimonie of the Lorde. Therfore let the Brownistes and al other wicked schismaticks barck that we have no ministrie, etc."[1]

This reason hangeth upon the same thread with this other last before, and is built upon the same popish and Anabaptistical grounds. Touching the persons of these martyres, we have alreadie in our first replie unto your answeare,[2] set downe our christian opinion and judgment. Yet can this argument of their persons no more justifie this antichristian ministrie of lord bishops, parrish parsons, merceanarie vagrant preachers, than it hath pleasured the pope heretofore, who had as manie godlie predecessors and martyres to boast of as they. The forgerie of their whole administration, preaching, worship, sacramentes, is furder discovered, than these winde-shaken fig-leaves can hide the shame therof. The truth is, howsoever the Lord doth reserve the canonical Scriptures, and some other doctrines of the Godheade, the suffring, resurrection, and glorie of Christ, of the judgment and [156] life to come, etc., in the false church and ministerie, and by his secret power and wil can use the said Scriptures and doctrines to the salvation of some, yet these effectes are not to be ascribed to the

---

[1] *A Short Treatise,* p. 82.
[2] " A Brief Summe of the Causes of Our Seperation," printed in Carlson, *The Writings of Henry Barrow, 1587-1590,* pp. 118-150 and especially pp. 125-6.

A Plaine Refutation

false ministerie or their corrupt ministration, adulterate sacraments, etc., which have no promise of blessing. And therfore those inward motions and comfortes receaved by them, are delutions, without grounde or warrant of God's worde, the actions as they doe them not being acceptable, but accursed in God's sight. The faith and repentance wrought by their ministerie appeareth in the general estate and life of their people, yea, of their whole church. As to that christian zeale, courage, and constancie to dye for the testimonie of the truth (which he popishlie caleth resolution)[1] and saith is wrought by their ministrie, we shal beginne to believe it, when they beginne to walcke in the truth, and to shake off that antichristian yoke they stand under; but whilest in this maner they betray their whole ministrie and gospel, the whole power and libertie of the church into the handes of these antichristian bishops, standing their sworne and marcked souldiours, administring and preaching after their prescription and limitation, being bownd by oath not to preach against anie thing by publick aucthoritie established,[2] how odious or enormous soever, but for feare and filthie lucre stand ministers of al these abhominations, we are warned by the Holie Ghost not to be deceived with their "swelling wordes of vanitie," promising us libertie, whilest they themselves stand the bond servants of corruption. And for the aucthor of these blaspheamous books, Mr. Giffard, who is apostatate and fallen away even from that litle faith and light which he sometimes seemed to have, building now againe the thinges he sometimes destroyed, retourned with the dogge to his owne vomite, and as

II Thes. 2:9, 10, 11, 12
Esa. 66:3, 4
Jer. 6:19, 20, 21

II Pet. 2

---

[1] Popish, because the argument emphasizes the role of man and the efficacy of his own resolution. Pelagianism and semi-Pelagianism teach that man can contribute toward his own salvation or his meritoriousness — the doctrine of works. Synergism, as held by Melanchthon, is the teaching that man can collaborate with God. Barrow holds to the view of Calvin and Augustine that even the resolution is a gift of God.

[2] See "Protestations to Be Made, Promised, and Subscribed, by Them That Shall Hereafter Be Admitted to Any Office, Roome, or Cure in Any Church, or Other Place Ecclesiasticall," in *Advertisements* (1584), B 3 *verso*. See also "Articles for Doctrine and Preaching," *ibid.*, A 3 *recto* and *verso*.

the washed sowe to the wallowing in the myre, yea, most cursedlie blaspheaming the truth of God and the poore witnesses therof, as a most bitter and professed enimie fighting in most hostile maner against the kingdome of Christ, for and under the kingdome of Antichrist, we shal believe that he wil suffer for the gospel of Christ when Queen Marie retourneth againe to persecute. In the meane while we say with the Holie Ghoste: It had bene better for this man never to have knowen the truth, than after he had acknowledged it, to tourne from the holie commandement given unto him.¹

Yet remayneth an other odd popish reason of Mr. Giffard his old store, brought by him in his first answeare unto certaine articles of ours, as the onlie proof he then could finde for his ministrie, *vzt*: [namely], the affirmation and consent of other pastors and churches, sending such as doubted, to enquire of these strangers their judgment of the church and ministrie of England, and in the mean tyme councelling them to suspend their judgment.² This reason and councel because we rejected as insufficient, unsound, and popish, requiring rather some proof by God's worde of themselves (wherin we wholly rested, and not in the opinions [157] of men) than thus to be sent in this case from the learned ministrie of England unto strangers to knowe what they thincke of their ministerie, as appeareth in our replie, to which we refer the reader for our answeare to this argument.³ Hereupon Mr. Giffard, in his first publick treatise against the Donatists of England, reneweth this old argument or quarrel 'rather by contriving this odious question, Whither the people in these controversies ought to be sent unto such hereticks and schismatickes as we are, or unto the learned pastors of other churches.⁴ This question after he had thus charitablie framed, he as gravelie and reverentlie discusseth

---

¹ II Peter 2 : 21.
² "A Brief Summe of the Causes of Our Seperation," in Carlson, *The Writings of Henry Barrow, 1587-1590*, p. 136.
³ *Ibid.*, pp. 136-143.
⁴ *A Short Treatise*, p. 78.

A Plaine Refutation

with these and such like holie christian passages. " See how sottishly ye cavil." " Blind presumptuous heretical schismatickes." " Yours is the course of al arrogant proude heretickes and schismatickes which covet to have the people depend uppon them, that they might have fame." Or unto " unlearned rashe Brownistes, intruding themselves without caling and running before they be sent." As the harlots and whoores of the stewes that " boast and glorie of their chastitie." " Who is more fierce and outragious, more uncharitable in condemning than the Brownistes ? And yet ye bragg of such patience and charitie as can not be overcome." " The Divel conterfaiting Christe's voice in heretical schismaticks should not be able to allure and cal away the sheepe from their shepheardes," etc., part of 78 and of the 79 page of his first booke ?[1] How thinck you, hath not this clarcke bene wel nourtured and brought up, that can thus learnedlie devise and handle a question and refute his adversaries in lesse than one page of his booke ? He that findeth not these those mightie weapons through God to cast downe holdes and reasonings, and to the captivating al understanding into the obedience of Christ. He that findeth not this, that quiet and gentle spirit, that heavenlie peaceable wisedome from above, that lenitie and meeknes wherwith the minister of Christ instructeth the contrarie minded, might even herebie doubte of Mr. Giffard his ministrie.

And see after this storme is a litle blowen over, and he hath somewhat discharged and eased his ful stomacke, in the end he alloweth of our course and councel for the tryal and proofe of their ministrie by the Worde of God only, and not by the opinions of anie men whoesoever; saying that " it is the same in effect " (if we could see) that himself gave before.[2] Peradventure Mr. Giffard meaneth, if we could see into his minde, for in his writing there was no such matter. But wel, seeing we are agreed of this course and tryal of their ministrie by the Scriptures, whie are we thus reviled and reproched for con-

[1] Ibid., pp. 78, 79.
[2] Ibid., p. 79.

senting unto, demaunding, and expecting this tryal? Yea, whie is not this christian peaceable course taken, this tryal and proofe made? Whie hath not Mr. Giffard at the least approved his ministerie in the office, entrance, and administration by the evident Scriptures? And therby both have approved themselves and convinced us, before he had pronounced this blasphemouse sentence against us, who acknowledg with reverence everie worde of God, therunto submitting our whole faith and life to be tried, corrected, directed in al things, which reproachful sentence Michael himself, that head of angels and men, durst not give even against the Divel in controvercie betwixt them. These controvercies betwixt them and us being of no lesse momente than Moses' bodie, [158] and none of us our owne judges in this case, but al standing to the judgment of God by his Worde, ought to have bene more soberlie and reverentlie handled. Wherein what Mr. Giffard hath failed wee leave him to his accomptes before that dreadful judge, where the consent and applausion of the bishops and cleargie of England shall not excuse him for al or anie of these despiteful reproches and fowle sclanders that he hath brought up and published in these his blasphemouse bookes, upon the Lorde's faithful servantes and poore witnesses in bandes against this antichristian ministrie and their ungodly proceedings. Which if here with all the deipe learning of Sathan cannot be hid or defended, how should they stand before his face " that hath his eyes like a flambe of fire," that " searcheth the hartes and reynes," and giveth everie man according to his worckes.[1] And for us, seeing wee finde this their whole ministrie by examining them by and comparing them unto the rules of Christe's Testament, to be false, forged, and antichristian in their office, entrance, administration, and maintenance, to have no place or mention in Christe's church; seing we before our eyes see them to have served in and belonged unto Antichriste's even the pope's kingdome and

Revel. 2

---

[1] Revelation 2 : 18, 23. Reynes, or reins, indicates the seat of the feelings and passions.

A Plaine Refutation

throne, the false church, with all the abhominable idolatries therin, wee dare boldlie affirme and conclude, that they keeping these offices cannot nowe belong unto or serve in Christe's kingdome, his church, neither be kint [knit] unto Christ as their heade. But as the Holie Ghost witnesseth of them, they have a kinge over them, the angel of the bottomlesse pit, whose name in Hebrewe, Abaddon, and in Greek Apollyon, in all languages and places, the destroyer.¹ And as we finde them, so according to the commaundement of God, we leave and avoide them: turning our eye and speach now a litle to the fourth principal cause of our dislike of, and separation from the Church of England.

Revel. 9:11

THE FOURTH PRINCIPAL CAUSE OF OUR SEPARATION FROM THE CHURCH OF ENGLAND, IS:

4. *For that their churches are ruled by, and remaine in subjection unto, an antichristian & ungodly government, cleane contrarie to the institution of our Savior Christ.*

> From this proposition is this argument manifestlie and directlie drawen.
>
> No true established church of Christe may willingly receive, or wittinglie stand subject under anie other ecclesiasticall government than Christ hath prescribed and instituted.
>
> But the Church of England willinglie receiveth and willinglie standeth subject under a strange ecclesiasticall government, other than that Christ hath prescribed and instituted.
>
> Therfore the Church of England is not the true established Church of Christ.

The chardge and argument being so evident and inevitable, as Mr. Giffard in [159] his first answeare (whilest he stoode of the Reformistes' side, a sutor for

---

¹ See Revelation 9 : 11.

Reformation)[1] durst neither for shame denie, nor yet for feare affirme, he sought by moving, and after his maner proving, a newe question, to obscure and tourne away, at the least (until he sawe furder howe the tymes would goe) to shift off the present proposition that pressed so sore, with such ambiguous doubtful Delphicke words and speaches, as might be interpreted in what sense himself list. And he falsly tourne to that side that were likest to prevaile and carrie the credit in the world. First by way of supposition and admission, in these wordes. " If it were admitted that there is some yoke of antichristian governement, under which the poore church may groane, is it therfore no longer the spouse of Christ?"[2] Mr. Giffard having thus entrenched himself, might issue out of his skonce[3] and turne to which side he would. As wel might he from hence have stoode of the Reformistes' faction, by saying that he never sought to plead for, or to defend this governement of these prelates (but even in these wordes he doth affirme and pronounce it to be a " yoke of antichristian governement," a bondage, an oppression of the church, etc.)[4] As now being revolted to the pontifical side, and saith he did but propounde it by way of question, supposition, admission. For the present government, he holdeth it the true and very government of Christ, in substance and matter, howsoever it have not the same forme, and be not executed in that maner which Christ hath prescribed; of which forme there is great question, whether it be permanent or variable.[5] Neither wil he meddle with the discussing therof, be-

---

[1] In 1588 Gifford wrote his manuscript reply to the Separatists. In the next two years some of the leaders of the Reformists, or Presbyterians, were brought before the Court of High Commission and the Star Chamber Court. Nine of their leaders were imprisoned, 1590-2, viz.: Thomas Cartwright, Humphrey Fen, Melanchthon Jewell, Andrew King, Edward Lord, John Payne, William Proudlove, Edmund Snape, and Daniel Wight.
[2] " A Brief Summe of the Causes of Our Seperation," in Carlson, *The Writings of Henry Barrow, 1587-1590*, p. 143.
[3] Bulwark, screen, protective device.
[4] *Ibid.*
[5] *A Short Treatise*, pp. 89-90.

cause he wil displease neither side. But this he held, and holdeth, that the true church may be oppressed and remaine under some yoke of antichristian government. That it is the lot of the church to be oppressed with outward bondage, to be made to keep the vineyarde which is not her owne, to be beaten of the watchmen, etc.[1] Mr. Giffard was answered unto these, that there is great difference betwixt civile bondage, and ecclesiastical bondage: betwixt outward oppression or persecution, and an antichristian yoke or government. That the church had beene or might be in civile bondage unto, outwardly oppressed and persecuted by either civile magistrates, as Pharao, Nebuchadnezzar, etc., or by false ecclesiastical ministers, proud antichristian usurpers, as Pashur, Caiaphas, Annanias, etc.[2] But yet that the church of God may never by the one or the other sorte be brought into bondage of, and wittingly remaine in subjection unto, anie yoke of antichristian governement, not even to the least lawe, tradition, or devise of man, which they see to be contrary to the word of God. For this was shewed to be a losse of christian libertie, if they should by the will or power of anie mortal man or men whosoever, be again entangled in any yoke of bondage, or brought in subjection of anie lawe, devise, or tradition of man, seeme it never so holie or expedient, be it circumcision, daies, feastes, fastes, meates, etc. To be so contrary to the gospel, as the truth therof should not contynue amongst them, if they should give place to anie man in the least of these things by way of subjection for the space of an howre, Galatians 2:4, 5. To add unto [160] the Worde of God, to superordeyne unto the Testament of Christ, yea, to abrogate the Testament of Christ, Galatians 3:15. To worship God in vayne, Matthew 15:9 Not to hold the head, but to be rashlie puffed

Gal. 4:9, 10
Gal. 5:1, etc.
Col. 2

---

[1] "A Brief Summe of the Causes of Our Seperation," Carlson, *The Writings of Henry Barrow, 1587-1590*, p. 143.
[2] Passhur was a prince of Judah, and an opponent of the prophet Jeremiah. Caiaphas was the high priest in Jerusalem from about 18 to 36 A.D. Ananias was a high priest when Paul was arrested and sent to Rome — about 57-60 A.D.

up in the sense of their owne fleshe, Colossians 2 : 18, 19. It was shewed that Christ is the onlie lawe-giver, kinge, husband, and Lord of and in his church. That one kingdome cannot receive two kinges, one marriage bed, two husbands, one house, two Lordes, so contarie as Christ and Antichrist, at one and the same instant. And that one neck cannot be said to beare two yokes, and drawe in them both at one instant. Neither [can] one person be a faithfull subject, wife, servant to two so divers and contrarie kinges, husbands, lords, as Christ and Antichrist are. Christ divideth not, neither hath part, fellowship, or communion with Antichrist. There is contynuall warre betwixt their kingdomes and subjectes, betwixt the false and true church, the false and true seede, they that are borne after the fleshe, persecuting them that are borne after the spirit. It was shewed that wee are his servantes and subjectes to whom wee obeye. That this yoke and bondage of Antichrist breaketh the wedlocke, breaketh the covenant with Christ; Christe's love and covenant beeing no longer bounde or plight to us, than wee keepe faith to him. Which faith is forfeited, and warre ended, by yeilding and standing in bondage to Antichrist, by taking and bearing his yoke. Which bondage and yoke was shewed and proved to be the badge of Antichrist, the marcke of the beaste, which al the miserable multitudes upon which the harlot, the false church, sitteth, are compelled to receive in their foreheades or in their handes, wherebie the children of Mounte Sina are knowen from the children of Jerusalem that is above and is free with al her children. For al which children our Saviour Christ hath purchased a ful and perfect libertie at a deare and pretious price, having given unto al his children the *arrhabon*[1] of his spirit, not the spirit of bondage but the spirit of adoption as sonnes. And where this spirit is, there is libertie. For if wee be sonnes, then are wee free and no bond servantes. For the bond servant abideth not in the house for ever, but the sonne abideth for ever. It was also shewed him to

---

[1] Arrabōn — earnest money or cautious money.

A Plaine Refutation

be a blasphemous error to say, that to beare Antichriste's yoke and governement, is the lot of Christe's church.[1]

To conclude, it was made plaine unto him, how fowllie he misunderstoode, abused, falsified, and perverted those places of the Songe[2] by him alleadged to prove that blasphemous error. So that if Mr. Giffard would either have bene advertised or advised, to make and put difference betwixt civile bondage and subjection, and an antichristian bondage and yoke, betwixt bodilie oppression and spiritual subjection, or would dulie have pondered our opinions, reasons, and proves, or would have bene admonished of his former dotages and errors, he could not againe in these poyntes thus boldlie have resisted the evident truth, turned away the direct Scriptures, unjustlie chardged and blasphemed us, persisted in his old detestable errors, runne headlonge into newe and more, and unsufferably [161] abused and perverted the holy Scriptures thereunto.

We never denied, and therfore may evil be chardged to hold, that the church might not be held in civile bondage, bodily oppression, persecution, etc., by wicked ungodly guides both civil and ecclesiastical.[3] But what of this? May it hereupon be concluded, that therfore the church may be held under Antichriste's yoke in ecclesiastical or spiritual bondage? There is no such consequence of this. Yet this is the state of the question propounded by Mr. Giffard in his first answeare. And this he there endevored to prove by this reason, as also by the places of the Songe. And nowe againe laboureth to bring to passe by an odde subtile distinction or division of his owne devising, and by sondry mo[r]e places of Scripture.

He divideth this antichristian yoke into two sortes, a strict yoke and a lardge yoke. His strict or proper yoke, he saith, "is only spiritual and inwarde, where

---

[1] "Brief Summe of the Causes of Our Seperation," in Carlson, *The Writings of Henry Barrow, 1587-1590*, p. 144. See also *A Short Treatise*, p. 83.
[2] Song of Solomon 1 : 6 and 5 : 6. Gifford mentions 5 : 6, but this becomes 5 : 7 in the later versions, since 4 : 17 is changed to 5 : 1.
[3] *A Short Treatise*, pp. 83-88.

the faith and conscience are burdened and be in subjection to receive Antichrist his lawes and worship." The lardger yoke is, " when the pastors of the church doe usurpe more than they ought in externall government, or tyrannously abuse the power committed into their hands." This he calleth " som[e] antichristian yoke." The first he saith " cannot be borne without falling from the freedome we have in Christ." The second (as the lot of the church) may be willinglie suffred and wittinglie borne, and yet remayne the church of Christ; and this by sondrie places of Scripture he endevoreth to prove.[1]

First unto his distinction or division of an antichristian yoke into straight and lardge, outward and inwarde, we acknowledge it without the compasse of our reading, or understanding. We still affirme that no yoke or government but only Christe's, may be borne or received of the true church. We furder saye, and already have proved, that al the lawes and ordinances of Christe's Testament (howe outwardly and smale soever they may seeme) concerne the conscience: and that the wilfull omission and transgression therof, bindeth both bodie and soule unto judgment, without repentance. So likewise we hold, that everie antichristian yoke chardgeth and bindeth the conscience, both bodie and soule, it being opposite unto, and a transgression of Christe's lawes and ordinances. And therfore wonder how these academical divines, these pleaders for iniquitie, dare hatch us these poysoned distinctions, of lardg and straight antichristian yokes, the one binding, the other not concerning the conscience. Except they can shewe God's lawe. Or ells some transgression of God's lawe that bindeth and chardgeth not the conscience. Until Mr. Giffard can doe this, he must give us leave not to receive his curious distinction of lardge and straight yoke, outward and inward. Wee thincke also his reason somewhat hardlie constrayned, when he concludeth, because Antichrist's yoke is spiritual, therfore onlie inwarde. Wee call it spirituall because it cometh (as also [162]

[1] *Ibid.*, pp. 83, 84, 88.

A Plaine Refutation

Antichrist himself doth) by the effectual worcking of Sathan. As also because it is wholly about spiritual and ecclesiastical actions and procedings. But shal we therfore say it is onlie inwarde? Might not by these reasons the whole visible church it self, al the publicke ministration, actions, and ordinances therof, as also everie person and member therof, be said only inward, because they are al said spiritual? Againe it seemeth that Mr. Giffard litle understandeth what an antichristian yoke is, that termeth everie sinne and disorder arising in the church, an antichristian yoke. We confesse the church may transgresse of negligence or ignorance, yea, and so suffer such ungodlie presumptuous persons and ministers to abuse their power for a ceason; yet this is not willingly to beare, or wittingly to receive, anie antichristian yoke; neither cease they hereupon to be true churches, whilest they despise not admonition, neither refuse to repent being reproved. Yet this we saie, the church greatlie sinneth in suffring such presumptuous inordinate persons, whom they ought to cast out. And if so be the church either want [lack] wil, and refuse to cast them out being admonished; or want power and be not able to cast them out being discovered, but is brought in subjection and remayneth in bondage to these guides, it ceaseth in this estate unto our judgment to be the true church of Christ.

And nowe to the Scriptures Mr. Giffard bringeth, that the true church may wittingly and willinglie be brought into bondage of some antichristian yoke, Ezechiel 34 :[4]. Jeremiah 5 : 31. Jeremiah 20 : 1. John 7 : 13. John 9 : 22. First wee say, that these ministers were by office and caling true ministers of the temple, but their ministers by office and calling are not, and so no comparison. Then we say, that these were now so wholly degenerate and apostatate in Jehoiakim and Zedechiah's tymes,[1] and the whole state so corrupted and fallen from God into most execrable

---

[1] Jehoiakim's reign as king of Judah extended from 608 to 597. Jehoiachim ruled for three months in 597. Zedekiah was king of Judah from 597 to 586. Jerusalem was captured by Nebuchadnezzar and the Babylonian army in July-August, 586 B.C.

idolatries, as they were not to be held the true churches of God, but were pronownced by the Holy Ghost whores, murtherers, idolaters, so commanded to be judged, esteamed, and forsaken of al the faithful. As everie where in those prophecies of Ezechiel and Jeremiah appeareth, and we have lardglie in the Second Principal Transgression proved, and himself in that estate confessed, that they ought to be abandoned by the godlie. For the generall estate in the time of our Saviour Christ's ministrie and suffringes, wee have also proved, that they were that malignant persecuting church, which did excommunicate Christ and al that confessed and believed in him: from whom our Saviour and his disciples separated.

And now to the place of the third epistle of John.[1] " I wrote to the church, but of them Diotrephes loving the primacie receiveth us not. For this if I come, I wil bring to remembrance the worckes which he doeth, prating against us with malitious wordes, and not content in these, neither himself receiveth the bretheren, and them that wo[u]ld he forbiddeth, and casteth them out of the church." These verses I have thus Englished to the worde, because me thinckes the usuall translation (though in it selfe not evil) seemeth a litle too much to nourish some false collections, [163] which neither the wordes nor circumstance of the text will beare.[2] But now what wil Mr. Giffard gather or conclude from this place? Diotrephes, he saith, abused the power of government ambitiouslie. If he meane the power of the whole church, the power of [ex]communication, it would be shewed and proved wherein. If he say, in that he cast the bretheren out of the church, we would first knowe of him what bretheren the Apostle

---

[1] III John 1 : 9, 10.
[2] This is a translation not from the Latin but from the Greek. Barrow may have used one of Theodore de Bèze's Greek editions which appeared from 1565, or he may have used the Greek New Testament first printed in England in 1587 by Thomas Vautrollier. This edition was based on that of Henricus and Robertus Stephanus (Estienne, Stephen), but was collated with that of Theodore de Bèze. Barrow also used *Testamenti Veteris Biblia Sacra*, by Immanuel Tremellius and Franciscus Iunius. Barrow may have had a Greek New Testament edited by Erasmus.

A Plaine Refutation

there speaketh of, whether those strangers, or such members of that congregation as were willing to receive those strangers, and whether they were caste out by waye of excommunication. If he say those members that were willing, etc., we affirme the whole context, the argument of the Epistle precedent,[1] the faultes of Diotrephes reckoned up, and the admonition subsequent, to shew the contrarie, that he meaneth of the other godlie strangers, Gaius in the premises being commended for intertaignement of those strangers. Diotrephes here blamed for these faultes, of an ambitious humor, loving and aspiring to be chief or first, and could not endure to be under the Apostles.

1. Therfore he received not the Apostle's letter. 2. He pratled against them with evil wordes. 3. Neither himself received these strangers. 4. But forbad them that would. 5. And so kept or caste them out of the church. The admonition was, that they should not imitate evil, but good, etc.

Manie reasons might be drawen from these circumstances, from sondrie wordes in the original, but especially by the right dividing of these two verses it wil appeare, not to be meant of the abuse of anie censure of the church, of excommunication. As also by the exhortation drawen from these faultes. For how could Gaius or anie other of the church imitate him in this, when there was no more pastors of that congregation but Diotrephes (if he were a pastor as they suppose) and by their rule onlie the pastor maie excommunicate? But what now if it were admitted (which can never by this Scripture be proved) that Diotrephes did both usurpe and abuse the power and government of the church, what wil Mr. Giffard collect and enforce from hence? First that this tyrannous oppression did not make them to be no longer Christe's church which remayned under him. Wel, and what wil he conclude hereupon? That these parishes which wittinglie remaine in bondage under the yoke of these popish prelates, which receive this false antichristian

[1] II John 1.

ministrie, this popish idolatrous worship and ordinances, etc., are the true churches of Christ ? As ther is no consimilitude (except in this one poincte of evil, wherin yet these parishes far exceed) so is there no consequent or comparison betwixt a church and no church, a true church and ministrie, and a false church and ministrie. Neither have we a better argument in al Mr. Giffard his booke to approve the ministrie and procedings of the Church of England, than the most odious sinnes and faultes of other churches; which were not recorded by the Holy Ghoste for us to imitate or to pleade for sinne by, so much as left for examples, and as it were lande markes, to flee sinne by. Againe this church here remayned not wilfullie under this tyrannie of Diotrephes; they never had bene reproved and admonished therfore. Howsoever we justifie not [164] or tollerate the least sinne that God condemneth in his worde, yet we make not anie sinne, until impenitencie and obstinacie be joyned therunto, to disanul and breake the covenant with God. Neither doe we make everie inordinate and presumptuous part (when the ministers of the church extend themselves beyonde their lyne and the limites of their office) straight waye an antichristian yoke, if they be not seene or repressed at the first. For as it is said, both the church and ministers may sinne in such thinges and transgresse the rule of ignorance or of negligence. And so what wil this example helpe their church, which standeth wilfullie and wittinglie in seene bondage unto these antichristian prelates ?

But Mr. Giffard saith the Apostle did not will the faithful to separate themselves, or not anie longer to obeye Diotrephes in anie thing.[1] We, and even this his owne fonde collection [foolish deduction] doth shewe, that Diotrephes' sinne was neither so prejudicial, heynouse, or publicklie knowen to the churche, as he would make it. For if Diotrephes had either usurped the whole power, or abused the publique government of the church so far, as to caste out of his owne sole aucthor-

---

[1] *A Short Treatise*, p. 85.

itie in his owne name what bretheren he luste, yea, those of the most vertuous and charitable, he had not to have bene suffred in the church, must lesse to have remayned a minister with such publicke heynouse sinnes upon him. This had bene contrarie to the lawes and rules of Christe's Testament, to the practize and procedings of the other Apostles, to the safetie of the church. To al which it is not credible or audible, that this Apostle would be so contrarie, neither may it be inferred from this place without grievous perverting the Scriptures, and injurie to the Holy Ghost. If Diotrephes' fault had bene in this nature so heynouse and publick, what needed the Apostle to say: "If I come, I will declare or bring his workes to remembrance," the Greeke worde is *hupomneso, submonebo*, I will submonish. Againe the beginning of the tenth verse, *dia touto, propter hoc*, for this, sheweth an other cause, an other matter, an other fault.[1]

Mr. Giffarde's other place, John 16, verse 2, serveth his tourne as evil. "They shal caste you out of their synagogues, yea, the hower cometh that everie one that killeth you shal thinck he doth God good service." It is strange that Mr. Giffard should thinck and use this as spoken of the true church, when the verie next verse hath these words. "And these thinges they wil do unto you, because they have not knowen the Father nor me." I hope these are no marckes of the true church, not to knowe God nor Christ, or to use such barbarous hostilitie towardes the disciples and faithful servantes of Christ. If then these marckes, this tyrannous usage, and the bloode of the sainctes be founde upon the Church of England, they shal by this glasse and place descrie [detect, discover] her to be the malignant persecuting synagogue, and not that persecuted church consisting of Christe's true disciples and faithful servants and witnesses. As to his other shoteancker [sheetanchor] and fundamental usual place at all assaies, II Thessalonians 2 : 4 (from whence he draweth

---

[1] III John 1 : 10. The Greek verb means "I shall remind"; the Latin and English words have also the meaning of gently reproving.

a maine argument from the Church of Rome and of England, to prove them both the churches of God, because it is there said that Antichrist shal sit in the temple of God, and Antichrist sitteth in [165] the Church of Rome and England, therfore the churches of Rome and of England are the churches of God), I doe refer the reader to the Seconde Transgression for answeare, which place and argument he shal there find lardglie handled and discussed.[1]

In the next poincte Mr. Giffard in his bad conscience finding the litle consequent from civile to antichristian bondage, quite forgeteth, forsaketh, and tourned the question, and would now make us or at least make others believe that we hold that the church maie be in no outwarde bondage, wheras we hold it may not beare Antichriste's yoke, or be brought into anie antichristian bondage. Having fullie set downe this opinion as ours, he pronounceth us Anabaptistes, and wondreth how so prowde a spirit could be in rotten flesh, so flatlie to contradict the spirit of God in these places, Genesis 15, Exodus 20, and al the places of the prophets, where the Lorde threatneth that they should be ledd into Babilon, and be there in bondage.[2] To take awaye his wonder though not his follie, we give him againe and againe to understand, that we never denied but that the church might be in civile bondage, in bodilie oppression, but never might be brought into anie antichristian bondage, either lardge or straight, outward or inwarde, as he distinguisheth. And therfore willed him to put difference betwixt civile and antichristian bondage, betwixt bodilie oppression, persecution, etc., and anie ecclesiastical antichristian yoke. Wee acknowledge the church to have bene in civile bondage, in great persecution and bodilie oppression in Egipt and Babilon; but that they were there in anie ecclesiastical bondage, or received anie antichristian yoke, we utterlie denie. And demande of Mr. Giffard where he can shew that anie of

---

[1] Barrow, *A Plaine Refutation*, [51], pp. 102-183.
[2] *A Short Treatise*, p. 86.

the faithful there bowed downe to their idolatries, received anie newe lawes and ordinances at those tyrantes for the worship of God, the administration and government of the church. Or if he can shew that anie did thus, whether those persons were by the worde of God to be esteamed members of the church? And as to the place by him alleadged, I Corinthians 7: 21, 22: "Art thou caled [being] a bond servant, care not for it; for the bond servant caled in the Lord, is the Lorde's freeman," it fullie sheweth that difference which we are driven so often to inculcate unto him betwixt civile and antichristian bondage. The one here shewed to be an holie estate and calling, no prejudize to the kingdome of God, or to the libertie of the sainctes. The other in al those places above recited to be contrarie to the kingdome of Christ, to our christian libertie and faith, to be intollerable, and not to be borne or suffred of the church, or any member of Christ. In as much as Antichrist is an adversarie, an opposite and lawlesse fellowe, that lifteth himself up not onlie against, but above God, shewing himself that he is God, II Thessalonians 2: [4], causing al both smale and great, riche and poore, to receive his marcke, Revelation 13: [16]. Which marcke we have declared from sondri places to be bondage and subjection to his statues and decrees, even as christian libertie is the marcke of the children of the free woman, of the heavenlie Jerusalem. Which bondage and subjection being the [166] marck of the beast, all the men that receive the same either upon their fore-heade or upon their hand, "shal drinck of the wyne of the wrath of God," of that pure wyne mixt in the cup of his wrath, and "shalbe tormented in fire and brimstone before the holie angells and before the Lambe, and the smoke of their torment shall ascend evermore, and they shall have no rest day nor night, which worship the beast and his image, and whosoever receiveth the prynt of his name." Revelation 14: [9-11]. And it followeth immediatlie. "Here is the patience of the sainctes, here they that keep the commandements of God and faith of Jesus."[1] Whereupon we may conclude, that no antichristian yoke, not even in the least things, is to be borne or suffred in Christe's church by waye of subjection not for the space of one hower. But all thinges rather to be undergonne, than to stoope down to the beast to beare his marcke, or worship his image.

By this tyme Mr. Giffard having shot off al his newe ordinance to litle purpose, retireth himself againe to his old skonce [bulwark], and wil by no meanes be driven from his two places of the Songe.[2] Wherbie (when he before so missed to prove the church in anie antichristian bondage) he nowe letteth that matter fal, and bringeth these places to prove the church to stand in outwarde bondage. Which doctrine thoughe it was never by us denied, but that the church might be in civile and bodily bondage, yet wee affirme nothing lesse to be proved by these places.

Cant. 1
[Canticles or Song of Solomon]

In the first, wee hope Mr. Giffard wil not be so grosse to take those vineyardes for locall vineyardes, and that setting or putting to keepe them, for civile or bodilie bondage. For besides that nothing could be more grosse or divers from that heavenlie spirituall argument of Salomon in that Songe, soe would Christ never wil the church or anie member of the church, to shake off anie lawfull or civile yoke in that maner, to depart from their earthlie lords and masters, to refuse such lawfull service and honest labour as they shoulde enjoyne them.

Cant. 5

Likewise to the seconde place. There may great difference be put betwixt bondage, and persecution or oppression. That the church there was in grievous persecution is evident, but that it was in anie bondage we cannot by that text or anie circumstance therof perceive. Thus Mr. Giffard everie way misseth his marcke, and as a giddye droncken man he reeleth from one side to the other. Sometimes endevouring by these

---

[1] Revelation 14 : 12.
[2] Song of Solomon 1 : 6 ; 5 : 6, 7. To a modern reader, who interprets the Song of Solomon as a Hebrew love song, it is surprising to see the extent of spiritualizing of its verses both by Barrow and Gifford. The subjectivity involved in the interpretation weakens the argument.

A Plaine Refutation

places to prove the church in bondage to some antichristian yoke, yet not daring to affirme those vineyardes (which her mother's sonnes put her to keepe) to be Antichriste's vineyardes, which if he affirme and prove not, there is no antichristian yoke to be dreamed on in that place, al the strength of his reason or rather delusion lying in these wordes: " The sonnes of my mother were incensed against me, they set me the keper of the vineyardes, my vineyarde that [belonged] to me I kept not."[1] The true interpretation wherof it here booteth not to stande upon, sufficeth that no antichristian yoke or bondage can from this place, or from anie one worde therof be drawen and inforced. But yet Mr. Giffard doth herein presse us with these places of the Songe, in that the faithfull did not here separate themselves from under these evil pastors [167] and governours, as heretickes and schismatickes doe.[2] And this he againe proveth by the example of our Saviour and his disciples, who did not separate themselves from the high priestes, scribes, and Pharasies, so long as the vineyarde was not taken from them, etc. To which proof he hath in the Second Transgression his ful answere. To these places: in the first the church hath an absolute and direct commandement from God himself, to goe foorth, not to staye in the steps of that flocke, to feede her kids above the tabernacle of those sheepheardes. In the second we can but wonder to see Mr. Giffard so insensate and grosse to imagine, that these persecuting watchmen were ministers or members of the true church. Especiallie seing the two churches so livelie in that place described, the one malignant and persecuting, the other the true church and persecuted. Betweene which I weene there is as great a separation as betwixt light and darcknes, betwixt hel and heaven. Neither did the church there staye with, or was stayed by those watchmen, but went to the daughters of Jerusalem to seek and enquire for Christ; much-lesse (as this man doteth) stayed in their fould in their tentes, or

---

[1] Song of Solomon 1 : 6.
[2] *A Short Treatise*, p. 88.

remayned under the government and bondage of those persecuting watchmen that openlie opposed against Christ, and could not endure that the church should seek him. Neither can anie thing be imagined more false or contrary to the argument of that heavenlie Songe, than that the church of Christ may at anie hand beare or stand in anie bondage to the yoke of Antichrist. Whose neck Christ adornes with chaynes, and she againe her doore postes with garlandes for him. Song 1 : 9 and 6 : 13. Under whose head Christe's left hand alwaies is, and his right hande embraceth her. Songs 2 : 6. Songs 3. She layethe holde of Christ, and bringeth Him into her mother's house, into the chamber of her that conceived her. There also is his bedde set up muche more glorious than the marriage bedde of Salomon, about which bedd sixtie valiant men of the mightie men of Israel are said to stand and guarde, all of them handling the sworde, expert in warre, [every man] with his sword upon his thighe from the feare by night. Songs 4 [3 : 7, 8].

The necke of the church is likned to the tower of Daniel [David] built for the armorie, where a thowsand shieldes doe hange, al the targetts of the stronge men [Songs 4 : 4]. And Songs 8 [verse 12], Christ saith his vineyard is allwaies and wholly before him, he chalendgeth and gathereth al the revenue therof himself, he divideth them not nor imparteth them to anie other as Salomon or other earthlie princes are constrayned to doe. What part or right then, what honor, or homage, especiallie what bondage is left here to Antichrist? But thus they are broken that thus wilfullie and of set purpose stumble at the Worde, as this man doeth.

Yet procedeth this graceles man furder, and is not afraide to affirme, that the church and everie member therof is in some spiritual bondage to sinne, and draweth an argument from this position, that therfore much more may it be in some outward bondage to Antichrist.[1] This execrable position and argument, the

---

[1] *Ibid.*, p. 88.

holie bishops and [168] learned priestes of England are content to let publiquelie passe from their viewe and corection, because it pleadeth for the antichristian usurpation of the one, and the servile bondage of the other. But when this argument shal never so litle by the Worde of God be skanned, it shalbe found most heretical and blasphemouse. For verilie if after our faith in Christ, wee be now left in anie bondage to sinne, then doth sinne stil live and raigne in us, and we stil bounde unto and with it, then hath not Christ fullie freed us from the curse of the law, death, and hel. Then was not Christe's death a sufficient ransome for, neither extended to al our sinnes, neither hath he subdued or set us free from al our enimies, neither have we as yet anie perfect peace or reconciliation with God. And then was his comming vayne, then can no flesh be saved therbie, then must wee looke for an other redeemer, or ells looke for him to come againe to dye for our sinnes that remaine and raigne in us. For the rewarde of the least sinne is death, being a transgression of God's lawe; and if wee be in bondage to sinne, then are we not kinges and priestes unto God. Is not this a meete minister of the gospel, that knoweth not yet the worck of our redemption, the benefite of Christe's death, the priveledge of the sainctes, that cannot and will not learne to put difference betwixt the frailtie or pronenes to commit sinne, which is in this mortal flesh of all the faithful, and that bondage and subjection to sinne which is never found in anie of the faithfull, after they have once trulie acknowledged and embraced Christ? Howsoever the ministrie of the Church of England may allowe and publish these doctrines, yet are they most odious and execrable to the soule and conscience of all that knowe, feare, or love the Lorde Jesus Christ.

[THE FOURTH PRINCIPAL TRANSGRESSION]

Nowe at length we are come to the second proposition of our argument, or rather to the Fourth Transgression wherewith their Church of England is chardged, *vzt.*,

Henry Barrow

"*that their churches are ruled by and wilfully remaine in subjection unto an antichristian and ungodly government, contrarie to the institution of our Saviour Christ.*" This wee shewed in our first writing by the publicke and present estate of the Church of England, in their whole ministrie, worship, administration, ordinances, ceremonies, censures, cannons, customes, courtes, to be antichristian, even the same yoke and government that the pope sometimes exercised by these his naturall children and unfaithful servants the bishopps, who nowe have gotten this power into their owne handes.[1] Most of these (if not all) have bene alreadie in this present treatise declared and proved to be idolatrous, popish, blasphemous, false, and antichristian, wholly swarved from the rules of Christe's Testament. Anie of these howe Mr. Giffard hath by the Worde of God approved, let the unpartial reader judge. This their ecclesiasticall government which nowe is in question, he saith is the same in matter though it varie in forme from Christ's government.[2] Wherof nowe is arisen a great question in their church, whether that apostolicke forme of discipline which they prescribed to the [169] churches, should be perpetuall, or variable. The Reformistes that hold it perpetuall, sue and complaine to the parliaments for the same apostolicke forme to be established, and to have this present government of these bishopps

---

[1] Carlson, *The Writings of Henry Barrow, 1587-1590*, p. 144.
[2] *A Short Treatise*, p. 89. Gifford agrees "in the matter" — i.e., that Christ hath given to his church the power to ordain pastors and teachers, and to admonish, suspend, and excommunicate. On the form or manner of exercising this power, he hesitates. He admits that in apostolic times the power belonged to presbyteries consisting of pastors, teachers, and elders. Some think that this form is perpetual and invariable, but others believe that "this forme is variable, and that it is the most safe and quiet way, that the power belonging to the presbyterie, be committed into the hands of the byshop." If this latter group — the Church of England — is wrong, as Gifford implies, nevertheless it does not stand under the yoke of Antichrist, because even as a church may err in points of doctrine and still not become antichristian, *a fortiori*, a church may err in external government and still remain the spouse of Christ. This represents the view of Gifford, who is a kind of crypto-Presbyterian, but it is also espoused by some Anglicans. Thomas Cooper, Bishop of Winchester, took the position that the Apostolic model was not perpetual and invariable (*An Admonition to the People of England* [pp. 79-81 in the 1589 edition of 245 pages; pages 73 ff. in the 1589 edition of 252 pages]).

A Plaine Refutation

and their false hierarchie with their courtes and offices quite remooved out of the church and abolished.[1] The prelates that holde it arbitrable at prince's pleasures according to the variable estate of tymes and countries, holde fast that popish inordinate usurped power which they have gotten into their handes, and therbie incarcerate, silence, sequester, depose al such of the contrarie faction as speake against their power, and present government, with al possible hostilitie. Yet al this deadlie debate Mr. Giffard covereth in a worde, calling it but a question about the outward forme of discipline. As also hideth all the other most heynouse and detestable enormities that arise and flowe from their monstruous antichristian governement, under the same title of outward forme of discipline.

For both sides he saith doe agree in the matter, "that Christ hath left a power to his churche to chuse, to trye, and to ordaine pastors and teachers. And likewise that he hath given the power of admonition, suspension, excommunication. Onlie here is the difference, that the one side woulde have this power exercised by presbiteries of pastors, teachers, elders, as in the Apostles' tyme. The other hold it the more salf [safe] and quiet waye to commit this power to the handes of the bishop."[2] Which side holdeth the truth, you shall hereafter knowe Mr. Giffard's minde; when the battell is fought he wil then tell you of which side he wilbe. Till then he wil take the bishops' side against the Brownists, tooth and nayle, and affirme their government to be the holie government of Christ, and the defaultes therof not such as make it to become antichristian, or a yoke of bondage, as the Brownist with open throte exclaymeth. And for the other side (wherof he sometyme was) they, howsoever they woulde have it removed, yet are far from the Brownistes' opinion; for they for the peace of the church had rather stand under it, than under Christ's

---

[1] See J. E. Neale, *Elizabeth I and Her Parliaments, 1559-1581*, Chapters II, III, Part 7; *Elizabeth I and Her Parliaments, 1584-1601*, Chapters IV and V of Part I and Chapter III of Part 2.
[2] *A Short Treatise*, p. 89.

Henry Barrow

crosse by witnessing against it [the prelatical power and episcopal discipline].[1]

Concerning the opinions of both these sides, for the execution of this discipline they speake of, wee have alreadie shewed both sides to erre, and fully refuted their several opinions by the way in the Second Principall Transgression,[2] where we have declared that the execution of the censure and power of the church belongeth neither to such a sequestred withdrawen presbiterie, nor yet to anie one man, but unto the whole church joyntlie, etc. Wee have also in that Second Transgression shewed the forgerie of their idol suspension, and of the popish excommunication of these bishops, and how the Church of England hath no power to excommunicate any person for any sinne or heresie whatsoever: but only abuse this most high judgment of God upon earth, to their filthie lucre and pompe, excommunicating for nothing but for contempt of their antichristian courtes, or for not paying their ravenous fees and extortions, as also absolving them for money when they please.[3] Wherupon whilest they want [lack] this power of excommunication, it

---

[1] Barrow sharply criticised Gifford and Cartwright and the other Presbyterian reformers for inconsistency, for failure to implement their beliefs, and for lack of courage. Both Presbyterians and Separatists agreed on the need for alteration but disagreed on the nature and degree and timing of reform. Luther's attitude toward Carlstadt and the Peasants' Revolt, Fourier's differences with Marx, and the conflict between revisionists and absolutists, socialists and communists — these illustrate the same problem. So near and yet so far.

[2] Pages [51] — [101], pages 102-183.

[3] See F. Douglas Price, " The Abuses of Excommunication and the Decline of Ecclesiastical Discipline under Elizabeth," *English Historical Review*, January, 1942, pp. 106-115. See also Wilfrid Hooper, " The Court of Faculties," *English Historical Review*, October, 1910. See further Great Britain. Ecclesiastical Courts Commission. *Report of the Commissioners Appointed to Inquire into the Constitution and Working of the Ecclesiastical Courts, with Minutes of Proceedings, Evidence, Returns, Abstracts, Historical and Other Appendices, etc.* This report is Command Paper 3760, Parliamentary Papers, 2 vols. (London, 1883). Canon Stubbs' valuable contribution is in volume I, 21-162. See an excellent recent work by Ronald A. Marchant, *The Puritans and the Church Courts in the Diocese of York, 1560-1642* (1960). See also Thomas Cooper, *An Admonition to the People of England* (1589); [Richard Cosin], *An Apologie: of, and for Sundrie Proceedings by Jurisdiction Ecclesiasticall* (1591); Franciscus Clerke, *Praxis Francisci Clarke*, ed. Thomas Bladen (1666, but written about 1596); Henry Consett, *The Practice of the Spiritual or Ecclesiastical*

A Plaine Refutation

followeth, [170] that admonitions were vayne and fruictlesse amongst them, when they cannot have their due power, processe, and effect. Sondrie of them also, as these bishops, the whole rabble of their false hierarchie and priestes being incorrigible, such as wilbe subject to no censure, neither receive admonition; but be more readie to smite and blaspheme such as reprove them.

Moreover, in the Third Principal Transgression we have shewed, how their churches have no power in themselves to elect or ordaine them any ministers, but are inforced to receive them from the patrone and the bishop, whether they will or no. Where we have also set downe the counterfeight and false maner of the ordination and institution of their ministers or priestes. Whereby evidentlie appeareth what kinde of government this their discipline of the Church of England is. So that here remaineth the lesse to be spoken of this poyncte, the chief matters being alreadie handled. Onlie here we wil a litle entreate of this controversie betwixt these bishops and priestes about their forme of discipline, and somwhat generallie of their courtes in fewe wordes, and so put an end to this poyncte.

This controversie Mr. Giffard affirmeth to be about the forme and not about the matter of discipline, wherin both sides agree " that Christ hath lefte a power to his church," etc. Doth not Mr. Giffard deserve high commandations, that with one logicall distinction can both defend all the pope's hierarchie, courtes, canons, etc., and make also these two opposite factions the bishops and priestes to agree in matter? So that now belike al this long bitter hostilitie, contention, and controversie amongst them hath bene about no matter. And then wil not this rare distinction hide or excuse the blame of either partie? Againe (save that we wil have no strife about inanitie of wordes) we alwaies tooke the forme to have given the being to the thing, and to

Courts (1685, 1708); Thomas Oughton, *Ordo judiciorum*, 2 vols. (1728-38), trans. in part by James T. Law, entitled *Forms of Ecclesiastical Law* (1831, 1844); James T. Law, *Lectures on the Ecclesiastical Law of England* (1861).

have bene so principal a parte therof, as it might never be severed from the same,[1] howsoever in way of discourse the forme and the matter may for argument sake be distinguished. For even common sense teacheth, that no man or creature may be separate from their peculiar and natural forme or shape. Neither anie member of them from that forme, place, and office, which God hath given and appoincted to that member. But al men hould it monstruous to have a mixte or false shape. How much more impossible and intollerable were it, but to admit anie other forme, or to change that forme which God hath given and appoincted to anie action of the church? Either that forme which God hath given and prescribed is no true and right forme, or ells those actions without that true and right forme, cannot be said those true actions of the churche. Howe monstruous then is their presumption that dare undertake to change, yea, to abrogate those formes, rules, ordinances, that Christ hath prescribed to his church in his Testament? Howe shamelesse and blasphemous their impudencie, that dare pronownce this adulterate monstruous discipline of their church, the same in matter and effect with that government [171] Christ hath prescribed? Is not this of the one sort to sit in the temple of God as God, to change the ordinances, etc? Is it not in the other with the false prophet to dawbe and uphold the throne of the beast? If God unto Moses prescribed an exact paterne in al thinges that belonged to that tabernacle, even to the least pinne, tape, hooke, utilence [utensil], with the due forme, shape, measure, waight, place, tyme, use, etc., and left nothing to his wil or discretion (but his praise was that he was founde faithful in al the Lorde's house, and had made and donne all thinges according to the paterne shewed him in the mounetaine). If the worde spoken by angels was made sinne, and everie transgression and disobedience received just retribution of reward, how

Exo. 25:40
Hebr. 8:5
Hebr. 3:5
Hebr. 2 and 12:25, etc.

---

[1] So Aristotle. See his views in W. D. Ross, *The Works of Aristotle*, volume VIII, "Metaphysica," (2nd edition; Oxford, 1928), Book Z, sections 3 and 8. See also Werner Jaeger, *Aristotle*, translated by Richard Robinson (Oxford, 1948), pp. 301, 340, 341, 403.

A Plaine Refutation

shal they escape, and where shall they stand, that neglect, yea, reject, that heavenlie arch-type, and onlie perfect paterne of Christe's Testament, delivered by the Holie Ghost to the Apostles, by the Apostles to the churches, confirmed by the death of Christ, and by divers signes and wonders from heaven: that take boldnes to innovate, change, and alter the inviolable perpetual ordinances of Christe's Testament, and to set up a new leitourgie, and to bring in a newe ministrie and government according to the same? If God were so jealous over the ordinances and utilences of that material temple, which consisted but of wood and stone, that he permitted not anie thing to those excellent servantes, Moses, David, Salomon, in al that busines, which they received not by divine oracle from his owne mouth, neither suffred wilful transgression in anie that drewe neare to administer before him, but executed most fearefull examples upon sondrie, as Nadab, Abihu, Corath [Korah], Uzzah, Uzziah, etc., how much more jealouse and seveare shall he be over the ordinances and administration of this spiritual house, which consisteth of the soules and bodies of men, over that kingdome of his Sonne which cannot be shaken, over that tabernacle which cannot be removed, the stakes wherof can never be taken away, neither shall anie of the cordes therof be broken for ever? Shal not the Lord destroye them which thus misbuilde and destroy his temple? Can they thinck themselves wiser, or more in favour with God than Moses, David, Salomon? To have greater priveledge than the Apostles? Who delivered not anie thing which they had not received, and bownde all builders and churches to that which they delivered, unto the worlde's end, teaching them to observe all things whatsoever Christ had commanded them, to keepe the true paterne and that holie commandement undefiled and without blame, until that appearing of our Lord Jesus Christ. Yea, can they thinck themselves wiser and fuller of eyes within and without, to have greater sight and providence of things present and to come, things inwarde and outwarde than the Lorde and builder of the house himself, that they dare

_{I Chron. 28:11, etc.}
_{I Kings 6 and 7 chapters}
_{Levit. 10}
_{Numb. 16}
_{II Sam. 6}
_{II Chron. 26}

_{Heb. 12:28}
_{Esa. 33:20}

_{I Cor. 3:17}

_{I Cor. 11}
_{I Cor. 4:17}
_{Mat. 28:20}

_{II Tim. 1:13}
_{I Tim. 6:13, 14}

_{Zech. 3:9}
_{Hebr. 3:6}

thus presumptuouslie violate and innovate the ordinances, the outwarde forme of government and administration (to use their owne wordes) which he hath instituted for his church and kingdome? Thinck they these of lesse moment and value, than those ordinances [172] and outward formes belonging to the tabernacle and temple under the lawe? Or is not this to prefer that material temple and the ordinances therof to the spiritual temple and the Testament of Christ? The person and ministrie of Moses, to the person and ministrie of Christ? To make Moses more faithful and absolute in his house than Christe? In as much as the ordinances of the temple were perfect and inviolable, such as no prince or priest might add to, alter, innovate, or breake the least of them. But the ordinances and formes of Christ in his church so imperfect, weake, insufficient, yea, so incongruent and unmeete, as they are left arbitrable at the discreation of men, conformed to the wil of princes, to polecies, times, and states? Yea, doe not these men that hold the forme or maner of the administration of Christe's discipline (as they terme it) variable and arbitrable, and that presume to prescribe an other maner of executing the same, hold their owne waies and devises more wise, equal, and convenient than the Lord's waies, and thrust their owne into the place of the Lord's? Which formes and devises of theirs can no more agree or be joyned to the Lorde's ordinances in his government, order, administration, than heaven and earth can be mingled. Neither may they without sinne be compared togither. The Lord's forme that he hath given and disposed to everie part, action, and exercise of his church only and best fitting and agreeing to the same, neither suffring or receiving any other.

Revel. 21:16 For as it is written, the forme of this citie is fowre square, most firme, immoveable, and proportionable, the height, length, and brea[d]th therof being equal. Yea, as our

Cant. 4, 6, 7 chapters Saviour pronounceth with his owne mouth most gratiously and often in the Songe, al the members, features, and proportions of his church, are most beautifull, amiable, and even ravishing the senses to behold, as we see there from top to toe described; not only in the

A Plaine Refutation

several partes, members, and joyntes, but even in the proper peculiar formes, proportions, features of each.

How wicked then and divelish is the opinion of these bishops and their side, that hold the formes, order, and maner of the actions, administration and government of the church prescribed in Christ's Testament, and together joyned and commanded with the actions, etc., not to be perpetual, alwaies meete or convenient, but to be variable at the disposition and will of men? But how monstruous is their presumption, and barbarous their havocke, that dare not only to bereave the church of that heavenly forme which Christ hath prescribed in his Testament, but in stead therof, set up and impose their owne leitourgie, their owne ougly [*sic*], deformed, and monstrous shapes, which can no more agree to the offices and actions of Christe's church, than the pawes of a beare, the mouth of a lyon, etc., can agree and be joyned to an humane bodie, which strange shapes and false members agree and belong rather to the monstruous bodie of that beast than unto the heavenly bodie of Christ. For if the great Creator have not permitted or given power to any mortal man to make or give shape to the least member or part of an humane natural bodie, not to make one hayre, or being made to give it colour or shape, white or blacke, short or long; muchlesse then hath the Lorde and great Archi-[173]tect of the church his spiritual bodie, given power to any angel or mortal creature to make or change the least part or action therof in matter or forme. But as he hath not called anie man to councell concerning these thinges, but hath delivered unto all men a perfect paterne in his Worde, where we have his whole minde, howe he will have al thinges donne in his church, so it behoveth al men soberly to rest in, and carefully to beware not to change, transgresse, or swarve from the same at any hand willingly: knowing that even the Lorde our God is a consuming fire, and wilbe served also of us in this his kingdome to his owne good liking with reverence and feare.

Now seeing we finde the forme and paterne which Christ hath instituted and given most perfect and absolute, such as cannot be corrected or amended by anie

Revel. 13

Esa. 14:13, 14, 15

Rom. 11:34
I Cor. 2:16
II Tim. 3:16, 17
Acts 20:32
Heb. 12:28, 29

humane devise or ingenie [cleverness, ingenuity], such as cannot be separate from the partes and actions unto which Christ hath joyned them, neither may those places or actions receive anie other forme, but that therbie they become adulterate, displeasing to God, pernitious to men. It is evident that this government which the bishops exercise over the church, cannot be the true government or discipline of Christ, because by their own confessions it is executed after an other forme and maner than Christ hath instituted, seing (as we have by manie reasons and expresse Scriptures proved) the forme is injoyned and joyned together with the action by the same aucthority, neither may by any mortal man be changed or separate from the same. So [that] Mr. Giffard his owne confession in that their government wanteth the true forme (for here we reason not of faultes in a true forme, but of a divers and false forme) is reason enough to shew, that it is not that true government which Christ hath instituted. And then must it needes followe to be a false and antichristian government. And consequently all that stand under it to stand under the yoke of Antichrist, and not to have Christ their kinge and governour. Moreover the Brownist with whom he hath to doe, hath learned and doth fully believe, that Christ ruleth in his church by his owne officers and lawes, and not by any such popish officers, courtes, and canons, as these bishops doe in the Church of England. All which he hopeth Mr. Giffard will not say to be of the forme of discipline. For sure he holdeth a true ministrie and the rules of the Bible to be of such necessitie, as the true church may never receive anie other ministers or lawes for their administration and government. We have likewise lardglie alreadie proved this whole ministrie, administration, ordinance, and maner of government, not to be according to the rules of God's worde, but forged, popish, and false.[1] Only in this place we

---

[1] The Third Principal Transgression, pp. [101-158], *supra*, pp. 183-285. See also *A Brief Discoverie of the False Church*, printed in Carlson, *The Writings of Henry Barrow, 1587-1590*, pp. 335-361, for the ministry; pp. 361-553 for the administration, worship, and preaching; pp. 553-672 for the ecclesiastical government and discipline.

A Plaine Refutation

would knowe of Mr. Giffard if the bishopps and their false hierarchie, courtes, jurisdiction, government were of God, how then these learned Reformist preachers may sue and seeke to have them utterly removed out of the church. I would not here be understood of their persons (wherof might be some colour and reason enough) but of their offices, courtes, jurisdiction, government. Al which they would have utterly abolished and taken away; which if they were of Christ could not be donne without [174] most heynouse impietie and sacriledge, without a most grievous wound and mayme in the body of Christ, by cutting off such pretious and principal members and officers of Christ, and that for ever. If those bishops, their accomplices, courts and government were of Christ, then are these Reformistes which sue and labour to have them removed and abolished, most dangerous and pestilent seducers, that perswade the prince and realme to doe this violence to the bodie of Christ his church, to reject the holy government and ministrie of Christ, which who so despiceth or putteth away, despiceth and putteth away Christ himself; and so perswade and drawe they their prince and the whole land into the assured wrath and vengeance of God. But nowe on the contrarie, if these bishops, officers, courtes, government be not of Christ, then belong they not unto, neither have anie thing to doe or to intermeddle with the ministrie or government, or anie action of the church of Christ. How great then on the other side is the perfidie and apostasie of these Reformistes, that knewe and pronounced in open parliament that they were not of God,[1] and sought to have them utterlie removed. Yet now for filthie lucre, and for feare of persecution, subscribe, sweare, and submit to their antichristian hierarchie, power, courtes, jurisdiction, and to al the detestable enormities that flowe from their throne? That dirive their ministrie from, and exercise it under them? Yea, that exercise

---

[1] Probably references to the parliaments of 1584-5 and 1586-7. See J. E. Neale, *Elizabeth I and Her Parliaments, 1584-1601*, chapters IV and V of Part I, and chapter III of Part 2.

their ministrie and keep the whole land under their yoke, and so in the knowen wrath of God? How odious is the hypocrisie and apostasie of this graceles man, that sometimes knewe and stood against these enormities, yet now as a withered fruictlesse tree twice deade, plucked up by the rootes, is fallen and apostatat from al faith, light, savoure, conscience, and feeling, as that starre wormewood[1] that poysoneth and maketh bitter and deadly al the waters he faleth into: now pleading and fighting for that apostatical throne of iniquitie, terming that [to be] nowe the government and power of Christ in matter and effect, which he himself page 56 and 58 of his booke[2] confesseth not to binde in heaven, not to be just as in respect of them that doe excommunicate, etc., colouring al the abhominations that flowe from this throne, and al the controversies about their government with a divers outward forme.

I hope he will admit the Testament and ministrie of Christ to be of the matter and substance. And then shall his halting on both sides, and double dissimulation appeare to all men, that durst not set downe so much as the controversie amongst themselves trulie. Which yet T.C. [Thomas Cooper] his lord [bishop] of Winchester dealt more rowndly in, flatlie deniing the apostolick discipline to be either perpetual or necessarie: but especially elections, excommunication, etc., by the people to be either expedient or tollerable, bringing sondrie fleshly reasons and politicke inconveniences and impediments to the contrarie, the refutation of whose blasphemies belongeth to an other place.[3] But this man thincking to keepe in with both sides, setteth downe the controversie to be onlie about the forme and not about the matter of discipline, although the bishops abash not in playne wordes to the veiwe of the world,

---

[1] The plant *artemisia absinthium*, known for its bitter taste.
[2] *A Short Treatise*.
[3] See *A Brief Discoverie of the False Church*, pp. 187-225, for Barrow's refutation. Thomas Cooper's views are given in his *An Admonition to the People of England*, pp. 79-94 in the edition of 245 pages, and pp. 73-84 in the edition of 252 pages.

A Plaine Refutation

and to the face of Christ, to denie the verie matter it self. As both sides also doe in deedes and effect; whilest they acknowledg that Christ hath given unto [175] his church the power of elections and censures, yet both of them withdraw this whole power from the church. The one into their sequestred synodes, the other into their popish courtes. If so be this power wilbe graunted to be of the matter of discipline. But this question is soone put to an end, whilest the bishops denie the apostolick discipline it self as tollerable in the common wealth, and flatlie denie Christ to reigne over them or over this church by his owne officers and lawes. And therfore except he wil give their persons, accomplices and trayne, as immunitie from al ecclesiastical censures, not to be subject for anie transgression or error to the reproof or power of the church; yea, except he wil resigne his right into their handes, and give them leave to reigne and rule over al the churches in this land, or that by their owne officers, courtes, canons, constitutions, injunctions, etc., he is no kinge or Christ for them. Nay, if he wil not bowe downe to al these and take their yoke upon him, he is no subject for them, he may not buy and sell, not live in this market, in this church. Which officers, courtes, cannons, etc., if Mr. Giffard had proved to have bene of the matter of Christe's discipline (for of the forme we wil al graunt him they are not) and had approved and justified them by the Worde of God, then had he some colour to ask this question, whether some faultes in their discipline should make it antichristian.[1] But seeing these bishopps and their courtes, officers, canons, etc., were by us affirmed unto him to have no foundation or mention in God's worde, no place nor use in Christ's church, but to be contrarie to the one, most prejudicial and dangerous to the other, and he in all this space could bring us no defence for them, wee cannot see by his owne reason (seing they have neither the true matter nor the forme of Christe's government) howe their government should be held and esteamed the true

Tit. 1:16
I Cor. 4:20

Luke 19:14, etc.
Math. 21:33

Rev. 13:17

---

[1] *A Short Treatise*, pp. 89, 90.

and holie government of Christ. And then must that sequel (which he so feareth) needes followe, that it is an antichristian government and yoke, such as the true church and servantes of Christ may not beare and wittinglie stand under.

To perticulate all the severall corruptions, abuses, enormities of the government of these antichristian bishops, is not in mie skil or power, not knowing in anie measure their cannons, customes, orders, priveledges, proceedings. Onlie this in general I may affirme, that of such pompeous, stagelike, popish, mixt courtes, handling both civile and ecclesiastical causes judiciallie, I never read through al the book of God, or to belonge to Christe's church. Especiallie exercising such absolute power and jurisdiction over al churches, causes, and persons ecclesiastical; yea, usurping, assuming, and executing the whole power, offices, and dueties of al churches, yea, even the proper prerogatives and priviledges only belonging to Christ himself. To make, impose, or abrogate lawes. To give or rather sel licences and dispensations, to have more benefices than one, to marrie, to eate flesh at tymes of restrainte, etc. To cal, sommon, and fetch by constrainte al causes and persons of the church before them, there to determine and decree, to censure, silence, suspend, [176] sequester, depose, incarcerate, punish by mulct what minister or member of the church they lust of their owne absolute auctoritie without any controlement, reprofe, or redresse. The church having no power or libertie to reproove or refuse, no, not so much as call into question anie thing they do or decree, to rebuke or censure these inordinate lawlesse fellowes for anie thing they doe either publickly or privatly. The church must receive and obey as most holie, whatsoever they decree or impose with al reverence as the oracles of God, though they be never so contrarie to the Worde of God. The church or any other member of the church in these courtes be not permitted so much as to propounde or pleade their owne cause; but are by them compelled to their Romish litigious course and procedinges, to speak and pleade by a feed [fed] advocate or proctor, after their popish order and custome. Where for bribes and fees al causes (be they never so fowle and corrupt) are handled, pleaded, and proceede, that I say not succeede. And without such bribes and fees, no cause (be it never so just, and the partie never so poore or innocent) hath audience or help. Here being so many officers, catchpolles, attendantes to be feed [fed] and pleased. To all these ravenous birdes with fingers the suetors and sommoned become a pray [prey]. But especially the faithful, such as speak against, and will not of conscience and faith unto God stoope downe unto their antichristian power, or obey their ungodly decrees; these shalbe worse used than any trayterous papists or facinorous [wicked] persons whatsoever; who shall all of them by their purse or freinds escape well enough and find favour, when these poore soules shall never geat out of their handes without wrack either of bodie or soule, either death or denying the faith. These though there be no direct matter, evidence, witnesses, or accusers against them, yet shall themselves be inforced to a corporal oth (as they call it) upon and by a booke, to answeare directly and truly to such articles and poyncts as shalbe propownded unto them.[1] If they denie or make conscience either of the maner or matter of this oth, then instead of godly instruction or christian persuasion, they are forthwith committed to prison, yea, for the most parte to close prison, there to remaine shut up from al ayre, exercise, friendes, dueties, callings, etc., untill they either yeild to take this idolatrous, blasphemous, and impious oth, or dye under their handes. No baile, maineprise, help, benefite, or redresse by lawe, by the Queene's royal writtes or courtes allowe to any, that are committed by the leaste of this hellish anarchie.[2]

---

[1] See Albert Peel and Leland H. Carlson, *Cartwrightiana*, pp. 28-46. See also "The History of the *ex officio* Oath in England," by Mary Hume [Maguire], a Ph.D. thesis (1923) at Radcliffe College, Cambridge, Massachusetts.

[2] During the 1580's the ecclesiastical commissioners, with the strong support and prodding by Archbishop Whitgift, developed into a powerful permanent Court of High Commission. Barrow knew this court at its

Henry Barrow

Whose lawlesse and insolent dealinges, oppressions, injuries, violence, may not be caled in question or examined by anie civile magistrates or courtes. All which they patronize by her majestie's high or especiall commission unto them. Although her majestie suffreth her roial preogative to be handled and considered of in some of these civile courtes; yea, and graunteth to all her free borne subjectes the benefite and free use of her Highnes' lawes even in anie cases or causes betwixt her Highnes and them according to the great charter in the *Magna Charta*, wherunto her majestie is sworne. Which [177] Charter also these lawlesse prelates most presumptuouslie and tyrannously violate and breake under colour of her majestie's commission; thus setting her majestie's commission against her majestie's prerogative and courtes royal, against that great charter of the land, against all her Highnes' lawes, yea, and against al the lawes of God and the Testament and kingdome of Christ. But to say as it is, their procedinges are both against the[i]r commission (if they might be dulie examined and conferred therunto) and against her majestie's meaning. Whose milde, peaceable, and just government in al causes that procead from her self, assure us, that she would never wittingly graunt such a commission as shoulde be so prejudical to her owne crowne and royal dignitie, to the estate of the church and of the whole common wealth, as this, wherby these prelates beare themselves and their ungodly procedings, is.[1]

height and its worst. After his death (1593) the court increasingly became the object of attack by Puritans, lawyers, judges, and the House of Commons. Common-law judges were able to limit the power and jurisdiction of the Court of High Commission by means of writs of prohibition on the grounds that ecclesiastical cases involved temporal matters. Inasmuch as the common-law judge issued the writ and decided what constituted temporalities, he possessed an effective weapon. Sir Edward Coke strongly and ably opposed the efforts of Archbishop Bancroft to enlist the unqualified support of King James I. See Stuart Barton Babbage, *Puritanism and Richard Bancroft* (1962), pp. 259-293. See also Roland G. Usher, *The Rise and Fall of the High Commission*, pp. 15, 46 *et passim*. There is an interesting manuscript of twenty folios in the Huntington Library, Ellesmere MS. 1988, dated June 20, 1589, which constitutes a new Court of High Commission — probably at the suggestion of Archbishop Whitgift.

[1] Barrow seeks to extenuate the role of the Queen in the Court of High Commission, but he is indulging in wishful thinking.

A Plaine Refvtation

That power graunted unto her majestie by parliament, to appoinct and aucthorize whom she shal thinck meet to execute under her " al maner jurisdictions, priviledges, and preeminences " concerning ecclesiastical causes to her belonging, is, as also al other her princely power and aucthoritie alwaies to be understood in the Lord, so far as shalbe found consonant to his word.[1] For neither is there given, neither may or wil her majestie take or exercise any furder or other power than the Lord her God giveth her. In whom kinges reigne, of whom their power is dirived and holden, by whom it is circumscribed and limited, to whom they shal as anie other persons, accompt.

If then these prelates and their antichristian hierarchie, these Romish courtes and their popish procedinges in the same, be not fownde to be of God, to have anie warrant in his word, or to belong to the ministrie and government of Christe's church, then can no commission or humane aucthoritie whatsoever make them lawfull, impose, or enjoyne them upon the church. Neither ought anie Christian to obey them at the commandment of any mortal man. Men must alwaies be obeyed in the Lord. Unto whom, when, or wherein they be fownd contrarie or opposite, there must God rather than men, be obeyed. His indignation that can cast both body and soule into hel fire, is more to be feared than theirs, that can but touch the body only. To obey God's commaundements, and to refrayne from al thinges that are fownd contrary to the same, is no disobedience to princes, neither to withdrawe or derogate from their sacred power, as this malignant clergie would persuade. But they rather, that encroch upon and openly impugne the prince's royal prerogative; that so highly abuse their prince, and that [abuse the] trust she committeth unto them; that breake and violate al the publicke lawes and charters of the lande; that usurpe the civile sword, aucthority, and jurisdiction, which are utterly prohibited them by God; that usurp

Acts 4:19
Mat. 10:28

---

[1] See the Act of Supremacy, I Elizabeth, *caput* 1, section VIII, *Statutes of the Realm, IV,* Part 1.

place above al in aucthoritie under her majestie whoesoever, to whom by the lawe of God they ought to be subject; that wil not submit their lawes, doings, and persons to any civile tryal at the prince's royal judgment seates, but rather seek to withdrawe some of the most high and chief causes from her royall courts and judgment seates into their owne courtes; that usurpe the proper [178] peculiar place, titles, privileges, power of Christ himself, exercising absolute aucthoritie over al churches, doctrines, causes, persons, to being in or cast out, erect or abrogate, what lawes, ordinances, ministrie, ministration, government they lust without controlement; that wil not submit their publick ecclesiastical decrees and procedings, nor yet their private lives and conversation to the tryall and censure of Christ in his churche by the Worde of God; that make such barbarous havocke, mis-rule, and confusion both in churche and common wealth; that seduce and deceive their soveraigne prince, their nobles, majestrates, and the whole land, leading them in the wayes of death and destruction, tourning them out of the straight waies of life and peace; that with their utmost endevour and skil oppose against the Testament and kingdome of Christ; that molest, spoile, and persecute in al hostile maner the Lord's most faithful servants, her majestie's most loyall and true hearted subjectes, for refrayning from their idolatries and enormities so contrarie to the gospel of Christ, which flowe from their antichristian government and ministrie; that nourish, favour, and support the Lorde's and her majestie's pernitious knowen enimies, the papistes, those idolators, those conspirators and traytors,[1] who they say are not such enimies to their pontifical estate and regiment as these faithfull Christians are; that are of nothing so jealouse, vigilant, and careful, not even of their soveraigne prince's life, or of the peace and prosperitie of the whole land, as of their owne usurped ruynous kingedome, lest the light of the gospel should break forth, and discover their apostaticall

---

[1] Perhaps Barrow is thinking of Edmund Campion (1581) or of Anthony Babington and Mary Queen of Scots (1586-7), with their supporters.

throne, and antichristian procedings. And therefor with al their might and mayne they strive to suppresse this light, and to oppresse all such as in anie sinceritie and good conscience professe and practize the gospel, tollerating and chearishing rather anie mischief, anie vile flagitious and dissolute persons, as by daylie experience is seene.[1]

So that by these markes and fruicts let the christian or but indifferent reader judge, whether these prelates and their antichristian hierarchie be to be held troublers of the church and state, abridgers of the prince's power, usurpers of publick aucthoritie without lawful caling like Corath [Korah], Dathan, and Abyram, or wee, as this accuser, this trompe[2] of Sathan (to bleamish our holie profession and glorious suffringes) shameth not to give out of us. Although they all hitherto have not, neither shal ever be able (in the confidence of God's grace, and of a cleare conscience we affirme it) justlie to detect, or so much as to suspect us of anie such crime, endevoure, or intent. We reverence and are subject to everie humane creature for the Lorde, whether unto the kinge as having aucthoritie over all, or unto rulers as sent by him, for the revenge of evil doers, or for the praise of them that doe well, that according to the wil of God, by doing wel, we might put to silence the ignorance of unwise men. Yet hold wee not the offices, courtes, and jurisdiction of these prelates and their hierarchie within the compasse of this commandement, or to be the ordinance of God; but finde them that verie throne of Sathan, that anarchie of Antichrist opposite to [179] the kingdome and Testament of Christ, most pestilent and pernitious both to the church and common wealthe. And therfore may not by princes be suffred in churches or common wealth, muchlesse by them be established over the church and common wealth, with- 1 Pet. 2

Revel. 17

---

[1] Perhaps the best treatment of ecclesiastical courts is to be found in William Stubbs, *Report of the Commissioners Appointed to Inquire into the Constitution and Working of the Ecclesiastical Courts*, in *Parliamentary Papers* (1883), vol. I. See also William Holdsworth, *A History of English Law*, I, 580-632 (London, 1903).

[2] Trump, trumpeter, proclaimer.

out giving their sacred power to the beast. Neither may anie faithfull Christian be brought in subjection to this their antichristian power and yoke, without bowing downe and worshipping the beast.

<small>Revel. 13:15</small>

To discusse or perticulate the severall and innumerable errors, faultes, abuses, corruptions, enormities, in the cannons, constitutions, customes, procedinges of the severall courtes that belong to these prelates' antichristian regiment, I am not (as I have said) able, neither were it in this place expedient. By this which hath bene here generally said of them, their courtes, and proceedinges, appeareth, how contrarie they are to that government, and to those ordinances which Christ hath established and set over his church for ever. Christ's scepter is an everlasting scepter, a scepter of righteousnes. He hath set downe a most perfect and absolute government to his church. He hath perticularly and exactly prescribed what officers, lawes and ordinances he requireth in his church. He cannot be separate from his owne government. He ruleth not his church by anie other officers or lawes, than by his owne which he hath instituted. These godlesse prelates, then, that appoinct other officers and lawes unto him and over his church, wrest not only the scepter, but the kingdome out of Christe's handes. And al such as stand under the antichristian government of these presumptuous idol shepheardes, stand not under Christe's staff, amenitie, under his scepter of grace, as the sheepe of his fould within his covenant and protection; but as the sheepe of destruction under his iron rodd, wherwith they shalbe broken as a potter's vessel. Here is our controversie touching this Fourth Principal Transgression, fully decided and determined by God's owne mouth; that all which stand under anie false ecclesiasticall government, stand not within the covenant, but under the wrath of God. All the mitigations then, reasons, and delusions of the false prophets, shal never be able to make voide, tourne away, or diminish these judgments, otherwise than by their unfaigned repentance and speedie conversion from their evil wayes.

<small>Zech. 11</small>

<small>Psal. 2</small>

A Plaine Refutation

Hitherto hath Mr. Giffard brought us not one reason or place of Scripture to proove the present government of these prelates and their hierarchie, to be that heavenly government which Christ hath instituted in his church, but hath grievouslie perverted manie Scriptures to proove that the church might stand under some antichristian yoke, although we in our first writing[1] in this Fourth Principal Transgression blamed it, as false and antichristian. In our second[2] shewed it to be such in the officers, courtes, cannons, proceedings. Now at length for a [180] conclusive reason to proove and determine all the poyncts at once, and to shut up his booke, he hath hatched and brought us foorth this worthie reason to rest upon. " If the execution of discipline by bishops be the yoke of Antichrist, and if all the churches which doe stand under the same doe worship the beast and be not Christians, it must needes follow that such as did ever execute this power, were Antichristes, and no children of God at that time or before thei repented." But by your owne confession manie of them died blessed martyres. " I conclude therfor, that the Brownists cannot but with heresies and most heinous injurie and inordinate dealing condemne a church as quite divorced and separate from Christ for such corruptions and imperfections in God's worship as be not fundamentall, nor destroy the substance; for that wicked men come with the godly to the publick exercises of religion; for some wantes in calling and ordaining ministers, and in ecclesiastical discipline."[3]

Be like Mr. Giffard is hard driven when this old popish reason alreadie by us answered, and now by him not over wel repayred, is fayne to become his cheif corner stone to approve this church in all these chardges, and the only reason he can bring for the hierarchie and regiment of the Church of England. By this reason his holie father the pope was wonte to defend his triple crowne and apostaticall chaire. Because in the same

---

[1] " A Breefe Sum of Our Profession," Carlson, *The Writings of Henry Barrow, 1587-1590*, pp. 81-85.
[2] " A Brief Summe of the Causes of Our Seperation," *ibid.*, pp. 118-150.
[3] *A Short Treatise*, p. 90.

have sit [sat] manie godly bishops and blessed martyres, etc., so that if the office, power, and dignitie of his popedome be antichristian, then must all these godly learned men that have executed the same needes be Antichrists, and not true members of Christ, untill they repent. But they never were founde to have repented these thinges, yet are confessed by al that knewe them in that age to be learned and godly. Therfore Mr. Giffard and all this horned cleargie and lordly hierarchie of England, cannot without schisme revoult from, without heresie pronownce, this holie sea [see] and office antichristian, etc. Let Mr. Giffard, now he seeth the fordge and issue, bind or loose, followe or leave this argument, at his owne pleasure and perill. If he suppose to escape by shewing discrepance betwixt these godly predecessors and ungodly successors in manie circumstances and vertues; and so thinck this reason wil not presse him half so sore as it doth us; yet let him consider (though I will not be the pope's advocate) that they here reason of the same office, and not of the same circumstances, and that these godly predecessors executed the self same office with these their bad successors. Yea, so might the example be put, as it should be without anie great difference in circumstance also. And as to the difference betwixt the persons of the one and of the other (if that may be a solution to this argument), we shall not greatly need to feare, finding this viperous generation, these idle, proude, wordlie, fleshlie, persecuting, blasphemous prelates, nothing so like these their godly predecessors these martyres, in laboures, humilitie, bowntie, spiritual and holie conversation, faith, patience, love of the truth, of the sainctes of Christ, etc., as they are in that which is evill in these antichristian titles, offices, courtes, jurisdiction, revenues, pompe, etc. Which (as we before said unto you), so say we againe, that no men or [181] angels can justifie where God's worde condemneth, though all the martyres in the worlde should dye in and for them. We may not be leed [led] or drawen by the examples and persons of men (how good soever) from one iote of God's reveiled [revealed] truth. The best men we see doe erre and

A Plaine Refutation

sinne, there never was or shalbe anie man, that erreth and sinneth not in manie thinges. But should we because good men have donne evill and erred, therfore justifie sinne and error? That were high presumption greivouslie to tempt God, and to abuse the holie Scriptures, which recorde not men's faultes to that end. What sinne or error might not so by the example of some good man or church be justified? Yet these are Mr. Giffard his best reasons for his church, ministrie, etc., and here his only reason, to approve the government of these bishops and hierarchie.

But now as we here justifie and allowe not any sinne by the examples and persons of the godly; so condemne we not these godly men's persons for sinne and error, until obstinacie be joyned therunto, which Mr. Giffard cannot shew in these holie martyres. And therfore we denie the consequent of his major or first proposition; that because the office and jurisdiction they executed were antichristian, therfore the men that exercised them were Antichristes, and not children of God. We may utterly condemne the sinne, and yet not so peremptorily condemne the sinner.[1] It is a sure position that everie sinne is of the devil, yet is there no consequence therof, that everie one that sinneth is of the Devil. We see no such necessitie as Mr. Giffard would persuade of that matter.

The godly may sinne of ignorance, of negligence, of fraylety, yet not therupon untill obstinacie be added unto sinne, cease to be Christians. The godly martyres so lately escaped out of that smokie fornace of the popish church, could not so clearly discerne, and sodenly enter into the heavenly and beautiful order of a true established church. It is more than one daye's worcke, to gather, to plante and establish a church aright, much

---

[1] This paradoxical sentiment is seen in later writers. John Dryden (1631-1700) wrote: " She hugg'd the offender, and forgave the offence " (" Cymon and Iphigenia," line 367). Alexander Pope (1688-1744) said: " And love the offender, yet detest the offence " (" Eloisa to Abelard "). And Thomas Buchanan Read (1822-1872) expressed this antithesis as follows: " I hate the sin, but I love the sinner " (" What a Word May Do," Stanza I).

more so manie thowsand severall churches as are supposed in this land. It can be no wonder that those godly men being so unexpert and unexercised in his heavenly worcke, never having lived in, seene, or hearde of any orderly communion of sainctes, anie true established church upon earth of so many hundreth yeeres, ever since the general defection under Antichrist so much foretold of in the Scriptures, no marvaile, I say, if they erred in setting up the frame. But what then? Should we therfore justifie or persist in their errors? Especially should we reject the true paterne of Christe's Testament which reproveth our workes, and sheweth us a better course? Should we not suffer our worckes to burne, after the maner of these deceitful workmen of these tymes? God forbid. For then should we receave their reward and perish with our worckes.

Now to the second proposition of this argument we have alreadie expressed our minde concerning the suffringes, faith, and death of these martyres. We finde them obstinatly to have resisted no part of God's worde or truth he gave them sight of at anie tyme, but to have bene [182] verie faithfull and constant even unto bandes and death in that truth they were come unto. Furder, we doubt not but they truly repented them of al their sinnes knowen, and faithfully laid hold of God's mercie in Christ Jesus for al their secrete and unknowen sinnes. God's grace we are assured is so much greater than all our sinnes, as the sea is greater than one dropp of water. Therefore we doubt not of their happie and blessed estate; all their sinnes and these false offices and ministrie, which they executed in their ignorance amongst the rest, being forgiven them. The example then and errors of these martyres will not approve the antichristian offices and government of these prelates, nor yet justifie the publick worship, ministrie, confusion, sacriledge of the Church of England.[1]

Muchlesse wil these two lame propositions of Mr. Giffard, his final argument, beare upp his forged conclusion, where he concludeth the Brownistes [to be]

---

[1] *A Short Treatise*, pp. 98-100.

A Plaine Refutation

heretickes, etc. Because they " condemne a church as quite devorced and separate from Christ, for such imperfections and corruptions in God's worship, as are not fundamental, nor destroy the substance; for that wicked men come with the godly to the publicke exercises of religion; for some wantes in calling and ordayning ministers; and for some wantes in ecclesiastical discipline."[1] If Mr. Giffard had taken the wise man's councel, he should not have answered a matter before he understood it, much lesse would he (if he had bene ledd by the spirit of God) have blasphemed the truth or condemned the innocent without cause.

But as he began his booke without councel, continued it without grace, and ended it without truth; so hath he herebie but purchased to himself shame, and brought upon his owne head the judgments due to an accuser, a blasphemer, a false witnesse and judge. What opinion the Brownistes hold of the Church of England, their worship, people, ministrie, government, we neither knowe nor regard, neither is there cause whie we should be chardged or condemned for their errors and faultes.[2] For which themselves, and this Church of England that receiveth and nourisheth all sectories, hereticks, wicked and abhominable persons whatsoever, shall accompt. For us, whom it pleaseth Mr. Giffard to terme Brownistes, and whome he endevoreth to confute in this treatise, we never condemned any true church for anie fault whatsoever, knowing that where true faith is, there is repentance; where true faith and repentance are, there is remission of all sinnes. Far be it from us to condemne anie whom Christ justifieth.

---

[1] *Ibid.*, p. 90.
[2] Barrow and Greenwood constantly repudiated any connection with Robert Browne, whom they regarded as an apostate for his recantation and his return to the Church of England. See Albert Peel and Leland H. Carlson, *The Writings of Robert Harrison and Robert Browne*, pp. 507-8. See also Stephen H. Mayor, " The Political Thought of the Elizabethan Separatists," a Master's thesis at the University of Manchester, 1951, and B. R. White, " The Development of the Doctrine of the Church among the English Separatists with Special Reference to Robert Browne and John Smyth," Ph.D. thesis at Oxford University, 1961.

1. And for the Church of England we neither did or doe condemne it (as this accuser suggesteth) "for such imperfections and corruptions in their worship as be not fundamentall or destroy the substance ";¹ but we condemned the publick worship of their Church of England presently injoyned, received and used, as devised by men, popish, superstitious, idolatrous, abhominable, not such as God commandeth, requireth, or accepteth, and therfore not such as anie faithfull Christian may offer up unto God, be [183] compelled, or consent unto. This wee shewed in the First Principall Transgression: This we have proved in the first part of this treatise.²

2. Secondly, wee condemne not the Church of England as separate from Christ, "for that wicked men come with the godly to the publick exercises of religion."³ But rather as never rightly gathered to Christ, for that al the prophane and wicked ar received and retayned as members of their churche. Wee gladlie acknowledge that Christ came a light into the world, to offer salvation unto all men, to have built his church upon an hil, there to be lifted up by the preaching of the word as a standard to al people and passengers, there to have made a feast to al nations, and thither to invite them. Neither were we ever so envious of the salvation of others, or of the glorie of God (as having founde mercie, and being entred our selves) to shut the doore or stop the fountaine of God's grace against others; yet God is witnesse with what heartie desire we long after them all, that they, even our greatest persecutors, might be partakers of the same salvation, joy, comfort, and happines with us. And howe wee intermit not,⁴ much lesse exclude, anie meanes therunto that God putteth in our power (though it were with the hazarde of our owne lyves) to bring them of the water of the wel at Bethelem [sic].

---

¹ *A Short Treatise*, p. 90.
² *A Plaine Refutation*, pp. 25-50; *supra*, pp. 60-102.
³ *A Short Treatise*, p. 90.
⁴ And we desire you to know that we do not interrupt or skip over any means God gives us to promote the salvation of others.

A Plaine Refutation

But now though we affirme that al the unbelieving and prophane not onlie may, but ought to resort to the publick exercises of religion in the church, as the most excellent meanes to call them to the faith; yet do we not therfore believe or affirme, that the prophane or unbelieving may be received or admitted as members of the church, before they have made voluntarie publick profession of their owne faith and obedience; or being entered by such profession, be permitted longer to stand or remayne of the church, than they contynue orderlie to walke in the same faith and obedience. And therfore we blamed these parish assemblies of England, as consisting of a confuse multitude of al sortes of prophane and wicked people indifferentlie; where they are al received, nourished, and retayned, as members of the church, though they were never called and gathered by the power of the worde, entered and received by the profession of their own faith, neither walke orderlie in the faith, or in anie dueties either publick or private. And so are al guiltie of most high sacriledg and prophanation of the holy things of God. No such assemblie or communion of sainctes, as Christe's faithful servantes ought to repaire or joyne unto. This wee shewed in the Second Principal Transgression. This we have lardgly proved in the second part of this treatise.[1]

3. Thirdly, we condemne not the Church of England " for some wants in calling and ordayning ministers ";[2] but for having, maintayning, and retayning a false and antichristian ministrie imposed upon them, with a false and antichristian calling and ordination, even the self same that the pope used and left in this realme; which false offices and ministrie cannot be joyned unto, or exercised in the true church of Christ. This wee shewed in the Thirde Principal [184] Transgression. This we proved in the third part of this treatise.[3] And therfore with an evil and corrupt

---

[1] *A Plaine Refutation*, pp. 51-101; *supra*, pp. 102-183.
[2] *A Short Treatise*, p. 90.
[3] *A Plaine Refutation*, pp. 101-158; *supra*, pp. 183-285.

conscience hath Mr. Giffard sought to hide this transgression under some wantes in the calling and ordaining ministers, and thus boldlie and falselie therupon to accuse us. Wee knowe there may be faultes either of ignorance or negligence in the calling, ordination, etc., yet these not to disanul the action, much-lesse the covenant, so longe as they are not obstinatlie held and persisted in. But our assertion and controversie here is not of a faultie ministrie, caling, ordination, etc., but of a false ministrie, caling, ordination, etc., which we have proved theirs to be, and that no such belongeth unto, may be imposed, received, or retayned in the church of Christ.

4. Fourthly, in like maner wee reason not of some wantes in the government and order of their church, but of a false and antichristian government set over the church. Neither condemne we the Church of England for some faultes in a true ecclesiasticall government, but for having and standing under a false and antichristian government, even the self same hierarchie, officers, courtes, cannons, customes, privileges, proceedings, that the pope used and left. This wee also have shewed in the Fourth Transgression, and have nowe in this fourth parte, and through this booke, fullie proved their present ecclesiastical government to be.[1]

To which fower principall transgressions a willfull obstinacie, an open rejecting and resisting the truth and al reprofe, a violent and most hostile persecution of all such as either refraine, speake against, or reprove their communion, ministrie, worship, government, being joyned, we may by all these reasons, severally, and have by them altogether, proved these parrish assemblies in this estate not to be the true established churches of Christ, to which the faithful servants of Christ ought to resort and joyne.

So then all men maie see how falsly this accuser hath sclandered us, and howe far he hath strayed from the present matters and transgressions in question, both

[1] *Ibid.*, pp. 158-186; *supra*, pp. 285-331.

A Plaine Refutation

through his whole booke, and in this conclusion of his booke,[1] where he chardgeth, pronownceth, and condemneth us as heretickes, etc., for condemning a church for some light imperfections in their worship, wantes in their discipline, etc., wheras we for their idolatrie, confusion, sacrilege, false and antichristian ministrie, and government, obstinacie in all these sinnes, hatred of the truth, and persecution of Christe's servants, have proved the Church of England not to be the true, but the malignant church. Therfore wee condemne no true church as he accuseth, neither for such causes as he surmiseth. Nor yet do wee, but rather God himself, condemne them. Wee but discover their sinnes, and shew them their estate by the Worde of God, refrayning and witnessing against their abhominations, as we are commanded by that voyce from heaven, " Go out of her my people, that ye communicate not in her sinnes, and that ye receive not of her plagues, etc." [185] Reve. 18:4

In the same love, knowing this terror and irrevocable decree of the Lorde against the false church and all her children, wee most earnestly exhorte and instantlie beseech, even so manie, to whom the truth of the Lorde and their owne salvation is deare, to flee out of the middest of her, and to save themselves from this perverse generation, and to deliver everie man his soule from the fierce wrath of the Lord, according to the councel of the prophets and apostles of God. And not to be stayed by the vayne persuasions, titles and promises of these false prophets, of thinges present, as of the church, worde, ministrie, sacraments, etc., or deluded by their vayne hope of things to come, as reformation, salvation, etc., or deterred with their vayne threates of schisme, heresies, daunger, persecution, etc., from obeying the voyce of God, whilest He yet speaketh and calleth unto you, and offreth grace, lest you despise the acceptable tyme of the Lorde, the day of his salvation, and He sweare in his wrath that you shal not enter into his rest for your disobedience, and then hereafter your II Cor. 6:17, 18
Acts 2:40
Jere. 50 and 51 chaps.
Zach. 2:7

---

[1] *A Short Treatise*, pp. 90, 106-110.

flight be in the wynter or on the Sabboth, when the wrath of God is come upon you, and there be no meanes or way to escape.

For the vaine boasting of these prophetts of things present, and promises of things to come, reade Revelation 18 : [2, 8], where the Holie Ghost sheweth their church to become " the habitation of divells, the prison of everie uncleane spirit, the cage of everie uncleane and hatefull birde," howsoever she boast her self a queene; to be no widowe, to see no sorrowe. " For this, in one day shal her plagues come, death, and sorrowe, and famine, and she shalbe burnte in fire, because the God that condemneth her is a mighty Lorde." You there reade how neither her shipmasters, marchantmen, princes, or multitudes, shalbe able to reserve her wares, or preserve her from the burning of this heavenly fire. No lamentation can ease or diminish her sorowe and grief. No balme can cure her woundes, no arte reforme or repaire her breaches, no arme or power shield her from the weight of that great milstone that shall presse her and all her children to the deapth of hell, being lifted up over her by that mightie angel. The Lord hath pronownced and his decree is irrevocable. The voyce of his heavenlie harpers and musitions, the psalmes and spiritual songes and laudes of his saincts, shal never be heard in her anie more; the skil and art of any heavenlie artificer, worckman, or builder, shal never be found in her any more; the voyce of the milstone that grindeth foode for the soule, shal never be heard in her any more; the light of a candle, much-lesse the burning lamps of God's spirit, shal never shine in her any more to keepe out darcknes; the heavenlie and comfortable voice of the brideg[r]ome, and of the bride; of Christ speaking to his church in instruction, exhortation, comfort, of Christe's church speaking to him in prayers, prayses, etc., shall never be heard in her anie more. Let her ship-masters, then, her mariners, marchantmen, enchanters, and false prophets utter and retayle her wares, deck and adorne her [186] with the skarlet, purple, gold, silver, jewels, and ornaments of the true tabernacle. Let them in her offer upp their sacrifices, their beastes, sheepe, meale, wyne, oyle, their odors, oyntements, and franckencense. Let them dawbe and undershore [support] her, builde, and reforme her, until the storme of the Lorde's wrath breake foorth, the morning wherof al these divines shal not foresee, muchlesse eschue or withstand the terror therof, until the wall and the dawbers be no more. But let the wise that are warned and see the evill, feare and depart from the same, so shall they preserve their owne soules as a praye.[1] And the Lorde shall bring them amongst his redeemed to Sion with praise, and everlasting joy shal- be upon their heades, they shall obtaine joy and gladnes, and sorrowe and mourning shal flee away.

Ezech. 13
Esay 47
Prov. 1:24, etc.

FINIS

---

[1] That which one saves or preserves. See Jeremiah 21 : 9, 38 : 2, 39 : 18, 45 : 5.

II

[A REFUTATION OF MR. GIFFARD'S REASONS CONCERNING OUR PURPOSES IN THE PRACTISE OF THE TRUTH OF THE GOSPEL OF CHRIST]

This treatise by Barrow is printed in his *A Plaine Refutation*, pp. 187-206. It was written in 1590 or 1590/1 and printed in 1591.

In 1587 Barrow wrote a brief Separatist manifesto, in manuscript, entitled, "A Breefe Sum of Our Profession." Gifford wrote an answer, also in manuscript, to which Barrow wrote a manuscript reply, entitled, "A Brief Summe of the Causes of Our Seperation, and of Our Purposes in Practise," perhaps in the early months of 1587/1588. Gifford did not produce his second answer until the spring of 1590, when his printed work appeared — *A Short Treatise*. In the closing pages of this work Gifford discusses five articles or Separatist purposes, and it is to these articles that Barrow makes his second reply — the present treatise. For the earlier phases of the statement, answers, and replies, the reader may consult the items printed in Carlson, *The Writings of Henry Barrow*, 1587-1590, pp. 81-85, 118-150.

[A REFUTATION OF MR. GIFFARD'S REASONS CONCERNING OUR PURPOSES IN THE PRACTISE OF THE TRUTH OF THE GOSPEL OF CHRIST][1]

[187] As we shewed in these four principal transgressions, in the worship, communion, ministri, and government of the Church of England, the causes of our separation

---

[1] This title is in the 1605 edition but not in the 1591 edition of *A Plaine Refutation*.

A Refutation

from their publick assemblies in this estate; so at their instance we in like maner set downe unto them our purpose and intent, what we now indevoured and meant to doe, in certaine briefe Articles. Of those transgressions and chardges, how this champion hath defended and cleared their church, by that which hath bene written now on both sides may appeare.

The Articles of themselves are so just and holie, as no divel can impugne or denie, no man of religion, conscience, or shame gaynesay or resist anie one of them: yet hath Mr. Giffard (instigated by the spirit of vayneglorie and envie) in a singular zeale enterprised to answere and confute them all, as you may see in his first writing.[1] The cavills and vanitie wherof, as also his unjust suspitions, calumniations, reproches against us therupon being layd open in our first reply unto him,[2] so far hath he bene from desisting to sporne against the pri[c]kes, to sclander, accuse, and rayle on us, or to take a more sober and christian course for the discussing and deciding these controversies betwixt him and us, as he hath burst forth yet into furder malice and madnes, blaspheming us in everie sentence of this his second answere[3] to these our Articles with such store of contumelious and odious wordes, as if that corrupt synck of his heart could never be emptied, the malice of his minde and venome of his tongue never satiate or uttered against us, even now as fresh as if he had not rayled enough or at all in his writings and booke before.

But seing his reproches want both profe and truth, they deserve neither refutation nor repetition. Neither can they prejudize our holie profession, or us, or anie way justifie or excuse him before God or man; but rather add to his fearful accompt before God, and evidently shew unto all men, by what spirit his heart

---

[1] Gifford's manuscript reply to "A Breefe Sum of Our Profession," is partly reprinted in his own *A Short Treatise* and in Barrow's "A Brief Summe of the Causes of Our Seperation;" see Carlson, *The Writings of Henry Barrow, 1587-1590*, pp. 118-150.
[2] "A Brief Summe of the Causes of Our Seperation," in Carlson, *The Writings of Henry Barrow, 1587-1590*, pp. 118-150.
[3] *A Short Treatise.*

and pen were guided at the writing of these contumelious answeres. Wherin yet most strange it is, how he could take occasion to lade us with all this vituperie, for propounding these godly Articles and holy dueties, especially having shewed withall such just causes of our separation from their assemblies. But let us nowe take a viewe of his reasons wherewith he hath disproved our endevours in these articles, and see whether they be of as great validitie, as those wherewith he hath approved their assemblies in the transgressions by us objected. The Articles, answeres, and our former replie I will not here againe insert, referring to the copies above.¹

Article 1   His cavilling and trifling about these wordes (Christe's Kingdome) in his former answeare to our first article,² together with his hypocrisie in seeming to labour for Christe's government, were by us layde open in our replie:³ as also his unjust surmize, that we should hold that Christe's kingdome could not be in anie, except they had that his outward ecclesiasticall government, was there by us fullie answe-[188]red and cleared. He nowe in his second answere⁴ as vaynely endevoreth to cleare himself of his former cavilling and hypocrisie, by deniing the necessarie sense of his former wordes; and by propounding two newe questions unto us instead of answering our two questions unto him, which we rather expected. Let the indifferent reader judge whether to all intendement he made not Christe's kingdome only inwarde, and his ecclesiasticall government but an help for the preservation of his inward kingdome, in the first parte of his former answere,⁵ howsoever afterward he vouchsafed it to be a part of his kingedome.

Unto his contumelious blasphemous questions we answere, that when he shal have dulie convinced us of heresies, or schisme, to have condemned a true ministrie,

---

¹ They are included in "A Brief Summe of the Causes of Our Seperation, and of Our Purposes in Practise," which was prefixed to *A Plaine Refutation*.
² *A Short Treatise*, pp. 90-1, where this "former answeare" is printed. See also "A Brief Summe of the Causes of Our Seperation," in Carlson, *The Writings of Henry Barrow, 1587-1590*, pp. 118-150.
³ "A Brief Summe of the Causes of Our Seperation."
⁴ *A Short Treatise*.
⁵ Printed in *A Short Treatise*, pp. 90-1.

A Refutation

to have falslie accused a true church, then we will confesse our selves to be more than ignorant and rash; till then all these reproches shall but followe his other sinnes into God's sight to hasten his owne judgment. Our questions also whilest they remaine unanswered, (and as we thincke unanswerable), must still lay open their bad estate and hypocrisie, in that whilest they remaine antichristian ministers in the false church, and have so longe continued under Antichriste's yoke and ecclesiasticall government, they cannot be said either to have or sincerelie to labour for Christ's ecclesiasticall government, as he and they then pretended.

And here by the way I must drawe two dangerous positions, and in the same observe great contrarietie in Mr. Giffard unto himself. First, in that they and he pretended to laboure, and had so long sued to parliamentes for Christe's government or discipline, they confesse the absence and wante of the same. For a fond [foolish] thing it were to labour and sue for that which alreadie they have. Then if they wante and have not Christe's ecclesiasticall government; and receive an other ecclesiasticall government over their church and ministrie which is not his, it must needes be a false and antichristian government. And so they and their whole church by their owne confession stand under Antichriste's yoke and government, and have not Christ their Kinge to rule over them, except they can shewe that Christ doth rule in his church by Antichriste's officers and government, which I thinck will be harde to proove; and then are they and their church in a bad estate. As also Mr. Giffard herein contrarie to himselfe, who erewhile affirmed this present government of these bishops their hierarchie and courts to be the true ecclesiasticall government of Christ. And that they were not antichristian.[1] Furder he hath observed and reserved one special poyncte in our replie: "that the kingdome of God may be in the scattered faithfull, which as yet have not the ecclesiasticall discipline."[2] This

[1] *Ibid.*, pp. 83-90.
[2] *Ibid.*, p. 92.

we graunt and never denied; although Mr. Giffard whatsoever he now say, then surmized the contrarie of us, or ells had smale cause so vehemently to have refuted this opinion. But we are content that it shall now remaine to his use. [189]

Article 2 The second article of seeking God's true worship, he granteth that al men ought to approve. Being demanded in our replie, howe then he continued in idolatrie, a minister of idollatrie, prophecied in Baal, and pleaded for Baal, or howe he could approve our article, and yet condemne us of schisme and heresie because we forsake their false, devised, idolatrous worship, and seek to worship God according to his worde.[1] To those he answereth that when we have proved their worship to be idolatrie, and that they prophecie in Baal, and pleade for Baal, then he is content that men take us for no schismatickes or hereticks.[2] And this I hope we have in this treatise[3] donne, having shewed their worship to be devised by man, idolatrous, abhominable, their ministrie to be as false, dirived from and exercised under their Baals these bishops. And how earnestly Mr. Giffard hath pleaded for these Baals, their throne and all the enormities proceding from the same, these his owne bookes shall testifie. So that I hope we are now cleared with all men, and shal hereafter be spared of him, from the odious accusations of schisme and heresie.

Articles 3, 4, 5 The third, fourth, and fifth articles (after Mr. Giffard his division) tending to one effect, and begetting but the same common difficulties, may together be handled. The chief controversies about the same are these two. 1. Whether these publicke assemblies of their parishes be antichristian and Babylonish. 2. Then whether the church consisting but of private men, may in this estate erect and establish amongst them such offices and ordinances of Christ, as he hath instituted to the ministri and government of his church.

---

[1] *Ibid.*, p. 93.
[2] *Ibid.*
[3] *A Plaine Refutation.*

A Refutation

Of the first, both Mr. Giffard and I have now lardgly set downe our mindes; so that I leave it as fitter for judgment, than anie furder discussing in this place. The reasons here repeated.
1. How their churches are from antient discent within the covenant.
2. And how their church in this estate hath begotten and nourished children unto God, as the martyres,[1]

have bene alreadie often propounded and urged by him in his book. I hope by that time he hath wel considered of the heresies, sacrilege, and absurdities of the first, and of the vayne assumption and litle consequence of the second, as they are set downe in our answeres, he shal have little cause to use them so often, or to urdge them with such confidence and bitternes. For when Mr. Giffard shal proove, that a nation so highly apostate and fallen from the faith, so deiply plunged into such execrable idolatries, abhominations, and hardnes of heart, as in the papistical corruption, stil continueth in this estate a true established visible church, within the outward covenant of God, so far as we may and ought to judge by his worde, then doubtlesse for mie part I wil grcount it a sound major proposition. And if he shal bring the church of Rome for instance in the minor, I must then yeild to his argument. Because the church at Rome was sometimes rightly gathered, established, and within the covenant. Yet even then I suppose it wilbe harde for him to make the like assured proof, that ever her daughter of England was rightly established [190] into that christian order and within the covenant. But I doubt rather, and by her present estate judge, that she was among the children of her mother's fornications, and therfore without the covenant.

To the second reason it will also hardly followe, that because some faithful men have bene called to some generall knowledge of God and of Christ in this estate, and because they in their ignorance continued in the same estate, that this should therfore justifie the out- Rev. 17:2
Deut. 23:2

---

[1] *A Short Treatise*, pp. 94, 97-100.

ward estate of the church which the worde of God condemneth, or proove it in this estate the true established church of Christ, when they have nothing aright according to Christe's ordinance, as we have prooved in this treatise, whether [to which] I refer for a more ful answeare of these reasons, hasting to the second poyncte.

Wherein I before shewed how God commandeth al his faithful servantes (of what estate or degree soever) to flee out of Babilon the false church, and being escaped not to stand still, to remember the Lord a far off, to let Jerusalem come into their minde, to goe up to Sion, to seeke out and to repaire unto the place where God hath put his name. To seek the church and the kingdome of Christ, to take his yoke upon them, to assemble together in his name, with his promise of direction and protection; and with his authoritie to establish his offices and ordinances amongst them, given by him to the ministrie and government of his church unto the worlde's end, there to leade their lives together in all mutuall duties, in his holie order, faith and feare. Now as we shewed all perticular and private men whosoever, to be called out of the false church from confusion, and out of the world from dispersion, unto the true church, unto order. So likewise shewed we, that all these faithfull persons whosoever, were as yet but private men at their first comming out of the false church and gathering together, none of them being as yet called to anie ecclesiasticall office or function in the church, it not being as yet established into order. Whereupon we concluded, and still of necessitie enforce, that seing God calleth all his servantes out of confusion, and will not have them live in dissipation or disorder, but only in this order which he hath prescribed in his worde; and hath given his church aucthoritie and commandement, to erect, retaine, and observe this order unto the worlde's end. And seeing in this estate the church now consisteth but of private men; that therfore the faithfull being as yet but private men, ought by the commandement of God to assemble and joyne themselves together in the name and faith of Christ, and in all mutual dueties orderly to proceede according to the rules of the worde, to a holy

A Refutation

choice and use of such offices and ordinances as Christ hath ordayned to the service and government of his church. And sure were not Mr. Giffard as forgeatful as he is ignorant of the Scriptures, he could not but have seene by the verie phrase the first proposition confirmed by many Scriptures; the second by many prophecies of this general defection; and if not verified in these present times, yet he cannot denie but in [191] some former not long sithence. Therefore whilest he fighteth with the conclusion, he but spurneth against the prickes, bewraieth [revealeth] the folly of his owne heart, and no waye avoydeth or defendeth the daunger therebie.

His best answeare to this reason, or rather manie reasons summed up, is (as he thinketh) to tourne it away by two questions, and by manifold contumelies against our poore persons; or (to say as it is) by inaudible blasphemies against the church of God: likening the assemblie of the faithful gathered in the name, and joyned together in the faith of Christ, proceding to the establishing and exercise of Christe's ordinances, to the rebellious company of Corath [Korah], Dathan, and Abyram, to a rowte of mutynous prentices assembled without leave of their prince to chuse a lorde mayor, etc.[1]

His first question is, that if all were private at the first comming out of the false church, who they were that caled them together? Or whether their comming together doth make them otherwise than private?[2] We answeare, that for anie thing we can see, or may judge by the word, they were but private men that first caled them out of the false church, and that caused them to assemble together, howsoever peradventure indued with more excellent giftes, and more rare graces than other. Furder, that being thus assembled, they ceased not to be private men, until they were lawfully caled unto some true ecclesiastical office in and by the church. Yet al this notwithstanding, the church in this estate nowe consisting onlie of private men, ought to procede

[1] *Ibid.*, pp. 102-3.
[2] *Ibid.*, p. 102.

to a right choice of minister, etc., according to the commandement of God.

His next stombling-block or question, is: who should ordaine these pastors and elders? And whether we "ever read of any ordained but by apostles, evangelistes, pastors, teachers, and governours?" And whether that "power was not at the first derived from the extraordinarie ministers to the Ordinarie"?[1] To this we have above answered, where wee entreated of the ordination of the ministers of England, and here againe doe answere, that the church had alwaies the power to chuse and ordaine their owne ministers, whereunto it ought to use the most fit instruments, whether these pastors, teachers, elders (if such be to be had) or ells where they be not to be had to use the fittest meanes and instrumentes that God exhibiteth. For this power of ordination is not (as Mr. Giffard and the unruly cleargie of these dayes suppose) derived from the apostles and evangelistes unto the permanent ministrie of pastors and elders, neither belongeth it by anie peculiar right to their offices and persons segregate from the church. But it is given by Christ and properlie belongeth unto the church, whereunto their ministrie and persons also belonge, and are by the church to be used unto this worck as occasion is administred. And thus (if a vaile were not laide over Mr. Giffard his heart at the reading of the Scriptures) he might finde that those cheife builders the apostles and evangelistes themselves used this power, not to take it from the church, but therein to assist the church, as we reade, Acts 13. Where the church being assembled unto fasting, prayer, and other holy exercises, it is there said also, that they [192] layde handes upon the apostles, and sent them out,[2] though wee doubt not the church did it by some one or mo[r]e of the prophets or elders, and unto the church at their returne the apostles declared the successe of their journey.[3] In which journey

<small>Acts 14:26, 27
Acts 14:23</small>

---

[1] *Ibid.*, pp. 102-3.
[2] Acts 13 : 3.
[3] Acts 14 : 27.

A Refutation

also, the apostles ordayning or rather helping the churches to chose and ordaine elders, the word *cheirotonesantes*, lifting up handes, whereby the whole action of chusing and ordeyning is expressed, doth clearly give the propertie and right therof unto the churches, and not unto the apostles only, who, as also the evangelistes, did but instruct, direct, help, and assist the church herein, and not pluck away this power from the churches.[1] Likewise the rules for the choice and ordination of ministers in the Epistles to Timothie and Titus, and other places of the Scripture, as Romans 12, I Corinthians 12, Ephesians 4, are not perticularly directed or committed to the consistorie of Elders, as they cal it, sequestred and withdrawen from the church, but unto the church consisting of al the members, which is thereunto to use (as in all other publicke and waighty causes) such meet and fit instruments as the Lorde affordeth and apoyncteth.[2] Neither is this action of approbation, and acception, or ordination of ministers so severed or disjoyned from the election as these men dreame; or so tyed to the office or persons of the elders, as the church might either not ordeyne, or not ordeyne without elders. And aswel might the elders take unto their hands the elections, excommunications, etc., of the church, as the ordination in this maner; againe if the ordination were thus of necessitie tyed to the handes and office of elders, how then should the church after this general defection and corruption under Antichrist (where al the starres were fallen to the earth, and the whole shape of the heaven departed away as a booke wrapped up, a new and strange ministry brought out of the bottomlesse pit with him, as wee reade) ever recover or have anie true ministrie againe in this world? Where should they have true elders to ordaine their ministers? In the false and papisticall church there can be no true elders or ministers of Christ. The true

Rev. 6:12, 13, 14
Rev. 9:[1, 2]

---

[1] Acts 14 : 23. Barrow's exegesis is debatable, inasmuch as the subject of the Greek participle cheirotonesantes is "they" — Paul and Barnabas.
[2] See Romans 12 : 6-8; I Corinthians 12 : 4-10, 28-30; Ephesians 4 : 11; I Timothy 3 : 1-10; 4 : 14; Titus 1 : 5, 7, 8, 9.

members of Christ can not be made the members of that beaste, the members of that harlot. The true ministers of Christ cannot belong unto, neither can administer in the false church, but only belonge unto and administer in the true stablished church of Christ. But now in the tyme of this general apostasie and papistical corruption Mr. Giffard cannot shewe anie where anie true visible established church upon earth, with the true ministrie, government, worship, sacraments, ordinances of Christ, howsoever in a singular conceipt of his owne, he have pleaded the church of Rome, and her daughters in their deipest apostasie, to be in the true church, they and al theirs within the covenant from antient discent, to have the true seale therof, namelie, baptisme, there given unto them all. Yet here not being to be founde anie true christian ministers or elders, who shal now ordaine their ministers, at their first comming out of popery and departing from the Romish church? For nowe we wil transfer the cause from our selves (who are so odious in Mr. Giffard his eyes as no good thing wilbe allowed in or to us) unto themselves.
[193]

When they first came out of poperie, were they then Corah [Korah] his companie, an assembly of mutinous prentices? Were they not all private men? Or which of them was otherwise? Ordinary or permanent ministers they could not be: because there was no true visible established church upon earth, and for a thowsand reasons that might be drawn from the forgery of their office, administration, etc., in the popish church. Extraordinarie ministers, apostles, or evangelistes they could not be, because (as we have above proved) they were ceased after the foundation was once laide, and the worck rightly erect according to the true paterne. Neither finde we to any one established church, the offices of apostles or evangelistes perticularly given, belonging, or erected in anie of them as a ministri of contynuance. Neither had these men the caling due to apostles and evangelistes. Nor yet did they chalendge or execute anie such office, as appeareth by their writings and profession, where they would not have bene ashamed

A Refutation

of the ministry God had caled them unto to have published themselves as they were. But if so be they had donne this, yet their practize being so discrepant from the apostolike paterne and worcke of the former evangelistes, we might not at any hand accept them for such. Thus then at their first comming out of the false church, and gathering together, they were but private men. What then, were they hereticks and schismaticks for departing out of the false church ? Were they conventiclers, sectories, etc., for assembling together ? Were they usurpers and intruders without caling, mutiners, rebels against princes, and abridgers of their power, and withdrawers from their obedience and allegeance for dissuading the people from the false church, the yoke of Antichrist and al their detestable idolatrys and enormities, for caling them to the communion of sainctes, to procede to the choice of ministers, and to the practize of Christe's Testament as the Lorde shoulde reveale unto them ? Al this they did, or at the least professed and endevored to doe. Yet I hope Mr. Giffard that so buildeth their tombes and garnisheth their sepulchers, wil not thus say of them, howsoever he rayle on us that doe and protest to doe no whit more. If they were faithful Christians, such are we: holding the same commune faith with them and al sainctes, not (as yet) truly chardged, or duly convinced of any one error contrary to the faith. They left the false church, so do we. They assembled and joyned together in the faith of Christ, so do we, or at the least would doe.[1] They were but private men, and so are we. They herein are not judged to have offended God or their prince, and why should wee for the same ? They herein did more, than to come out of Babilon.

---

[1] The Barrowists had met in private homes since 1587 and possibly earlier. It was difficult to hold meetings because of the law of the land, the persecuting policies of Whitgift, and the vigilance of the Bishop of London and the ecclesiastical pursuivants. It was not until September, 1592, that the Barrowists were able to organize a church in London, with Francis Johnson as pastor and John Greenwood, who was then out of prison, as teacher. Daniel Studley and George Kniveton were elected elders, and Christopher Bowman and Nicholas Lee were selected as deacons.

Henry Barrow

They did more than sweepe or repaire the house, for they proceeded to the choice and ordination of ministers, to the building of the house, etc. Or ells Mr. Giffard by his owne reasons must condemne them, the church, and al the ministrie of the land, yea, of al Europe, as wel as us.

If he alleadge that though they left their popish administration, and to administer in the popish church, yet they left not that ministerie they there had; we answere (as we have answered) that they received [194] no better ministrie in the false church, than the false church could and did give them; neither could they bring anie better out, than they there received. But the true ministerie belongeth not to the false church, neither can the false church ordaine true ministers.

Againe, whosoever leaveth the publick administration of his ministrie, forsaketh his ministrie: but they left the publick administration of their ministrie. The like argument may be drawn for leaving the church wherof they were ministers. And yet to stop his mouth farder, if the martyres and first witnesses had a true ministrie, such also have sondrie of us whom he termeth Brownistes, etc., yea, by so much a better, as he holdeth the ministrie of the Churche of England better than the ministrie of the church of Rome. Yea, if Mr. Giffard his owne ministrie be good, such and the same have divers of us had, and are as yet undisgraded, otherwise than by unfaigned repentance of so detestable a ministrie. So that if they lost not their ministrie by forsaking the churche they received it of, and exercised it in; why shoulde Mr. Giffard be so severe to judge others, that may make the same plea? If they saye they left not the church of Rome but the corruptions therof, what should let [hinder] us to alleadge the same nowe against them, if we would stand upon those shiftes and doublings? But we use no such coloured excuses, neither relye upon men's persons and doinges. Wee have the expresse commandement of God for our warrant of al those thinges we doe, or refuse to doe, and stand to make proofe and tryal therof by the same word, gladly submitting our selves, al our actions and whole faith unto this tryal. Although also we have and use the examples

A Refutation

and practise of these faithful, that first came out of the popish churche, and enterprised the erection and practize of Christe's ministrie and ordinances amongst themselves, according to that measure of knowledge God gave them. Whose errors though wee shunne (neither will mainetayne our owne when they shalbe shewed us, cleaving onlie to the true paterne of God's word), yet make we their president [precedent] a bulwark for us against these cavilling enimies; who must, for doing these thinges, either condemne them, and so themselves, and their whole church and doings with them, or ells with no shame or justice condemne us of heresie, schisme, sectes, presumption, intrusion, rebellion, etc., for doing the self same thinges they did, or at the least professed to doe; yea, for doing them better and nearer the true paterne than they did. If they in this doing neither intruded without caling, nor presumed above their caling, why are we judged for this doing to doe both? Yea, for this saying, to have put an halter about our neckes?[1] Doth not this our hange-man and executioner (that with joye speaketh of the chaynes and fetters,[2] that these bloodie bishopps lay upon the faithfull servantes of Christ, for leaving their antichristian yoke and seking Christ's heavenlie government) put with the same hande, and trise [draw] the halter about these godlie martyres' neckes, yea, about his owne and his lorde bishops' neckes, and al the ministers' neckes of the land? That have no other defence for their ungodly ministry and doings, than the [195] erroneous practize of these godly martyres, who (as hath bene proved) were but private men at their first comming out of popery and erection of these churches, as we now be? Mr. Giffard had not best shew us manie of these trickes of *legier du main* [sleight of hand, deception], lest he ensnarrle and choke himself with the same halter he would cast about our neckes, and kil himself and his whole church with that sharpe weapon wherwith he would kill us at once in his furious moode.

[1] *A Short Treatise*, p. 96.
[2] *Ibid.*, p. 102.

For sure if it be unlawful for private men to assemble, and in this estate to proceede to the election and ordination of ministers, then by the same lawe was it unlawful for them so to doe. Then are all these bishops and ministers [nothing more than] private men, usurpers; [they are] no more true ministers, than such a one as the mutinous prentices should make mayor [elect as lord mayor] were [would be] a true mayor.¹

Yea, let me goe furder, if the church consisting of private men, may not in this estate erect and ordaine Christe's true ministrie amongst them, then is there no true ministri upon earth, neither ever can be, until God raise up new apostles and evangelistes, and buildeth a new church upon a new foundation, which shalbe when we have a newe Christ. And then Mr. Giffard shal have his dreame. For he saith that when God will have his worcke donne, he will raise up extraordinarie workemen therunto.² But where read Mr. Giffard this position, if not amongst the Anabaptistes? Sure he never founde it in the New Testament, where we have the minde of Christ, a perfect foundation, an accompleat [accomplished or complete] ministrie, until Christe's comming. So that we neede not to say in our heartes, who shall ascend up to heaven for us, or descend from heaven unto us, or goe over the sea for us to bring or teach us the commandement of our God, when the worde is so neare us, even in our mouthes and in our heartes for to doe it. Therfore when Mr. Giffard shall make his proofe of this assertion, and shew his warrant and promise that God will now raise up to his church extraordinarie worckmen, and that til then no private men ought to proceede to the choice and ordination of ministers, but to tarye and expect this promise of the Lorde; then surelie we will acknowledge

Deu. 30:11, 12, 13, 14
Rom. 10:6, 7, 8

---

¹ In *A Short Treatise*, p. 103, Gifford had argued that " if all the Brownists in the land should come together, and choose a minister, and ordeine him, should it make him anye more a minister indeede before God, than if all the apprentices in London taking upon them to choose a lord mayor of the citie, and to minister an othe unto him, should make him a lord mayor "?

² *A Short Treatise*, pp. 103, 106.

A Refutation

him no false prophet, no Anabaptisticall dreamer, and that we have presumed over far upon the Lorde's authoritie and commandement given to his church unto the worlde's end, to chuse and ordaine his ministerie, and to practize amongst them whatsoever he hath commanded. But nowe because this were to bring Christ from above, and againe from the deade, because also we have God's direct commandement to goe out of the false church; being come out, to assemble and joyne together; and being so joyned, to proceede to the erection of his ministrie and practize of his ordinances, and have his authoritie and promise of blessing to these proceedings, because we have the practize of Christe's apostles in planning the primative churches, and now latelie the examples of such as endevored to build this church they live in, we dare not by any vayne hope or threates of this false prophet be drawen to neglect so great salvation, to continue either in apostasie or disorder, and to transgresse or neglect the Lorde's commaundement. [196]

The next objection against us is drawen from an especiall observation in our first Article, where we confessed the universal church and kingdome of Christ to extend to all such as by true faith apprehend and confesse Christ Jesus, howsoever they be skattered, and wheresoever dispersed upon the face of the whole earth. Hence Mr. Giffard concludeth, that seing the faithfull may be in state of grace and have Christ their Kinge, though they live not under that government and order that Christ hath established in and to his church, therfore it is not necessarie for private men to set it up.[1]

Sure this is a weake argument, and not worth half the noting and observation he hath made of it; we must for all this denie it; and finde no more consequent, than if he had therfore concluded that the communion of sainctes, the ministrie and ecclesiasticall government of Christ are not to be sought of the faithfull, because some faithfull may be saved that live not in an established church, *vizt.*, such as are in captivitie, sicknes,

[1] *Ibid.*, p. 102.

^{Luke 17:22, etc.} age, or in such times and place, as they knowe not where to finde "one day of the Sonne of man." He might aswel conclude, that because God is able and doth save some in the false church, therfore private men ought not to forsake the false church. God is able to save some in dispertion out of the established church, therfore private men ought not to seek the established church.[1]

The last and greatest matter is, that we runne before the prince's commandement, whose dutie it is to reforme churches. Private men might not so much as sweepe them, much-lesse build them. For this is to erect a state and government, because "the power of the church is both publicke and greate."[2]

We have above shewed, that the church hath God's commandement and authoritie alwaies, to erect Christe's ministri and government amongst them. That the church in this estate consisteth only of private men, neither are there anie true ministers anie where to be found upon the earth: neither any extraordinarie ministers to be looked for, seing they are long since ceased. Therfore the church in this estate, consisting only of private men, ought to erect this ministerie and government: ells should they also cease and never be had againe upon the earth: and so should there never be any established church, ministrie, sacraments, etc., agayne in this world. Yet here must be noted by the way, that Mr. Giffard runneth too much upon, and wresteth too far, these wordes (*private men*) when we speake of the church consisting only of private men. Now unto his crimination, the church having this commandement and aucthoritie given of God unto the worlde's end, we before shewed him that no prince might take it away, or without great wronge hinder them from the performance hereof. Yea, that the

---

[1] If "out of" means from within the established church, then the conclusion should be that "private men ought not to *forsake* the established church." If "out of" means outside of the established church, as seems in keeping with the irony of the preceding sentence, then the conclusion is valid.

[2] *A Short Treatise*, pp. 97, 106.

A Refutation

servantes of God ought not to be staied from doing the commandements of God, upon anie restrainte or persecution of any mortall man whosoever. For this we alleadged the examples and practize of the apostles, who then had bene guiltie of the same disobedience and rebellion, if princes in this busines had bene to be stayed for, or their restrainte [197] had bene a sufficient let. Yea, that persecution and the crosse of Christ were utterly abolished, if the church and faithfull were not to proceede in their duties, untill princes give leave. We shewed also, that the obedience and practize of God's will was no disobedience or prejudize to the prince. That we attempted nothing beyonde our calling, neither transgressed in our calling, we medled not with the reformation of anie publick abuse either in the common wealth or in their church, otherwise, than by prayers unto God, and godly exhortation. We only according unto God's commandement refrained from their idolatrie and other publicke evils, and assembled together in all holy and peaceable maner to worship the Lord our God, and to joyne our selves together in the faith unto mutual duties. This we shewed to be the duetie of everie private man that would be saved, to leave the false church, and to seeke the true church. And being thus assembled and joyned in the faith, we shewed it to be their duetie together to seeke that ministrie and government which Christ hath left unto his church, and for the church to erect the same.[1]

Unto the apostles' proceeding without the licence of princes he maketh a double answere. One in respect of the persons of the apostles, that they were furnished with a special commission and authoritie from Christ himself to set up his kingdome: which commission and power the pastors and teachers successively received and delivered over to others, so that

---

[1] This paragraph is a summary of the Third Principal Transgression — a false antichristian ministry imposed upon the church — and of the Fourth Principal Transgression — an antichristian and ungodly government or ecclesiastical discipline.

private men may not have this power.[1] The other in respect of those princes in the apostles' tyme, which were all heathen, and therfore it had been bootlesse to sue to them. But where there is a christian prince that holdeth the fundamentall poynctes of the christian faith (though otherwise " this christian prince doe erre in some matters of doctrine, or touching the rules of discipline), everie godly private man is to keepe a good conscience, not breaking the unitie and peace of the church. But not to take publicke authoritie to reforme."[2]

These instances of the persons of the apostles and princes as they are litle to the purpose, so doe they him as litle good. If the commandement of God were sufficient warrant to the apostles to doe their worke, though al the princes of the world resisted; then must the commandement of the same God be of the same effect to all other instrumentes, whome it pleaseth the Lorde to use in their callings to his service also, though all the princes in the world should withstand and forbid the same. For neither dignitie of the persons that are used, make the commandement of God of more authoritie or necessitie to be donne: neither yet the greatnes or the goodnes of the persons that withstand this commandement of God, make it of lesse authoritie or necessitie. Onlie let the servantes of God be sure to have the commaundement and calling of their God for that [which] Rom. 13: [1-5] they doe, and then they neede not feare the powers that are placed [198] of God for the praise and not for the punishment of the good. Our question then is not whether private men may doe that which is not their dutie, to which they have no commaundement, as this accuser surmizeth to bring us into danger and hatred; but whether they may not doe that which God commaundeth them, within the limites of their caling. As to forsake idolatrie and the false church, to seke the true worship of God in the true church, though all the princes of the world, whether believers or infidels, should forbid

---

[1] *A Short Treatise*, pp. 103, 104.
[2] *Ibid.*, p. 105.

A Refutation

the same. And this we affirme to be the duetie of everie perticular person, whosoever forbid. We say not now that private men may reforme the false church, abolish publick idolatrie, or depose a false ministrie that the kinge setteth upp. This were to breake the boundes of their calling, to intrude upon the prince's office; and great cause had they then to feare, for he beareth not the sworde in vayne.

Againe, our question is not whether it is the office and dutie of the princes to see abuses reformed both in the church and common wealth (which we thinck no man to be so ignorant or barbarous to denie, except the Anabaptistes), but whether the church ought not now amongst themselves freely to practize Christe's Testament, either in erecting his officers and ordinances, or in reforming or correcting anie fault or abuse that ariseth amongst them, without staying for the prince's licence; yea, though the prince should upon the paynes of death Mat. 18: etc. forbid. This we affirme to be the dutie of everie per- 28:20 ticular congregation, Christ having therfore given unto each and all of them his sacred power and aucthoritie to binde and to loose in earth, and to doe all thinges whatsoever he hath commaunded them, with promise to be with them unto the end of the world. He hath II Cor. 10 given them the two edged sworde of his mouth to cut downe all sinne, the mightie spirituall weapons of his II Cor. 10:[4, 5] worde to bring "in captivitie everie thought to the obedience of Christ," to the overthrowing of all munitions, reasonings,¹ and sublimitie lifted up against the knowledge of God, "and to have in a readines to revendge all disobedience." To cast sinne into the epha,² and the talent of God's judgment upon it, and Zech 5: [8, 9] to remove it out of the church with all power and celeritie, "with the winges of a storke and the wynde under their winges, and to lift up the epha betwixt the

---

¹ The reading in the 1591 edition is "munitious reasonings," but the correct reading is "munitions," which is the actual word used in the Rheims version of 1582. Other versions have "strong holds."
² The ephah was a Hebrew dry measure, with a capacity of four to nine gallons; it was sometimes equated with a Hebrew liquid measure — the bath, which contained about six and one-half gallons.

heaven and the earth" in the eyes of all men. Christ hath given this aucthoritie to his servantes whom he hath left in his house, and hath commanded them all therfore to watch together, to observe and avoide them that cause anie divisions or offenses contrarie to the doctrine that they have learned, to contende for the maintenance of the whole faith. Not to intermit [omit, suspend] or be withdrawen from anie part of the same by anie man or angell, for persecution or anie thing that man can doe unto them; everie where warning, instructing, and exhorting his servantes not to feare persecution for righteousnes' sake, to take up and beare his crosse daylie, etc. Likewise, for the neglect of those thinges God reproveth and stirreth up the churches [199] to repent and to doe the first workes, or ells he wil come against them speedily, and remove their candlestick. To repent or ells he wil come against them speedily and fight against them with the sworde of his mouth, commending those churches that kept that they had, the worde of his patience in persecution, promising them the crowne of life, if they remaine faithfull unto the death: to make them that overcome pillers in the temple of God, etc.

<small>Mark [13:] 34, etc.
Rom. 16:17
Jude 3
Gal. 1:8</small>

<small>Rev. 2:10 and 3:10 etc.
[Rev. 2:5]</small>

Mr. Giffard he is contented, that under heathen or popish princes the church now may reforme or proceed in the practize of the whole will of God, but at no hand where the prince professeth the faith in the fundamental poinctes, though otherwise he erre and mis-leade the whole churche in some matters of doctrine, or touching the rules of discipline. In these abuses and corruptions " everie private man is to keepe a good conscience, but none to take publick aucthoritie to reforme ": because these kinges are " principal members of the church."[1] What cleare conscience any private man that yeildeth to these publick seene errors or transgressions, or the whole church, whilest it wittinglie doth, or soffreth these things to be donne, can keepe, we have above shewed in the Second Principal Transgression.[2] How

---

[1] *A Short Treatise*, p. 105.
[2] The Second Principal Transgression is discussed in *A Plaine Refutation*, pp. [51] — [101], *supra*, 102-183.

A Refutation

expreslie contrarie this leavened traditionall proposition of Mr. Giffard is to all these Scriptures and doctrines above recited, is so evident to all men, as it needeth no furder or lardger refutation. If God have committed his whole worde unto his church, as the foundation of their faith and of everie action they doe, commanding them to stand to the death for the maintenance of the whole truth and the holy practize of the same; and to cast out in his name and power all, that publicklie and obstinatlie hold anie opinion, or that so commit anie transgression contrary to his worde. If God for the neglect hereof have menaced [threatened] to come in judgment, and exhorteth the churches upon the first discoverie hereof to speedie repentance; howe can Mr. Giffard persuade the churche to continue wittingly in open errors and publick transgression, or in this estate promise them peace? The Holie Ghost hath not set downe this as a note of a true prophet; neither hath God promised anie peace to them, that wittingly continue in any error or transgression, until they repent. Doth not one deade flie putrifie and cause to stincke the whole oyntment of the apothecary?[1] " A litle leaven make sower the whole lumpe?"[2] Wee would knowe of him therfore, whether that divelish distinction of fundamental errors and transgressions, and such errors and transgressions as he holdeth not fundamentall (wherebie he turneth away the practize of what part of God's worde he lusteth, and justifieth [or at the least tollerateth] what open errors and publick transgressions of God's worde he lusteth) will excuse him, or anie that wittinglie breake the least of God's commandements? And whether the aucthoritie or Christianitie of anie princes wil in that daye excuse before the Lorde anie man, that hath at the prince's commandment committed, much more continued to committ, anie transgression, without unfaigned repentance? [200] But if the least error be contrarie to true faith, the least transgression sinne, and no knowen sinne or error to be committed or continued

Deut. 13
Jer. 6:8, 23

---

[1] Ecclesiastes 10 : 1.
[2] I Corinthians 5 : 6 ; Galatians 5 : 9.

in: howe can he persuade the churche to commit or to contynue in anie error or transgression? So highly to tempt and provoke the Lorde?

And now to the poynct. We would know of him whether anie prince, much-lesse a christian prince, may abrogate the commandement of God, or take away that power and aucthoritie that God hath given to the church unto the worlde's end. If not, but that the commandements of God remaine alwaies the same, and the churche hath the same power under a christian magistrate, that [it hath] under a heathen, why then it ought not to proceede to the obedience and practize of God's Worde, whether in correcting and redressing faultes, or in going forewarde in the wayes of God as they are reveiled [revealed] unto them, as well and freely under a christian prince as under an heathen? Is it because a christian prince is the principall and greatest member of the church? Why by so much the rather ought and the better may the church doe it, having now such a singular help and rare accomplement [fulfillment, completion] of so pretious a member. Everie true member is given for the help and comfort, and not for the hindrance and hurt of the body. We may then much better conclude, that the church under a christian prince may procede with all freedome in the sincere practize of Christe's gospel, because he is a member of Christ and of the church, than under an infidel prince, that is an enimie to Christ and to the church.

An other reason he bringeth, why the churche under a christian prince may not reforme without his licence, or untill he will; because it is the office of a christian prince to reforme the church, and therfor the churche in taking such a publicke worke upon them, should but usurpe and encroch upon his office.[1]

Because wee are so apt to mis-understand one an other, and to take words in too lardge or straight a sense, it were good wee set downe what is meant by this reformation here spoken of, before we proceede. Wee meane then by reformation to reduce all thinges and

---

[1] *A Short Treatise*, pp. 104-109.

A Refutation

actions to the true antient and primative paterne of God's Worde. This we graunt to be the office and duetie of the prince to doe aswel in the church as in the common wealth. The prince's eye may suffer no transgression of God's lawe, he is to oversee, and see everie one to doe their dueties in the office and caling God hath placed them. Yet is this no prejudize to the christian libertie and power of the church, no impediment to anie member therof, but rather a singular preservation of all duties, and an excellent instigation of them all to doe the wil of God in their calings. For in all this here is no power given the prince to restraine anie jote of the libertie and power of the church, or to with-hold anie one person from doing the whole will of God in their caling. Much-lesse is here anie power given the prince to drawe or compel the church or any member therof to the least transgression or error; yea, when the prince shal in [201] anie thing be founde contrarie to God, God is then to be obeyed rather than man. And this is no disobedience to the prince's soveraigne and supreame power over al persons and causes ecclesiastical or civile, is no prejudize or impediment to the church, or to anie member therof, from doing the whole will of God in their calings. So in like maner are not the proceedings of the church according to Christe's Testament, any derogation from or encrochment of the royal power and prerogative of princes, as this false prophet out of the mouth of Sathan woulde perswade; but rather a singular preservation and most rare illustration therof. Whose reignes are never so glorious as when, or glorious but when, God is worshipped and obeyed according to his reveiled [revealed] words, and those most chearished and favored, that are most faithful therin.

In the church of Christ are al duties most faithfullie taught, and no knowen transgressions of anie knowen duetie suffred, either to God or man. Howe then can Sathan himself say, that the proceedings of the church, or rather of Christ in his church, are contrarie to, or derogate from the royall power of princes? They cannot be of God that thus set at variance these blessed powers which God hath so conjoyned and contempered for the mutual help each of other, and the service of his glorie. No, it is the false church and this antichristian hierarchie that are prejudicial unto, encroch upon, and usurp the royall aucthoritie, power, jurisdiction, titles, honors, prerogatives, lands, palaces, pompe, etc., of princes. The true church both knoweth howe to obey the Lorde, and their prince in the Lorde. They usurpe not the prince's office when they reforme anie publick fault in the worship, administration, government ecclesiastical, etc., but execute their owne office. For this is not the prince's office to doe in person, but to commande the church to doe it by such instrumentes as God hath therunto ordayned. This commandment of the prince doth neither give the church more power, or make the action more lawful. Neither doth the prohibition of anie prince take away this power of the church that God hath given, or make the action that God hath commanded more unlawful. How then doth the church more sinne in doing these duties in reformation and correction of publick faultes, and proceeding in the practize of God's will (which God hath commanded to be donne by his Church), than anie private man sinneth, when he correcteth anie fault in himself or in his family, or beginneth to doe anie duetie (which he before neglected) without his prince's licence? Seing the prince's eye, power, and office extendeth aswel to civile as to ecclesiastical dueties, aswel to private as to publick reformation. Yea, the prince's licence in al christian consideration, extendeth to al godly duties and honest actions, even to as many things either to be donne or to be left undonne, as the commandements of God extend unto. For he is the minister of God for the praise of them that do wel, and for the punishment of them that doe evill. When the prince resisteth or suffreth not the worde of God to have free passage, he sinneth and doth [202] not his duety. But this can be no excuse for us to cease to doe the wil of God, or to intermit [suspend, discontinue] our duetie. If he drawe the sword and smite us for wel doing, that but augmenteth his sinne, and the blessing of God resteth

A Refutation

upon us that suffer for righteousnes sake. Wee may not for feare of persecution, or for the indignation of princes leave the commandments of God undonne. For that were with this false prophet to mancipate [subject] the lawe of God to the wil of princes, and utterly to abolish the crosse of Christ out of the world. For princes never punish men for obeying, but for breaking their hestes [commands].

Beastly then and hellish is the speach of this man, that saith, the church refuseth the peace of their prince, and provoketh him to strike, when they either reforme such faultes as are in the church, or proceed to doe such things as God hath commanded them, though the prince forbid and wil not give licence. But especiallie where the blasphemer is not afraide to say, that the church when it procedeth to the establishing and practize of Christe's ordinances, erecteth a state and government of their owne.[1]

Doe they erect anie thing of themselves, or that Christ himself hath not erected? Is not this to accuse Christ of treason, because he said he was a King? And his servants of sedition, because he saith he is a Kinge? And his servants of sedition, because they set up his kingdome without the licence, and against the will of princes, though it cost them their lives for the same? Is not this man a faithfull servant of Christ, a faithfull subject of his prince, that so reprocheth Christ's heavenlie kingdom, rejecteth his ordinances and commandments to make them depend upon the wil of princes, that so seduceth his prince, and would drawe her into battell against God Almighty and his church?

Yea, if to set up Christ's kingdome in a christian estate without the leave or licence of the prince or state, be rebellion and disobedience, a derogation from their sacred power, an intrusion into their high office, how then will he excuse our saviour Christ himself? Who being borne in the flesh, but in the estate of a subject

---

[1] *Ibid.*, pp. 97, 105, 106, 109. For Barrow's views on the role, powers, and obligations of the magistrates, see Carlson, *The Writings of Henry Barrow, 1587-1590*, pp. 13, 25, 64, 80, 158, 159, 229, 326, 405, 554, 640-646.

and a private man (he neither being minister of the temple, nor magistrate in the common wealth, and that in a godly state under faithful magistrates, as himself acknowledgeth), did notwithstanding by al meanes indevour to set up his kingdome, preached, baptized, caled al men unto him, although the whole estate and governours earnestly forbad and resisted him. Those governours were to be obeyed, and he himself was obedient in al things, as became a true subject. If it be answered that he did it by the especial commission and commandment of God; wee readilie graunt that [to be] a sufficient warrant unto him before God and men; as also unto all others that have the commandement of the same God for that they doe. But what is this to our question? Whether the church or such as have aucthoritie from God, ought to be stayed from doing the commandment of God, by the inhibition of a christian prince or state? Wee graunte it high sinne and intollerable presumption for anie that have not aucthoritie of God, to enterprise to doe anie thing in the church, whether with or without their prince's licence. But if it be unlawful for the church, or [203] such as have aucthoritie of God, without the licence of their christian prince or governours, then verilie our saviour and his disciples offended herein, who stayed not to doe the will of his heavenlie Father for the threates and laying wayte of the rulers.[1] Furder, if it be unlawful and derogatorie to a christian prince's office and aucthoritie, for anie to doe God's wil in their callings, and for the church to proceede in the practize of Christe's Testament, though against his wil, then is it also unlawfull under a heathen prince. For the christian and heathen princes have one and the same aucthoritie, office, duetie, to see all thinges both in the church and in the commune wealth donne according to the will of God. There is the same reverence and obedience

---

[1] See Robert Browne, " A Treatise of Reformation without Tarying for Anie, and of the Wickednesse of Those Preachers Which Will Not Reforme till the Magistrate Commaunde or Compell Them," in Albert Peel and Leland H. Carlson, *The Writings of Robert Harrison and Robert Browne*, pp. 150-170.

A Refutation

(though I say not the same bowells of love) due to the heathen, that is due to the christian prince in regarde of their office. The heathen prince shall answere aswel as the christian [prince] for the neglect of their duetie, for the abuse of their power and place. And thus also if Mr. Giffard's doctrines be sound, the apostles likewise sinned against the aucthoritie of princes, in erecting Christ's kingdome, and the churches in proceeding to receive the same, and to doe the wil of God, without their prince's licence, and notwithstanding their prohibition, seing that the unbeleeving princes have the same place, office, and aucthoritie, and ought to have the same obedience in respect thereof, that christian princes have, or ought have.

And sure most divelish and detestable are these two published and generallie received opinions of these contrarie factions of our English cleargie men; the one giving out, that the forme of ecclesiasticall government prescribed in Christ's Testament, practized by the apostles and primative churches in the tymes of persecution, is not nowe necessarie or tollerable under a christian prince. The other giving out, that those ordinances and that government which they acknowledge Christ to have instituted and prescribed to his church unto the worlde's end, may not nowe, under a christian prince, be put in practize by the church, if he forbid the same, as they might, ought, and were under heathen princes by the faithful in all ages.[1]

With the one of these blasphemous positions, the prelates defend their outragious government, and all their antichristian proceedings. With the other, the tyme-servers these counterfeite Reformistes, colour and

---

[1] Barrow has in mind Bishop Thomas Cooper as representative of the prelatical faction; see his book, *An Admonition to the People of England* (1589), pp. 73-84, in the edition of 252 pp. The other faction is the Presbyterian or Reformist group, represented by Gifford. See Gifford's *A Short Treatise*, pp. 97, 106. Other prelatical or Anglican representatives were Richard Bancroft, Thomas Bilson, Richard Hooker, Hadrian Saravia, Matthew Sutcliffe, Dean John Bridges, Bishop John Aylmer, and Archbishop John Whitgift. Among the reformed or Presbyterian leaders were Thomas Cartwright, William Charke, William Fulke, John Penry, William Perkins, Job Throckmorton and Walter Travers.

defend their perfidie, not witnessing unto and practizing the gospell of Christ, and their servile subjection to the government of Antichrist. By which positions both sides most impiously abrogate the heavenlie government and ordinances of Christ in his church, and intollerably seduce and abuse that most blessed and comfortable ordinance of the christian magistracie. Both of them hereby shut up the kingdome of heaven against all men, neither entring themselves, nor suffring such as would, but holding the whole land under the enormous government of Antichrist in the wrath of God, whose judgment therefore sleepeth not. [204]

Yet remayneth an other dangerous error which Mr. Giffard hath picked out of a certaine answere made by me Henrie Barrowe[1] to three greate bishops of this land, etc.,[2] where being demaunded whether the queene may make lawes for the church which are not contrarie to the worde of God. I (seeing wherat they aymed: *vzt.*: to maintayne al these popish reliques, devises, tromperies, etc., wherwith their worship and church is pestered) answered (as I remember) to this effect. That no prince, neither al the men of the world, nor the church it self, could make any lawes for the church, other than Christ hath left in his worde. But I thought it the dutie of everie prince (especially of everie christian prince) to enquire out and renewe the lawes of God, and to stir up all their subjects unto more diligent and careful keeping of the same.[3]

This answere Mr. Giffard after his accustomed maner pronownceth Anabaptisticall, deniing and cutting off a great part of the power God hath given unto princes;

---

[1] *Ibid.*, pp. 106-7.
[2] Archbishop Whitgift, Bishop Aylmer, and Bishop Cooper. Since Bishop Cooper was present at Barrow's examination on March 24, 1588/9, but not at the examination of March 18, 1588/9, when the other two were present, we may feel certain that the examination of March 24 is intended.
[3] See " Barrow's Fifth Examination, March 24, 1588/9 (Barrow's Version)," question number nine, in Carlson, *The Writings of Henry Barrow, 1587-1590*, p. 199. In " Barrow's Fifth Examination, March 24, 1588/9 (Register's Version)," the question is number eight — *ibid.*, p. 205. Barrow's memory is remarkably accurate, as may be seen by comparing the above passage with the same question in the examination.

A Refutation

and a great part of discipline.[1] Proof of these chardges he maketh none, except we must take these two assertions in way of proofe, untill he bring better. The first is, that Christ hath given " general lawes or rules for matters of circumstance that be indifferent and variable in the perticulars, and so to be altered and abolished, as the peace and edification of the church shal require. And therfore that princes with the church are to ordaine and to establish such orders by those generall rules, as may afterward for just cause be altered."[2] Mr. Giffard his antecedent here is so general and extendent, his conclusion so doubtful and indefinite, taking such roome to himself in both to escape and evade, as except he drawe nearer, and in his next booke[3] take the paynes to set downe what he meaneth in his proposition by (*general lawes and rules*) and by (*matters of circumstance*), and in his conclusion, what kinde of orders those (*such orders*) are the prince should ordeine and establish, he shalbe so far from distressing or convincing me, as I shall never perceive where he is, or where about he goeth.

This when he shal doe, then I shall knowe what to answere him. In the meane tyme I confesse many things of circumstance as the tyme and place of assembling, what Scriptures to reade or to interprete, how longe to continue in prayer or prophecie, etc., to be left in libertie at the discretion of the church, to be wisely used according to their present occasions, to edification, order, decencie. Of these and sondrie such like, the Lord in wisedome sawe it not good to set downe positive or permanent lawes for all churches and tymes; because the present estate and divers occasions of all churches, yea, of anie one church, are so divers and variable, that prescript definitive lawes could not be set of such things in perticular for the space of one moneth, without manifold inconveniences and great prejudize to the church. Of such things then as the Lord for these wise endes and

---

[1] *A Short Treatise*, p. 107.
[2] *Ibid.*, pp. 106, 107.
[3] Barrow anticipates rightly here, because Gifford published his "next book" in December, 1591, entitled: *A Short Reply unto the Last Printed Books of Henry Barrow and John Greenwood, the Chiefe Ringleaders of Our Donatists in England.*

waighty causes hath left in the libertie and discreation of the church to be used and ordered according to the present estate and occasions therof, etc., may man make no prescript positive lawes in particular, to enjoyne therby this forme, this tyme, etc., upon all or upon anie one church, without restrayning that, [205] which God hath left at libertie; yea, without controlling and contrariing the wisdome of God (which no doubt is most excellently perfect even in the least thinges) and without manie other grievous inconveniences and intollerable prejudize to the church of God. Much better therfore should the prince provide for the church to see them duly to observe the lawes that God hath given, and to use their libertie aright, or where they transgresse in either of these, to reproove or to correct accordingly, than to make and enjoyne new lawes of his owne devising, so contrarie to the libertie, yea, even to that order and discipline Christ hath given; which cannot be joyned unto, exercised, or preserved by anie other lawes than God hath made; as by due examination in perticular of the least or best thing they thus devise and enjoyne, will appeare.

Christ that great architect of his house hath left us a most absolute and exact paterne of all things belonging thereunto, unto which no humane devise can more be added or joyned, than heaven and earth can be commingled. Wherefore we may by better right esteeme Mr. Giffard a corrupter of Christ's discipline, or rather a fordger of a new discipline, for making and bringing in new lawes into the church other than God's lawes, than he may pronownce us denyers and cutters off of Christe's discipline, for allowing and receiving no lawes for anie action in the church, but God's lawes.

His other reason is this. Princes ought to establish the whole christian religion, to punish idolaters, wicked despisers, heretickes, schismaticks, blasphemers, etc. But this cannot be donne but by lawes made and established. Therfore princes ought to make lawes for the church. And I in deniing this, denie " a great part of that power, which God hath given unto princes."[1]

[1] *A Short Treatise*, pp. 107, 109.

A Refutation

His first proposition is no more than I have professed in mine answere. If he understand his second proposition of other lawes than God hath made, I then denie it as most false and untrue. Whereof untill he make proofe, he hath not obtayned his purpose, nor convinced mine answere. And therfore til then [he] must withdrawe his triumphant conclusions. I hold that God's true religion is only founded upon, and established by his owne holie worde and lawes, and not upon or by man's lawes; and that the prince may aswel make a newe religion, as newe lawes for religion. Furder, as I hold in God's Worde sufficient rules and directions for all actions of the church, so hold I in the same most just judgments and meete punishments to everie transgression. So that the prince can no way better advance and establish true religion than by, yea, can no way establish by, but it, the promulgation, and due execution of God's lawes; calling all men of all degrees to the hearing and sincere practize thereof in their calings, and dulie punishing al such as transgresse the same after such order proclamed and established. God hath incommended [intrusted] and injoyned the booke of his lawe to al princes, therbie to governe both the church and common wealth in al things, as we plentifullie read, Deuteronomy 17 : 18, 19 and 5 : 32 and 29 : 9 etc. and 4 : 6 ; Joshua 1 : 8 ; I Kinges 2 : 3 ; I Chronicles 28, and in sondrie other places. The kinge is not [206] made the Lord, but the minister of God's lawe, to which he is bownde, and for the transgression therof shall answer unto God, as anie other person. He is placed in the seate of God, and the worde of God committed unto him, not to alter or neglect the least part thereof, not to make newe lawes, but to keepe and see observed those lawes which God hath made. Greate then is their ignorance that thincke not that God hath given sufficient instruction and direction in his holie worde for all actions of his church. And greater their wickedness that knowing this, dare give mortal men leave to make lawes for God's church. If they say that the prince's lawe must be consonant to God's lawe, then I answere they have warrant and groundworke in God's worde, which if they have, then are they God's and no man's lawe. For God's lawe extendeth as farr as the equitie of his law extendeth. But what lawes soever have no warrant or groundworke in God's Worde, those cannot be said to be consonant to God's wil, because there we have the whole minde of Christ, and so are to be avoyded as superflous, burdenous, and contrarie to God's Word, how necessarie or expedient soever thay may seeme to humane wisdome.

And now let the christian reader judge what cause Mr. Giffard had to pronownce this mine answere to the bishopp's question Anabaptistical, when I therein acknowledged the whole lawe of God, the place, office, and whole power of princes that God hath given them, all which the Anabaptistes utterly denie. Or with what conscience he hath charged us as seduced by [Robert] Browne's writing.[1] And [to accuse me] to hold that princes ought not to compel their subjects to the true worship of God. Neither ought to reforme the church.[2] All which sclanders this my answere which he here endevoreth to confute, refuteth to his face.

FINIS

---

[1] See Robert Browne, "A Treatise of Reformation without Tarying for Anie, and of the Wickednesse of Those Preachers Which Will Not Reforme till the Magistrate Commaunde or Compell Them," in Albert Peel and Leland H. Carlson, *The Writings of Robert Harrison and Robert Browne*, pp. 150-170.

[2] This is an incomplete sentence. Barrow is asking Gifford how he can in good conscience accuse Barrow of denying the right of the prince to compel his subjects to true worship and to reform the church. Barrow believes the prince should do both, but the real problem is that of determining what is " true " worship and what is the extent and direction of " reformation." Catholics, Anglicans, Presbyterians, Separatists, Calvinists, Arminians, and Erastians provided various answers in Tudor and Stuart times, and they do so to-day.

APPENDICES

III

GEORGE GIFFORD'S CONTROVERSY WITH BARROW

The controversy with Gifford continued for five years, from 1587 to 1592. In 1587 the writings of Barrow and Greenwood were circulating in manuscripts. A copy came into the hands of a schoolteacher in Essex, who brought them to Gifford with the request that he reply to them. Gifford was reluctant to enter into the fray, according to his own account, but when many people became disturbed or influenced by the arguments for separation, he consented to reply to the articles and accusations. The controversy is rather complex because of manuscript and printed items, recapitulations and repetitions, and the admixture of answers to Barrow and Greenwood. The following outline will enable the student to see the entire controversy in perspective.

A. In 1587 several items of Separatist literature by Barrow and Greenwood were in circulation, in manuscript. These included:
1. " A Breefe Sum of Our Profession," in six articles.
2. " Four Causes of Separation," called principal transgressions, against the Church of England.
3. " Divers Arguments against Read Prayer."

We do not possess the first and third manuscripts, but they were printed in 1590, at least in summary form, in the course of the polemic.

AA. Gifford's first answer appeared in manuscript, late in 1587 or early in 1587/8. It is available, in part, in Gifford's printed work, *A Short Treatise* (1590), and also in Barrow's " A Brief Summe of the Causes of Our Seperation," printed in *A Plaine Refutation* (1591), pp. 1-20.

B. Barrow's first reply appeared early in 1587/8. It was in manuscript, but Gifford printed part of it in *A Short Treatise*

(1590). It was printed completely in "A Brief Summe of the Causes of Our Seperation," as a part of *A Plaine Refutation* (1591), pp. 1-20.

BB. Gifford's second answer appeared about May, 1590. It was a printed answer, entitled, *A Short Treatise*, of 110 pages. Pages 2-7 pertain to Article 6 of "*A Breefe Sum of Our Profession.*" Pages 7-90 relate to the subject of read prayers and the four principal transgressions. Pages 90-106 refer to Articles 1-5 of "A Breefe Sum of Our Profession," and pages 106-110 criticize the views of Barrow and Robert Browne on princes.

C. Barrow's second reply was *A Plaine Refutation*, printed in 1590/1. This was a reply to Gifford's *A Short Treatise*. Barrow defended the accusations made — the four principal transgressions, pp. 21-186, and also defended the six articles, pp. 187-206.

CC. Gifford's third answer was his book, *A Short Reply*, entered in the *Stationers' Register* 6 December, 1591, and printed about the same time. This was Gifford's last writing against the Barrowists.

D(1). Barrow's third and fourth replies were both written in manuscript. He probably received a copy of Gifford's *A Short Reply* about December, 1591, or January, 1591/2. From a statement that he had been in prison four and one-quarter years, we may conclude that he completed his third reply in February, 1591/2. This was a *general* reply, and was entitled, " A Few Observations to the Reader of M. Gifford His Last Replie." The manuscript was smuggled out of the Fleet prison, but it is unlikely that Gifford ever saw it. At least he never produced an answer to it. Gifford died in May, 1600. In 1605 a second edition of *A Plaine Refutation* was issued, most likely by Francis Johnson in Amsterdam. In this 1605 edition one significant change was made. Greenwood's "A Fewe Observations of Mr. Giffard's Last Cavills about Stinted Read Prayers, and Devised Leitourgies," pp. 235-255 in the 1591 edition of *A Plaine Refutation*, was eliminated and replaced by Barrow's " A Few Observations to the Reader of M. Gifford His Last Replie." The reason

Appendices

for this change was that Greenwood's "A Fewe Observations" had been printed in 1591 and re-printed in the 1603 edition of his work, *An Aunswer to George Gifford's Pretended Defence of Read Prayers*, pp. 45-66. Thus, without injury to Greenwood, the editor in 1605, Francis Johnson, who most likely was also the editor of the 1603 book, published for the first time Barrow's "A Few Observations." Therefore, Barrow's third reply — his *general* reply — was first printed thirteen years after it was written, twelve years after Barrow's execution in 1593, and five years after Gifford's death in 1600.

D(2). Barrow's fourth reply, also to Gifford's *A Short Reply*, was in manuscript and was a *detailed* reply. It was completed after his *general* reply, and may be dated about March, 1591/2. Unlike the *general* reply, the *detailed* reply was written in the margins of Gifford's book, *A Short Reply*. In 1588 Barrow had written a series of marginalia to Robert Some's book, *A Godly Treatise Containing and Deciding Certaine Questions, Moved of Late in London and Other Places, Touching the Ministrie, Sacraments, and Church.* This volume had been seized by the prison authorities. Again, Barrow set to work on an interleaved copy of the same book — some friend having provided a copy with inserted blank pages. When Barrow reached page 12, his copy was again confiscated in one of the periodic riflings of his prison chamber. Once more in 1592 he suffered the same misfortune, when his copy of Gifford's *A Short Reply* was seized. But this time he had completed the entire task of refutation. Gifford's book contains 98 pages, and on all except four of them Barrow has written his replies in a very small but legible hand. The book eventually made its way to the Cambridge University Library, perhaps via the Bishop of London, or the Archbishop of Canterbury, and Lambeth Palace Library. The marginalia have never been published, but they will be printed in Volume VI, about 375 years after Barrow wrote them. Thus the long controversy comes to an end.

IV

GEORGE GIFFORD'S CONTROVERSY WITH GREENWOOD

Since Gifford's controversy with Greenwood closely parallels his polemic with Barrow, it may be of help to present the following outline.

A. In 1587 Greenwood's manuscript writing on the subject of read prayer was in circulation. The manuscript is not extant, and only parts of the argument can be obtained from later controversial writings, especially pp. 17-18 of Gifford's *A Short Treatise*.

AA. Gifford's manuscript answer was written late in 1587 or early in 1587/8 Some hints of his argument may be obtained from page 19 of his *A Short Treatise* and from his opponent's arguments.

B. Greenwood's manuscript first reply, probably issued early in 1588, is briefly summarized in pp. 19-21 of *A Short Treatise*.

BB. Gifford's second answer, this time in print, which appeared in the spring of 1590 after more than a two years' interval, was his *A Short Treatise*. Pages 17-46, which relate to the subject of read prayers and spiritual worship in the Church of England, concern Greenwood.

C. Greenwood's second reply appeared in print during the summer of 1590. It was entitled, *An Answere to George Gifford's Pretended Defence of Read Praiers and Devised Liturgies with His Ungodlie Cavils and Wicked Sclanders Comprised in the First Parte of His Last Unchristian and Reprochfull Booke, Entituled, A SHORT TREATISE AGAINST THE DONATISTS OF ENGLAND*. This second reply relates to the "first parte" — that is, pp. 17-46. It was re-printed in 1603 and 1640.

CC. Gifford's third answer appeared in print about the latter part of 1590, with the title: *A Plaine Declaration That Our Brownists Be Full Donatists — Also a Replie to Master Greenwood*

Appendices

Touching Read Prayer. This work consists of two parts. The first section — pages 1-69 — sets forth the renewed accusation that the Brownists are Donatists, and seeks to draw specific parallels from the actions of the Donatists in the fourth and fifth centuries, in the time of Augustine. The second part — pages 72 [70]-126 — is an answer to Greenwood's *An Answere to George Gifford's Pretended Defence of Read Praiers*, and relates to the issues of worship, reading from the *Book of Common Prayer*, and spiritual devotion.

D. When Barrow's *A Plaine Refutation* was published in the spring of 1591, it contained two treatises by Greenwood. The first treatise (pp. 207-234) was entitled " A Breife Refutation of Mr. George Giffard His Supposed Consimilitude betwene the Donatists and Us." This was a reply to the first part of Gifford's *A Plaine Declaration*. Greenwood's second treatise (pp. 235-255) was entitled "A Fewe Observations of Mr. Giffard's Last Cavills about Stinted Read Prayers, and Devised Leitourgies." This was a reply to the second part of Gifford's *A Plaine Declaration*. In 1603 a second edition of Greenwood's *An Aunswer to George Gifford's Pretended Defence of Read Prayers* was printed, and appended to it was Greenwood's " A Fewe Observations of Mr. Giffard's Last Cavils about Stinted Read Prayers, and Devised Leitourgies " (pp. 45-66). Therefore, when the 1605 edition of *A Plaine Refutation* was issued, Greenwood's " A Fewe Observations " was omitted and replaced by Barrow's " A Few Observations," which had never been printed.

DD. Gifford replied to Greenwood and Barrow in his third and last anti-Separatist book, *A Short Reply unto the Last Printed Books of Henry Barrow and John Greenwood*. This work, entered in the *Stationers' Register* on December 6, 1591, was an answer to Barrow's *A Brief Discoverie of the False Church* and to Barrow's *A Plaine Refutation*, which also contained two treatises by Greenwood. For Gifford and Greenwood, this marked the end of the controversy, but in 1591/2 Barrow issued a general reply and also a detailed marginal reply, both in manuscript, the former printed in 1605, the latter confiscated by his jailer and not printed until in the present edition, in Volume VI, *The Writings of John Greenwood and Henry Barrow*, 1591-1593.

V

SIR ROBERT SIDNEY TO BURGHLEY, 21 APRIL 1591, FROM FLUSHING

" Right Honorable. There was information given me the last day of bookes of Barrow and Greenwood's writing, which should secretly be conveied into England. Wheruppon I made search for them and fownd them; the party likewise that should have caried them, whom I now send over unto your Lordship. His name is [Scipio] Billott, a gentleman as he saith, and was by Barrow and Greenwood imploied for the prynting of the books at Dort and to se them conveied unto England. The books be of two sorts, the one [*A Plaine Refutation*] dedicated unto your Lordship, which is in answer of a booke written by Dr. [Mr. George] Giffard and should have bin, as he saith, presented unto your Lordship. Of that sort he confesseth 1,000 to have bin printed. The other is caled *A Breef Discovery of the Fals Church*. Of that sort there were printed 2,000 but, as he protesteth unto me, was resolved should have bin quite suppressed and some he sais already to have bin sent into England and burnt. I thinck I do not want many of the nomber and he protesteth he doth not know where any one more is than he hath delivered unto me. I send your Lordship half a dozen of eyther sort. The rest, because of the greate bulk of them, I have not sent til I heare further of your Lordship's pleasure. I have likewise [349 *verso*] committed to prison a soldior of this garrison caled Bonnington, whoe was confederate unto him for the carrying over of the books. I expect likewise your Lordship's pleasure what shall be done with him. I cannot find by this Billot other than a simple zealous man; and truly without any force in the world he confessed where the bookes were. And sure I thinck he deserves rather pitty than anger. I beseech your Lordship that I may know your directions heerein, which I will very humbly obey and will ever pray to God. I send your Lordship prosperous succes of all your honorable and most vertuus desyrs. Your Lordship's most obedient to do yowr service."

R. Sydney. At Flushing the 21 of April 1591.

[State Papers, Holland, XLI, ff. 349 *recto* and *verso*; S. P. 84/41]

VI

SIR ROBERT SIDNEY TO BURGHLEY, 31 MAY 1591, FROM FLUSHING

". . . and wil onely add that according to the order in your letter of [May] the 12, I wil cause Barrow's books to [be] burnt. It seems your Lordship hath written another letter to the same effect, but I have not received it. And so beseching your Lordship to pardon me if I have bin to long I wil pray God to send you long and happy lyfe. At Flushing the 31 of May 1591. Your Lordship to do you humble service."

R. Sydney.

[State Papers, Holland, XLII, f. 82; S.P. 84/42]

VII

SIR THOMAS BODLEY TO SIR ROBERT SYDNEY

"To your Lordship's letter, with the booke of Barowe, for which I thanke you very hartely; I sent a present answear the next day after, which I cannot nowe remember to whom I delivered, nor what other mater it contened. And though I thinke there were nothing that could turne me to anger, yet, in truth, I am angrie that any letter should miscarrie."

From the Hage

May 20, 1591.

Arthur Collins, *Letters and Memorials of State* (London, 1746), I, 323.

VIII

GOVERNOR BRADFORD'S ACCOUNT OF
A PLAINE REFUTATION

There are two editions and possibly three printings of *A Plaine Refutation*. The first edition was printed in 1591, either at Dort or Middelburg. There is an interesting story in connection with the printing of this volume which deserves notice. Governor William Bradford writes:

"Mr. [Francis] Johnson himself, who was afterwards pastor of the church of God at Amsterdam, was a preacher to the company of English [Merchants] of the Staple at [the Gasthuis Kerk in] Middelburg, in Zealand [Middelburg, on the island of Walcheren, Zeeland], and had great and certain maintenance [£200] allowed him by them, and was highly respected of them, and so zealous against this [Separatist] way as that [when] Mr. Barrow's [*A Plaine Refutation*] and Mr. Greenwood's [*A Breife*] *Refutation* of Gifford was privately in printing in this city, he not only was a means to discover it, but was made the [English] ambassador's instrument [Sir Robert Sidney] to intercept them at the press, and see them burnt; the which charge he did so well perform, as he let them go on until they were wholly finished, and then surprised the whole impression, not suffering any to escape; and then, by the magistrates' authority, caused them all to be openly burnt, himself standing by until they were all consumed to ashes. Only he took up two of them, one to keep in his own study, that he might see their errors, and the other to bestow on a special friend for the like use. But mark the sequel. When he had done this work, he went home, and being set down in his study, he began to turn over some pages of this book, and superficially to read some things here and there, as his fancy led him. At length he met with something that began to work upon his spirit, which so wrought with him as drew him to this resolution, seriously to read over the whole book; the which he did once and again. In the end he was so taken, and his conscience was troubled so, as he could have no rest in himself until he crossed the seas and came to London to confer with the authors, who were then in prison, and shortly after executed. After which conference he was so satisfied and confirmed in the truth, as he never returned to his place any more at Middelburg, but adjoined himself to their society at London [in 1592], and was afterwards committed to prison [December 6, 1592], and then banished [to Ramea, in the Magdalene Islands, near Newfoundland, in April, 1597]; and in conclusion, coming to live at Amsterdam, he caused the same books, which he had been an instrument to burn, to be new printed [in 1605] and set out at his own charge. And some of us here present testify this to be a true relation, which we heard from his own mouth before many witnesses."[1]

This is indeed a fascinating story and in most respects seems to be true. The *Short-Title Catalogue* lists only one known copy of the 1591 edition of *A Plaine Refutation*, which came to the Huntington Library with the purchase of the Duke of Bridgewater collection. Very likely this book was in the possession of Francis Johnson, and came into the hands of Attorney-General Thomas Egerton, who was created Baron Ellesmere and Viscount Brackley, and thus it came to be a part of the famous Bridgewater collection. But the account speaks of two copies saved from the fire. After searching in numerous libraries, some of which erroneously claim to have the first edition, I was fortunate in finding the second copy at Lambeth Palace Library, and rejoiced that the 1591 edition was also available in England. Later, I discovered that David Ramage lists first editions in the Norwich Public Library and the Lincoln Cathedral Library.

The difficulty inherent in the story is that allegedly the printing and seizure occurred at Middelburg. But Robert Stokes testified that the book, *A Brief Discoverie of the False Church*, and *A Plaine Refutation*, were printed at his expense at Dort, beginning about Christmas, 1590, and that all three thousand copies were seized at Flushing [Vlissingen, on the island of Walcheren, and near Middelburg] and Brill [Brielle, near Rotterdam]. Futhermore, these two books seem to be printed with the same type used in the first edition (1589) of *A True Description out of the Worde of God, of the Visible Church*, in *A Collection of Certaine Sclaunderous Articles*, in *A*

---

[1] From Governor William Bradford's Dialogue, in Alexander Young, *Chronicles of the Pilgrim Fathers of the Colony of Plymouth, from 1602 to 1625* (Boston, 1841), pp. 424-5.

Appendices

Collection of Certain Letters and Conferences, and in Greenwood's *An Answere to George Gifford's Pretended Defence of Read Praiers*. This would indicate that the books came from the same press and the same printer, one Hanse [Hans Stell?] in Dort.

In the testimony of Robert Stokes there is an ambiguity. When he says that all the books were taken at Flushing and Brill, it is not clear whether he means both *A Brief Discoverie of the False Church* and *A Plaine Refutation*, or only the latter. When he says three thousand were printed, he is speaking of 2,000 copies of *A Brief Discoverie* and 1,000 copies of *A Plaine Refutation*. If Barrow's book, *A Brief Discoverie of the False Church*, was seized at Brill [Brielle], it is not true to say that all were confiscated. I have examined six different copies of this work, and there may be other copies extant. The book is indeed scarce, but some copies must have escaped seizure.

It seems certain that *A Brief Discoverie* was printed at Dort about December, 1590. Possibly some copies of this book were seized at Brill [Brielle] — farther down the river Maas, which is linked with the Merwede, on which Dort is located. If so, the printer at Dort, who was continuing with the work on *A Plaine Refutation*, possibly became alarmed and went to Middelburg or sent the sheets thither. Upon hearing of the work being carried on at Middelburg, or possibly on learning of the arrival of printed sheets at Flushing [Vlissingen] (the port town near Middelburg), Francis Johnson and the English ambassador seized upon the illegal printed matter. Such a reconstruction does not entirely accord with Governor Bradford's account, but the governor may have garbled a detail or two, and his version of 1648 must be checked by Robert Stokes' testimony of 1593.

There is a bit of contemporary evidence going back to November — December, 1591, the year of the seizure. Writing a reply to *A Brief Discoverie of the False Church* and to *A Plaine Refutation*, Gifford said: "They [Barrow and Greenwood] have replyed and published in print their defence, but their bookes are intercepted, yet some few have escaped, and are dispersed among theyr fellowes. Wherefore I hold it needfull to publish some answere, not dealing with every error and absurditie (for that would aske the travaile of some yeares), but onely with the chiefe grounds of their schisme."[1]

[1] Gifford, *A Short Reply*, A 2 recto.

Henry Barrow

There is one other bit of contemporary evidence, about February, 1591/2, when Barrow was writing "A Few Observations to the Reader of M. Gifford His Last Replie."

"Yet, beholding this *Replie* of Mr. Gifford unto certaine intercepted books of ours . . . . I thought it good, towching this *Replie* of Mr. Gifford to the said intercepted book [*sic*], to signifie these " few obervations unto the reader." The rather for that the books here pretended to be refuted, ar[e] not common or easie to be come by of the reader, who without the same might be easily deceived and greatly abused by this author."[3] These statements are ambiguous, but I interpret them to mean that a few copies of *A Brief Discoverie of the False Church* were dispersed, and that at least eight copies of *A Plaine Refutation* were saved.[4] There may have been more, but in the absence of further copies, the story which Governor Bradford received from Francis Johnson seems substantially true.

Besides the rare 1591 edition, mention should be made of the second edition of 1605. Ironically enough, this was issued by Francis Johnson, who had been an instrument for the destruction of the first edition. Because the last line of the title page carried the date 1591, some libraries have erroneously claimed to possess a first edition, but the "Advertisement to the Reader" is dated 1605, in the copies owned by the British Museum and Dr. Williams's Library. But the copies in the McAlpin Collection in New York, the Prince Collection in the Boston Public Library, and the Lambeth Palace Library are dated 1606. Since the books are the same except for this variation, I conclude that either there were two printings or that the printer or editor changed the date in the course of printing the books.

I have reproduced the rare 1591 edition, but have also collated it with the 1605 edition. The variations are usually minor differences of spelling, punctuation, extension or contraction of words. But one major difference exists in the two editions. The 1591 edition includes Barrow's *A Plaine Refutation*, Greenwood's *A Breife Refutation*, and Greenwood's *A Fewe Observations of Mr. Giffard's*

---

[1] Barrow, *A Plaine Refutation*, p. 237 in the 1605 edition. Barrow's "A Few Observations," of 1591/2, will be printed in Volume VI.
[2] Two copies for Francis Johnson and six copies sent to Lord Burghley by Sir Robert Sidney, the English ambassador.

Appendices

Last Cavills about Stinted Read Prayers and Devised Leitourgies. The 1605 edition eliminates Greenwood's *A Fewe Observations*, which had been reprinted in 1603 with Greenwood's *An Answere to George Gifford's Pretended Defence of Read Praiers and Devised Litourgies.* In its place, the editor inserted Barrow's " A Few Observations to the Reader of Mr. Giffard His Last Replie," written in 1591/2, but not previously printed. The editor also inserted a one-half page " An Advertisement to the Reader," which is not found in the 1591 edition.

In the 1591 edition there are two pages numbered 64 and two numbered 123. In this edition, therefore, pages 1-234 correspond to 1-236 in the 1605 edition. Thereafter, in the 1591 edition, follows Greenwood's " A Fewe Observations " (pp. 235-255), but in the 1605 edition, we find Barrow's " A Few Observations " (pp. 237-260). A summary of the contents and pagination of the two editions will indicate the differences:

1591 *Edition*	1605 *and* 1606 *Editions*
1. Title page, Dedication	1. Title page, Dedication, Advertisement to the Reader,
Wisdome to the Reader.	Wisdome to the Reader.
2. A Brief Summe (pp. 1-20).	2. A Brief Summe (pp. 1-20).
3. A Plaine Refutation (pp. 21-206 [208]).	3. A Plaine Refutation (pp. 21-208).
4. A Breife Refutation (pp. 207 [209]-234 [236]). By Greenwood.	4. A Breife Refutation (pp. 209-236). By Greenwood.
5. A Fewe Observations (pp. 235 [237]-255 [257]). By Greenwood.	5. A Few Observations (pp. 237-260). By Barrow.

IX

GEORGE GIFFORD'S WRITINGS

Fulke, William. Praelections upon the Sacred and Holy Revelation of S. John, Written in Latine by William Fulke, Doctor of Divinitie, and Translated into English by George Gyffard. London: Imprinted by Thomas Purfoote, 1573.

A Briefe Discourse of Certaine Points of the Religion Which Is among the Common Sort of Christians, Which May Be Termed the Countrie Divinitie, with a Manifest Confutation of the Same, after the Order of a Dialogue. London: Toby Cook, 1581 and 1582. London: Imprinted by Richard Field and Felix Kingston, 1598.

A Sermon upon the Parable of the Sower. London: Tobie Cook, 1581 or 1581/2. Also 1584 and one ed. without date.

A Dialogue betweene a Papist and a Protestant, Applied to the Capacitie of the Unlearned. London: Imprinted for Tobie Cooke, 1582. Also 1583. Also 1599.

Foure Sermons: upon the Seven Chief Vertues or Principall Effectes of Faith, and the Doctrine of Election: Wherein Everie Man May Learne, Whether He Be God's Childe or No. Preached at Malden in Essex by Master George Gifford, Penned from His Mouth, and Corrected and Given to the Countesse of Sussex, for a New Yeere's Gift. London: Imprinted for Tobie Cooke, 1582. Also 1584. The sermons are on II Peter 1:1-4; 1:5-7; 1:7-9; 1:10-11.

A Godlie, Zealous, and Profitable Sermon upon the Second Chapter of Saint James. [Verses 14-26]. Preached at London, by Master George Gifford, and Published at the Request of Sundry Godly and Well Disposed Persons. London: Imprinted for Tobie Cooke, 1582, or 1582/3.

A Catechisme, Conteining the Summe of Christian Religion, Giving a Most Excellent Light to All Those That Seek to Enter the

Appendices

Path-way to Salvation: Newly Set Forth by G. G. London: 1583. Also 1586.

A Sermon on James 2 : 14-26. London, 1583. In Brook, *Lives*, II, 278; in Wood, *Athenae*, II, 292. Probably a reprint, 1586.

A Dialogue, Concerning the Strife of Our Churche. 1584. This is a manuscript attributed to Gifford in the McAlpin Catalogue, p. 104. The attribution is doubtful.

A Brief Treatise against the Sacrifice and Priesthood of the Church of Rome. London: H. Middleton for Toby Cook, 1584. Also, 1634 and 1635. Not listed in the *S.T.C.* with Gifford's works, but the reissues are included under G.G., Nos. 11494-5. The first edition, unrecorded in the *S.T.C.*, is at Lambeth Palace Library.

A Sermon on II Peter 1 : 11. London, 1584. In Brook, *Lives*, II, 278.

A Discourse of the Subtill Practises of Devilles by Witches and Sorcerers. By Which Men Are and Have Bin Greatly Deluded: the Antiquitie of Them: Their Divers Sorts and Names. With an Aunswer unto Divers Frivolous Reasons Which Some Doe Make to Proove That the Devils Did not Make Those Aperations in Any Bodily Shape. London: for Toby Cooke, 1587.

Eight Sermons, upon the First Foure Chapters, and Part of the Fift, of Ecclesiastes, Preached at Maldon. London: Printed by John Windet for Toby Cooke, 1589.

A Short Treatise against the Donatists of England, Whom We Call Brownists. London: Printed by John Windet for Toby Cooke, 1590.

A Plaine Declaration That Our Brownists Be Full Donatists, by Comparing Them Together from Point to Point Out of the Writings of Augustine. Also a Replie to Master Greenwood Touching Read Prayer, Wherein His Grosse Ignorance Is Detected, Which Labouring to Purge Himselfe from Former Absurdities, Doth Plunge Himselfe Deeper into the Mire. London, 1590 or 1590/1.

Henry Barrow

A Sermon Presented at Paul's Cross, 30 Maie 1591 on Psalm CXXXIII. London, 1591. In Arber, *Stationers' Register*; in Wood, *Athenae*, II, 291; in Brook, *Lives*; not in *S.T.C.*

A Short Reply unto the Last Printed Books of H. Barrow and J. Greenwood, the Chiefe Ringleaders of Our Donatists in England: Wherein Is Layd Open Their Grosse Ignorance, and Foule Errors: upon Which Their Whole Building Is Founded. London, 1591.

A Dialogue Concerning Witches and Witchcraftes. In Which Is Laide Open How Craftely the Divell Deceiveth not onely the Witches but Many Other and So Leadeth Them Awrie into Many Great Errours. London: Printed by John Windet for Tobie Cooke and M. Hart, 1593. Also, Printed by R. F. and F. K. and Are to Be Sold by Arthur Johnson, 1603. Reprint of 1593 ed. by the Shakespeare Association. London, 1931. Reprint of 1603 ed. by the Percy Society. London, 1842.

A Treatise of True Fortitude. London: Printed for John Hardie by James Roberts, 1594. Reissue by R. M. and Abergavenny, Miners Press, 1922.

Sermons upon the Whole Booke of the Revelation. London: Printed for Thomas Man and Toby Cooke, 1596. Also 1599.

Certaine Sermons upon Divers Texts of Holie Scripture. London, 1597. McAlpin Collection in N.Y. and Library of Congress.

Two Sermons upon I Peter [5]: verses 8 and 9. London, 1597. Brook, *Lives*, has 1598; Wood, *Athenae*, has 1598; T. W. Davids, *Annals*, has 1598.

Fifteene Sermons upon the Song of Saloman. London: Printed by Felix Kingston for Thomas Man, 1598. Also 1600. Printed by John Windet, for Thomas Man. Also 1612. Also 1620, Printed by Barnard Alsop, by the Assignes of I.M. and G.N., and Are to Be Sold at His House, by St. Anne's Church Neere Aldersgate. T. W. Davids, *Annals*, lists an ed. of 1610.

Foure Sermons upon Several Parts of Scripture. London, 1598.

Exposition on the Canticles. London, 1612. Probably a reprint.

X

BARROW'S CITATIONS FROM SCRIPTURE

It is sometimes asserted that the Puritans were more interested in the Old Testament than the New Testament. This may be true of certain individual writers, but it does not apply to Henry Barrow.

In his work, *A Plaine Refutation*, Barrow has 111 marginal citations to the Old Testament. In the text of his work are some 58 additional citations from the Old Testament, for a total of 169.

His marginal citations from the New Testament number 297. In the text there are 80 additional citations, for a total of 377 — more than twice as many as to the Old Testament.

Barrow refers to the four gospels 43 times, to the Pauline letters 179, and to the Book of Revelation 49.

XI

GEORGE GIFFORD'S WILL

The will of George Gifford is in the Greater London Record Office, DL/C/359, folios 210 *verso* and 211 *recto*. The specific register of wills is called " Sperin," named from Thomas Sperin, whose will is the first one in this volume. (Sperin had interviewed Barrow and Greenwood in prison, and had died in 1592). Volume 358 includes wills for persons dying 1559/1560—1591; volume 359 includes wills for the years 1592—1609; volume 360, for the years 1609—1621; and volume 361, for the years 1621—1630/1631.

The records of the Consistory Court of London were transferred from the Principal Probate Registry, Somerset House, in January 1956, to the London County Record Office, County Hall, Westminster Bridge.

Gifford's will establishes clearly that he died in 1600, not in 1620 as the *Dictionary of National Biography* states. The will also gives information about Gifford's wife, children, friends, and property.

* * * * *

[210 *verso*] In the name of God, Amen. The eighte daie of Maie in the yeare of our Lord one thowsande and sixe hundred, and in the twoe and fortiethe yeare of the reigne of our Soveraigne Ladie Elizabeth by the grace of God nowe Queene of Englande, etc., I George Giffard, clarke, preacher of God's Worde in Mauldon in the countie of Essex, beinge weake and sicke in bodie, yett of good and perfecte memorie, thancks be unto God, knowinge that all men (by nature) are borne to die, doe therefore make, publishe and declare this my laste will and testamente in writinge in manner and forme followinge:

First, I comend my sowle into the handes of Almightie God (that blessed Trinitie), the Father, the Sonne, and the Holie Ghoste, assuredlie beleevinge by the mightie worke and wittnes of the Holie Spirritt in me that all my synnes of God's great mercie by and throughe the pretious merrittes, sufferinges and passion of Jhesus Christe my alone Saviour and Redeemer (in whome I have beleeved, whome I have professed and whome I have preached and tawghte accordinge to the guifte and grace of God bestowed on me), are fullie pardoned and donne awaie. And my bodie I comytt to christian buriall.

And as towchinge the worldly possessions, benefitts, and blessings bestowed on me of the bounteous kindnes and goodnes of God for this mortall lief, my mynde and will is thereof as followeth: firste, I will and devise by this my will that Agnes my welbeloved wief, for and duringe the terme of her naturall lief, shall have and enjoye all that parcell of lande and pasture contayninge by estimacion three acres [(] nowe in the occupation of Edwarde Faunce or his assignes) lyinge and beinge in Maldon aforesaid. And I will and devise aswell the revertion or remaynder of the said parcell of lande and pasture with the appurtenaunces, as alsoe my coppiehould, tennement, and orchard with the appurtenaunces nowe in the occupation of John Courtnoll in St. Peter's parishe in Maldon aforesaid, after the deathe of the said Agnes my wief, in which tennement and orchard with the appurtenaunces she hath alreadie an estate for lief, unto theise my righte trustie and welbeloved freinds, Raphe Breeder, one of Her Majestie's bayliffs of the said burrowghe towne of Maldon, William Dernon [Vernon?], Elizabeth Garington, John Brooke, Christopher Henworthe, and William Burles of Maldon, gentlemen, and John Gaywood the elder of Mutche Tottenham [Great Totham], yeoman, their heires and assignes. To this verely end, intente, and purpose that they the said Raphe, William Darnon [Vernon?], Eliza, John Brooke, Christopher, William Burles, and John Gaywood or the survivors or survivor of them or the heires or executors of the survivor of them, after the deathe of my said wief or before yf necessitie shall soe require, whiche therefore I leave to their discreations and wisdomes, shall make sale of the saide parcell of lande and of the said tennement and orchard with the appurtenaunces for the beste price and to the moste advantage they maie or can make thereof. And the sommes of monney to be made and rise of sutche sale thereof, I will to be paide and distributed by my said trustie freinds or the survivors or survivor of them or the executors of sutche survivors, unto and betwixte all my children then lyvinge, exceptinge onelie my sonnes John and Daniell Giffard and my dawghter Marie, to every one sutche parte and portion as his or her estate, imbecillitie, or necessitie shall [211 *recto*] (less or more) require at the good discreation of my said freinds or the survivor of them aforenamed.

And yt is my earnest desire that yf the said Agnes my wief fortune to decease owte of this lief duringe the terme and lease which my right worshipfull freind John Butler, esquire, hath of and in the said tennemente and orchard with the appurtenaunces, that then the said Mr. Butler doe use and imploye the lease and intereste of and in the said tennement with the appurtenaunces then to come and not expired for and to the benefitt of my said children, exceptinge the said John, Daniell, and Marie as aforesaid, in sutche mannor and sorte as my good meaninge appeareth in this my will.

Item, I give unto my saide two sonnes John and Daniell Giffard all my library and bookes equally betweene them to be devided att the discreation of my good freinds Mr. Raphe Hawden of Langford and Maister John Leake of Woodham Ferrers.

Item, I will and give unto the said Marie Gifford my dawghter twentie pounds of lawfull monney of Englande, to be paide to her by the executrix of this my testamente att her daie of marriage or within one yeare after my deathe, which firste happen.

Item, I will unto the forenamed John Brooke my lease and intereste whiche I have of the demise and graunte of Robert Palmer, clarke, vicar of All Sainctes and St. Peters in Maldon aforesaid, by indenture of and in the vicaradge howse, tithes, proffitts and other things thereby letten and demised.

And yt is my will and mynde that the said Agnes my welbeloved wief shall have the use and occupation of the messuage wherein I dwell, with the orchards and gardeyne and other the appurtenaunces thereunto belonginge, for and duringe soe manie yeres and soe longe time of my lease and terme as the said Agnes shall live. And after her decease I will the lease, interest, and terme of yeres of and in my said dwellinge, howse, orchards, and other the appurtenaunces thereunto, shalbe sould by my said freinds, afore speciallie named and appoynted in this my will for the sale of my lands, or the survivors or survivor of them or the executor of sutche survivor. And the monney to come and growe thereof to be paide over and distributed unto and betwixte theis my children, Samuell, Jeromie,

Appendices

George, William, and Martha Giffard and of the childe wherewith my wief nowe goeth yf ytt please God she be with childe, or to the survivors or survivor of them then livinge, everie one of the said sonnes to have his parte and portion at his full age of one and twentie yeres and the dawghter at her age of twentie yeres or daie of marriage, whiche firste happen.

And I doe make, constitute and ordaine the said Agnes my wief sole and onelie executrix of this my laste will and testamente, to whome I give all my howshould stuffe and my readie monney and debtes to me owinge and whatsoever ells I have that is testamentary (not before in this my testamente otherwise bequeathed) for and towarde her better maintenaunce, bringinge upp and education of the same my younger children. And I desire and intreate my said good freinds Mr. Raphe Hawden and Mr. John Leake and the said Raphe Breeder, William Dernon [Pernon?], Eliza Garington, John Brooke, Christopher Hanworthe and William Burles to be overseers of this my testamente and laste will and to see the same performed soe farr as in them liethe.

In wittnes hereof I have hereunto putt my seale and subscribed my name the daie and yeare firste abovesaid in the presence of us George Giffard, Thomas Albert, John Burton, and Thomas Cheese.

* * * * * *

Probatum fuit huiusmodi testamentum coram venerabili viro magistro Edwardo Stanhope legum doctore, reverendi patris domini Richardi London-[ensis] Episcopi vicario in spiritualibus generali et officiali principali, etc., ultimo die mensis Maii, anno domini 1600. Juramento magistri Galfridi Clarke, notorii publici, procuratoris Agnetis Gifford relicte dicti defuncti et executricis in huiusmodi testamento nominat[e] cui in persona dicti procur[ator]is comissa fuit ado [administrando, administratio] etc., de bene etc. [de bene et fideliter administrando eadem ac de pleno et fideli inventario]. Jurat etc. Saluo iure cuiuscumque, etc.

INDEX

Abergavenny, 380
Abihu, 307
Abiram, 319, 339
Abraham, 8, 115, 118, 119, 170
Absolution, 5, 79, 80, 81, 141, 155, 351
Act of Supremacy (1559), 6, 9, 317
Act of Uniformity (1559), 6, 9
Adiaphora, Things Indifferent, 2, 15, 43, 85
Aesop, 185
Ainslie, James L., 145
Ainsworth, Henry, 126, 140, 213
Albert, Thomas, 385
Alexander, 140
Alexandria, 75
Alison, Richard, 30
All-Hallows, 4, 70, 72
All-Saints, 72
All Saints and St. Peter's, Maldon, 384
Almanacs, 215, 216
Alsop, Barnard, 380
Ambrose, 218
Amsterdam, 373, 374
Anabaptism, 2, 48, 64, 65, 66, 124, 280, 360, 364
Anabaptists, 1, 7, 31, 51, 54, 66, 83, 124, 296, 346, 347, 351, 364
Ananias, 287
Anderson, Anthony, 226
Andrewes, Lancelot, 260
Anglicans, 5, 7, 8, 16, 20, 302, 359, 364
Antichrist, 34, 44, 45, 57, 65, 126, 127, 131, 132, 133, 202, 203, 207, 209, 212, 223, 225, 244, 265, 266, 288, 290, 296, 297, 319, 321, 335, 341

Antinomianism, 57
Antioch, Church of, 19
Apocrypha, 6, 101
Apostasy, 1, 2, 342
Apostles, 10, 188, 340, 341, 342, 346, 350
Aquinas, Thomas, 218
Arber, Edward, 268, 380
Archbishops, 11, 18, 43, 191-196, 199, 200, 202, 203, 210, 229, 322, 367
Archdeacons, 10, 11, 12, 16, 18, 80, 97, 135, 191, 208, 209, 210, 241
Arches, Court of, 18
Archippus, 138
Aristotle, 12, 214, 215, 306
Arminianism, 9, 364
Arminius, Jacobus, 9
Arnold, Thomas, 228
Asia, Church of, 57, 157, 172, 279
Atchley, Cuthbert, 265
Aubrey, William, 208, 209
Audience, Court of, 18
Augsburg Confession, 278
Augustine, 9, 218, 281, 369, 379
Authority, 3
Aylmer, John, Bishop of London, 3, 7, 15, 44, 54, 77, 111, 117, 118, 188, 203, 229, 242, 243, 343, 359, 360

Babbage, Stuart Barton, 197, 316
Babington, Anthony, 318
Babylon, 35, 46, 125, 129, 157, 250, 255, 296, 336, 338, 343
Bacon, Francis, 197
Baillie, Robert, 140

Index

Bainton, Roland H., 171
Bancroft, Richard, Archbishop of Canterbury, 7, 15, 140, 197, 245, 316, 359, 385
Baptism, 5, 8, 41, 84, 85, 87, 88, 89, 92, 105, 110, 114, 115, 124, 125, 126, 129, 130, 131
Baptists, 124; *see also* Anabaptists
Barnabas, 19, 341
Barrett, William, 99
Barrow, Henry, ix, x, 1-21, 25-31, 34, 37, 38, 41, 51-53, 60, 61, 64, 96, 100, 102, 104, 106, 114, 126, 141, 144, 148, 157, 158, 169, 183, 188, 191, 205, 208, 210, 211, 213, 221, 225, 227, 228, 232, 243, 247, 259, 265, 266, 268, 269, 272, 279-281, 286, 287, 289, 292, 296, 298, 304, 310, 312, 315, 318, 325, 332, 341, 357, 359-361, 364-373, 375-377, 380-382
Barrow, *Barrow's Fifth Examination*, 360
Barrow, *Barrow's First Examination*, 210
Barrow, *A Breefe Sum*, 158, 187, 321, 333, 365, 366
Barrow, *A Brief Discoverie*, 29, 30, 100, 126, 160, 310, 312, 370, 371, 374, 375, 376
Barrow, *A Brief Summe of the Causes*, 25, 28, 41, 53, 60, 67, 68, 96, 104, 114, 118, 157, 158, 187, 213, 221, 266, 279, 280, 282, 286, 287, 289, 302, 321, 333, 334, 365, 366, 377
Barrow, *A Few Observations*, 26, 29, 366, 367, 376, 377
Barrow, *The First Part of the Platforme*, 1
Barrow, *Four Causes*, 279, 365
Barrow, *Letter to Mr. Fisher*, 227
Barrow, *A Plaine Refutation*, 1, 19, 25, 26, 28, 29, 37, 53, 157, 326, 327, 332, 334, 336, 365, 366, 369, 370, 371, 373-377, 381
Barrow, *A Refutation of Mr. Giffard's Reasons*, 19, 25, 51
Barrow and Greenwood, *A Collection of Certain Letters*, 30, 375
Barrow and Greenwood, *A Collection of Certaine Sclaunderous Articles*, 30, 374
Barrowists, 343, 366
Bellott, Arthur, 213, 370
Bernard, Richard, 206
Beveridge, Henry, 235
Beza, Theodore, 3, 140, 145, 218, 292
Bibles, 292
Billott, Scipio, or Arthur (?), see Bellott
Bilson, Thomas, Bishop of Worcester (1596) and Winchester (1597), 99, 140, 200, 220, 359
Bindoff, S. T., vii, 50
Bingham, William, 208
Bishoping, 5, 84, 89, 90
Bishops, 10-13, 16, 18, 20, 37, 43, 89-91, 102, 133, 136, 137, 138, 155, 156, 191-196, 199-203, 207, 229, 232, 237, 238, 239, 246, 271, 305, 309, 311, 313, 317-319, 322, 335, 336, 360, 364
Bladen, Thomas, 304
Bodley, Sir Thomas, ix, 372
Bohun, William, 260
Boleyn, Anne, Queen, 278
Boniface VIII, 12
Book of Common Prayer, 3, 4, 14, 40, 42, 66, 75, 79, 88, 90, 96, 98, 155, 156, 231, 237, 246, 369
Bosanquet, Eustace F., 215, 216
Boston Public Library, 376
Bowman, Christopher, 343
Bradford, John, 280
Bradford, William, ix, 373-376
Bradshaw, William, 86
Breeder, Raphe, 383, 385

Brewster, Samuel, 211, 260, 265
Brewster, William, 8
Bridge, William, 213
Bridges, John, Dean of Salisbury, 200, 225, 359
Bridgewater Collection, 374
Brill or Brielle, 374, 375
British Museum, 376
Brook, Benjamin, 44, 379, 380
Brooke, John, 383, 384, 385
Broughton, Hugh, 99
Browne, Robert, 212, 213, 217, 325, 358, 364, 366
Browne, " A Treatise of Reformation," 358, 364
Browne, " A Treatise upon the 23. of Matthewe," 217
Brownism, 2, 213
Brownists, 37, 41, 44, 47, 51, 54, 86, 124, 126, 172, 203, 213, 251, 280, 283, 303, 310, 321, 324, 325, 344, 369, 379
Bucer, Martin, 218
Buckminster, Thomas, 215
Burghley, William Cecil, Lord, ix, 1, 25, 29, 31, 32, 33, 237, 370, 371, 376
Burials, 82, 83
Burles, William, 383, 385
Burroughes, Jeremiah, 213
Burton, John, 385
Butler, John, 384

Caiaphas, 287
Caley, John, 231
Calvin, John, 3, 145, 169, 218, 234, 235, 276, 281
Calvinists, 7, 9, 364
Cambridge University, 3, 13, 31, 367
Campion, Edmund, 318
Candlemass, 4, 70, 72
Canisius, Peter, 218

Canne, John, 213
Canterbury, Archbishop of, see Parker, Matthew; Grindal, Edmund; Whitgift, John; Bancroft, Richard; Laud, William
Cardwell, Edward, 135, 199
Carlile, Christopher, 99
Carlson, Leland H., vii, 25, 41, 53, 60, 67, 96, 104, 114, 126, 160, 187, 205, 210, 212, 213, 217, 218, 221, 227, 266, 279, 280, 282, 286, 287, 289, 302, 310, 315, 321, 325, 332, 333, 334, 357, 358, 360, 364
Carlstadt, Andreas Rudolf Bodenstein of, 304
Cartwright, Thomas, 3, 15, 102, 140, 145, 218, 286, 304, 359
Catabaptists, see Anabaptists
Catechisms, 89, 90, 219, 378
Catholics, 364. See also Papists
Cecil, William, see Burghley
Cessations, 71, 72, 73
Chaderton, Laurence, 187
Chaderton, William, Bishop of Chester, 198
Chambers, Robert, 73
Chancellors, 10, 11, 12, 16, 18, 155, 191, 207, 208, 241
Chaplains, 237
Charke, William, 359
Charles, R. H., 130
Chatterton, see Chaderton
Cheese, Thomas, 385
Childermass Day, 73
Christie, James, 265
Christmas, 4, 41, 71
Chrysostom, 218
Church Fathers, 218
Church Government, see Polity
Church of England, 2, 6, 9, 10, 15, 16, 18, 19, 20, 28, 37, 41, 49, 63, 100, 101, 106, 107, 126, 132-135, 138, 153, 157, 173, 198,

Index

209, 214, 215, 252, 258, 269, 270, 274, 285, 296, 302, 325, 326, 344
Churchill, Irene Josephine, 208
Churching, 4, 77, 78
Churchwardens, 11, 80, 97, 192, 264
Chwolson, Daniel A., 171
Circumcision, 125, 166
Clapham, Barbara, vii
Clare College, Cambridge, 13
Clark, John, 209
Clarke, *see* Clerke
Clarke, Galfridus, 385
Clarke, M. L., 224
Classis, 10, 15, 44, 102, 148, 149, 203; *see also* Presbytery
Clerke, Franciscus, 304
Clifton, Richard, 213
Coke, Edward, 197, 316
Coleman, Christopher B., 193
Collects, 69, 76, 81, 83, 84, 91
Collins, Arthur, 372
Collinson, Patrick, 50, 102, 199
Colwell, E. C., vii
Comber, Thomas, 260
Comminations, 4, 69, 75, 85
Commissaries, 10, 11, 12, 16, 18, 80, 97, 135, 155, 191, 207, 208, 241
Communion, Private, 5, 79, 81
Communion, Public, 5, 9, 69, 91, 114
Confirmation, 5, 41, 84, 89, 90
Conscience, 16, 30, 42, 44, 205, 206, 352
Consett, Henry, 304
Consistory Court of London, 382
Constantine, 193
Contributions, 258, 259, 261, 262
Convocation, 59
Cook *or* Cooke, Tobie *or* Toby, 203, 378, 379, 380
Cooke, Mildred, wife of Lord Burghley, 1
Cooper, Charles Henry, 224

Cooper, Thomas, Bishop of Winchester, 15, 60, 188, 200, 220, 228, 249, 302, 304, 312, 359, 360
Cooper, *An Admonition*, 60, 220, 228, 249, 302, 312, 359
Cope, Anthony, 44
Corinth, Church of, 57, 79, 157, 172, 173, 177, 279
Cosin, Richard, 140, 188, 209, 225, 304
Costello, William T., 224
Cotton, John, 8, 140, 206
Courtnoll, John, 383
Covenant, 8, 19, 47, 110, 114-120, 122, 124, 126, 131, 159-163, 234, 288, 337, 342
Crane, Nicholas, 213
Cranmer, Thomas, 278
Cross, F. L., 59
Curtis, Mark H., 224
Cyprian, 218

Dale, Valentine, 209
Darnon, *see* Dernon
Dathan, 319, 339
David, 307
Davids, T. W., 50, 242, 380
Davies, J. G., 211
Deaconesses, 10, 188, 189, 190, 211
Deacons, 10, 11, 12, 16, 188-191, 210, 211, 225, 237, 238, 242, 343
Deans, 11, 13, 18, 211, 224, 225, 241
Decius, 20
Delegates, Court of, 208
Denck, John, 124
Dernon, William, 383, 385
Dexter, Henry M., 186
Dickens, Charles, 208
Diocletian, 20
Diotrephes, 293, 294
Discipline, 2, 5, 9, 14-19, 38, 40, 76, 104, 123, 135-143, 152, 153, 205, 207, 302-305, 310, 312, 313, 321, 335, 361, 362

Ditchfield, Peter Hampson, 265
Divinity, Study of, 218-224, 248
Donation of Constantine, 193
Donatism, 2, 49
Donatists, 1, 28, 31, 37, 49, 51, 54, 279, 282, 369, 379, 380
Dort *or* Dordrecht, 373, 374, 375
Dove, John, 140
Downame, George, 140
Dr. Williams's Library, 376
Dryden, John, 323

Easter, 41, 71
Easterby, William, 260
Edersheim, Alfred, 142
Education, 12, 13, 212-224, 248
Edwards, Jonathan, 9
Egerton, Stephen, 187
Egerton, Sir Thomas, 26, 374
Elders, 10, 16, 66, 141, 143-147, 188-191, 198, 233, 234, 235, 302, 340, 341, 343
Eldership, 233, 234, 302, 341
Election, 6, 9, 120, 124, 164, 165, 232, 236, 274, 312, 341, 346, 378
Elizabeth, Queen, 1, 2, 15, 20, 34, 109, 126, 135, 197, 247, 304, 316, 382
Embers, 4, 41, 68, 69
Erasmus, Desiderius, 292
Erastianism, 15, 364
Estienne, *see* Stephanus
Euphrates, 35
Evangelists, 10, 188, 195, 340, 341, 342, 346
Ex-officio Oath, 12, 18, 315
Excommunication, 10, 16, 105, 107, 108, 134-141, 147, 150-155, 160, 169, 179, 292, 293, 302, 304, 312

F., R., [Field, Richard], 380
Faculties, Court of, 18

Faith, 47, 55, 110, 115, 119, 161, 180, 275, 288, 343, 353, 378
Farel, William, 145
Fasts, 4, 41, 68, 69, 70, 72
Faunce, Edward, 383
Feasts, 4, 41, 70, 71, 72
Fen, Humphrey, 187, 286
Field, John, 15, 50, 140
Field, Richard, 140
Field, Richard, printer, 378
Finegan, Jack, 125
First Principal Transgression, 60-102, 207, 326
Fisher, Mr., 205, 227
Fleetwood, William, 209
Fludd *or* Floyd, William, 187
Flushing, 370, 371, 374, 375
Fourier, F. C. M., 304
Fourth Principal Transgression or Cause, 285-331, 301, 320, 321, 328, 349
Franck, Richard, 242
Frere, W. H., 208, 226
Frith, John, 276
Fulke, William, 359, 378
Fussner, F. Smith, 260

Gabriel, Richard C., 50
Galatia, Church of, 57, 79, 279
Gnostics, 57
Gaius, 293
Garington, Elizabeth, 383, 385
Gaywood, John, 383
Gibbon, Edward, 13, 191
Gibson, Edgar C. S., 98
Gibson, Edmund, 59
Gifford, Agnes, wife of George, 383, 384, 385
Gifford, Daniell, son of George, 383, 384
Gifford *or* Giffard, George, ix, x, 1-5, 8, 9, 14, 15, 17-19, 21, 25, 26, 28-32, 37-39, 41-51, 53, 54, 57, 60-64, 66, 68, 77-81, 86, 87,

Index

89, 95, 99, 100, 102, 104-107, 112-114, 117, 118, 122-124, 131, 133, 134, 149-151, 156-159, 165, 167, 170, 172-174, 182, 185, 188, 194, 202-204, 206, 207, 215, 216, 218, 221-223, 227-230, 234, 239-243, 248, 256, 258, 266, 267-269, 272-276, 279, 280, 281, 283-286, 289, 293-296, 298, 299, 302-305, 310, 313, 321-325, 328, 332, 333, 335, 339, 340, 342, 343-348, 352, 353, 359, 361-370, 375-379, 382-385

Gifford, *A Briefe Discourse*, 185

Gifford, *A Plaine Declaration*, 31, 37, 42, 43, 44, 203, 368, 369, 379

Gifford, *A Short Reply*, 240, 268, 361, 366, 367, 369, 376, 380

Gifford, *A Short Treatise*, 31, 37, 40, 43, 45, 48, 51, 54, 56, 61, 64, 65, 68, 70, 71, 74, 76-79, 81, 84, 86, 87, 91, 96, 98, 99, 102, 103, 106, 109, 110, 111, 115, 118, 126, 128, 129, 131, 133, 134, 136, 138, 150, 151, 156, 157, 158, 160, 162, 163, 165, 173-175, 177, 178, 185, 188, 203, 207, 213, 223, 227, 240, 248, 249, 267, 268, 270, 272, 273ʻ 277, 279, 280, 282, 283, 286, 289, 290, 294, 296, 299, 300, 302, 303, 313, 321, 324, 325-327, 329, 333-337, 339, 340, 345-348, 350, 352, 354, 357, 359-362, 365, 366, 368, 379.

Gifford, George, son of George, 385

Gifford, John, son of George, 383, 384

Gifford, Jeromie, son (or daughter?) of George, 384

Gifford, Marie, daughter of George, 383, 384

Gifford, Martha, daughter of George, 385

Gifford, Samuell, son of George, 384

Goodman, Gabriel, Dean of Westminster, 225

Goodwin, John, 213

Goodwin, Thomas, 213

Government, Church, *see* Polity

Graetz, Heinrich, 142

Gravett, William, 188

Gray's Inn, 18

Great Totham *or* Mutche Tottenham, 383

Green, E. Tyrrell, 99

Greenslade, S. L., 218

Greenwood, John, ix, 25, 26, 29-31, 34, 37, 49, 102, 186, 187, 205, 213, 259, 268, 272, 325, 343, 365, 367-370, 373, 375-377, 379, 380, 382

Greenwood, *An Answere*, 102, 203, 367, 368, 369, 375, 377

Greenwood, " A Breife Refutation," 25, 28, 37, 49, 369, 373, 376, 377

Greenwood, "A Fewe Observations," 25, 26, 28, 29, 366, 367, 369, 376, 377

Gregory of Nazianzus, 218

Grindal, Edmund, Bishop of London and Archbishop of York and Canterbury, 198, 237

Hague, Haag, Den, 372

Half-Way Covenant, 9

Hanse *or* Hause (?), *see* Stell

Hanworthe, *see* Henworthe

Hardie, John, 380

Harrison, Robert, 212, 213, 217, 325

Hart, Mihil, 380

Hatch, Edwin, 232

Hatton, Sir Christopher, 31

Hawden, Raphe, 384, 385

Henry VIII, 13

Henry E. Huntington Library, 26, 374

Henworthe, Christopher, 383, 385

Heresy, 1, 29, 56, 57, 58, 67, 104, 115, 128, 150, 159, 160, 162, 163, 164, 201, 322, 325, 334, 336, 343, 345, 362
Herod the Great, 73
Heylyn, Peter, 73
Heywood, James, 224
Higgins, John, 99
High Commission, Court of, 11, 12, 18, 191, 197, 209, 286, 315, 316
Hilary of Poitiers, 218
Hildersham, Arthur, 218
Hill, Adam, 99
Hill, Christopher, 260
Hitchcock, Roswell D., 232
Hobart, Henry, 197
Hoenig, Signey B., 142
Hoffman, Melchior, 124
Holdsworth, William, 319
Hooker, Richard, 7, 140, 200, 220, 228, 359
Hooper, John, Bishop of Gloucester and Worcester, 280
Hooper, Wilfrid, 304
Hopton, Owen, 209
Hosius, Stanislaus, 218
Howell, Wilbur S., 212
Hubmaier, Balthasar, 124
Hume, Mary, 315
Hunt, R. N. Carew, 145
Hunter, A. Mitchell, 145
Hunter, Joseph, 231
Huntington, Henry E., 26, 374
Hurstfield, Joel, vii, 50
Hus, John, 276
Hutchinson, William, 188, 225
Hymenaeus, 140

Induction, 239
Innocent III, 11
Innocents' Day, 73
Institution, 239, 240, 242, 305
Iunius, see Junius

Jacob, Henry, 99, 213
Jacobs, Henry E., 278
Jaeger, Werner, 306
James I, 197, 316
James, the Apostle, 20, 83
James, Margaret, 260
James, Montague Rhodes, 245
Jehoiachim, 291
Jehoiakim, 291
Jeremiah, 167, 287
Jeremias, Joachim, 171
Jerome, 218
Jerome of Prague, 276
Jewell, Melanchthon, 286
John of Leyden, 124
John the Baptist, 72, 109, 170
John the Seer, 1, 130, 378
Johnson, Arthur, 380
Johnson, Francis, 29, 58, 126, 140, 213, 343, 366, 367, 373-376
Johnson, Francis R., 215
Jordan, W. K., 206
Josephus, 142
Joshua, 192
Junius, Franciscus, 292

K., F., 380, see Kingston, Felix
Keeling, William, 76
Keim, Theodor, 142
Kennedy, William P. M., 201, 208, 265
King, Andrew, 286
Kingston, Felix, 378
Knappen, Marshall M., 102
Knipperdolling, Bernhard, 124
Kniveton, George, 343
Knox, John, 145
Kocher, Paul H., 215
Korah, 307, 319, 339, 342

Lady Days, 4, 41, 70, 72
Lambeth Palace Library, 367, 374, 376, 379

Index

Langford, Essex, 385
Lathbury, Thomas, 59
Latimer, Hugh, 280
Laud, William, Archbishop of Canterbury, 9
Law, James T., 305
Leake, John, 384, 385
Lecler, Joseph, 206
Lectureship, 242, 243, 245
Lee, Nicholas, 343
Legg, J. Wickham, 265
Lent, 4, 41, 68, 69, 76
Lewin, William, 208, 209
Lightfoot, J. B., 232
Lincoln Cathedral Library, 374
Littell, Franklin H., 124
Liturgies, 28, 38, 39, 56, 57, 66, 76, 92, 93, 100, 101
Lombard, Peter, 218
London, Bishop of, see Aylmer, John
Lord, Edward, 286
Lord's Day, 251
Lord's Prayer, 98, 99, 279
Lord's Supper, 5, 8, 9, 91, 114, 131, 152, 177, 178, 182
Luke, 216
Luther, Martin, 218, 234, 276, 304
Lutherans, 7, 278, 279

M., I. [Mann, Joane ?], 380
M., R., 380
Mackinnon, James, 145
Magdalen College, Oxford, 13
Magistrates, 7, 16, 19, 20, 21, 112, 150, 201, 228, 348-360
Magna Carta, 316
Maguire, Mary, 315
Maintenance, 256-264
Maitland, F. W., 109
Makower, Felix, 135
Maldon, Essex, 3, 203, 230, 242, 382, 383
Man, Thomas, 380
Marchant, Ronald A., 209, 243, 304

Marriage, 85, 86
Marshall, John, 278
Martin Marprelate, 200, 201, 237, 245
Martinists, 245
Martyr, Peter, 218
Martyrs, 3, 20, 276, 278, 280, 321-324, 337, 344, 345
Marx Karl, 304
Mary Queen of Scots, 318
Mary Tudor, Queen (1553-1558), 20, 280, 282
Mather, Richard, 140
Matthews, Hazel, 50
Maundy Thursday, 70
Maxwell, William D., 145
Mayor, Stephen H., 325
McAlpin Collection, Union Theological Seminary, 376, 379
McNeill, John T., 145
Melanchthon, Philip, 278, 281
Melchizedek, 115
Membership, 2, 6-10, 18, 38, 46, 102, 106, 156, 162, 182, 183, 184
Meyer, Carl S., 109, 278
Mentz, Georg, 278
Middelburg, 373, 374, 375
Middleton, Henry, 379
Ministry, 2, 10-14, 18, 20, 21, 28, 32, 38, 39, 40, 57, 78, 101, 183, 207, 211, 237, 256, 266, 268, 269, 272, 273, 327, 344, 346, 349
Moloch, 120, 122
Molyns, John, see Mullins
Montagu, Richard, 260
Moore, George Foot, 142
Mornay, Philippe de, 140
Moses, 17, 307, 308
Mosse, George L., 206
Munzer, Thomas, 124
Mullinger, J. B., 224
Mullins, John, 210, 225

N., G. [George Norton], 380
Nadab, 307

Neale, Sir John E., v, vii, 44, 50, 109, 303, 311
Nebuchadnezzar, 287, 291
Nero, 20
Nettles, Stephen, 260
Nicholas, 57
Nicolaitans, 57
Noah, 115, 202
Norwich Public Library, 374
Nowell, Alexander, 225
Nye, Philip, 213

Oecolampadius, Johannes, 218
Oesterley, William O. E., 123
Ordination, 235, 237, 239, 270, 271, 302, 305, 340, 341, 346
Origen, 9
Orwin, Thomas, 203
Oughton, Thomas, 305
Overton, William, Bishop of Lichfield and Coventry, 237
Owen, John, 213
Oxford University, 13, 31

Paget, John, 140
Palmer, Robert, 242, 243, 384
Papists, 28, 66, 74, 80, 108, 273, 279, 318, 378
Parker, Matthew, Archbishop of Canterbury, 97, 199
Parker, Robert, 86
Parkhurst, John, Bishop of Norwich, 198
Parish Clerks, 4, 11, 76, 85, 192, 264, 265.
Parliament, 3, 17, 18, 20, 43, 50, 271, 311, 317
Parsons, 11-14, 106, 107, 155, 227, 228-232, 241, 242, 250, 263
Passhur, 287
Pastors, 10, 14, 16, 102, 147, 188, 189, 190, 196, 228, 230, 231, 232, 240, 241, 302, 340

Patron, 235, 238, 239, 240, 305
Paul, 31, 75, 140, 141, 201, 287, 341
Payne, E. A., 124
Payne, John, 286
Pearson, A. F. Scott, 102
Peel, Albert, 44, 50, 97, 205, 217, 218, 242, 245, 315, 325, 358, 364
Pelagianism, 281
Pelagius, 9
Penry, John, 186, 213, 359
Pentecost, 41, 71
Perfectionism, 2, 48, 67
Perkins, William, 99, 206, 359
Perne, Andrew, Master of Peterhouse, 3
Peter, the Apostle, 20, 90, 140, 141
Pierce, William, 200, 201, 237
Pilate, 31
Polity, 14-17, 19, 38, 39, 56, 206, 228, 285-290, 320, 328, 334, 335, 349, 359
Pontificales, 245, 250, 286
Pope, Alexander, 323
Porter, H. C., 224
Prayer, 6, 28, 82, 94, 102, 255, 361, 366, 368, 369, 379
Preaching, 243, 249, 250, 268, 269, 273, 280
Prebendaries, 11, 13, 192, 211, 226
Prebends, 13, 211, 226
Precisians, 244, 245
Presbyterians, 7, 8, 15, 16, 44, 102, 203, 286, 302, 359, 364. *See also* Reformists
Presbytery, 10, 16, 44, 148, 149, 179, 235. *See also* Classis
Price, F. Douglas, 135, 304
Prisons, 1, 3, 15, 18, 30, 52, 54, 99, 187, 205, 315, 343, 345, 366, 367, 369, 370, 374
Prophesying, 7, 198
Prophets, 10, 32, 43, 122, 123, 130, 168, 188, 195, 198, 211, 259, 273, 320

Index

Prothero, G. W., 150
Proudlove, William, 286
Prynne, William, 260
Purfoote, Thomas, 378
Purifications, see Churching
Puritans, 244, 245, 271, 316

Queen's Prerogative, 1, 2, 12, 18, 20, 21, 29, 43, 48, 50, 228, 257, 316, 317, 319, 348-364
Questmen, 11, 264

Ramage, David, 375
Ramea, 374
Read, Thomas Buchanan, 323
Rectors, 11
Reformation, 6, 349, 354, 364
Reformists, 250, 253, 254, 285, 286, 302, 311, 359. See also Presbyterians
Relievers, see Deaconesses
Roberts, James, 380
Robinson, H. W., 124
Robinson, John, 213
Robinson, Richard, 305
Robinson, Theodore H., 123
Rogations, 4, 41, 75, 76
Rogers, Thomas, 99, 200
Roman Catholic Church, 2, 6, 9, 20, 45, 49, 100, 126, 128-131, 133, 235, 248, 258, 296, 337, 342, 344
Ross, W. D., 214, 215, 306
Rothmann, Bernard, 124
Rupp, E. Gordon, 278

Sadolet, Cardinal [Sadoleto, Jacopo] 235
Saint Athanasius, 113
Saint George, 4, 73
Saint John the Baptist, 72, 109, 170
Saint Michael, 4, 73, 92
Saint Peter's Parish, 383

Saint Stephen, 73
Saints, 4, 70, 72, 73, 75, 343, 347
Saints' Days, 70, 71
Saints' Eves, 4, 41, 68, 69, 71
Salvation, 6, 326
Sanhedrin, 142, 143
Saravia, Hadrian, 140, 359
Saul, 19. See Paul
Scambler, Edmund, Bishop of Peterborough, and of Norwich, 198
Schaff, Philip, 171
Schism, 2, 7, 20, 29, 47, 48, 54, 104, 122, 124, 126, 169, 244, 279, 322, 334, 336, 343, 345, 362
Schurer, Emil, 142
Schweizer, Edward, 232
Scripture, 3, 4, 6, 7, 13, 19, 29, 34, 36, 37, 41, 62, 98, 100, 101, 117, 139, 197, 217, 248, 250, 271, 280, 353, 381
Second Principal Transgression, 102-183, 292, 299, 304, 327, 352
Sectaries, 1, 29, 169, 244, 245, 343, 345
Sedition, 1, 29
Segal, J. B., 171
Selden, John, 260
Separatism, 8, 28, 31, 38, 48, 49, 103, 159, 160, 166, 175, 187, 235, 278, 279, 343, 344, 347, 365
Separatists, 1, 2, 8, 16, 18, 20, 188, 271, 278, 279, 286, 325, 364, 373
Sermons, 241
Settle, Thomas, 213
Sidesmen, 11, 264
Sidney or Sydney, Sir Robert, ix, 370, 371, 372, 373, 376
Simpson, Sidrach, 213
Sir Halley Stewart Trust, vii
Six (or Five) Articles, 19, 51, 332, 333, 334, 336, 347, 366

Smith, John, see Smyth
Smyth, John, 213, 325
Snape, Edmund, 286
Solomon, 17, 307
Some, Robert, 1, 29, 30, 31, 126, 186, 188, 211, 223, 248, 249, 259, 273, 367
Some, *A Godly Treatise Containing and Deciding*, 30, 31, 186, 367
Some, *A Godly Treatise, Wherein Are Examined*, 31, 223, 249, 259, 273
Some, *A Godly Treatise Whereunto One Proposition*, 186
Spelman, Henry, 260
Sperin, Thomas, 382
Spiritual Courts, 18, 314-320, 335
St. John, Wallace, 206
Stanhope, Edward, 188, 208, 209, 385
Star Chamber, Court of, 286
Starkey, Thomas, 278
Stell, Hans, 375
Stephanus, Henricus, 292
Stephanus, Robertus, 292
Stoddard, Solomon, 9
Stokes, Robert, 374, 375
Storch, Nicholas, 124
Strype, John, 44, 99, 198, 199, 237, 242
Stubbs, William, 304, 319
Studley, Daniel, 30, 343
Subdeans, 11, 13, 192, 226
Suspension, 16
Sussex, Countess of, Frances Sidney, second wife of Thomas Radcliffe, third earl of Sussex, 378
Sutcliffe, Matthew, 140, 200, 211, 225, 359
Sylvester I, pope, 193

Taylor, *or* Cardmaker, John, 280
Teachers, 10, 16, 188, 189, 190, 198, 230, 241, 302

Tertullian, 218
Thiele, Edwin R., 125, 158
Third Principal Transgression, 183-285, 207, 310, 327, 349
Thirty-Nine Articles, 99
Thompson, Craig R., 224
Thorndike, Lynn, 215
Throkmorton *or* Throckmorton, Job, 186, 248, 359
Throkmorton, *Master Some*, 186, 248
Tillesley, Richard, 260
Tilley, Morris Palmer, 248
Timothy, 141
Tithes, 4, 14, 78, 79, 256-264
Titus, 141
Toleration, 7
Torrance, T. F., 235
Tramz, Mrs. Orin, vii
Travers, Walter, 140, 145, 228, 359
Tremellius, Immanuel, 292
Tyndale *or* Tindale, William, 276

Udall, John, 15, 140
Underhill, Edward B., 206
Uniformity, 7
Universities, 12
Unwin, Sir Stanley, vii
Usher, R. G., 102, 209, 316
Uzzah, 307
Uzziah, 307

Valla, Lorenzo, 193
Vautrollier, Thomas, 292
Vicars, 11, 12, 14, 192, 211, 227, 229, 232, 241-243, 250
Vlissingen, *see* Flushing

Walker, John, 208
Walton, Brian, 260
Wendel, François, 145
Wernham, R. B., vii

Index

Weske, Dorothy Bruce, 59
Wesley, John, 9
White, B. R., 325
White, Francis O., 201, 237
Whitgift, John, Archbishop of Canterbury, 1, 7, 8, 15, 140, 188, 197, 199, 200, 210, 237, 242, 315, 316, 343, 359, 360
Wiersdale, Mark, 242, 243
Wight, Daniel, 286
Williams, C. H., 50
Williams, George H., 124
Winchester, Bishop of, *see* Cooper, Thomas

Windet, John, 379, 380
Wolf, John, 203
Wood, Anthony, 379, 380
Woodham Ferrers (*or* Ferris), Essex, 384
Worship, 2, 3, 4, 6, 18, 19, 28, 32, 38, 40, 42, 61, 63, 336, 368, 369
Wright, Thomas, 224
Writs, 135, 197, 240, 315, 316

Young, Alexander, 374

Zedekiah, 291

For Product Safety Concerns and Information please contact our EU representative GPSR@taylorandfrancis.com
Taylor & Francis Verlag GmbH, Kaufingerstraße 24, 80331 München, Germany

www.ingramcontent.com/pod-product-compliance
Lightning Source LLC
Chambersburg PA
CBHW051623230426
43669CB00013B/2163